CW01262880

IRISH WRITING ON LAFCADIO HEARN AND JAPAN

Lafcadio Hearn in his early 20s as a general reporter on the Cincinnati Enquirer, *c.1873*

IRISH WRITING
on
LAFCADIO HEARN AND JAPAN

Writer, Journalist & Teacher

EDITED BY
SEAN G. RONAN

GLOBAL ORIENTAL

IRISH WRITING ON LAFCADIO HEARN
AND JAPAN

Edited by Sean G. Ronan

First published 1997 by
GLOBAL ORIENTAL
P.O. Box 219
Folkestone, Kent, UK CT20 3LZ

*Global Oriental is an imprint
of Global Books Ltd*

© GLOBAL BOOKS LTD 1997

ISBN 1-901903-05-2

*The publication of this book has been
supported by a grant from the Ireland Funds*

All Rights reserved. No part of this publication
may be reproduced or transmitted in any form or by
any means without prior permission in writing from
the Publishers, except for the use of short extracts
in criticism.

British Library Cataloguing in Publication Data
A CIP catalogue entry for this book is available
from the British Library.

Set in Bembo 12 on 13pt by Bookman, Slough
Printed and bound in England by Bookcraft Ltd, Midsomer Norton, Avon

For Brigid, Deirdre, Maeve and Emer

Contents

―――― oOo ――――

Foreword		*xi*
Preface		*xiii*
Acknowledgements		*xxi*
List of Contributors		*xxiii*
List of Illustrations		*xxix*
1	Matsue Tribute by the President of Ireland MARY ROBINSON	1
2	A Shrine for Lafcadio Hearn 1850-1904 SEAN DUNNE	5
3	Lafcadio Hearn and His Relations in Dublin LILO STEPHENS	7
4	A Profile of Lafcadio Hearn (Koizumi Yakumo) CHARLES V. WHELAN	12
5	Grandfather Lafcadio Hearn and I TOKI KOIZUMI	30

6	Two Celts in Japan: Enigma of the East SHERLEY McEGILL	38
7	Irish but as Japanese as the Haiku ULICK O'CONNOR	42
8	Lafcadio Hearn in New Orleans ULICK O'CONNOR	46
9	Lafcadio Hearn and Some Irish Writers ROGER McHUGH	52
10	The Loose Foot of Lafcadio Hearn ROGER McHUGH	57
11	East Irish MICHAEL DISKIN	65
12	Lafcadio Hearn: A Spiritual Odyssey CIARAN MURRAY	69
13	Lafcadio Hearn, W.B. Yeats and Japan BARBARA HAYLEY	75
14	Opening of the Lafcadio Hearn Library in the Embassy of Ireland, Tokyo ANTHONY J.F. O'REILLY	97
15	An Irishwoman's Diary: A Visit to Matsue LORNA SIGGINS	100
16	Lafcadio Hearn and Japanese Poetry GERRY O'MALLEY	104
17	The Literary Criticism of Lafcadio Hearn PETER MCMILLAN	108
18	Lafcadio Hearn and Early Irish and Japanese Mythology and Literature PETER MCMILLAN	121
19	Hearn's Japan: A Visit to the Oki Islands JAMES A. SHARKEY	135

20	The Horror and Ghostly Writings of Lafcadio Hearn SEAN G. RONAN	140
21	Lafcadio Hearn's Interpretation of Japan PAUL MURRAY	154
22	Lafcadio Hearn and the Irish Tradition PAUL MURRAY	172
23	W.B. Yeats and Lafcadio Hearn: Negotiating with Ghosts GEORGE HUGHES	188
24	Hearn, Yeats and the Problem of Edmund Burke GEORGE HUGHES	204
25	Lafcadio Hearn's First Day in the Orient PETER McIVOR	216
26	Kokoro – A Century Later SEAN G. RONAN	226
27	The Achievement of Lafcadio Hearn ALLEN E. TUTTLE	245
28	Some New Hearn Primary Source Material PAUL MURRAY	255

Notes & References — *316*

Appendices
I	LAFCADIO HEARN: PRINCIPAL DATES	*333*
II	HEARN'S TRAVELS IN JAPAN	*335*
III	CHRONOLOGICAL LIST OF WORKS	*336*
IV	HEARN'S FAMILY TREE	*337*
V	HEARN'S TERM MARKS AT USHAW COLLEGE	*338*
VI	KUMAMOTO TEST PAPER	*339*
VII	LEINSTER SQUARE, DUBLIN, C.1850	*341*

Index — *344*

Foreword

In 1988 I invited the former Prime Minister of Japan, Yasuhiro Nakasone, to Pittsburgh to deliver the annual Heinz Foundation lecture. Although uncomfortable with English, he made an excellent speech and spoke, almost like a prize fighter balanced on his feet, in a forceful and aggressive way. Afterwards, we repaired for drinks and I sought some common ground on which we could converse. I mentioned Lafcadio Hearn. His eyes lit up and he said, 'Ah, Lafcadio Hearn-Koizumi', for that was his Japanese name, 'he made my childhood, and that of almost every other child in the Japan I grew up in.'

I was stunned at his reaction – amazed that an Irishman like Lafcadio Hearn could have had such an influence on an enclosed society like Japan was then, and strangely gratified at the wonderment of it all.

Since then I have followed with fascination the rediscovery of the Greek-Irish boy who became, in time, the man who unlocked the door to the unfathomable.

Conceived by an Irish surgeon-soldier and a Greek lady, the boy moved to Dublin when he was one, and lived in Dublin until he was 19. He then went to America and lived there until he was 40. Only then did he go to Japan, and thus began the great odyssey of his life. In some uncanny way he became, in our idiom, 'more Japanese than the Japanese themselves', and in so doing he took us on a journey into the riches of the Japanese mind and lifestyle. In a phrase, Lafcadio Hearn distilled the essence of an impenetrable world and made it real for Western eyes.

In 1988 Sean Ronan was our ambassador in Tokyo and had the wonderful idea of creating a Lafcadio Hearn Library at the Embassy there. He invited Heinz to contribute to it, and I had the honour of opening it on 19 September 1988. It has been a great and continuing success linking our two countries.

It is, therefore, with great pleasure that I pen a short foreword to a fascinating book and enjoin The Ireland Fund in contributing to it and to our understanding of an unsuspected period in our history.

Tony O'Reilly
20 June 1997

Preface

*Afterwards, he was a story still told, set
Firmly as rocks in a Zen garden.*

SEAN DUNNE

---------- oOo ----------

It is a tribute to the particular genius and literary achievements of Lafcadio Hearn (Koizumi Yakumo, 1850-1904) that his works are read, analyzed and appreciated a century after his time. In fact, no writer on Japan is receiving more attention these days than Hearn. By the time of his death he had achieved an international reputation as a foremost interpreter of the emerging Japan for the West. He remains one of the most quoted writers on Japan to this day.

His reputation declined after World War II, particularly in America, when he was perceived to have been too sympathetic to all aspects of Japanese life although his relationship with that country was somewhat troubled.

In Japan, his enthusiasm for the Old Japan was at variance with modernization policies but he was embraced again by other generations when Japanese interest in their inherited cultural values revived. His interpretation of Japan was focused on a sympathetic view of the *kokoro* or heart and inner life of the country.

The 1980s and 90s have seen a revival of interest in Hearn and a re-evaluation by both Japanese and Western scholars of his life and work which reached a watershed at the Matsue centennial celebrations in 1990, marking Hearn's arrival in Japan. Hearn is now more widely recognized as a multi-dimensional figure whose fascinating life and work demand serious recognition and whose career is by no means limited to his writings on Japan.

There are a number of purposes for the present anthology, bearing in mind the above background, viz.-

a) to honour and commemorate Lafcadio Hearn by the land where he spent his formative years, as well as those Irish authors who have written about him;
b) to give a perception of the knowledge and written coverage of Hearn by Irish authors over the years;
c) to promote more information about Hearn and his work in Ireland and abroad;
d) to focus attention in the re-evaluation of Hearn of the importance of his Irish background;
e) to make an Irish contribution to current Hearn scholarship, including publication of new primary source material, and
f) to ensure that Hearn's Irish dimension is fully acknowledged and analyzed.

The anthology includes most of the known articles about Hearn written by Irish authors at home or abroad or published in Ireland. In addition, it includes a summary of a

Preface

talk on Hearn given in Dublin in 1993 by his grandson, Toki Koizumi, which shows the extent of Lafcadio's memories of his childhood in Ireland and the effects of Irish folklore, culture and customs on his Japanese stories of spirits, fairies and ghosts.

Toki Koizumi and his son, Bon, and their families have been assiduous in researching and promoting the life and works of their distinguished forebear in Japan and elsewhere. They have visited most places outside Japan associated with Hearn and come to Ireland regularly to meet their relatives here.

The papers in this collection are in general in chronological order except where considerations of presentation or subject matter would indicate a different placement. Some articles are more of historic interest and biographical details in them may differ in some respects, reflecting the fact that research on Hearn has improved, especially in recent years. I hope therefore, that the reader will accept these various accounts for their historiographical merits in the context of this collection and refer to modern bibliographies as required. I should add that because of his nomadic tendencies most writers will see a need to explain Hearn's wanderings. The Wandering Irish (*scotti peregrini*) theme continues to be popular in Ireland.

Since 1990, however, there has been much less emphasis on biographical aspects and more on analyses and interpretation of Hearn's personality and work. The anthology includes some new Hearn material generously contributed by Paul Murray, his most recent biographer. Murray's comments on the letters which Lafcadio wrote to his half-sister, Minnie Atkinson, should be of great interest to Hearn scholars, also other letters and material made available from family sources and archives.

The following extract is from a letter to Paul Murray from Toki Koizumi, dated 23 May 1997:

Your work contains some material quite new even to the Hearn family in Tokyo including myself. For us such material is not just academic but is 'significant to our understanding of Lafcadio', as you said. New material, especially relating to Lafcadio's younger days, always calls forth something emotional both in me and in my son, Bon.

Just to make sure, please take this letter as proof of my permission to publish, insofar as the copyright of some of the material under my control is concerned.

I enclose short comments on the new material which you kindly invited me to prepare (see p. 256ff). While I am a lineal descendant of Lafcadio, English is not my native tongue, so I hope that you will make allowance for that in what I have written.

Bon joins me in expressing our warmest thanks to you for the fruit of your hard labour and in hoping that all goes well with the forthcoming publication.

The appendices also include some lesser-known material, such as Hearn's term marks at Ushaw College and copy of a manuscript of term tests set by Hearn at the Fifth Higher School in Kumamoto in 1893.

An emerging theme in the re-evaluation of Hearn is the importance of his Irish background. His contacts during his formative years with relatives, tutors, countryfolk and fishermen in Dublin, Cong and Tramore familiarized him with Irish folktales, ghost stories, legends and songs which enabled him to enter easily into the world of Japanese fantasy.

He grew up in Dublin in the atmosphere that nurtured Charles Maturin, Sheridan Le Fanu and Bram Stoker, who was a contemporary. Indeed, genealogical relationships have been traced between Hearn and Le Fanu, Stoker and Synge. He was interested in the Irish literary revival and the old Celtic tales and fairy literature of W.B. Yeats and Samuel Ferguson. These traditions and the strong sense of the supernatural in everyday life were of great significance for Hearn when he came to Japan.

Irish people who are aware of the Lafcadio Hearn literary connection with Japan are surprised when they come to Japan to learn that he was almost universally regarded not only as British but specifically as English and that this extended to Japanese encyclopaedias and reference books. His Irish background was either unknown, ignored or regarded as unimportant.

Another reason for the neglect of Hearn's Irish background may have been his own tendency of trying to distance himself from the unhappy part of his childhood and forge a new identity for himself by fabricating details of his past. This attempt might well be a key to his complex personality. This lacuna in Hearn studies requires further research.

Hearn did not belong exclusively to any of the societies in which he lived. There can be no question of any country laying claim to Hearn as he was truly a citizen of the world. However, there is no reason why he should not be honoured by each of the countries in which he lived and wrote. More than most he established a bridge of understanding between East and West, specifically between Europe, America and Japan.

Defining his own life and the consequences of its nomadic course, Hearn considers himself to be

> ... the civilized nomad whose wanderings are not prompted by the hope of gain, or determined by pleasure, but simply controlled by certain necessities of his inner being, – the man whose inner secret nature is totally at variance with the stable conditions of a society to which he belongs only by accident.
> ('A Ghost' by Lafcadio Hearn, *Harper's Magazine*, 1889)

Nevertheless, that part of Hearn that was Irish is now more widely recognized and researched. His formative years were spent in Ireland so that, in any event, his Irish background had an important influence on his character and attitudes to life and contributed significantly to his literary interests and achievements.

The nature and extent of Irish interest in Hearn is also worth recording. The United States where his work was published was always the principal outlet for his writings. To a much lesser degree they were read in Britain; they were also translated into some European languages, notably French and German. Inevitably, therefore, his work was not so widely known in Europe as in the United States and Japan.

While no obituaries of Hearn have been traced in Irish newspapers or magazines, a review of a *Japanese Nightingale* by Onoto Watanna (Constable & Co., London), in *The Irish Times* of 4 November 1904 says:

> Lafcadio Hearn has given us some delightful books on Japan, its people and its folklore as seen by the eyes of the Western world, but the fiction written by Japanese authors for Japanese readers is worthy of attention especially as it seems likely enough that fifty years hence the ways of life and modes of thought they treat of will be as obsolete and foreign to the Japanese of the day as our seventeenth century is to our twentieth.

Austin Stack, who had been Irish Volunteer Commandant in Tralee, Co. Kerry, in 1916, was interested in Asian literature including books by Lafcadio Hearn. In 1923 he presented a copy of *Glimpses of Unfamiliar Japan* to Ernie O'Malley, Southern Commander in the War of Independence and author of *On Another Man's Wound*, who was also interested in Eastern literature. O'Malley wrote in one of his letters that Hearn's book had given him much pleasure.

Those early references to Hearn would indicate some general knowledge of his status as a writer and of his writings in Ireland in the first quarter of the century.

On books by Irish writers about Hearn, it should be mentioned that Nina Kennard (1844-1926), who wrote *Lafcadio Hearn* (Kennikat Press Inc., New York, 1912), was born in Belair, Kings Co. (now Offaly), the eleventh of fifteen children of Frances Sophia (Berry) and Thomas Homan-Mullock. In 1886 she married Arthur Challis Kennard, of Eaton Place, London. Her life of Lafcadio Hearn sprang from her friendship with Hearn's half-sister, Minnie Atkinson, with whom she visited Japan in 1909 and met Hearn's widow, Setsu, and family. Her book on Hearn is a valuable primary source.

In 1991, as a contribution to the centenary celebrations of Hearn's arrival in Japan, the Ireland Japan Association in Dublin published *Lafcadio Hearn (Koizumi Yakumo) His Life, Work and Irish Background* by Sean G. Ronan and Toki Koizumi. This was the first book on Hearn published in Ireland. Its third revised edition was issued in 1996.

A Fantastic Journey: The Life and Literature of Lafcadio Hearn, by Paul Murray, was published by the Japan Library, Folkestone, Kent, in 1993 with a Foreword by Professor Roy Foster, Carroll Professor of Irish History at Oxford, and an Introduction by Professor Sukehiro Hirakawa, Professor Emeritus, Tokyo University. Paul Murray, through his profession as an Irish diplomat, was by chance able to follow in Hearn's footsteps, particularly in Japan, where he was posted, and knew its language and culture well. His book is undoubtedly the best researched of all the Hearn biographies and the most definitive.

The present volume is a further step in honouring Lafcadio Hearn in Ireland where we have been slow at times in the past in honouring our writers and creative people. It is also an Irish contribution to Hearn studies. Scholars and researchers may find it useful to have in one volume most of the Irish written views and analyses of Hearn and his work.

The anthology does not contain a bibliography but rather notes after each article. Readers interested in a bibliography are referred to those in the biographies of Hearn, particularly in Paul Murray's book referred to above.

I wish to thank all the contributors to the anthology for their cooperation and generosity in agreeing to the inclusion of their articles or papers. They or their estates own the copyright and have sole responsibility for what they wrote. I am most grateful to the President of Ireland, Mary Robinson, for agreeing to the inclusion of her tribute to Hearn in Matsue during her State Visit to Japan in February 1995. I am grateful to other contributors for their reminiscences of places associated with Hearn and to George Hughes, Peter MCMillan, Paul Murray and Ulick O'Connor for their extended treatises.

I am also glad that the publication of this volume affords an opportunity of honouring some writers on Hearn who are no longer with us – Sean Dunne, Barbara Hayley, Roger McHugh and Lilo Stephens. *Ar dheis Dé go raibh a n-anamnacha.* It has not been possible to identify Sherley McEgill or Allen E. Tuttle. Although they published articles on Hearn in Ireland the names they penned must have been pseudonyms.

I should like to thank my publisher, Mr Paul Norbury, for his patient and constructive guidance and to wish him success with his new series on Lafcadio Hearn which commenced with publications by Professor Sukehiro Hirakawa, Mr Yoji Hasegawa and Mr Paul Murray.

I wish also to express appreciation to The Ireland Funds for their financial grant which made the publication possible. I am also very grateful to Dr Tony O'Reilly for contributing the Foreword and a chapter to the book as further tributes on his part to the memory of Lafcadio Hearn and the promotion of understanding and culture between Ireland and Japan.

Finally, I should like to quote from an address given by Dr Rudolph Matas, a close friend of Hearn, delivered at the dedication of the Lafcadio Hearn Room of the Howard-Tilton Memorial Library in Tulane University, New Orleans, on 17 March 1941:

> In closing, we may claim for him the crowning title of the greatest prose poet of his time, with a marvellous capacity for choosing harmonious words with which to convey imponderable niceties of meaning; of all modern writers in English the exponent of the most polished, beautiful and lyrical prose, and, from this viewpoint alone, worthy of a niche in the pantheon of the immortals.

Acknowledgements

―――――――――― oOo ――――――――――

The Editor wishes to thank all the contributors, or their literary estates, as the case may be, for the use of their copyright material reproduced in this anthology. Specifically, grateful acknowledgement is made of the kind permissions given by the following:-

PUBLISHERS
THE GALLERY PRESS for 'A Shrine to Lafcadio Hearn 1850-1904' by Sean Dunne taken from *Time and the Island* © 1996.
Eigo Seinen Henshubu (The Rising Generation), Tokyo, Japan, for 'Lafcadio Hearn and His Relations in Dublin' by Lilo Stephens.
The Examiner for 'Two Celts in Japan – Enigma of the East' by Sherley McEgill.
The Sunday Independent for 'Irish but as Japanese as the Haiku' by Ulick O'Connor.
The Dublin Magazine (ceased publication 1958) for 'Lafcadio Hearn in New Orleans' by Ulick O'Connor, and 'The Achievement of Lafcadio Hearn' by Allen E.Tuttle.
Yomiuri Shimbun, Tokyo, Japan, for 'Lafcadio Hearn and Some Irish Writers' by Roger McHugh.
The Irish Times for 'The Loose Foot of Lafcadio Hearn' by Roger McHugh; 'East Irish' by Michael Diskin and 'An Irishwoman's Diary – A visit to Matsue' by Lorna Siggins.
COLIN SMYTHE, Gerards Cross, Bucks, for 'Lafcadio Hearn, W.B.Yeats and Japan' by Barbara Hayley, and 'The Literary Criticism of Lafcadio Hearn' by Peter McMillan .
RADIO TELEFIS EIREANN Sunday Miscellany Programme (RTE Radio 1) which broadcast the first version of 'Lafcadio Hearn and Japanese Poetry' by Gerry O'Malley.
THE HEARN SOCIETY, MATSUE, JAPAN, publication *Centennial Essays on Lafcadio Hearn* and its Editor, Professor Kenji Zenimoto, for 'Lafcadio Hearn and Early Irish and Japanese Mythology and Literature' by Peter McMillan, and 'The Horror and Ghostly Writings of Lafcadio Hearn', originally 'Lafcadio Hearn Wandering Ghost' by Sean G.Ronan in the Bram Stoker Society Journal, Dublin, No.5, 1993.
Nihon Keizai Shimbun (in Japanese), *The Nikkei Weekly* (in English) and Kenkyusha's 'The Rattle Bag – Readings in English Cultures' for 'Hearn's Japan – A Visit to the Oki Islands' by James A.Sharkey.
THE JAPAN SOCIETY, LONDON, (Proceedings No.124, Autumn 1994) for 'Lafcadio Hearn's Interpretation of Japan' by Paul Murray.
The Irish Studies Review, Bath, for 'Lafcadio Hearn and the Irish Tradition' by Paul Murray.
GLOBAL BOOKS LTD, Folkestone, Kent (*Rediscovering Lafcadio Hearn – Japanese*

xxi

Legends, Life and Culture) for 'W.B.Yeats and Lafcadio Hearn – Negotiating with Ghosts' by George Hughes.
The Japan Quarterly, April-June 1996, published by Asahi Shimbun, Japan, for 'Lafcadio Hearn's First Day in the Orient' by Peter McIvor.
SIR DEREK OULTON, LT.CMDR.BASIL HEARN AND DENIS S.STEPHENS for making their private collections available to Paul Murray, and their permission to include in this anthology the results of his research on the material in Ch. 28 'Some New Hearn Primary Source Material'.

PHOTOGRAPH COLLECTIONS
Lafcadio Hearn Collection (#6101), Clifton Waller Barrett Library, Special Collections Department, UNIVERSITY OF VIRGINIA LIBRARY, for the miniature of the John Henderson Garnsey cartoon of Lafcadio Hearn featured on the jacket of this book.
SEAN G. RONAN, former Ambassador to Japan, for the picture of 30 Leinster Square, Dublin (photo No.2) and the picture of Tramore (photo No.28)
MARGARET CLARKE, Cong, Co. Mayo, for the picture of Strandhill House, Cong (photo No.4)
NANCY KHEDOURI, Tramore, Co.Waterford, for the picture of Belair House (photo No.5)
LT. CMDR. BASIL HEARN and PAUL MURRAY respectively for the provision of and research on photographs Nos. 1, 8-11.
DUBLIN TOURISM and DR PAUL BYRNE for the picture of Lafcadio Hearn's memorial plaque (photo No.6)
GRICHI GALLWEY, Tramore, Co.Wexford, for the pictures of Henry Hearn Molyneux (photo No.7) and Sarah Brenane (photo No.25)
SIR DEREK OULTON and PAUL MURRAY respectively for the provision of and research on photographs Nos. 12-14, 16
TOKI KOIZUMI and the JAPAN IRELAND LAFCADIO HEARN EXCHANGE ASS'N of Tokyo for the frontespiece and photographs Nos. 15, 17-24, 26, 29
SUNDAI IRELAND INTERNATIONAL SCHOOL, Curragh, Co. Kildare, for photograph No. 27

APPENDICES
APPENDICES I-III
The Japan Ireland Lafcadio Hearn Exchange Association of Tokyo and the Lafcadio Hearn Library Ireland

APPENDIX IV
Hugh Rudkin, 'Lafcadio Hearn and the Hearn Family' in *Notes and Queries*, London, 9 December 1939, pp 420-1

APPENDIX V
Ushaw College Library, Durham

APPENDIX VI
University of Kumamoto Library, Kyushu, Japan

APPENDIX VII
Ann Lavin, architect, Dublin, and Sean G. Ronan

NOTE: The Editor and Publishers have used their best efforts to trace all copyright-holders and have sought and received permission from each contributor to this anthology. The appropriate arrangements will be made with any who have been inadvertently overlooked and who choose to make themselves known to either the Editor or Publishers.

List of Contributors

———— oOo ————

Michael DISKIN
Studied at University College Galway (B.A.) and Strathclyde University (M.Sc. and Ph. D.) 1985. His doctoral thesis was on the subject of 'Democratic or Official – The Competition for Unionist Votes in Northern Ireland'. He was a tax consultant with Price Waterhouse & Co. 1985-7; a researcher in the Embassy of Japan, Dublin, 1987-89; Manager of the Galway Arts Festival 1990-92; Director of the Galway Arts Council 1992-95 and Manager Town Hall Theatre, Galway, 1995 to date.

Sean DUNNE (1956-95)
Poet, author and journalist. Born in Waterford but lived and wrote in Cork. His published work includes the highly praised memoir *In My Father's House* (1991) and *The Road to Silence* (1994); collections of poetry *Against the Storm* (1985), *The Sheltered Nest* (1992) and *Time and the Island* (1996). He was Editor of *Poets of Munster* (1986) and the *Cork Anthology* (1993) containing poetry and prose of Irish life written over twelve centuries. He died just as he was beginning to realize his great literary potential.

Barbara HAYLEY (1938-91)
Educated at Trinity College Dublin and the University of Kent at Canterbury. At the University of Cambridge she was a Gulbenkian

Research Fellow and later a Fellow of Lucy Cavendish College. She became Professor of English at St Patrick's College, Maynooth. Her books include *Carleton's Traits and Stories of the Irish Peasantry and the Nineteenth Century Anglo-Irish Tradition*; *A Bibliography of William Carleton*; *Carleton's Traits and Stories: An Appendix*. She has co-edited *Irish Theatre Today* and was writing *A History of Irish Periodicals, 1800-1870*, at the time of her premature death.

George HUGHES
Educated at University of Sussex and Queen's College, Cambridge. He is Visiting Professor of English Literature at Tokyo University. He is international representative of IASIL-Japan and editorial board member of *HARP*. His books include *Contemporary British Poetry* (Tokyo: 1989), *In Comparison: Essays on England and Japan* (Tokyo: 1993). Editor of *Corresponding Powers* (Cambridge: 1997), joint editor of *International Aspects of Irish Literature* (Gerrards Cross: 1996) and *Gleanings of the Writings of Lafcadio Hearn* (Tokyo: Yushodo, 1991). He has written many articles on Hearn in English and Japanese and on literary topics – in Irish literature, particularly on Yeats, Synge, MacNeice, Heaney and Brian Friel.

Toki KOIZUMI
Born in Tokyo, he was the only child of Kazuo Koizumi, the eldest son of Yakumo Koizumi (Lafcadio Hearn). He studied at Denki-Tsushin University and worked for a Sea Liner Company. Later, he was employed in the public relations sector of the American Forces in Japan until his retirement. He now researches and promotes the life and work of his distinguished grandfather, Yakumo Koizumi.

Roger McHUGH (1908-87)
Critic, prolific author and lecturer. He was the first Professor of Anglo-Irish Literature at University College Dublin. His books include *Henry Grattan* (1937); *Trial at Green Street Courthouse* (1945); *Rossa* (1948); *Universities and European Unity* (1955). He contributed many articles on Irish literature and drama to newspapers, encyclopaedias and learned journals including *The Bell, Studies, Envoy, Threshold, University Review* and *Irish University Review*.

Peter McIVOR
Educated at Trinity College, Dublin, and at Leeds University. He joined the Irish Foreign Service in 1982. In addition to assignments

at Headquarters in Dublin, he has served as Second Secretary at the Embassies of Ireland in Bonn and in Tokyo. He is presently serving as First Secretary in Tokyo.

Peter MCMILLAN
He is a Professor of English and Irish Culture at Kyorin University in Tokyo and is currently on a two-year sabbatical at Princeton, Columbia and, in second year, at Oxford. He was educated at University College Dublin (B.A. and M.A.) and at the University of South Carolina (Ph.D.). He has lectured in literature and philosophy at the Universities of Maryland, Waseda, Meisei and Tooritsu. He is a member of the Executive Committee of IASIL-Japan, and was the Director of the IASIL International Conference at Otani University, Kyoto, 1990. His current interests are in Japanese art history and art appreciation in Japan, and he is engaged in research in those topics during his sabbatical. He has published many articles in the Japanese media, in English and Japanese, and appeared on Japanese television and radio on several occasions.

Ciaran MURRAY
He took his M.A. while writing for *The Irish Times*, and his Ph.D. while working in Japan. He has published extensively on the Japanese sources of romanticism, a subject on which he has lectured in Asia, Europe and America. He is currently Professor of English at Chuo University.

Paul MURRAY
Graduated from Trinity College, Dublin, with an M.A. in History and Political Science and joined the Irish Foreign Service. His assignments have included London, New York, Ottawa and Tokyo. While serving in Tokyo in the early 1980s he was well placed to research the career of Lafcadio Hearn. His biography *A Fantastic Journey: The Life and Literature of Lafcadio Hearn* (1993) was awarded the Koizumi Yakumo Literary Prize in Japan. An American edition has been issued by the University of Michigan Press (1997) and a Japanese translation is also due to be published in 1997. He has contributed articles on Hearn to recent books and journals. He is currently working on a biography of Bram Stoker to be published by Jonathan Cape.

Ulick O'CONNOR
Biographer, poet and playwright. His biographies include Oliver St John Gogarty, Brendan Behan and *Celtic Dawn*, a biography of the Irish Literary Renaissance. He has published three books of poems

Lifestyles (1975); *All things Counter* (1986) and *One is Animate* (1990) and a translation of Baudelaire's *Les Fleurs du Mal* (1995). His plays include *The Dark Lovers* (Swift and Stella), *The Dream Box*, *The Oval Machine Execution*, *A Trinity of Two* (Oscar Wilde and Edward Carson) and *Joyicity*. His book *Biographers and the Art of Biography* (1991) was widely acclaimed. He is well known for his verse plays in the Noh form. He has visited and lectured in Japan where his play *Deirdre* was directed by the famous Noh actor, Hideo Kanze.

Gerry O'MALLEY
Retired engineer and now a full-time writer. His plays and stories have been broadcast on RTE and BBC. He is a contributor to the 'Sunday Miscellany' radio programme on RTE 1. Lives in Bray, Co. Wicklow.

Anthony J.F. O'REILLY
Chairman and Chief Executive of H.J. Heinz Co. A native of Dublin, he joined the Heinz organization as Managing Director of its English subsidiary in 1969. He has served as CEO of the company since 1979 and as Chairman since 1987. Dr O'Reilly is Chairman of Fitzwilton Plc, Independent Newspapers Plc, Waterford Wedgwood and Matheson Ormsby Prentice in Dublin; and a Director of Georgetown University. He is past Chairman of the Grocery Manufacturers of America and currently a member of its Executive Committee. Educated at Belvedere College, Dublin, University College Dublin and the Incorporate Law Society of Ireland, he earned his Ph.D. degree in Agricultural Marketing from the University of Bradford in England. Dr O'Reilly is active in many cultural and charitable organizations and has received numerous honours and awards. He is Chairman of The American Ireland Fund.

Mary ROBINSON
United Nations High Commissioner for Human Rights 1997–. President of Ireland (1990-97). A graduate of Trinity College, Dublin, (M.A., LL.B.), King's Inns, Dublin, (B.L.) and Harvard University (LL.M.). She has had a very distinguished legal and political career and acquired a world reputation as President of Ireland. She was a Senator 1969-89 and a member of the Irish Parliamentary Joint Committee on EC Secondary Legislation 1973-89. She became a member of the English Bar (Middle Temple) 1973, Senior Counsel 1980. She was Founder and Director of the Irish Centre for European Law, Reid Professor of

List of Contributors

Constitutional and Criminal Law TCD 1969-75, Lecturer in European Community Law TCD 1975-90. She was member of Dublin City Council 1979-83, of the New Ireland forum 1983-84, of the International Commission of Jurists, Geneva, 1987-90 and of the Royal Irish Academy. She has received numerous honours and awards.

Sean G. RONAN
Graduated from University College Dublin with M.A. and LL.B. Was Ambassador of Ireland to Germany, Greece and Israel (non-resident), Japan and Korea (non-resident) as well as a Director General in the EC Commission 1973-77. He is active in promoting Hearn scholarship. He co-authored the book *Lafcadio Hearn (Koizumi Yakumo) His Life, Work and Irish Background* and has written and lectured on historical and literary subjects.

James SHARKEY
Educated at St Columba's College, Derry, University College Dublin and Birmingham University. A member of the Irish Foreign Service since 1970, his foreign assignments included Moscow, Rome and Washington. He was Ambassador to Australia and Japan and is currently Ambassador to Denmark, Norway and Iceland. He was closely associated with the celebration in Matsue in 1990 of the centenary of Hearn's arrival in Japan. He accompanied President Mary Robinson to Shimane Prefecture in 1995 where, during the course of her State Visit to Japan, she paid tribute to Hearn's special place of honour in the Japanese imagination.

Lorna SIGGINS
She is an *Irish Times* staff reporter specializing in marine and environmental issues. In 1989 she participated in the Journalists in Japan Fellowship sponsored by NSK, the Japanese Newspaper and Publishers' Association, in Tokyo.

Lilo STEPHENS (1888-1982)
She was the wife of Edward M. Stephens, who was a nephew of John Millington Synge. She encouraged the first biography of Synge by David H. Greene and her husband (1959), who was also a second cousin to Lafcadio Hearn. She was active in promoting knowledge of Hearn at home and abroad.

Charles V. WHELAN
Educated at Christian Brothers School, Synge Street, Dublin, Rockwell College, Co. Tipperary, and the University of London

(B.Sc.Econ.). He entered the Irish Foreign Service in 1949 and served in Spain, the United States and Great Britain. He was Ambassador to Spain, Japan, Greece and the Soviet Union. On his retirement in 1990 he was appointed Co-Chairman of Anglo-Irish Encounter (1990-96). His interest in Lafcadio Hearn commenced at school in Dublin and was later encouraged by a film of Hearn's work, *Kwaidan*, shown in Dublin at the Irish Film Society in 1968. On appointment to Tokyo, he familiarized himself with Hearn's life and work and his Irish background.

NOTE

It has not been possible to date to identify Sherley McEGILL (not known in Cork) or Allen E. TUTTLE (not known to the Charles E. Tuttle Company). Although they published articles on Hearn in *The Cork Examiner* and in *The Dublin Magazine* respectively, the consensus is that the names they penned must have been pseudonyms.

List of Illustrations

---000---

PLATE SECTION NUMBERS (*Between pages 161/162*)

1. Lafcadio Hearn, photographed in Kobe, Japan, 7 April 1895. (Writtten in his own handwriting).

2. Leinster Square, Dublin, c.1850, where Lafcadio lived in No.21 (now renumbered No.30) with his great-aunt, Sarah Brenane (see Appendix VII).

3. No.48 Lower Gardiner Street, Dublin, where Lafcadio and his mother Rosa Antonia, lived with his grandmother, Mrs Elizabeth Hearn, when they arrived in Dublin in August 1852.

4. Strandhill House, Cong, Co.Mayo, residence of Lafcadio Hearn's aunt, Mrs Catherine Elwood. It was featured in the film *The Quiet Man*. Demolished in the 1960s.

5. Belair House, Tramore, Co.Waterford, a house of the Molyneux family, where Lafcadio and his great-aunt, Sarah Brenane, stayed during the summer holidays in the 1850s and early 60s.

6. Lafcadio Hearn memorial plaque on 73 Upper Leeson Street, Dublin, where he lived with his great-aunt, Sarah Brenane, 1856-1863.

7. Henry Hearn Molyneux, 1837-1906. Distantly related to the Hearns. He affected Lafcadio Hearn's destiny through his influence over Lafcadio's great-aunt Sarah Brenane.

8. Richard Holmes, father of Lafcadio's grandmother, Elizabeth Hearn, of Streamstown, Co.Westmeath.

9. Richard Hearn d.1890 unmarried, brother of Charles Bush Hearn and uncle of Lafcadio; artist and friend of Millet.

10. The Rt.Revd.Alexander Arbuthnot, Bishop of Killaloe and nephew of Primate Stone. A great-uncle of Lafcadio's grandmother, Elizabeth Hearn née Holmes. Related to Dr John Arbuthnot, the subject of Alexander Pope's *Epistle*, and Queen Anne's doctor.

11 Major Robert Thomas Hearn (1823-62), brother of Charles Bush Hearn and uncle of Lafcadio. Was a Major in the 26th Cameronians, and afterwards in the 76th Regt.

12 Lafcadio's aunt Jane (1832-1906), daughter of Lt.Col.Daniel James Hearn and Elizabeth Holmes. Married Henry Colclough Stephens of Dublin, solicitor, 1850.

13 The Rt. Revd. Robert Thomas Hearn, Bishop of Cork, Cloyne and Ross, grandson of Lafcadio's uncle, Major Robert Thomas Hearn (No.11).

14 Mrs Catherine Frances Elwood d.1861, sister of Charles Bush Hearn and aunt of Lafcadio. Known to the family as 'Aunty Fanny'.

15 James Daniel Hearn (1854-1935), Lafcadio's younger brother who lived in Ohio and Michigan.

16 Elizabeth Hearn, née Holmes (1791-1861), Lafcadio's paternal grandmother.

17 Lafcadio's half-sister Minnie Charlotte Atkinson, b.1859.

18 Lafcadio's half-sister Posey Gertrude Brown b.1860.

19. Lafcadio's half-sister Elizabeth Sarah Maud (1858-1938), unmarried.

20 Robert James Hearn, Lafcadio's great grandfather (1734-92).

21 Daniel James Hearn, Lafcadio's grandfather (1768-1837).

22 Surgeon-Major Charles Bush Hearn, Lafcadio's father (1818-

List of Illustrations

66) in late middle age.

23 Lafcadio Hearn in the 1870s.

24 Lafcadio Hearn aged about eight with his 'adopted mother', great-aunt Sarah Brenane, Dublin, late 1850s.

25 Portrait of Sarah Brenane.

26 Lafcadio Hearn aged about 16 at Ushaw College, near Durham.

27 The Lafcadio Hearn Museum and Library, Sundai Ireland International School, Curragh, Co.Kildare.

28 Tramore, Co.Waterford, where Lafcadio and his great-aunt, Sarah Brenane, spent summer holidays with the Molyneux family up to the early 1860s. Here he learned to swim and took a parting walk with his father in 1857.

29 Lafcadio Hearn and his wife Setsu with their eldest son Kazuo at the age of two, Kobe November 1895.

1

Matsue Tribute to Lafcadio Hearn
by MARY ROBINSON, PRESIDENT OF IRELAND

――――――― oOo ―――――――

Mr Governor, Mr Mayor, Ladies and Gentlemen

It is a very special pleasure to have this opportunity to visit Shimane Prefecture and its capital, Matsue,[1] and I want to thank you sincerely for your most hospitable welcome.

I am here to acknowledge the unique association which exists between Ireland and this Prefecture through our shared pride in the life and work of Lafcadio Hearn – Koizumi Yakumo.

No writer before Hearn succeeded so sympathetically and so effectively in communicating a sense of Japanese civilization, tradition and folklore to the world beyond these shores. Perhaps no foreign writer since Hearn has won such a place of honour and distinction in the imagination of the people of Japan.

That he was Irish is a source of great pride to me, nowhere more so than here in this historic city, where his memory is especially prized. It is the city in which Lafcadio Hearn began his life of scholarship in Japan; the city in which he began a sustained engagement with all aspects of Japanese civilization; the city which provided so much of the material for his first great work on this country: *Glimpses of Unfamiliar Japan*.

We know from this book just how enchanted Lafcadio Hearn was with Matsue; with the great beauty of the natural scenery in the Izumo region and with its extraordinary cultural heritage. One of his most famous essays, which he called 'Chief City of the Province of the Gods' is about Matsue: a celebration of a day in the life of the city, beginning with the sounds of the morning and ending with the sun setting over Lake Shinji.

Characteristically, what excited Lafcadio Hearn about Matsue were the ordinary events marking the course of an average day: the booming of the temple bells, the pattering of *geta* over the Ohashi Bridge, the children in kimonos hurrying to school. Even the simplest sights touched a chord in his imagination: no event, however small, was without significance either in itself or for the lesson it might contain about Japanese civilization, tradition and sensibility.

It was this attention to the routines of ordinary life in Japan, together with a sure sense of the underlying currents of Japanese life, of religion, history and customs, which make Lafcadio Hearn's interpretation of Japan so compelling and convincing. It has also ensured that his works remain relevant down to our own day.

Although Lafcadio Hearn is undoubtedly the most famous Irish person to come to Japan in the wake of the Meiji Restoration, his contributions can be seen not only as a writer but also as one part of the wider contribution made by Irish people to the modernization of Japan at the end of the nineteenth century in areas as different as the development of the roads and the railways, industry and trade, university education and scholarship. There is a link here, I believe, between these early Irish pioneers and the new generations of Irish people, including those who are living in Shimane, who are now resident in Japan a century later. It is particularly pleasing that in more recent years the JET[2] programme has enabled Irish people once again to come to know the wonders of this special region.

When my visit to Japan was being planned, I asked that my programme should include Matsue because I wanted to honour not only the memory of Lafcadio Hearn but also to acknowledge your part in this prefecture in preserving that memory for future generations. This you have done through the sensitive preservation of buildings associated with the writer and through the work of Yakumo-kai, the Hearn Society which is based here in Matsue. I am delighted also to welcome the recent inauguration of the Japan-Ireland Society of the San'in and to wish them success in the years ahead in their enterprise of friendship. I also wish to register the important role played in the promotion of Hearn studies by Hearn's grandson Toki-san whom I had the pleasure of receiving in Ireland, and his great grandson, Bon-san who is here this evening. All of this endeavour enhances the special bonds of affection between Ireland and Shimane Prefecture which have been established through the great achievement of Lafcadio Hearn.

Tomorrow when I visit Izumo Taisha I will have the opportunity to travel further into the Province of the Gods and also to see something of the 'Chief City' itself. I am looking forward greatly to this. I want, in the meantime, to thank you for your great generosity in allowing me to renew this evening the ties of friendship and cooperation forged through Ireland's historic connections with this prefecture and to convey my warmest good wishes to all the people of this region and to everyone in Japan who takes pride in the name of Koizumi Yakumo – Lafcadio Hearn.

MESSAGE TO THE KUMAMOTO PREFECTURAL OFFICE[3]

It is a very special pleasure to congratulate the Kumamoto Prefectural Office in Tokyo on the occasion of the exhibition 'Koizumi Yakumo and the No.5 High School'.

The special ties which exist between Ireland and Japan through our shared pride in the life and work of Lafcadio Hearn are especially valued in Kumamoto where Hearn lived for almost three years in the early 1890s. In *Out of the East*, his second book on Japan, he left an unforgettable record of his experiences in this lovely prefecture, including his pride in the work of the students at the No.5 High School where he taught.

In the course of my State Visit to Japan I had the great pleasure of visiting Shimane Prefecture and of seeing there some of the locations which were especially important to Lafcadio Hearn. I am delighted to have this opportunity now to acknowledge the important part played by the people of Kumamoto in preserving the memory of Lafcadio Hearn in Japan. This exhibition is a very valuable contribution to that effort.

I congratulate everyone involved in making the exhibition possible and wish it every success.

Mary Robinson,
President of Ireland

2

A Shrine for Lafcadio Hearn, 1850-1904[1]

SEAN DUNNE

Like Hokusai painting on rice-grains,
He tried to trap Japan in a story:
His one good eye so close to the page
He might have been a jeweller with a gem.

So much to tell: kimonos and cranes,
Cemeteries to stalk at evening, slow
Shoals of candles like souls
Along rivers beneath a massive moon.

Even the sound of sandals on a bridge
Stayed in the mind for an evening,
Matching the shadow of fishermen
On still waters: a painted print.

Or a face smiling to hide its grief,
The touch of passing sleeves part
Of a plan that maps the future,
A heron seeking the heights on a wall,

Every act with its own ancestry.
He saw the singular made special:
A solitary spray in a vase
Far from childhood's opulent wreaths.

Loneliness ended in Matsue: that raw
Pain no longer gnawing like the Creole
Songs on a sidewalk in New Orleans.
Instead he heard a flute's clear note.

He was a lantern drifting from the shore,
Dissolving in the tone of a struck bell.
Sipping green tea in Tokyo, he heard
Ghost stories from an impossible past

And died past fifty from his Western heart.
Afterwards, he was a story still told, set
Firmly as rocks in a Zen garden.
Incense burns near cake at his shrine.

In the sound of sandals on a bridge
I hear him sometimes, or catch him
In the swift calligraphy of a scroll,
Smooth curve of a lacquered bowl.

A breeze through a bamboo grove,
His memory passes for an instant.
Snow falls on his grave and on plum blossom.
He is fading like a fisherman in mist.

DÁNTA ÚRA: NEW POEMS

3

Lafcadio Hearn and His Relations in Dublin

LILO STEPHENS

———————— oOo ————————

Lafcadio Hearn was a cousin of my father-in-law, Henry Stephens. The following is an account of Lafcadio and his relations in Dublin which I have put together from material collected by my late husband, Edward Stephens, from cousins of Lafcadio's and old letters.

Charles Bush Hearn, father of Lafcadio, was a Surgeon in the British Army, and in 1842, was promoted to the Staff. He was a dashing, handsome man, with a good tenor voice, and was an admired and adored son of his mother, Mrs Hearn. In 1846, before he left for service in the Ionian Isles, he fell in love with a Dublin girl, Alicia Goslin who because of her beauty was known as the Pocket Venus to whom, it is believed, he became engaged before he left for abroad. However, because of her father's opposition she broke off her engagement and it is said that Charles nearly went out of his mind when her letters ceased and one of his brother officers told him she was married to a Judge Crawford. Some years later while he was stationed at the Fort on Santa Maura, Charles Bush met Rosa Kassimati, a beautiful Greek girl, and fell in love with her. Her family was opposed to her marrying someone in the British Army, but in spite of this opposition they eventually married at Santa Maura in 1849. Their son Lafcadio was born there in 1850.

In the latter part of 1851, Charles Bush was assigned to duty in the West Indies where he could not bring his wife and child. As Rosa's family did not wish her to come home, and as Charles himself was concerned as to whether his mother would allow them to live with her in Dublin, he persuaded his brother, Richard, an artist living in Paris, to take Rosa and the little Lafcadio while waiting to hear from Mrs Hearn. Richard in the meantime engaged a companion for Rosa to teach her English and prepare her for the different way of life she would have to face in Dublin.

Charles' mother, Mrs Hearn, who was always devoted to him and would without hesitation have happily accepted his wife and child into her home, was naturally apprehensive as to how a wife from foreign parts, used to a completely different social milieu, and with a very slight knowledge of English, would adapt herself to the family life in Dublin. However, in August 1852, she warmly welcomed Rosa Kassimati, her companion and Lafcadio to her home, a large old-fashioned terrace house of seven stories in Lower Gardiner Street, on the north side of Dublin.

Mrs Hearn had been a Miss Holmes. Both the Hearn and Holmes families had belonged for seven generations to the Landed Gentry in Ireland, and were Protestants of the strict, narrow form of the period. At that time in Ireland there was practically no social contact between Protestants and

Catholics. Mrs Hearn (née Holmes) was a member of a large family, and it was a great blow to them when the youngest daughter, Sarah Holmes, became a Catholic in order to marry a Mr Justice Brenane. However, because of the strong affection between the sisters, they did not break off relations with her and she constantly visited Mrs Hearn in Gardiner Street. There is a story told in the family of the parrot trained to say: 'Have you seen the Priest,' a sentence which it shouted when Aunt Sarah Brenane arrived. Though in sympathy with the bird's attitude of mind, on one occasion some member of the family for propriety sake shook it off its perch, and it shouted: 'Oh, you dirty pirate.'

This was the family background to which Rosa Kassimati had to adapt herself. In spite of the warmth of Mrs Hearn's welcome, she found the restricted social life in the dark and rather gloomy house a frightening contrast to the freer social life in the warm and sunny countries where she had lived. As time went on, the situation became more impossible, and when Charles Bush returned he also realized the magnitude of the difficulties and the impossibility of their marriage continuing. A separation was agreed upon. Rosa Kassimati went back to the Ionian Islands and Charles Bush returned to his military duties abroad, leaving the responsibility of Lafcadio's future in the hands of his family. His grand-aunt, Mrs Brenane, a warm-hearted, kindly woman, disappointed at having no children of her own, suggested she would adopt him on condition that he would be brought up a Roman Catholic, and this is what happened.

Lafcadio was a delicate, nervous, highly-strung child, with poor eye-sight, and from the Hearn side of his family inherited their imagination and awareness of the supernatural. The fact that he never saw his parents again added to his feeling of insecurity. Mrs Brenane's own strict upbringing and strong belief in self-discipline prevented her, in spite of her kindness, from understanding how to deal with the fears and imaginings of a sensitive child, and she could not realize the cruelty of refusing him a light in his bedroom and locking him in. This, she felt, was necessary for self-discipline.

Because of the religious differences in the family, there was very little coming and going between Lafcadio and his young Protestant cousins, and so his life with an elderly grand-aunt was rather solitary. There were happy times, however, when his grand-aunt took him to visit his aunt, Mrs Elwood, who lived with her husband on his lovely estate in County Mayo, and sometimes during the summer to Tramore, a seaside place with wonderful stretches of sandy beach, ideal for children.

When Lafcadio reached the age to leave home to go to a boarding school he was sent to a Catholic one in England. After the death of Mr Justice Brenane, Mrs Brenane found herself in financial difficulties, and after her death the income she had settled on Lafcadio was no longer available to pay his school fees and he was sent to a distant relation in the United States. He never returned to Ireland again.

In 1856, when his father Charles Bush was passing through London from the Crimea, a fellow officer asked him to leave a travelling rug at a certain house. When he rang, the hall-door was opened by the butler who showed him upstairs to the drawing-room. The door opened and in came a lady in widow's weeds: the Pocket Venus, his early love! This happy encounter led to their marriage the following year (of which his mother strongly disapproved) after which he and his Pocket Venus sailed for India where in course of time three daughters were born. During the intense heat of the autumn of 1861, the Pocket Venus, who had been in poor health, had a still-born baby from which she was making a very slow recovery. Her husband returning home one afternoon found her, as he thought, resting as usual on the verandah, but when he bent over her she was dead and an open letter from her mother-in-law had fallen from her hand. After this tragedy Charles Bush brought his three daughters back to England.

Lafcadio's half-sister, Minnie Atkinson, the second daughter of Charles Bush and the Pocket Venus, was one of the close relations he allowed to write to him. She had always hoped to visit him in Japan but circumstances prevented her from making the journey before his death. Even after his death she was still anxious to keep in touch with his family and she and her daughter were able to visit his widow and children in Japan in 1909.[1]

4

A Profile of Lafcadio Hearn[1]

CHARLES V. WHELAN

———————————— oOo ————————————

He was a small dark man, 5'3" in height. He was blind in one eye and had a pale face with a drooping moustache. He was moody, resentful, suspicious and easily moved to anger. Begotten and born in inauspicious circumstances, he was abandoned and betrayed in his youth. His life-story has a compelling interest. It links Greece, Ireland, England, America and Japan.

As a writer he possessed a rare sensitivity for capturing both the beautiful and the ugly in life. Dogged by misfortune he persevered through an unbreakable faith in himself and his talent. He was a wanderer, a restless spirit, with an insatiable curiosity about peoples and their cultures, particularly the strange and exotic.

It is the story of a man who could be quite impossible at

times, who lost many friends but who won the deep affection of the country that finally adopted him as its own, and gave him wife and family, peace and happiness. His major achievement was to interpret that country – Japan – and its people to the Western World at a time of historic change.

☐

The ferry from Patras in Greece to Ancona in Italy passes through the seas surrounding two of the Ionian Islands, on one side Ithaca and on the other Lefkas. Ithaca brings to mind the wanderings of Ulysses and the modern Odyssey of Leopold Bloom. The view of Lefkas recalls the life of Patrick Lafcadio Hearn born in the principal town of the island on 27 June 1850. Travellers all three, but Patrick Lafcadio was fact, not fiction: a man, not a myth.

His father, Charles Bush Hearn, and Anglo-Irish Protestant from Dublin, a member of the minority ruling caste in Ireland, was an assistant surgeon and officer in the British forces who occupied the Ionian Islands for nearly half a century. His mother Rosa Kassimati was a native of the island of Kythira (then known as Cerigo) the most southerly of the Ionian group. Charles Hearn met Rosa early in 1848 during a temporary posting on that small island. On his being assigned a year later to Lefkas, then officially known by its Venetian name of Santa Maura, the couple faced a dilemma. Rosa was pregnant but her family strongly opposed the relationship and so the couple eloped to Lefkas where their first child, George Robert, was born and where they eventually married on 25 November 1849, in the ritual of the Greek Orthodox Church.

Rosa, like many young island women, had received no formal education and was not able to sign the marriage contract, a circumstance of ominous significance. On 27 June 1850 a second child, Patrick Lafcadio, was born to the couple. (The first child, George Robert, died shortly afterwards.) Named Patrick for his father's country and Lafcadio meaning native of Lefkas, he later believed he had two souls, one sensitive and impulsive like his Greek mother and the other proud and stubborn like his Anglo-Irish father. Later, as a young man, rejected by his father's family, he dropped the name Patrick altogether.

Soon, his father was assigned to the British West Indies and the mother and child were sent to Dublin to stay with the Hearn family and await Surgeon-Officer Hearn's return. It may be imagined what a cultural, social and psychological shock it was for the young unlettered mother from the warm south to have to adapt to living in a cold northern country where family life among the Anglo-Irish was stiff and formal, compared with that in her Greek homeland. The Hearns in turn found it difficult to accept this stranger who knew little English, whose reaction to events was often impulsive and emotional and who was unable to share the social and intellectual interests of her husband's relatives.

Rosa Kassimati became so unhappy that, following her husband's first home visit in 1854, it was decided that she should return to Greece for a visit to her family. The boy was left in the temporary care of his great-aunt, Mrs Sarah Brenane, a sister of Charles Hearn's mother. He never saw his mother again. About her he wrote later: 'I remember only my mother's face: it was delicate and dark, with large black eyes, very large.'

On return from the Crimean War in 1856, Charles Hearn decided to terminate the marriage with Rosa in her absence. He had discovered that the girl he had been in love with as a young man was now a widow and free to marry again. This was Alicia Goslin Crawford, who was known as the 'Pocket Venus' because of her petite beauty. Lafcadio remembered her on a visit with his father as 'all white-robed with very bright hair, very slender. I thought her beautiful as an angel. She gave me a beautiful book and a gun but my aunt took

A Profile of Lafcadio Hearn

them away saying she was a very wicked woman and he was a very wicked man'.

The young boy was now established permanently in his great-aunt's care. His father secured an annulment of his marriage to Rosa on the basis that she had not signed the contract but she may have accepted the failure of the union. Charles Hearn married his 'Pocket Venus' and he, with his new bride, departed for India, again on army service. In 1861 the second Mrs Hearn died of fever in India and Charles Hearn died of malaria on board ship in the Gulf of Suez in 1866. Both of Lafcadio's parents had disappeared from his life.

Rosa married again in Kythira but her second husband, Giovanni Cavallini, a prominent local official of Italian descent, later Governor of Antikythira island, made it a condition of the marriage that her children by Hearn would not remain with Rosa. Lafcadio's younger brother, James Daniel, who had been born after Rosa left Dublin, was sent first to Ireland and later to school in England. Lafcadio never met him but in the course of correspondence in later years he defended their mother against his younger brother's charge that she deserted them. Lafcadio informed James Daniel that Aunt Sarah Brenane and the servants in her household told him: 'Do not believe anything unkind about your mother. She loved you all as any mother could do. She just could not help herself.' Sadly, Rosa developed mental illness and died on 12 December 1882 in the mental asylum in Corfu at the age of 59.

Sarah Brenane was a widow and a Roman Catholic, having converted from the Anglican faith on marrying a wealthy landowner in County Wexford, Captain Justin Brenane, J.P. Now aged 64, she undertook the upbringing of Lafcadio in her own home with the assistance of a nurse maid in the early years. As a widow without any children, she took to regarding the boy as her own son, thus filling the void in her life left by her husband and her childless marriage. The boy had an impish nature and was not easily disciplined. Mrs Brenane was apparently rather liberal in matters of education and religion. The boy received no formal instruction and was left free to read from an extensive library and to listen to the folk-tales of the servants.

His imagination was already a fertile field for fantasy, auguring his future talent for story-telling. Lafcadio once imagined he saw a figure in the lonely top floor of the house. Thinking it was his cousin Jane, who used to tease him, he called to her. The figure turned towards him but it had no face, only a pale blur, and then vanished. His cousin later fell ill and died on that floor. He had constant nightmares caused by his guardian's decision that he should sleep alone in the darkness with the bedroom door locked. Memories of imagined horror returned in his later work as a writer.

Outside Dublin, he spent holidays at Tramore where he learned to swim, a pleasure he would retain all his life, and he also spent holidays in Connemara near Cong, both places where relatives had residences. Of that time he wrote later a short account of meeting a traditional singer and harper but curiously he places the scene in Wales and not Ireland although he gives the words of the harper's song as the well-known lines from Thomas Moore: 'Believe me, if all those endearing young charms.' Clearly, Lafcadio was not only rejecting the memory of his father but also of the country from which his father came. Indeed, he had little to say of the other Ireland, which had recently suffered a great famine, the land stalked by disease and death and the people, losing all hope, emigrating in tens of thousands.

He now had a tutor who, on discovering Lafcadio absorbed in a book on classical Greece, took it away from him. When it again appeared on the library shelf Lafcadio found that the gods and goddesses had been 'dressed', some of them with baggy bathing suits. He wrote later: this barbarism proved of some educational value, it furnished me with many problems of restoration and enabled me to develop a very artistic line for later use in drawing classes.'

Lafcadio's great expectations as the heir of great-aunt Sarah never were fulfilled. Mrs Brenane, now in her seventies, went to live in England with a relative, Henry Molyneux, and his wife. Lafcadio was sent to boarding school in France and then in England. The College Lafcadio attended in England was St Cuthbert's near Durham, the College of Cardinal Wiseman and of the poet Francis Thompson. There he was known as Paddy Hearn and was regarded as a 'wild Irish boy'. To some he appeared to be a leprechaun. His schoolmates later recalled his many pranks and tricks which made him quite popular except with his teachers. He began to read avidly – travel and adventure stories were his favourites. Thus, his literary interests developed. He let his right-hand index-finger nail grow so that he could use it as quill pen. He began to question accepted rules and beliefs and seemed to go out of his way to shock his English Catholic superiors.

While at St Cuthbert's he suffered a dreadful piece of bad luck that affected him for life. During a game in the school playground he was hit by a knotted rope which struck him in the left eye. Severe inflammation led to surgical treatment but the eye could not be saved. The boy had been nearsighted and now he had only his one good eye which he had to use even more as writing and reading became his main interests in life. The punishing use of this good eye caused it to become enlarged while the sightless eye remained covered with scar tissue. This most unfortunate accident affected Hearn's emotional balance for the rest of his life. He was always conscious of the disfigurement and reacted more than he might otherwise have done to any suspicion of rejection by others. In photographs he always posed in profile.

Meanwhile, his great-aunt had allowed Henry Molyneux to use her money in a business which went bankrupt.

Lafcadio was withdrawn from St Cuthbert's at the age of 17 and sent to live with his former nursemaid and companion, Catherine Ronan, who had married a dock worker named Delaney in London. This was a traumatic transition for the youth but his sudden descent into the lower depths may have heightened his capacity for realistic observation. In contrast, he took a growing interest in romantic writers whom he wished to emulate. Suddenly, Molyneux decided to eliminate the young man from his life and that of his guardian, Mrs Brenane. Lafcadio at the age of 19 was given passage money to America and was told to seek out a relative in the city of Cincinnati to help get himself a job. So, in the spring of 1889, Lafcadio Hearn journeyed across the Atlantic carrying with him a tremendous burden of resentments, hates and fears but also carrying a great reserve of personal pride, ambition and talent.

☐

He arrived in America when it was recovering from the Civil War. Cincinnati was at the cross-roads of North and South, divided by the great Ohio River. To the older stock of New Englanders, Germans, French and Irish, were now added the homeless and rootless emancipated blacks who brought from the South their plantation culture, their religious songs and stories. There were possibilities for work if one could get a good start. The young Lafcadio, however, had another setback. His relatives in Cincinnati gave him a small amount of money but made it clear that they wanted to have as little to do with him as possible.

Cast off completely on his own, he believed that he had been cheated by his father and all his father's relatives and the bitterness remained with him for the rest of his life. He found some menial work of various kinds and became a boarding-house servant, lighting fires and shovelling coal in exchange for food and sleeping on the floor of a small bare room.

Previously, he had slept in stables and so was grateful for this new 'luxury'. Later, he wrote to a half-sister on his father's side: 'My dear little sister has been very lucky, she has not seen the wolf's side of life, the ravening side, the apish side, the ugly facets of the monkey puzzle. I found myself dropped into the enormous machinery of life of which I knew nothing. I had to sleep for nights in the street only to be moved on by the police.'

However, the first good turn in his fortunes occurred when he met the owner of a small printing shop, Henry Watkin, who took him in as an assistant tidying up papers, sweeping the floor and sharing his meals. He now slept on a bed made of paper from the shavings of the book-binding department. Watkin provided an old man's advice and companionship in the evening and he and Lafcadio would sit and talk. Watkin was the first firm friend that Hearn met in America. Hearn would read to him from the serious magazines and they would discuss life and philosophy with complete freedom. In the public library of Cincinnati, which contained 50,000 books, Hearn educated himself even further, and made new friends who helped him to get ahead. Through Henry Watkin he met Captain Leonard Barney who took him on as an assistant for a trade journal.

He now moved to a boarding house as a lodger, no longer a servant, and there he met a young woman of mixed race called Mattie Foley who worked in the kitchen and had a four-year old son. He was attracted by her good looks and kindness and she listened to his tales of misfortune. Her mother had been a slave on a Kentucky farm and her father was the owner of the plantation. Her tales of misfortune coincided with his own and touched a chord in Lafcadio's heart. Before long, they found themselves entangled in an intimate relationship. However, Mattie was a simple and kind-hearted but uneducated girl with whom Hearn could not share his intellectual interests.

Meanwhile, Hearn got his first chance as a serious writer

when the principal Cincinnati newspaper *The Enquirer* published a review which he had written on Tennyson's *The Idylls of the King*. By 1874, he had become a regular journalist of *The Enquirer*, combining literary reviews with down-to-earth reporting. His powers of observation and description had been enhanced by the compensatory need to use the sight of one eye with greater intensity than if he had two. He became known as a realistic and sensational reporter, covering murders in the greatest detail and writing special articles on such diverse and grisly subjects as slaughterhouses, paupers' graves, lunatic asylums, poorhouses and executions. He also developed a great interest in the river community of Cincinnati. Along the great Ohio river, a tributary of the Mississippi, there were many distinct and colourful people of black, white and mixed race, with their own songs, dances and customs. Those from the South, both blacks and whites, held a particular fascination for Hearn.

Suddenly, in 1875, he lost his job on *The Enquirer*, apparently as a result of his relationship with Mattie Foley. He had decided that they must marry but at that time in Ohio a marriage could not be performed legally between a white person and a black. Lafcadio stubbornly insisted and secured a marriage licence without revealing the true facts. They were married in this fashion in 1874 but the case did not become known to the owner of the newspaper until the following year. By that stage the marriage was already falling apart. She turned to drink and bad friends and for long stretches they hardly saw each other. Later, she said that she had grown weary of his oddities and that their moods were not the same.

Hearn was then employed at a lower salary by *The Cincinnati Commercial* newspaper but was now disillusioned and decided to move down the Mississippi to the deep South, to a warmer and more exotic climate. He went first to Memphis and then to New Orleans. He had little money and only one recommendation to help him to become established. New Orleans, with its polyglot population, its Creole culture and nearby Indian reservation of the Choctaw tribe, was a fascinating city. Calling upon his early education in French he made translations of works of contemporary French writers such as Theophile Gautier and Gustave Flaubert. Before he left Cincinnati he had obtained an assignment from *The Cincinnati Commercial* to write from New Orleans a series of articles on life in that city. He wrote fourteen articles but then was told that a New Orleans correspondent was no longer required. Hearn, weakened by near starvation, fell victim of a fever and later wrote to his friend Henry Watkin: 'My face is as dry as a knife and my skin has become as dark as that of a mulatto.'

Fortunately, his only letter of recommendation enabled him to obtain employment in a small newspaper, a four-page sheet called *The Item*. He also entered into a partnership for the running of a '5 Cent-Restaurant' known as the Hard Times Restaurant. Again he was unlucky: his partner scooped up the profits for the first month and disappeared. However, Hearn soon established himself as a reporter and writer in New Orleans, especially in colourful accounts of the exotic side of life including voodoo and other primitive beliefs. He was attracted also by the oriental tales of Pierre Loti, the French naval officer, who wrote of his romantic – often amorous adventures – in the Orient.

By 1880, he became well-known in a wider sphere. *Chita*, a novella of Creole life, was published and well received. He had moved to the principal newspaper, *The Times Democrat*, and his circle of friends began to widen. (Behind his back, a door closed in Cincinnati in 1880: Mattie Foley remarried, this time legally.) As in Cincinnati his writing encompassed a wide range and he also brought out a book on Creole cooking. His best friends were his doctor, also a man of literary talent, Rudolph Matas, and a young woman journalist, Elizabeth Bisland, who both remained firm friends. The Irish-American writer W.D. O'Connor noticed his work and he and Hearn entered into regular correspondence. He admired the work of the Anglo-Irish writers Ferguson, Allingham and later W.B. Yeats and was much influenced by the Gothic tales of Maturin and Le Fanu.

Hearn became more attracted to oriental themes and brought out a book of Chinese folktales. Then came the event which determined the later course of his life and work. New Orleans staged a World Industrial Exhibition in 1884 and Hearn was greatly involved in his newspaper's promotion of this event. Visiting the exhibition grounds he was particularly attracted to the Japanese pavilion and made the acquaintance of the Japanese Commissioner, Ichizo Hattori. This proved later to be a most fortunate meeting when Lafcadio Hearn eventually arrived in Japan.

Hearn's interest in the exotic and oriental brought him to the island of Martinique in 1887, where he spent almost a year working on a novel and on various articles about the French West Indies. The result was *Two Years in the French West Indies*, a collection of his vivid accounts of the life and traditions of a people unspoiled by modernity. He also wrote *Youma*, a novella about a West Indian slave. It was not immediately accepted for publication. He caught a serious illness and had to return to the United States where he became increasingly restless. He moved to New York only to find it entirely unappealing despite the many friends he made in the literary and publishing world.

During his time in New York, he received a letter from James Daniel his brother, who had read about him and had seen his picture in a local newspaper. It turned out that James Daniel was now a farmer in Ohio. Suspicious as ever, Lafcadio replied to this approach very cautiously, addressing his brother as 'Dear Sir', and asked for his full name, his mother's name prior to her marriage, her native place and where she now lived. James Daniel Hearn knew less than Lafcadio the answers to these questions but convinced him that he was his brother. Lafcadio apologized and wrote: 'You ought to have on the calf of your leg three lines made by our mother at the time of baptism.' It turned out that his brother had been sent away separately to a school in England where he had stayed until the age of 16 and arrived in the United States in 1871, two years after Lafcadio. He had lost everything in the great Chicago fire in that year, at a time when Lafcadio was also having a bad time in Cincinnati. But James Daniel was practical and showed a business talent in various areas such as tobacco growing and milling. He had owned a farm and lost it and now was renting one. He sent a picture of his wife and baby. They corresponded but never met.

Lafcadio Hearn now loathed New York. He did not find enough work there to supplement his income from books. He was determined to go on his travels again and to make a break with his New York life. *Harper's Magazine* suggested that he go to Japan and accepted the outline of a book which he would write on that country. And so, together with an illustrator, he travelled from New York to Montreal and then crossed the continent on the Canadian Pacific Railway to Vancouver in British Columbia. He and his companion boarded the ship *Abyssinia* which began its crossing of the Pacific on St Patrick's Day, 17 March 1890. Eighteen days later Hearn, for the first time, saw the cone of Mount Fuji rising above the dark shore of Japan.

☐

Hearn's stay in Japan was meant to be temporary, one of a few months, to enable him to write a book which bore the name *Glimpses of Unfamiliar Japan*, but he fell out with his illustrator companion and then with his publishers. He decided that he would remain in Japan for a longer period and seek a new publisher, earning an income as a teacher of English. He had fallen in love with Japan: everything seemed so strange but so beautiful. Later, he wrote in the first chapter of his book: 'There is some charm unutterable in the morning air, cool with the coolness of Japanese spring and wind-waves from the snowy cone of Fuji. . . Everything, as well as everybody, is small and queer and mysterious. The little houses under their blue roofs, the little shop-fronts hung with blue, and the smiling little people in their blue costumes. . . .' He wrote to Henry Watkin: 'Here I am in the land of dreams surrounded by strange gods I seem to have known and loved from somewhere. I burn incense before them.' Indeed, his first weeks in Japan were spent visiting many shrines and temples. In the ancient city of Kamakura he swung a great beam to sound a bell 650 years old. He wrote: 'A sound deep as thunder rolls from the hills and far away.'

He ended his association with *Harper's Magazine* by writing an angry letter accusing them of underpaying him and of cheating him as regards travel expenses. Turning his back on the American publishers, he obtained introductions through new friends in Japan, notably Mitchell McDonald, the US Navy Paymaster at Yokohama and Ichizo Hattori, the friendly Commissioner of the New Orleans pavilion, who was now Vice-Minister of Education.

With this help, and that of the eminent Prof. Basil Hall Chamberlain of Tokyo Imperial University, Hearn obtained a teaching assignment in Matsue, a city far from Tokyo on the other side of the country by the Japan Sea. There, Lafcadio Hearn was to spend the happiest and most fruitful year of his life. He was given the task of teaching English to schoolboys from 12 to 16 years of age, some of whom were destined to be teachers themselves. He developed a close affectionate relationship with many of his students and became a popular local celebrity. He had won the support of both the Governor and the school authorities.

He was in a part of Japan know as the 'Land of the Gods', where all the consecrated dead were supposed to gather once a year. It was a country of ancient traditions, old stories and colourful customs and kindly people, but it was cold in winter-time and Hearn was not taking care of himself. His Japanese friends decided he needed a wife and in the way of Japanese tradition a teacher colleague acted as matchmaker and go-between. The young woman who was chosen was the daughter of a samurai who had come down in the world. In the old Japan, under the rule of Shogun, the class of samurai or noble warriors had a dominant position in Japanese society. They were not only highly disciplined as soldiers but also highly educated as administrators. This class was, however, abolished in the new Japan of the Meiji era which came into being some 20 years before Lafcadio Hearn arrived in that country. His wife's name was Setsuko meaning 'little true one' and her family name was Koizumi. In marrying Lafcadio Hearn, Setsuko was helping her family financially, as Hearn was well paid as a foreigner. The marriage took place in January 1891 according to Japanese law and custom. Hearn was now responsible not only for the upkeep of his wife but also her parents and grandparents. Later, his wife wrote: 'When I married him I found in his house only one table and a chair, a few books, one suit of clothes and a Japanese *kimono*.'

Their marriage was successful despite differences in character. Although Hearn loved Japan to extravagance, his manners did not conform to Japanese custom. He had little patience and never disguised his anger. In Japan this is quite contrary to normal behaviour. If he took a dislike to somebody he would say so and usually the cause of the dislike was not at all reasonable. From his unhappy early years he had been quick to take offence. On the other hand, his wife noted how kind he was with children and little animals. She took control of the practical side of his life and helped him gather and translate old Japanese folk-tales. She was no Mme. Butterfly to be loved and then discarded. For Hearn this marriage was a binding one and he intended it to remain so.

He was able to pursue his studies of local customs and

folk-tales, preparing for publication *Glimpses of Unfamiliar Japan*, which was published two years later. Hearn maintained contact with his friends in the US. He told them about his life and the various incidents when travelling about the countryside. One amusing story concerned his stay at a little hotel in a fishing village. A crowd gathered to stare at the foreigner and the hotel proprietor went out to chase them away. Hearn gives the following account of the proprietor's argument with the crowd: 'You there, what are you doing? What is so marvellous? This is not a theatre, he is not a juggler, he is not a wrestler, what is so amusing? He is an honourable guest.' But the crowd responded, pleading with the hotel owner: 'Please let us see, we want to see.' And then: 'He that we look at will not be worn out by our looking at him.'

After only one year in Matsue, Hearn was obliged to leave for health reasons. The winters in Matsue were notoriously very cold and he soon began to suffer from respiratory complaints. Reluctantly, he said farewell to Matsue, to take up a new teaching post in the city of Kumamoto in the warmer southern island of Kyushu. With him went Setsuko and her family. As the little boat left, some 200 students with their teachers assembled and Hearn describes his departure as follows: The little steamer shrieks . . . a long ah h h h h rises up from the uniform ranks and all the caps wave. I shout in English "goodbye" and there floats back to me a cry "Manzai, Manzai (ten thousand years to you, ten thousand years)"'.

The city of Kumamoto was different to Matsue where life had been relaxed and informal. Now in Kumamoto, an important administrative centre, Hearn found the school to be larger and the staff and students impersonal and less friendly. He made few new friends but concentrated on his second book for publication in the US. Both this work and the first book *Glimpses of Unfamiliar Japan* (1894) were published in Boston by Houghton Mifflin Co.

A Profile of Lafcadio Hearn

His first child was born in 1893 and he was most concerned that the little boy would have normal eyesight, although there was no reason why he should not. However, Hearn felt the loss of one eye as an enduring obsession. He wrote: 'Last night my child was born, a very strong boy with large black eyes; he looks more like a Japanese than a foreign boy but he has my nose but his mother's features. In other respects there is no fault in him and he promises to become very tall.' These remarks indicated Hearn's obsession with his small stature and his visual handicap.

After three years, unhappy with his situation in Kumamoto he and his family moved to the port city of Kobe where he had obtained, through his contacts in the English-speaking community, a position as editorial writer in the *Kobe Chronicle*. By this stage, his reputation in literary circles in the US had grown following the publication there of his books on Japan. In Kobe he continued to write and became established in the West as the foremost interpreter in English of Japanese life and culture.

In 1895, Lafcadio Hearn took Japanese citizenship in order to protect his family from an increasingly nationalistic xenophobia and to safeguard their inheritance rights. He adopted his wife's surname, Koizumi, and as his first name he chose Yakumo, meaning 'eight clouds', taken from an ancient poem associated with the 'Land of the Gods'. Hearn was now officially known as Koizumi Yakumo. Two more boys and a girl were born to the Koizumis.

His failing eyesight obliged him to give up his newspaper work in Kobe but his prestige was such that he was appointed to the Imperial University in Tokyo as Professor of English Language and Literature. He held this post for over six years and in 1904 accepted a similar position at Waseda University, also in Tokyo, noted for its interest in the liberal arts.

His general health had been deteriorating for some years and he reduced his social contacts to a few close friends. His relations with the foreign community soured, as he opposed the work of Christian missionaries and others who, in his view, were a disruptive influence in Japanese life. His own philosophical outlook was that of a rather dogmatic evolutionist for whom Darwin and Spencer were the guiding stars.

He died quite suddenly of heart failure at the age of 54 on 26 September 1904. His remains were cremated and buried at a Buddhist funeral in Zoshigaya cemetery in Tokyo, under trees in an area where he liked to walk with his family.

Shortly before he died, Hearn had brought together into one book his definitive analysis of Japanese history, culture and society. Entitled *Japan – An Attempt at Interpretation*, the book was constructed from lectures he had intended to give at Cornell University. Generally sympathetic to Japan and its people, the work also contained a warning of things to come.

With the outbreak of the war between Japan and Russia in 1904, Japan had entered a new age as a military power. For Hearn who had written 'that a man may do better service to his country by writing a book than winning a battle', this new development was ominous. He warned the Japanese against taking on too quickly and too easily the manners and customs and the industrial, commercial and military aspects of the Western powers.

Some forty years after his death, Hearn's interpretation and prophetic insight made a significant impact at the time of Japan's surrender at the end of World War II. A personal adviser to General MacArthur was a strong admirer of Hearn's work and a close friend of the Koizumi family. This was Brig. Gen. Bonner Fellers, a former West Point lecturer in English literature who had come across Hearn's books and lectures when at West Point in the twenties. He and his wife visited Japan in 1930 and called on Hearn's widow and family. In further prewar visits he befriended Kazuo, Hearn's eldest son. The friendship later extended to the next generation: Fellers' daughter Nancy became a Hearn scholar and co-edited a Hearn anthology with Kazuo Koizumi.

Brig. Gen. Fellers opposed efforts by the victorious Allies to have Emperor Hirohito placed on trial as a war criminal. In a memorandum to MacArthur he drew upon Hearn's interpretation of the symbolic role of the Emperor, which he insisted had a positive value in persuading the Japanese people to accept the surrender and the Occupation and also the subsequent democratic constitution and reconstruction of Japanese political and economic life. MacArthur took this advice and the Emperor was allowed to remain as Head of State, to be treated with respect as US-Japanese post-war cooperation developed.

Thus it may be said that Lafcadio Hearn reciprocated posthumously the debt of kindness and generosity that he owed to the Japanese people. They, for their part, have never forgotten the gifts of creativity and interpretation that he brought to an understanding of their life and culture. The work of Lafcadio Hearn as Koizumi Yakumo is still studied with admiration and affection in Japanese schools and colleges. In the West, including Ireland, there is a renewed interest in his work. During the State Visit to Japan of the then President of Ireland, Dr Patrick Hillery, in September 1983, the importance of Lafcadio Hearn in Irish-Japanese cultural relations was stressed in speeches by Emperor Hirohito and President Hillery.

5

Lafcadio Hearn and I

TOKI KOIZUMI

──────────── oOo ────────────

Firstly, I would like to convey my gratitude to H.E. Former Ambassador Sean G. Ronan, Mr Ronald Bolger the Chairman of the IJA [Ireland Japan Association][1], Mrs Yoshiko Ushioda of the Chester Beatty Library, and Mr and Mrs Seo of Sundai School, and also to H.E. Ambassador James Sharkey who helped me in Tokyo, in providing me with such a pleasant and honourable occasion to speak to all of you gathered here about my grandfather, Lafcadio Hearn in his country – Ireland. As a grandson of Lafcadio, I am so excited that no words can express how I am feeling now. I would first like to express my great appreciation to you all for coming here today to hear my talk.

Lafcadio Hearn died in 1904 when his first son, Kazuo, who was my father, was just 10 years old. I heard about

Lafcadio Hearn and I

Lafcadio through my grandmother Setsu, my father Kazuo, and my mother. My grandmother Setsu died when I was eight years old but I remember her quite well.

Today, with many anecdotes known in my family, I would like to talk about Lafcadio Hearn at home from the view point of one of his relations.

LAFCADIO HEARN AND HIS GRANDCHILDREN

You probably know already that Lafcadio came to Japan in 1890 and married Setsu Koizumi who was a daughter of the Mandarin class in Matsue. They had three sons and a daughter. I am the only son of Lafcadio's first son, Kazuo. My son, Bon Koizumi is my only son. Last year I had my first grandson, So Koizumi.

My father, Kazuo, was born when Lafcadio was teaching in a college in Kumamoto (Daigo Koto-Gagakko which is now the University of Kumamoto). He studied English literature in Waseda University in Tokyo. He wrote about the memories of Lafcadio, and published the letters of his father. Lafcadio's second son, Iwao, studied English literature in the Imperial University of Kyoto, and later taught English in Momoyama secondary school in Kyoto. He translated the complete works of Lafcadio into Japanese in 1933. He wrote some novels of his own as well. Lafcadio's third son, Kiyoshi, studied painting in an Academy and became a painter. He painted under the influences of Cubism. His works were not evaluated before World War Two. However, he was eventually awarded the Yomiuri Prize after the war. Lafcadio's only daughter, Suzuko, was not healthy throughout her life and never married. All Lafcadio's children are now deceased.

There are five grandchildren of Lafcadio, namely two sons and a daughter from Iwao, one from Kiyoshi, and myself.

'KWAIDAN' AND CELTIC PATTERNS

I would now like to tell you some stories about Lafcadio Hearn in relation to Ireland, some of which I told at the World Conference of IASAIL (International Association for the Study of Anglo-Irish Literature) in Kyoto in 1990. Unfortunately, in the very first biography of Lafcadio Hearn, in Japanese, which was written by Mr Yuji Tabe – one of Lafcadio's students – there was very little reference about the relationship between Lafcadio and Ireland. However, during the past four or five years, I have had some contact with Irish people and I have learned Irish folklore, culture and customs. Having heard these things, I have come to realize Lafcadio's Irish connections. I will give you some examples, though I am not sure at this stage whether my interpretation is reasonable or not.

Lafcadio was very much interested in stories of spirits, fairies, and ghosts in Japan and he published 'Kwaidan' in his later years. After settling in Japan, he heard many of these stories from his wife, Setsu. He did not have any dislike for them as a Christian, but tried to understand the spiritual world. This may be due to the time spent in his youth in Dublin when he was told Irish fairy stories. After he moved to America, Lafcadio's memories of these fairy tales made him even more interested in these. I do believe, however, that these interests had their culmination after his arrival in Japan, as he was caught by the attractiveness of the Japanese world of fairy tales, *Kwaidan*, and ghosts.

I heard from Mr Seo that Ms Mayumi Tsuruoka, who was the most distinguished expert of Celtic culture in Japan, had visited the Lafcadio Hearn Library at the Sundai School in Co. Kildare, in order to see the first version of *Kwaidan*. Actually, on the cover page of the first version, a special pattern drawn by Lafcadio himself is printed just below the title of the book. Ms Tsuruoka thought this special pattern might have its origin in traditional Celtic design. I think it is a really interesting discovery. I am looking forward to the release of her new book. Also one of my acquaintances, who is making a chronology of Lafcadio's works through careful examination of his hand-writing, mentioned about the possibility that the said special pattern might have some influences from Celtic designs. Taking these new facts into consideration, though some more research is required, we may deduce that when Lafcadio was writing *Kwaidan* in Japan, he recollected his memories of Irish fairy tales, mixed them with those of Japan, and put a Celtic pattern on the cover page.

SPECIAL WRITING DESK

In Tokyo, Lafcadio had a special writing desk made for his son, Kazuo. The desk was very tall with a sloped top. He made a sketch of the desk himself and ordered a furniture maker in Shinjuku-Yotusuya to make it. According to my father, Lafcadio took great care of his eyes and therefore, he made a special desk so that his children would not be short-sighted. Unfortunately, this desk disappeared.

However, some years ago when I was watching a quiz programme on TV, the very same desk was shown and it was stated that Lafcadio had used this desk in his childhood and that it still belonged to one of Lafcadio's relations. I was really surprised and quickly requested Ambassador Ronan to find out who owned the desk. Soon, we found that the desk belonged to Dr John Oulton Wisdom, a philosopher, who was a descendant of Lafcadio's aunt, Jane. Unfortunately, he passed away recently. I suppose that this desk was used by the young Lafcadio while he was being brought up by his great-aunt, Mrs Brenane. I think while in Tokyo, the design and shape of the desk occurred in his mind, and Lafcadio made the very same writing desk that he had used in his childhood for his own children.

If you allow me, I would like to refer to some other

relations of the Hearns. Lafcadio's aunt, Jane Hearn, who was the sister of Lafcadio's father Charles Bush Hearn had a son and daughter. Her son, Henry Francis, married the elder sister of a very famous Irish playwright – J.M. Synge. Therefore, the Hearn family is related to the Synge family.

TALES TOLD BY LAFCADIO TO MY FATHER

When I was a small boy, at the beginning of the Showa Era (1926-89), radios were just becoming popular in Japan. Therefore, our major pastime was to listen to tales told by our parents. My father often told me stories which were told by Lafcadio to my father. I can remember many of them very clearly, although some of them are now almost gone from my memory. Following my father's way, I also told my son some of these tales when he was a small boy.

Even after I had grown up, I automatically thought that these stories were from the tales of the 'Grimm Brothers' or from 'Andersen'. Of course, some of the tales which Lafcadio told my father were from these well-known books. However, there seemed to be quite a few stories from other sources, though I did not try to investigate their background.

About three years ago, I happened to encounter Prof. Tadaaki Miyake from the University of Kyoto at the Irish Embassy in Tokyo, and was given a book entitled *Irish Folk Tales and Legends*. To my surprise, I eventually found that many of the stories Lafcadio told my father, and I told my son, were Irish.

LAFCADIO'S LETTERS WITH SKETCHES

After Lafcadio settled in Tokyo he went to Yaidzu in Shizuoka Prefecture almost every summer until his death to enjoy some swimming for his own rest and pleasure, and to teach his children how to swim. Lafcadio, who was fond of the sea, enjoyed relaxation which he had not had since the time of Martinique. He would swim in the sea, teach Kazuo, and collect some local topics in that area. Everyday, while at Yaidzu, Lafcadio wrote letters in Japanese – of which he had very little knowledge – to his wife Setsu who was left in Tokyo. He wrote letters about their children, views of Yaidzu, tiny animals, insects, and flowers together with some of his sketches.

I heard that Lafcadio's father, Charles Bush Hearn who was a surgeon with the British Army, had been so strict that he had seldom smiled. However, I also heard that he had doted upon his children. When he was in India, he often wrote letters with sketches to Patricio Lafcadio Hearn in Dublin. Later in his life, Lafcadio told his own family that his father had written to him with stories of children's favourite animals such as tigers, elephants, or huge snakes, in simple sentences and in capital letters. To lonely Lafcadio who was separated from his mother quite early, these letters probably meant the only real warm affection of a family. I guess, this memory of letters from India was in Lafcadio's mind in Yaidzu, and therefore, he wrote a lot of letters with sketches to his wife. Moreover, the fact that he put most of his energy in writing Japanese, which was a foreign language to him, was backed by his sincerity. Speaking of Lafcadio's swimming, I would like to point out that he learned how to swim in Tramore, Co. Waterford, where he was brought every summer by his great-aunt and became very good at it.

OTHER ANECDOTES

Before finishing my talk today, I would like to relate a few more little anecdotes of Lafcadio's childhood. When Lafcadio was small, his mother Rosa made him wear a Greek-style cap with a long velvet tail. This cap was strange for Irish children, and when Lafcadio went outside the home, many of the neighbourhood kids pulled the tail. I imagine Lafcadio explained this old memory to his family as if he were showing a piece of still-photography.

One day, when he went out for shopping with a housekeeper, he came across a party of cavalry. He thought that his father must be in the party, and actually found his father. As he shouted to his father, his father pulled up Lafcadio and continued the parade with him in his arms. Lafcadio recounted later how he had never been so exultant as this time and he felt he had never been more proud of his father in his life. Later, while the officers were having their meal in an officers' club, Lafcadio was bored and crawled under the table. He was amazed as he felt as if he were in a jungle of boots. But soon, he began to go here and there under the table and kicked the boots.

Probably, the following story took place while Lafcadio was with his great-aunt. An old housekeeper bought a pretty porcelain doll in the shape of a cow and put it on the cupboard in the kitchen. Shortly after, Lafcadio found it, but he was told by her that the doll was not a toy and should never be touched. The doll was to keep milk in it and when the cork piece on the teats was taken off, the milk inside flowed out. Lafcadio was very excited with this mechanism and thought that if he continued to be a good boy, he could get the doll. However, some days later, this cow doll suddenly disappeared. When Lafcadio asked the housekeeper why the cow had disappeared, she answered that it was a birthday gift for her own child and not for Lafcadio. Lafcadio in his later days told his own family that he had never forgotten the great regret he had felt that time, and thus made everybody in the family laugh. Lafcadio's sons, Kazuo and Iwao, asked their father to buy such a cow, but such a cow was not available in Japan at that time. Therefore, when I found a milk pitcher in the shape of a Swiss cow made four years ago, I was really excited. I bought it and have been serving our guests with this pitcher ever since. I feel that I myself, a third generation descendant of Lafcadio, took revenge for Lafcadio's regrets.

Lafcadio said that although he will not forgive what his

father had done to him, he envied his father for being buried in the sea. Lafcadio wished to be buried in the clean sea and to have his eternal rest surrounded by corals, and various fish. What a poetic wish it was! I imagine how Lafcadio would feel if he saw many people enjoying skin-diving easily nowadays. I hear that Charles suffered from malaria in India and died on 21st November, 1866 near Suez on his way home. He was buried at sea.

Since the time of Lafcadio, it is our custom in my family to have Christmas Pudding on Christmas day. Ambassador Ronan and Mrs Seo were kind enough to provide me with Plum Puddings from Bewley's. Mrs Seo once pointed out that there is a possibility that the young Lafcadio had gone to Bewley's in a carriage with his grand-aunt to buy Plum Puddings, and I also agree with this assumption. My grandmother wrote that Lafcadio liked beef steaks and Plum Pudding very much until his death.

6

Two Celts in Japan: Enigma of the East

SHERLEY McEGILL

———————————— oOo ————————————

In many respects, there is a striking similarity between the careers of the late Professor Tadhg O'Conroy, who died on 5 November 1935, formerly Professor of English at Keio University, Tokyo, and Lafcadio Hearn, the eccentric Irish genius who was also a Professor of English in the Imperial University at Tokyo. O'Conroy died at the age of 52 and Hearn died at the age of 54. Both went to Japan full of high hopes. They were enthralled by the glamour of the Lotus land. They married Japanese girls of high caste and though both men lived very happily with their wives they eventually became disillusioned with Japan.

O'Conroy, however, made the tragic mistake of criticizing

the Japanese. They are an ultra-sensitive race, and the Oriental mentality objects to criticism of a destructive character. Unlike Hearn, he apparently did not attempt to make himself amenable to the customs of the country.

The life of Lafcadio Hearn in Japan is one of the romances of literature. During his earlier years in the country he was quite happy; but eventually he became baffled by the enigma of the East.

PARENTAGE

Hearn had an adventurous career before fate landed him in Japan. His father, Charles Bush Hearn, was an Irish doctor, who, when serving with the British Army, met and married a Greek girl named Rosa Tessima.[1] Their son, whom they called Patricio Lafcadio Tessima Carlos Hearn, was born in August 1850. Two years later, he was sent to Dublin when his father's regiment was drafted to the West Indies. Unfortunately, Mrs Hearn did not like Dublin. She could not speak English and as she was a Catholic while her husband's people were Protestants; there was a conflict of temperament. She eventually returned to her own country. When the marriage was eventually dissolved in 1856 poor young Patricio suffered mental torture in consequence of the domestic upheaval involved by the desertion of his mother.

Fortunately, a Catholic aunt, Mrs Sarah Brenane adopted the child and he had a happy childhood at 73 Upper Leeson Street, Dublin. In 1863, he was sent to the celebrated English Catholic College at Ushaw. Patricio's education was, however, interrupted by the financial reverses suffered by his aunt. In 1867 his relatives got rid of him by paying his passage to the United States.

Here his misfortunes began. In those days it was difficult for a sensitive and delicate boy to make a livelihood in America. He had a varied career for fourteen years, and it was not until 1881 that his mastery of the English language attracted the attention of editors. He became a journalist.

In 1890, he was sent to Tokyo as American correspondent. After a few months he deserted journalism and became a professor of English in a Japanese college. He subsequently obtained a similar position at the Imperial University, Tokyo. One of his colleagues in the school advised him to get married and actually selected his wife for him. Setsu Koizumi was quite philosophic about accepting the unassuming and not very prepossessing little middle-aged man of 42. However, she proved a loyal wife and she was undoubtedly the dominant partner.

Shortly after the marriage, Lafcadio discarded his European names and became Yakumo Koizumi. He wore Japanese garments and it has been asserted that he became a Shintoist. This is a religious system of nature and hero worship. His wife worshipped her ancestors while her docile husband probably made a pretence in order to avoid family friction.

REVERSES

When Hearn adopted Japanese nationality he discovered that he lost many privileges and rights which he formerly enjoyed. For instance, his salary as a professor was drastically reduced to the ordinary Japanese rate.

This was perhaps a good thing because it stimulated him to write delightful studies of Japanese life. The style is perfect. It is graceful and dignified. It conveys delicately worded pictures of facets of a civilization which is still a mystery to the occidental mind. *Out of the East* and *Glimpses of Unfamiliar Japan* are two of his best known books.

To the discerning reader it is obvious that his earlier life in Ireland influenced his literary work. Many of his word pictures of Japan are idyllic descriptions of sun-bathed shores and purple-clad hills in the Isle of the West towards which his thoughts frequently turned when he felt the exile's loneliness for home and kindred.

Towards the end of his life Hearn longed 'to smell once more the peat-laden atmosphere of his Irish home, to see the daisy-strewn meadows of Tramore and sunlit Lough Corrib'.

But his wish was not realized. He was driven out of his post in the University. This fanned the flame of his desire to leave the country. But failing health and his consideration for his young family compelled him to remain in Japan. His soul became sad. 'Never, dearest', he wrote, 'never shall we meet – not even when the stars are dead'. On 26 September 1904, the night came 'never to be broken by any dawn'.

The Japanese claimed him as their own. They gave him a Buddhist funeral in the Buddhist Temple of Jitoin Kobudera.

7

Irish but as Japanese as the Haiku

ULICK O'CONNOR

———————————— oOo ————————————

In 1953 I wrote my first literary essay for the *Dublin Magazine* then edited by one of the last survivors of the Irish Literary Renaissance, the poet Seamus O'Sullivan. He was generous in writing to me about the piece and seemed genuinely excited about the fact that I had fished up information about someone who was then little known. It was an essay on the Irish writer, Lafcadio Hearn, whose work I had come in contact with during a year's stay in New Orleans. My granduncle, James O'Connor, United States Congressman from Louisiana, had been in charge of the *Item* newspaper in that city in the 1890s and employed Hearn as a columnist.

When I first wrote about Lafcadio Hearn I took the view, from reading his letters (and as a result of not reading enough of his works), that his real creative output would have come

Irish but as Japanese as the Haiku

from his interest in Creole cultures of New Orleans and the West Indies, and that his last years, which were spent in Japan, where he became Professor of English at the Imperial University of Tokyo and a Japanese citizen, were barren from a creative point of view. How wrong I was. Today, Hearn is regarded by the Japanese themselves as one of the few writers who has managed to understand their culture and explain it to the outside world – superior to Pierre Loti, Rudyard Kipling, even Arthur Waley, whose translation of Japanese literature and plays are looked on in the West as masterpieces.

In 1984 Penguin issued an edition of Lafcadio Hearn's work from Japan edited with an excellent introduction by Francis King.[1] Why this book is so fascinating is that it makes a selection from the rather haphazard publications of Hearn and puts them together in such a way as to give us a picture of a culture that we are almost in total ignorance of.

For instance, can you imagine what insect music is? Well, in Tokyo Lafcadio Hearn discovered twelve varieties of musical insects sold in tiny wooden cages from booths illuminated like magic lanterns. Later, he was to learn that there is a whole literature, going back to Lady Murasaki of the eleventh century, which centred around the customs of keeping musical insects. Here, we cage larks and nightingales, but who would, amongst us, have thought of imprisoning a grasshopper?

In Tokyo, when Hearn arrived there, the majority of people wore clogs. He was puzzled as to why these Japanese clogs made the sound 'kring krang' till he discovered that the left clog was made differently from the right one so that the walker's step would have an alternative rhythmic structure. Another petite Japanese touch. Soon, he had accustomed himself to a new sound, that of a brazen gong being struck in the city streets. These were the gongs of pilgrims going on the traditional Japanese pilgrimage to one thousand shrines which might take a person two years to complete.

Hearn himself made the chief pilgrimage in Japan by climbing to the top of Fuji, the Japanese Knock,[2] which peak, eternally snow-covered, hangs like an inverted white cone against the sky. The Japanese Buddhist reveres Fuji because its form is like the white bud of the Sacred Flower and because the eight points which surround it are like the eight petals of the Lotus, symbolizing perception, contemplation, conduct, etc. All this fascinated Lafcadio Hearn and, after some years in Japan he had become Japanized, married a Japanese woman and absorbed himself in Buddhist teachings. A Japanese authority wrote of him that he was 'as Japanese as the Haiku'. He took the name of Koizumi Yakumo (Yakumo means 'eight clouds').

Japan, like Ireland, is an island and one wonders if it was the intense beauty of the landscape which lured Lafcadio Hearn into assuming the personality of the people who lived there. He has written that he was so struck by the filmy mist of the petals of the plum and cherry trees that he wondered if the trees had become so domesticated and caressed in this land of the gods that they had acquired souls of their own and were trying to show their gratitude to the men and women who had made them thus. On the other hand, he wondered if the beauty of the Japanese landscape had not itself somehow influenced the character of the people.

There is much in, for instance, the belief that a man can rediscover himself in nature, that spiritual fulfilment can be found through the contemplation of beauty, which reflects the culture of pre-Christian Ireland. The Samurai culture and the tales that it generated have much in common with the Cuchulain sagas and the Ulster Cycle. One wonders why Hearn, who was brought up in Dublin by a Catholic grandaunt, Mrs Brenane, and who severed his connection with Ireland when nineteen, never made a comparison between the culture of his native land and the one he adopted. Perhaps he knew little of the heroic past of his country! It was left to Yeats, less than a decade after Lafcadio Hearn's death (in 1904) to make the bridge between the two cultures with his plays based on the Japanese Noh form, thus establishing the two leading interpreters of Oriental culture in this century as Irishmen.

8

Lafcadio Hearn in New Orleans[1]

ULICK O'CONNOR

———————————— oOo ————————————

If you leave the main thoroughfares of New Orleans, you can slip quietly away into another world, hidden behind the facade of skyscrapers and neon lights. Here the streets are thin and winding, and the people move in a world of quiet shadows. Sometimes the sun breaks through, and catches the incredibly ornate metalwork which adorns the balconies of the houses. Antique shops conceal their priceless contents under a modest exterior, and proclaim themselves the only legitimate trade in streets like these. Here and there though, you may catch a glimpse of a bar, where the waiters with pale solemn faces move like acolytes in the gloom.

Somewhere in these ancient by-ways you can find the place where Lafcadio Hearn, poet and author lived. 'Îci la che demeura "Sieur Hearn"', the people will tell you in the strange patois, a mixture of the French, Italian and negro tongues, which is spoken in the French Quarter of New Orleans.

In this house Hearn lived for six years, making his living as a writer, but often driven to strange occupations in order to supplement his small earnings. At one period he owned of all things, a laundry, surely a unique occupation for a literary figure. Of mixed race himself, he found little difficulty in mixing and making friends with the native Creoles, who formed about fifty per cent of the population of the French Quarter. These Creoles had Latin and Negro blood in their veins. They were descended from the Spanish and French aristocrats who had intermarried with the Negro slaves. Their language and customs fascinated Hearn, and he spent many years in their midst, joining only occasionally in the more exciting life of the modern part of the city.

This strange Irishman was born on the Isle of Leucadia (Levkas) in the year 1850. His father was an Irish surgeon in the British Army who had met his wife while on duty in the Ionian Islands. She was a beautiful girl of Grecian birth, and they called their son *Patricio Lefcadio* after the island on which he was born. After marriage, Surgeon Hearn returned to the family seat in Ireland and Lafcadio grew up amid the brown and purple shadows of the Dublin hills.

The Hearns, the race from which his father sprang, were an Anglo-Irish family settled in Ireland for three centuries. One of them had been Dean of Cashel, a Dignitary of the same Church which has given the World of Letters Berkeley, Dean Swift and Oliver Goldsmith.

Before long, however, Surgeon Hearn's Irish temperament proved at variance with the Latin impetuosity of his wife, and when Lafcadio was four years old his mother left for Greece. As the father's duties kept him almost permanently away from home, he left his son to the care of a rich aunt, Mrs Brenane, an enthusiastic convert to Catholicism.

He was not an easy child to rear. A passion for Greek Sculpture is a startling trait in a child of seven, and Lafcadio's guardians were constantly perplexed at the strange habits of this precocious boy. At thirteen years of age together with an enormous trunk of books, he was sent off to the Ushaw Roman Catholic Seminary at Durham. Here, despite his leanings, he was a popular little boy, and if his theories were a bit radical, his humour and vivacity assured him of a devoted circle among these future sacerdotes.

One day, he announced his disbelief in the Bible to the horror of his cassocked friends, but sometime later confided he was quite convinced of the Divine Origin of the Holy Book. He was a pious youth and a non-Catholic cousin who did not bow to an image of the Blessed Virgin, was severely admonished to do so. Some years later, circumstance made him speak bitterly of the Church of his youth, yet he remained always attracted by the Latin background of Catholicism. Years after, writing to a friend in Japan, he stated that he considered the ecclesiastical system of education the best, because of its firm discipline and set form.

While in the seminary Hearn suffered an injury, which made him sensitive about his appearance for the rest of his life. One day at play a chain caught his eye, and the subsequent treatment left him with a thin film over the left iris.

In 1869, at the age of nineteen, we find him in New York, and then later in Cincinnati, where, curiously enough, he proved himself an intrepid crime reporter. He had already shown promise as a literary artist, but it was not until he moved to the gay, vivacious atmosphere of the South that he was to find a suitable background for his creative genius.

Inspired by the descriptions of a friend in 1877, he moved to New Orleans. And what a city this great port then was. Less than sixty years before Hearn arrived, New Orleans had been a province of France. The society life of the city was still in line with any metropolis in Europe, and during the season the gracious ante bellum mansions of Louisiana, were emptied as their occupants came down to taste the gay life of New Orleans. The Old French opera house was much patronized, and when the patrons had sufficiently indulged their musical taste, they could slip down to the French Market on the banks of the Mississippi. Here, cooled by the river breeze, they could drink the nectar of New Orleans, a brand of coffee still claimed as the finest in the world.

Duelling was popular under the flowing cypresses of Audubon Park, and the city was swarming with swashbuckling, rumbustious characters, some of them immensely rich. Hearn loved to meet and talk with these latter-day D'Artagnans, and he wrote often to his friends of the feats of the legendary Bob Howard. Howard was the richest man in New Orleans. Once, furious at being blackballed by the Metairie Jockey Club, he swore: 'I'll make that place into a goddam grave-yard.' Today the Metairie street car moves smoothly past one of the most ornate cemeteries in the world. On the gateway is a memorial to its founder – Robert E. Howard.

As a newspaper man, Hearn moved in the midst of this thrilling, and exciting life. But another part of New Orleans had already captured his imagination. In the afternoons, when his work at the office was over, he would retire to the French Quarter. Here at last, he had found a people, whose hearts beat in time to the movements of his Latin soul. The hours of evening were spent wandering at random, through the palm-shadowed squares near the old cathedral, watching the passing pageant of the Creole faces.

Hearn was painstaking in the study of these people and put together with great care a dictionary of Creole phrases and a collection of their songs and music. No detail escaped him and he constantly consulted his medical friends as to some peculiar vocal tone, or cast of feature which he had noticed during his walks in the Vieux Carré. He felt that by careful investigation of all aspects of Creole life, he could eventually place his finger on the pulse of their civilization. Then he could harness this material to his genius, and create a work of real merit.

This was Hearn's life dream, and day by day, he wrote prolifically, paring and polishing his literary style. Sometimes the strangeness of this miscegenated race filled him with a great passion, and he longed to follow their civilization down to the French West Indies, to places with exotic names like Martinique, Marianao and Guantanamo.

Despite the weight of his journalistic hack-work, Hearn was a faithful correspondent, and in one of his letters to his friends he has left us some pretty pictures of life in the Quarter. In one letter he tells of a female sorceress with two skulls on her desk: in another of Jean Montanet, the Voodoo doctor down the street. 'All my medicines is pure water,' confessed this intrepid Senegalese: 'Don't hurt noone, but if folks want to give me fifty dollars, I take fifty dollars every time.'

In a short story called 'Dead Love', Hearn was surely writing his own feelings, when he lay sick of fever in his house in the Vieux Carré. 'He heard always the far off drowsy murmur, made by the toiling of the city's heart. But the gold born days died in the golden fire, and blue nights unnumbered filled the land with indigo shadows – and the perfume of the summer passed like a breath of incense.'

In 1887, his desire was fulfilled, and he spent a year-and-a-half in the French West Indies producing a book, which is a minor classic of its kind. But his hope of a place among the immortals was never achieved. Like many another Irishman, his dream of greatness was but a phantasy, destroyed by the vacillating character of his temperament.

In 1890, he left America for Japan to do a series of articles for *Harper's Magazine*. He was never to see his beloved New Orleans again. Always enticed by strange civilizations, the East opened up endless vistas of mystery for him. In a year or two he had married and adopted the Japanese way of life.

Soon he had become famous in Japan and eventually succeeded to a professorship in Tokyo University. He never forgot the Creole culture he had left in New Orleans. In a letter he wrote to a friend 'Pretty to talk of my pen of fire, when I've lost it.'

Artists often yearn after what is most unattainable to them and we can imagine Hearn in Yokohama. When his eye caught the masts of trading ships in the harbour he would feel a nostalgic longing for the old French Quarter where you could see the masts of the ships, showing between the gaps in the houses. These were the magic galleons of his heart's desire, vessels to bring him to the half-forgotten lands of the Conquistadores, where 'the sandalled sentinels still cry, sereno alerto, in the night,' just as they did 200 years ago.

In an anguished letter to a friend, Ellwood Hendrick, he wrote: 'Ah, the tropics, they still pull my heart strings. Goodness, my real field was there in the Latin countries, the Indies and Spanish America. My dream was to haunt their crumbling civilizations getting romances none else could find.' He was proved very wrong.

9

Lafcadio Hearn and Some Irish Writers[1]

ROGER McHUGH

———————— oOo ————————

Many Irish visitors to Japan during EXPO '70 may have heard the name Lafcadio Hearn mentioned as one of the first writers of English who tried to reveal Japan as it was at the turn of this century to readers in the West. Struck by his Irish surname they perhaps recalled some vague connection with Ireland.

I remember reading some of his Japanese sketches when I was a student in Dublin, then some 20 years later coming across his traces in New Orleans, where he had lived and worked as a reporter. But these traces contained nothing about his Irish context and it was not until recently, as preparation for a lecturing visit to Japan, that I started reading him again and investigating his background.

I knew from Shotaro Oshima, Hiro Ishibashi and other Japanese scholars who had visited Ireland that Hearn is still highly regarded in Japan. Mrs Lily Stephens, a distant relative of his, was able to tell me more and to lend me some books which were most helpful; and so the main facts about Hearn and the lineaments of his interesting personality began to emerge.

Lafcadio Hearn was born on the island of Santa Maura in Greece in 1850. The name Lafcadio is a corruption of Leucadia, the island's older Greek name, and appropriately derives from the Greek verb meaning 'to wander'. But it was the second name given to him at his christening. The first was Patricio. His father was Charles Bush Hearn who was an Irish military surgeon in the British Army stationed in Greece.

He married Rosa Cassimati from the island of Cerigo (the ancient Cythera) in 1849. When Lafcadio was two his father was transferred to the West Indies and his wife and child lived with Charles Bush Hearn's mother and his sister, Mrs Henry Stephens, at 48, Lower Gardiner Street, Dublin.

This Dublin period of Hearn's life is perhaps not so well known to his Japanese readers. In fact, Ireland was his home for some seventeen years. His Greek mother returned to Greece when he was four and he lived with different relatives, some Protestant, some Catholic all (as far as one can judge) decidedly bigoted. This caused him a good deal of unhappiness and gave him a dislike of institutional religion.

It seems that his happiest days as a boy were spent in Tramore where, in a setting of sea and cliffs, he heard old tales and legends from fishing and farming people. His letters in later years tell of the retentiveness of Irish oral tradition and of his vivid recollections of Irish dance tunes and harp music.

At 13, he was sent to an English Catholic College where he signed his name 'Patrick L. Hearn'. His father died abroad three years later and, after a year or so in France, the boy returned to Dublin. By this time his guardianship had passed to a Mr Molyneux who disliked him and who suddenly shipped him off to Cincinatti, Ohio, leaving him thereafter unprovided for.

Hearn dropped the 'Patrick' after that and as Lafcadio Hearn worked as a newspaper man in New Orleans and Martinique before going to Japan as a correspondent for *Harper's Magazine*. The polyglot population of these two places had helped to interest him in Oriental subjects.

He was 40 when he arrived in Japan. Within the 14 years of life which remained to him he dropped *Harper's*, edited the *Kobe Chronicle*, taught in the little town of Matsue, where he married a Japanese girl of 22 the year after his arrival, lectured at the universities of Tokyo and Waseda and produced some 13 books on Japan between 1894 and 1904, when he died in Tokyo, the place of his burial.

He had wished to be buried at Matsue but the traditions of the Samurai family into which he married decreed otherwise. However, the Lafcadio Hearn museum is located at Matsue and now contains the piece of Connemara marble engraved with the figure of a salmon which I had brought with me from Ireland as a token of remembrance. I found Hearn an interesting writer for several reasons. He anticipated by 70 years the dilemma of Japan today, the choice between preserving older traditional values and virtues and accepting the Western system of competition, economic development and military strength.

He continually questioned 'the higher morality that the strong races should rob the weak – deprive them of liberties and rights . . . force upon them not only the higher pleasures but the deeper pains of an infinitely more complicated and more unhappy civilization' and looked forward with apprehension to the day when 'there will be no hearts – watches will be substituted instead'.

In this his attitude perhaps reminds one of that of

Lafcadio Hearn and Some Irish Writers

Mishima, the Japanese novelist and poet who, after an abortive military coup in Tokyo directed 'against the bureaucrats' recently committed suicide in the traditional manner, with its stern and terrible ritual. But Mishima believed in military power and Hearn did not.

What he repeatedly tried to do was show that in many ways Buddhistic and Western thought might be reconciled; that, for example Japanese 'ancestor worship' and 'cyclic recurrence' could tie in with Western thinking about evolutionary changes and the influence of heredity and environment. In this he was perhaps more idealistic than deep; but so was Yeats, for that matter. Hearn, incidentally, like Yeats was an enthusiastic reader of Berkeley and saw an intellectual support for the visionary approach to life in Berkeley's argument that nothing material really exists except through the perceiving mind; as Yeats puts it–

> 'And God-appointed Berkeley that proved all things a dream,
> That this pragmatical, preposterous pig of a world, its farrow that so solid seem
> Must vanish on the instant if the mind but change its theme.'

Like Yeats, Hearn's approach to literature was much influenced by the old beliefs and superstitions of the people around him. His most permanent work may indeed prove to be books like *Japanese Fairy Tales* (1898); *In Ghostly Japan* (1899) and *Kotto* (1902), which are full of Japanese legend and folklore.

He had some acquaintance with Yeats' early work and with an essay 'On Some Fairy Literature', praises the poem *The Host of the Air* (1899) as a wonderful fairy poem and alludes to Yeats' play *The Land of Heart's Desire* (1894).

One curious thing is that Hearn in his story 'The Dream of a Summer Day' retells the old Japanese story of the young fisherman, Urashima Taro, who is brought by a sea-maiden to a Land of Youth, revisits Japan many years later, breaks a taboo laid on him by his beloved and turns into an ancient and decrepit man. This is substantially the old Irish tale which in 1889 Yeats relates as 'The Wanderings of Oisin', but Hearn does not allude to it in this essay. How the same reached Ireland and Japan is as interesting a speculation as why ancient Irish 'spirals' are to be found also on Japanese stones, or why ancient Japanese 'tomoe' designs figure also in the *Book of Kells*.

Finally, Hearn, although not a creative writer in the sense that Joyce was, frequently reminded me of him, not because of the superficial resemblance of being Catholic-trained, anti-clerical and monkish in disposition by turns, handicapped by eye-trouble and so on, but because of their mutual enthusiasm for words.

'People cannot see the color of words, the tints of words, the secret, ghostly motions of words . . . cannot perceive the poutings of words, the frowning and fuming of words, the raging and racketing and rioting of words . . . are insensible to the phosphorescing of words, the noisomeness of words, the tenderness or harshness, the dryness or juiciness of words' wrote Hearn to his friend Professor Basil Hall Chamberlain in 1893.

The passage might have served as a model for a particular passage in *Portrait of the Artist*, published 20 years later. Hearn also has some interesting remarks on the use of foreign words in English which 'flows over into unimaginable lands of as yet unknown extent' and in discussing Lewis Carroll's 'nonsense poems' says that they really contain a profound psychological basis found in the non-sequitur flow of dreams.

Here I am heading straight for the polyglot dream-world of *Finnegans Wake* and it is time to bring this article to a conclusion. On St Patrick's Day I am sure that many Japanese will remember this particular Patrick, Patricio Lafcadio Hearn. In Dublin I shall certainly recall him, the beautiful country of his adoption and the many friends I made there.

10

The Loose Foot of Lafcadio Hearn[1]

ROGER McHUGH

———————————— oOo ————————————

Greece, Ireland, France, England, America, the West Indies; these are the principal countries over which the loose foot of Lafcadio Hearn travelled before it finally came to rest in Japan. The Hearns of Dorsetshire are said to have gypsy or Romany blood. One of them came to Ireland in 1693, became Dean of Cashel and settled in Westmeath. From his stock descended Lafcadio's grandfather, a military surgeon who served under Wellington in the Peninsular Wars. His eldest son, who followed the same profession, was Charles Bush Hearn, a surgeon-major of the 76th Foot. In the late 1840s the 76th Foot was ordered to Greece and Lafcadio's story began.

England at that time still occupied the Ionian Isles and the 76th Foot garrisoned the island of Cerigo. There Charles

Bush Hearn had a passionate love-affair with a local girl named Rosa Cassimati. Her male relatives are said to have reciprocated with an equally passionate attack on the surgeon-major, whom they stabbed and left for dead; a probable story, for in their eyes he would have appeared as a double-despoiler. At any rate, Hearn recovered, took Rosa with him, when transferred to the island of Santa Maura (Lefkas to the Greeks) and married her there according to the Greek rite. Their first son died in infancy. Their second was Patricio Lafcadio Hearn born in June, 1850, in Lefkas.

ROCKY ROAD TO DUBLIN

This mixed name may stand as a token of Hearn's later belief that he had two souls; one mutinous, impulsive, sensitive, the other proud and persistent. To his mother, whom he dimly remembered as dark-eyed and beautiful, teaching him his prayers or telling him fascinating stories, he attributes his artistic sensibility. His father was more dimly recalled as steely-eyed, impassive and taciturn, essentially a military type. Hearn's recollection of him is not sympathetic. This can be understood from what followed the departure of the British Army from Greece and the arrival of the Hearn family at Dublin in the 1850s.

In Dublin the marriage soon went to pieces. The relatives with whom they stayed were well-off but bitterly divided on religious issues. They never accepted Rosa, who was a foreigner, knew very little English and was Greek Orthodox in religion. Surgeon-Major Hearn was soon off on active service in the West Indies and rarely returned home during the next few years. Soon he developed another attachment and eventually secured separation by impugning the validity of his first marriage. Rosa his wife, returned to Greece, where she married again. At four years old Patrick Lafcadio was adopted by a great-aunt and found himself isolated from all other family ties.

Mrs Brenane, his great-aunt, was a well-off widow who lived in Rathmines. She was a convert to Catholicism and decided that Patrick Lafcadio should be brought up a Catholic. His formal education appears to have been undertaken for a brief period at a Jesuit College in Yvetot, Normandy, and for several years at St Cuthbert's College in Ushaw, near Durham. It was while at Ushaw that he had the bad fortune to lose the sight of his left eye through an accident in a school game. This eye filmed over and Hearn was always inordinately sensitive about it, shielding it with his hand when in close conversation and appearing *en profile* in photographs far later in life.

The chief fruits of his formal education were a fluent knowledge of French, a wide range of reading in books of travel and adventure, a love of the romantic poets, some talent in sketching and the development of a speculative turn of mind.

This brought him into conflict with his teachers, who censored the illustrations of the pagan gods in his art-books and were not amused when he announced that he wished that the devil would appear to him in the shape of the beautiful women who tempted the anchorites in the desert. Young Hearn, they considered, was a difficult boy.

LONDON POVERTY

When he was sixteen he left Ushaw. Mrs Brenane's money had dwindled through bad financial advice and the boy could count only on small sporadic sums from her. He appears to have spent two years as an invalid, followed by a hand-to-mouth existence as a servant in London. There were periods when he depended on charity for food, on the straw of stables for a bed and on the public libraries for his one luxury, reading. He reflected sadly that his stable-companions, the horses, had no understanding but earned their food and lodging, while he with some knowledge of the universe had no use in the world whatsoever. What was to become of him?

The gods decide by strange ways. Hearn was now an embarrassment to Mrs Brenane, who had promised to make him her heir, a promise that was never fulfilled. Probably on the advice of her financial friend, Henry Molyneux, he was shipped to New York in 1869. He was then nineteen. Penurious, delicate, half-blind, he seemed unlikely to become eventually one of the chief interpreters of Japan to the Western world.

Some time in 1869 Lafcadio Hearn, who had shed the 'Patrick' from his name, arrived penniless in New York, where sporadic employment enabled him to survive for a while. Then starvation forced him to go to Cincinnati, Ohio, where his great-aunt had sent a small sum of money for him. When it was spent Hearn drifted through a succession of jobs; messenger, peddler, library-clerk, proof-reader, before getting a foot into the newspaper world.

CRIME REPORTER

By 1874 he was beginning to make a reputation as a crime-reporter for the Cincinnati *Enquirer*. He wrote luridly about the half-burned corpse of one victim, discussed with cold scientific exactness the placing of a bullet in another, grew lyrical about a blood-bespotted rose on the body of a girl suicide. His reports were really feature-articles and the *Enquirer*'s circulation grew. Then Hearn committed what his employers considered a serious crime; he went through a form of marriage with a black girl who had befriended him. Her name was Althea Foley.

He was fired immediately and was lucky to find employment at a reduced salary with the Ohio *Commercial*, which in 1877 sent him as a political reporter to New Orleans. This seems to have terminated his connection with Althea Foley. We do not hear of her again until after his death in Japan in 1904, when she sued for a widow's share of Hearn's royalties. The court decided that her marriage was contrary to Ohio law, whatever form it had taken.

Meanwhile, Hearn found New Orleans a vast improvement on Cincinnati. It was warm and it had an exciting polyglot population. France, Spain and England had ruled it and had left their racial deposits; emigrants had come from most other European countries and from China, the Philippines and Malaya; the local Choctaw Indians represented the original inhabitants on their nearby reservation. This polyglot, colourful atmosphere suited Hearn perfectly, nourishing his interest in language and in the exotic. He was particularly interested in the Creoles and wrote a book on their foklore and music, another on Creole cookery. For his articles he had only to listen to their stories or to observe their colourful dress and conversation in 'Gumbo French' about voodoo practices.

By 1881, despite many hardships, he had become literary editor of the New Orleans paper *The Times-Democrat*. His chief feature consisted of extracts translated from Gautier, Baudelaire, Flaubert, Loti and other French writers, together with legends and tales from many countries. His power as a translator and story-teller drew many readers. Rival papers began to publish translations from the French, which Hearn mercilessly dissected when they were inadequate. He published books of stories drawn from his wide reading of the exotic books he collected, including *Some Chinese Ghosts* (1886) which did not please him because it 'tried to understand the Far East from books'.

LITERARY CELEBRITY

By this time this pint-sized, retiring, wall-eyed Hearn was a local literary celebrity. His friends included his editor-in-chief, Page Baker, who nursed him through many a fit of depression and rage induce by imagined insults. There was also Father Roquelle, a Creole priest who once had tried to marry a Choctaw princess and whose poetry about the Louisiana Savannahs had been praised by Ireland's Tom Moore. The more disreputable (and there were many) included Marie Laveau, a black dispenser of voodoo charms; some malignant, which she scattered by night on the doorsteps of houses; some benignant, which she sold as remedies to their affrighted owners.

Hearn's loose foot took him to the West Indies. He got a travel book out of his experiences, also *Youma*, a romance about Martinique. He had become dissatisfied with New Orleans' papers. Sending them a good essay, he said, was like offering a buzzard charlotte russe. He longed to write deeper studies of life and to collect tales which had the desirable quality of 'weird beauty' and folklore which he believed revealed the essential spirit of a people.

In 1890 his chance came, when a colleague on *Harper's*, which had begun to publish his work, suggested that he write a book on Japan. Within a few months he sailed from Vancouver, full of enthusiasm for the project. He may not have noticed that, oddly enough, it was St Patrick's Day.

IN JAPAN

In Japan Hearn found his true role, to interpret that country's way of life to the West. His assimilation was rapid. He supported himself by writing and by teaching, mainly at Matsue and Kumamoto. He adopted Japanese dress and lifestyle; within a year of his arrival he married Setzu Koizumi, a Japanese lady who, though poor, was of Samurai origin. Later, in becoming a Japanese citizen, he took her family name and became officially Koizumi Yakumo. Setzu was a devoted wife who bore him several children and also helped him in collecting traditional stories and folklore. His best pupils also helped him in this way so that Hearn had a steady source of material. By 1896 he had produced some

The Loose Foot of Lafcadio Hearn

half-dozen books about Japan and Tokyo Imperial University appointed him a lecturer in English. He held this post until 1903, when he transferred to the private university of Waseda. Before he died of a heart-attack in 1904 he had published all thirteen books on Japan and had become known as one of its chief interpreters to the Western world.

His books about Japan are mostly curious blends of stories, folklore, travel impressions and reflections. The stories are chiefly traditional supernatural tales. One of the best is 'The Dream of a Summer Day' which describes the visit of a fisher-lad to an underwater Land of Youth. It is the theme which Yeats used in 'The Wanderings of Oisin'. Yeats's early poetry was certainly known to Hearn, who considered him the representative poet of fairy literature and praised his poem 'The Host of the Air' and Ferguson's 'The Fairy Thorn' for their power to communicate pleasurable fear and weird beauty.

These are the very qualities which are to be found in the stories of Hearn himself. He often blends them with macabre incidents about malignant goblins of Japanese tradition but uses many of them to show the positive side of Buddhistic thought; how self-sacrifice can save lives of friends or how reincarnation can restore them to those they loved.

Hearn found the connection between the living and the dead an integral feature of Japanese belief. The older religion of Shintoism was based on ancestor worship, which involved placation of the gods of family, of the community, of the ruler. In the sixth century Buddhism added the idea that one's ancestors were constantly changing by metempsychosis and could pass into animals and objects. Through Buddhistic art, ancestor worship then took on a bewildering complexity of forms and shapes but it remained the fundamental belief behind folklore, custom and ritual. What Hearn's writing on folklore accomplished was to show the unity of spirit which lay behind such different things as the inherited skill of a child calligrapher, the custom of launching candle-lit boats on the Feast of the Dead or the symbolism of dragon-flies in Japanese painting.

Japan: An Attempt at Interpretation, which appeared in the year of Hearn's death in 1904, was his final effort to synthesize his thoughts about Japan. It is perhaps weak on the philosophical side, for Hearn who believed in the evolutionary philosophy of Herbert Spencer, endeavoured to find its endorsement in the Buddhistic theory of the alternative cosmic disintegration and renewal of matter. On the other hand, he argued that the Buddhistic teaching that external reality is in truth an illusion, was a confirmation of philosophical idealism. Incidentally, he had a particular regard for the Irish idealist philosopher, George Berkeley, thus anticipating a common interest of Yeats, Joyce and Beckett. He was himself essentially an idealist and a perceptive artist whose true achievement lay in his creative presentation of Japanese stories and in his many perceptive impressions of Japanese people and customs.

Today, he can be seen to have idealized Japan too much, probably out of conviction that she was doomed to go down before Western civilization. Yet, for his time he was in his own way one of its best interpreters.

Through the kindness of the Japan Foundation I had the opportunity to revisit Japan briefly last autumn. It is quite clear that Hearn is still honoured there. At Matsue his house is preserved and a Hearn Museum contains his books and manuscripts. Most of his works have been republished recently and several are prescribed texts in the schools. The numerous studies of Hearn by eminent Japanese scholars show a warm appreciation of this man with the loose foot and the enquiring mind.

11

East Irish[1]

MICHAEL DISKIN

———————————— oOo ————————————

Next week, the Irish background of Lafcadio Hearn will receive some belated recognition when the Mayor of Matsue, the city in Japan in which Hearn initially settled and which he regarded with great fondness, will visit Dublin and unveil a plaque at No. 73 Upper Leeson Street, where the young Lafcadio lived with his great-aunt. Hearn is a bizarre figure in the great Irish diaspora: celebrated in Japan, well known in America, at least in the pre-war decades, but virtually unheard of in his native Ireland.

Aside from his literary achievements, his own life story is not lacking in dramatic and even exotic interest. Lafcadio's father, Charles Bush Hearn, was of a Protestant middle class Dublin family. Commissioned as a surgeon in the British Army, he was posted in 1846 to the Ionian Islands. There, he fell in love with a local girl whom he married against the wishes of her parents. In 1850 they had a son, Lafcadio, but shortly afterwards his father was posted to the West Indies, where he could not bring his wife and child. They were sent instead to Dublin to live with Charles' mother, who occupied a terraced house in Gardiner Street. The limitations of Dublin's social life and climate proved too much for Lafcadio's mother, however, and she returned to Greece on her own. It was then decided that Lafcadio would be brought up by his great-aunt, a Mrs Brenane, who was something of a family outcast since she had converted to Catholicism some years previously.

By all accounts Lafcadio had an unhappy childhood. Because of the religious differences in the family he rarely met his Protestant cousins and his life with an elderly aunt was rather solitary. Mrs Brenane, moreover, believed in a strict upbringing and Lafcadio would recall in later years how she had refused him a light in his bedroom and locked him in. She sent him to Catholic schools in France and England but he was not able to adapt to the rigorous discipline. In addition, at the age of 16 he suffered a serious accident which left him permanently blind in his left eye. His few happy memories of this period were of his summer holidays in Tramore, Co Waterford, and on the Elwood Estate near Cong, Co Mayo. The Twelve Pins of Connemara would later feature in some of his writing.

Mrs Brenane fell on hard times towards the end of her life, and with no money to pay school fees Lafcadio was forced to cut short his education and emigrate to live with a relative in the United States. In 1869 he left for Cincinnati, never to return to Ireland. There, he began to write, usually small pieces for local newspapers, but also some translations of French literary works. From the beginning he displayed an interest in ethnic minorities and the 'undercultures' of American society, such as the blacks and the Creoles of New Orleans. In 1887 he was employed by *Harper's Magazine* and three years later they sent him to Japan. Lafcadio immediately was captivated with the life he witnessed. He left *Harper's* and took a job as an English teacher in the town of Matsue.

This small castle town, set by the sea, represented for Lafcadio a sort of oriental paradise. He liked it for its simple sentiments and its strong tradition of folklore. Here he met his future wife, Koizumi Setsu, the daughter of a samurai family. Since his knowledge of Japanese remained limited, she would read to him the old records of ghost stories and incidents in newspaper articles which he used as literary material. In 1896, in order to protect his family's citizenship, he became a Japanese citizen, adopting his wife's family name. For health reasons, he had to leave his beloved Matsue for a warmer region and after a spell as a staff writer with the *Kobe Chronicle*, he was appointed head of the English Department at Tokyo Imperial University. He was to hold this position for most of the rest of his short life. He died in 1904.

Hearn was certainly a prolific author. During his 14 years in Japan, he wrote two major works attempting to explain Japan to foreigners, *Glimpses of Unfamiliar Japan* and *Japan: An Attempt at Interpretation*. In addition, he wrote many volumes of Japanese folk tales and a study of Buddhism. In all, 13 books. Taken as a whole, his writing introduced Japan to the outside world and at the same time encouraged the Japanese to take a fresh look at their own country, which was only slowly emerging from centuries of complete isolation.

Perhaps because of his troubled and unsettled early years, Lafcadio had none of the great moral certainties of his British contemporaries of the Victorian era. He did not hold up Western and Christian civilization as superior and this enabled him to appreciate and analyse Japanese culture unburdened by such ideological baggage. In the preface to *Glimpses of Unfamiliar Japan* he set out his purpose (and the secret of his literary power) 'to capture . . . the inner life of the Japanese . . . their religion, their superstitions, their ways of thought, the hidden springs by which they move'. With all the zeal of the foreign ethnologist, he disliked the Westernizing and modernizing influences which were at the turn of the century creeping into Japanese society. But ultimately he is celebrated in Japan because he understood and expressed their culture from the point of view of the common man rather than an outsider.

Searching for the 'Irishness' in Hearn's writings is a difficult task. The common thread which does seem to link Hearn with his Anglo-Irish contemporaries who remained in Ireland, such as Yeats and Synge, was his interest in ethnic culture and folk mythology. Just as Synge found artistic inspiration in the Aran Islands, Hearn found it in the 'real Japan' uncontaminated by Western influences.

12

Lafcadio Hearn: A Spiritual Odyssey

CIARAN MURRAY

──────────── oOo ────────────

There is always a sense of the incongruous. You get it when you visit the apartment building in Zürich where Joyce lived and wrote. It is modern, faceless, antiseptic: difficult to believe that it was here he dreamt his dreams of a mythic, personality-ridden, odoriferous Dublin.

You get it again at Sankt-Gallen: the cloud-like library in white and gold, and in the middle of it the rustic Irish scribings out of which all the rest of it grew, and in which you touch the soil from which the pilgrim sprang a thousand years ago.

And you get it at Matsue, in the wooden Japanese house worn paper-thin by the years, with its melancholy garden and its memorial hall nearby. This time you hear a voice: but to explain that, I have to go back a bit.

My first encounter with Hearn was incongruous enough too: it was in the pages of a French magazine. I saw a picture of a shaven monk with hieroglyphs painted on his face, and read of how, blind, he sang the fall of the Heiké to an unseen audience, not knowing they were the ghosts of the Heiké dead. It was a review of a Japanese film, *Kwaidan*. Nothing could have seemed more exotic; but it traced the author to Ireland.

In the Ireland of the 1960s, his books were not easy to find. When I applied for some for students through the Central Library, one came to me from England, a second from Northern Ireland, and a third from Scotland. But Hearn, I discovered, was not a mystery; he was a secret. When I asked for him in the gloom of the rare-book sanctum, with its locked glass cases, at Hodges Figgis, a namesake of my own said: 'No, I haven't got any of his books; but I'll do something better for you – I'll introduce you to his family.' And so in 1969 I met Lily Stephens, who gave me the recollections of her father-in-law, who had known Hearn as a child.[1]

A family friend, in the meantime, had confessed to possession of the Stevenson biography; and here I was struck, as one must be, by the resemblances with Joyce: the combination of sexual and intellectual rebellion against a blackthorned and hobnailed theocracy.[2] Hearn now swam into focus against the perspective of Irish psychological geography.

When I came to Japan in 1972, my first pilgrimage was to his burial-place. I found ' a sad seventeenth-century temple, with dust swirling around its courtyard, and Zoshigaya, a Buddhist cemetery dense with trees and alive with the noise of cicadas'.[3] And in the bookshops, Hearn himself was up and alive. I felt ridiculous: I had treasured the slim volumes in blue and gold, that I had come upon from time to time on the Dublin quays. Here you could find him anywhere, in garish paperback. People knew about him too: though some thought him Japanese, and others American. Those who knew better knew he was British.

And so when the Irish embassy asked me to make a TV programme about Hearn in 1980, I thought it necessary to stress his status as an Irish writer, and in particular his parallels with Joyce.[4] To judge from the response to the programme, this was *terra incognita* to most.

I felt it all the more necessary to emphasize this because I had been reading Joyce with my students, and was amazed at their response. The quiet desperation of *Dubliners* appealed to them; *Portrait* by contrast, seemed unbridled donnybrook. what touched them in the lives of the Dubliners was what they saw as a poetry of *karma*: the sadness of inevitable fate. Joyce's characters were trammelled, of course, but at the same time sustained, by the web of their social relations. Stephen Dedalus, on the other hand, was a societal vandal, his flight beyond the nets unimaginable. This reflected their own experience at the time: then, a student who had gone abroad was a rarity; now it is rare to find one who has not. It is a development that has created its own literature, as in the novels of Ishiguro, and that harks back, I feel, to the older tradition in which the Japanese were great adventurers, making arduous pilgrimages to China and India, a possibility shut off when the country was closed. For a quarter of a millennium, there was nowhere to go; and my students were still in that mindset. For them, Stephen at the end had sailed off the edge of the world; had vanished, like the Cheshire cat, in the ghost of a gesture.

For the same reason, the myth of *Ulysses* meant nothing to them; but I saw it as crucial to Hearn. His association with it, after all, was privileged: he was a fellow-countryman of Odysseus, and he did not forget that fact. 'Greece', I said, 'was not an influence, as Ireland was; it was an impulse, and his deepest one.'[5] He thought he remembered it as a place of more intense light,[6] and he spent a great part of his life in the search for it. Had the search been merely regressive, he would have gone back to Greece. Instead he moved outward and on. It was a return as a spiral is a return; the remembrance of light as incentive to enlightenment.

The essential antithesis is drawn in a diptych of childhood scenes. In the first, he is taken into a Dublin church, and it induces a sense of nightmare. He experiences Gothic as terror, Christian aspiration as interfused with alarm.[7] Against this is to be set the second scene, in which his volume of the classical divinities, with their nude figures, is inked over by his tutor.[8] The sexual merges with the intellectual: the gods of nature glow for him against ecclesiastical gloom. Here he aligns himself with the broader current of European history:[9] a fact of which he is perfectly well aware. 'I had entered', he declares, 'into my Renaissance.' He was later to express the issue in epigrammatic form: 'You cannot', he said, 'make a Goth out of a Greek.'[10]

And so, while Jim steers a course for Tara via Holyhead, Lafcadio makes for the Acropolis by way of Cincinnati. He steeps himself in the counterculture, is drawn inexorably south. He studies Creole, hears African rhythm in Latin song, explores the Caribbean. When he describes himself at this time as 'Oriental', it is in the older sense of Mediterranean. But somehow, this is not what he seeks. He cannot, after all, abandon himself to the fullness of tropical light. He is morose and silent, dissatisfied.[11]

He senses, now, his own shadowings. And so, when another kind of Orient beckons, one that presents itself in variants of grey,[12] he goes. Arrived in Japan, he sees himself reflected in the mirror of a shrine, the phantom of the sea behind. He wonders whether that which he seeks has any external reality, or whether all is not the projection of a dream.[13] He feels he has lived here before,[14] a sensation easily fostered in the region of Matsue, where the skies are in constant commotion, and you have that Irish illumination that shifts between blackness and brilliance. And it is from the name of this region that he is to take his Japanese name: Yakumo, Crossroads of the Clouds.[15]

There was to be the same turbulence in his feelings towards Japan — as also in his feelings for the West. As Malcolm Cowley has pointed out, he is a phenomenon in Japanese history as well, interpreting the West to Japan through his lectures while he interpreted Japan to the West through his books.[16] He learned to see one through the other. The beauty of traditional Japan came to seem to him bound up with repression, a Joycean dominion of the dead;[17] while Western individualism appeared akin to aggression.[18] He knew, now, that the war of Greek and Goth is ubiquitous, that everywhere Apollo and Dionysus share the stage. He understood that there is no illumination without shadow: that, in the phrase of Sir Thomas Browne, 'light unto *Pluto* is darkness unto *Jupiter*'.[19]

When asked what I thought his greatest achievement, my answer was:

> The shape of his life. I see his books as the record of a voyage: as a spiritual odyssey.[20]

He was aware, at the end of that voyage, that his Ithaca was no earthly paradise. But then neither was the original. It is an outcrop of rock that offers Odysseus the opportunity to labour for his oil and his wine, and the presence of those who love him, and whom he loves. Hearn had learnt to see the light and dark in others; and he had learnt to see it in himself. He was grateful when his Japanese wife intercepted the letters he dashed off in those fits of Celtic irascibility that no change of citizenship could alter.[21] Through the medium of his adoptive country, the accents of the one which had orphaned him, but which he belonged to in spite of himself, rang through.

And that is what I heard in Matsue. Leaning over the case in which his seal was preserved, I felt a shock of recognition. He had had his family name engraved on it in the Japanese phonetic syllabary. Nowadays, this is rendered as *Haan*: that is, Hearn with a British accent. But what he called himself was *Herun*: two syllables, with a rolling of the 'r'.[22] It is an Irish voice, a voice that has resisted blandness and assimilation. There is no contradiction here: one is never more Irish than as a *scottus peregrinus*.

13

Lafcadio Hearn, W.B. Yeats and Japan

BARBARA HAYLEY

——————————— o0o ———————————

Though Lafcadio Hearn and W.B. Yeats approached Japan in very different ways and by very different routes, that country was source of vitality and inspiration to both, and both writers are of lasting interest to the Japanese. Yeats, like many late-nineteenth-century Westerners, was fascinated from a distance by Japanese art and artefacts. He never visited Japan, and what he took from its culture was specific and individual – more to do with the art of W.B. Yeats than with that of Japan. He quickly found in the Noh plays, via Ezra Pound and Ernest Fenollosa, what he needed, seeing the possibilities for his own work in an imaginative vision of an art that he had not experienced. The artistic use that Yeats made of his idea of Japan is paradoxically disproportionate to his first-hand knowledge of it. The scholarly interest that the Japanese take in Yeats had its beginnings in the fact that when Japan opened its gates to Western culture, a conscious decision had to be taken whether to begin to study contemporary Western literature and keep abreast of it, or to start at its beginnings and work forwards. The former course was decided upon; and the profusion of Irish writers in the last decades of the nineteenth century occasioned an enduring interest in Anglo-Irish writing.

Whereas Yeats, like many artists, stayed at home and received Japanese influence from afar, Hearn was unique. He was a solitary explorer who brought the East to the West, not by returning with travellers' tales but by staying in the East and sending back both his first lively impressions and the osmotic Orientalism of one who worked and settled in Japan, married a Japanese wife, lived a Japanese life. He became Japanese by naturalization, by adoption, by affinity. He wrote from a deep affection for the Japanese people as well as from an interest in their country.

There is a paradox in Hearn's Japanese-Irish connection too: to the Japanese, Hearn is seen as an Irish writer, whereas in Ireland he is only beginning to be claimed as such, and in fact he lived for only a few years in that country as a boy. The circumstances of Hearn's youth, even of his name and family, are somewhat obscure.[1] The Irish connection started with the first Hearn to come to Ireland in the seventeenth century as chaplain to the Lord Lieutenant; he became Bishop of Cashel and settled in County Westmeath. His descendant, Surgeon Major Charles Bush Hearn of the Seventy-Sixth Foot, was Lafcadio Hearn's father. He went to the Ionian Islands on garrison duty when they were still British possessions, and married a local girl; their son was born on the island of Santa Maura, in Modern Greek Lefcada, in ancient Greek Leucada. (The island's other claim to literary fame was that Sappho was supposed to have leapt to her death from the Leucadian rock.) Hearn always prided himself on his classical and mediterranean frame of mind, detesting all that was cold, Anglo-Saxon, northern.

The family returned to Dublin when Britain ceded the Ionian Islands; the parents separated, both remarrying; the sons were left with the father, and then taken in by various relatives, Hearn by an aunt, Mrs Brenane, who being a Catholic convert, sent him to a number of Catholic schools in France and England. He quarrelled with his aunt, left home, went to London and then to America, and drifted into journalism and travel writing. He never returned to Ireland, and seems to have kept in touch with only one member of his family, his half-sister Minnie Atkinson. His movement towards Japan was slow yet inexorable; his letters show him moving closer and closer to the Orient in his interests, his reading and his undefined yearnings. He loved Japan and its people from his first days there; and in return he is still widely studied not as 'English literature' but as one of the first folklorists of Japan.

To Hearn and Yeats, Japan offered a way out of a tired literary tradition: to Hearn a permanent and single way, to Yeats one of many interconnecting paths. They had much in common beyond and attraction to the East. Both were late Romantics, *déracinés*, who reached out towards the inaccessible. One of them found it and found himself – that one not being Yeats. Whether finding oneself as a man and as a thinker creates the finer literature is another question: it is the tension of reaching out and not grasping that makes Yeats's poetry great. But the freshness and sense of fulfilment in Hearn's Japanese writings convey one aspect of the late romantic spirit shared by these near-contemporaries (Hearn was born in 1850 fifteen years before Yeats).

Neither was a true *fin de siècle* decadent willing to push literary or other experience to the limit, although Yeats's years in Paris and Hearn's in Cincinnati, where he had a brief illegal marriage to a mulatto woman, and later in New Orleans suggest a certain breaching of frontiers. Both wished to go beyond jaded conventional material and belief. Hearn found his new world already existing and hallowed by tradition; Yeats had to invent or resurrect his. When each searched beyond Christianity, Hearn found a philosophy living all around him in Japan, in priests, in shrines, in temples, expressed in gardens and houses and in Japanese people; Yeats had to create his own philosophy and had to invent the rituals of the Golden Dawn with his confrères as they went along. (Hearn is scathing about esoteric Buddhism, 'which is damnable charlatanism'.[2]) Hearn did not need to revivify the Japanese myths and legends as Yeats did the Celtic; they were alive in the minds of the Japanese.

Hearn was interested in many of the same things as Yeats: folklore, myth, legend, the dance, dreams, the occult, the genius of the race, Buddhism. In these materials each found a rich symbolism. Here again, Yeats had to construct his own symbols or at least to reinterpret such symbols as the Rose and Cross, the Platonic skein, the Hermetic path. He had to build his own Byzantium. But Hearn's objects were already symbols; his Byzantium was all around him. One might think that the forging of the symbol would make for the greater literature: but is the found symbol any less potent than the forged one?

Yeats regretted 'the romantic movement with its turbulent heroism, its self-assertion'. In 'The Autumn of the Body' (1897) he analyses the idealism of the 'old romanticism', and warily acknowledges decadence:

> I see, indeed, in the arts of every country those faint lights and faint colours and faint outlines and faint energies which many call 'the decadence', and which I, because I believe that the arts lie dreaming of things to come, prefer to call the autumn of the body.[3]

One way out of this autumnal vapour was by way of the East: 'Europe is very old and has seen many arts run through the circle and has learnt the fruit of every flower and knows what this fruit sends up, and it is now time to copy the East and live deliberately'.[4] This sense that the fruit of Eastern philosophy was both new and restorative had much to do with Yeats's interest in Japan. He received the Noh drama circuitously through Pound and Fenollosa (whom Hearn knew and quarrelled with). He wrote in 1927 that he had read some Japanese literature including D.T. Suzuki's *Essays in Zen Buddhism*, Arthur Waley's translation of *Genji Monogatari*, Lady Murasaki's tenth-century novel of aristocratic life; and Toyohiko Kagawa's *Shisen O Koete* (*Before the Dawn*) which he expounds in *Explorations* and recalls at the end of *A Vision*: 'I remember the Apocalyptic dreams of the Japanese saint and labour leader Kagawa, whose books were lent to me by a Galway clergyman'.[6] He wrote in 1928 to Kazumi Yano:

> I do not think my interest in your country will ever slacken, especially now that I have found this new interest – its philosophy. Whether I shall ever see Japan is another matter . . . Since I have met you I have felt a door open into Japan; you have told me so much, and given to me the means of further knowledge.[7]

One tends to think of Hearn only as the Japanese Hearn; but it is easy with hindsight to see him moving towards Japan throughout his early life and literary career, pushed by an undirected romanticism. In 1869, having left Ireland and Europe behind for ever, he turned up in New York. He wrote later in 'Intuition':

> I was nineteen years old, and a stranger in the great strange world of America, and grievously tormented by grim realities. As I did not know how to face these realities, I tried to forget them as much as possible; and romantic dreams, daily nourished at a public library, helped me to forget.[8]

Here are the two main axes of Hearn's existence: the 'grim realities' are often there in his letters, but Romanticism is there as well; not, always as here, escapist, but idealistic and literary. The letters[9] and articles[10] written before his arrival in Japan show a nostalgia for romanticism, a loathing for realism, and a wary admiration for the decadents: 'What our age really needs is not more realism, but more of that pure idealism which is founded on a perfect knowledge of the essential facts of human life', and 'the most imminent danger . . . lies in the loss of idealism', through 'debauching realism' ('Realism and Idealism'). In 'Decadence as a Fine Art', he sees the *décadents* as the 'jewel in a dung hill' (that is, the 'enormous putrid mass of realistic rhyme and fiction which has been created by the pessimistic philosophy and morbid feeling of certain French writers'). The decadent writers 'affect to worship only the crumbling, the effete, the ruined, the medieval, the Byzantine', but are admirable in having an ideal, even if it is still 'spectral'. He detests Zola's 'revolting realism', despises Matthew Arnold, has no patience with Emerson or with Whitman's 'Calibanish shagginess'. He praises John Addington Symonds and Algernon Charles Swinburne in 'Eclecticism in Literature'; Gustave Flaubert, especially for *Salammbo*; Gerard de Nerval (for his *Voyage en Orient* and his Abyssinian wife); Charles Baudelaire (for his 'intense passion for exotic singularity' and the black madonna figure of his 'savage mistress') in 'Idol of a Great Eccentric'. He admires Edgar Allen Poe, Dante Gabriel Rossetti, George Borrow, Ernst Hoffman; Thomas De Quincey's *Spanish Nun* and Théophile Gautier's *Mademoiselle de Maupin*. The author he most reveres is Pierre Loti, for his 'elegance of tinted words', and for 'reflecting the romance of an Oriental country' ('A New Romantic').

From his earliest criticism onwards, he seeks out 'the new, the strange, the exotic, the amorphous, the bizarre'. He is physically and intellectually restless in the West, writing in 1883: 'Surely all mysteries seem to issue from the womb of nations – from the heart of Asia'. In 1887, he writes: 'I am trying to find the Orient at home, – to apply the same methods of poetical-prose treatment to modern local and living themes'. By 1889 he has 'a library of Oriental books'. In 'A Peep at Japanese Poetry' he says 'The more the Western world learns of the extreme East, the more are the antiquated notions of Oriental inferiority weakened'. These were the interests that drew him Eastwards.

When Hearn arrived in Japan in 1890, he had feared that his literary career might end 'without a single flash of brightness or a solitary result worthy of preservation'. He had made his way up from typesetter to journalist in Cincinnati on a variety of *Enquirers*, *Gazettes* and *Commercials*; then in New Orleans had worked on the cheap *Daily Item*, and from 1881 on the 'quality' *Times-Democrat*, to which he had contributed a weekly translation from the French, and literary articles in which he displayed romantic idealism and exotic reading.[11] He had published *One of Cleopatra's Nights* (six translations of Théophile Gautier, 1883); *Chita, a story of Last Island* (1884); travel sketches from the Windward Islands for *Harper's Magazine*; and , as a result of living in Martinique, *Two Years in the French West Indies*; a small output for one who had high literary aspirations. He was forty, and had fourteen more years to live. He had accomplished little so far, but he was now about to produce a distinctive body of work, perceptive, reflective and full of integrity. In those fourteen years he was to produce thirteen books about Japan and the Japanese which would make a bridge between East and West. His openness to Oriental tradition, religion and philosophy made them accessible to him. He was no detached observer; he had an affinity with and love for the Japanese people.

His first Japanese book, *Glimpses of Unfamiliar Japan*, penetrating gazes rather than glimpses, established his way of looking at the country.[12] Anyone familiar with his work will remember 'My first Day in the Orient'; but for Hearn it is not just the first impression that is important, it is the reflection afterwards, the movement outwards from the immediate shrine to its history, to present beliefs surrounding it, to the lives of its thousands of worshippers. 'In a Japanese Garden' moves from Hearn's own garden to the philosophy of the garden and the relationship of landscaping to Buddhism; to the legends and literature of Japanese gardens; to plants and trees, butterflies, lizards and toads; concluding that 'the art that made the beauty of this place was the art, also, of that faith to which belongs the all consoling text, "Verily, even plants and trees, rocks and stones, all shall enter into Nirvana"'.[13] The early 'Pilgrimage to Enoshima' gives some idea of the number of associations encompassed in each object that Hearn looks at:

> 'And this,' the reader may say, – 'this is all that you went forth to see: a torii, some shells, a small damask snake, some stones?' It is true. And nevertheless I know that I am bewitched. There is a charm indefinable about the place, – that sort of charm which comes with a little ghostly thrill never to be forgotten. Not of strange sights alone is this charm made, but of numberless subtle sensations and ideas interwoven and interblended: the sweet sharp scents of grove and sea; the blood-brightening, vivifying touch of the free wind; the dumb appeal of ancient mystic mossy things; vague reference evoked by knowledge of treading soil called holy for a thousand years; and a sense of sympathy, as a human duty, compelled by the vision of steps of rock worn down into shapelessness by the pilgrim feet of vanished generations. And other memories ineffaceable: the first sight of the sea-girt City of Pearl through a fairy veil of haze; the windy approach to the lovely island over the velvety soundless brown stretch of sand; the weird majesty of the giant gate of bronze; the queer, high-sloping, fantastic, quaintly gabled street, flinging down sharp shadows of aerial balconies; the flutter of colored draperies in the sea wind, and of flags with their riddles of lettering; the pearly glimmering of the astonishing shops. And impressions of the enormous day, – the day of the Land of the Gods, - a loftier day than ever our summers know; and the glory of the view from those green sacred silent heights between sea and sun; and the remembrance of the sky, a sky spiritual as holiness, a sky with clouds ghost-pure and white as the light itself, – seeming, indeed, not clouds but dreams, or souls of Bodhisattvas about to melt forever into some blue Nirvana.[14]

Glimpses of Unfamiliar Japan was the product of a happy

year at Matsue, a remote town almost unchanged since the fourteenth century, where Hearn taught in the Middle School, married Setsu Koizumi, a girl from an impoverished Samurai family, and took her family name, becoming Yakumo Koizumi ('many clouds', 'little spring'). Matsue was the formative influence of his life in Japan, but ill-health forced him to move. His next book, *Out of the East*, written in Kumamoto, a more modern, less sympathetic town, shows a fiercer race than the gentle, smiling people of Matsue. Later books included *Kokoro* and *Gleanings in Buddha-Fields*, written when he lived in the open port of Kobe. As Professor of English at the Imperial University of Tokyo he wrote *In Ghostly Japan*, *A Japanese Miscellany*, *Kotto*, *Kwaidan* and *Japan: An Attempt at Interpretation*.

Hearn's minute observation in describing the Japanese is one of the most attractive features of these books. 'From the Diary of an English Teacher', for example, lovingly scrutinizes each of his pupils. But it is in his generalized observations that he is most remarkable. He vividly conveys specific features of the Japanese: their complexion, their musculature, their 'small symmetrical, tilted feet'. He devotes an entire essay ('Of Women's Hair') to ways of washing, dressing, oiling, cutting and combing the hair, and to the conventions underlying each degree of elaboration. He considers the subtlety of Japanese etiquette, and his conclusions are much the same as Yeats's: 'How but in custom and in ceremony/Are innocence and beauty born?' His sensitive attitude to the Japanese can be seen in the essay 'The Japanese Smile', in which he explains the stoicism, politeness, sensibility and self-abnegation behind the smile, which shows 'the difficulty of mutual comprehension between the Eastern and Western races'. Westerners, suspecting insincerity, often misinterpret, say, the smile that masks pain. Hearn often reverts to the smile, never suspecting, never resenting:

The country-folk gaze wonderingly at the foreigner. At various places where we halt, old men approach to touch my clothes, apologizing with humble bows and winning smiles for their very natural curiosity, and asking my interpreter all sorts of odd questions. Gentler and kindlier faces I never beheld; and they reflect the souls behind them; never yet have I heard a voice raised in anger, nor observed an unkindly act.[15]

The sympathy and openness of this passage give some idea of Hearn's attitude as observer and observed; always, one senses an affection for the people of Japan and not merely an interest in their country, their beliefs and their customs:

> Regret for a single individual smile is something common to normal human nature; but regret for the smile of a population, for a smile considered as an abstract quality, is certainly a rare sensation, and one to be obtained, I fancy, only in this Orient land whose people smile forever like their own gods in stone. And this precious experience is already mine.[16]

Such love of 'a population' is never evident in the work of Yeats, who loves the peasantry and the aristocracy but not many in between.

It is in their collecting of folklore that Hearn and Yeats correspond most closely, though even here their purposes differ. Yeats mentions in 1893 the 'noteless Gaelic poet' who made a bird-story into a 'forgotten ballad, some odd verse of which my white-capped friend remembered and sang for me', but comments in a footnote in 1924: 'There is a ballad in my *Wind Among the Reeds* on this theme' ('The Host of the Air').[17] Myth and legend to Hearn were to be absorbed, retold, and thus preserved: to Yeats they were a source for his own creative work. In religion the two writers held similar beliefs but had different aims. In Yeats's exploration of the occult, of Rosicrucian, Hermetic, Kabbalistic and finally Buddhist doctrine, he was looking for a personal experience, a moment of revelation which he never achieved (hence the panic and fury of the late poetry). Hearn sought no personal revelation; his own faith was a modified Spencerian

Evolutionism which he reconciled happily with the Buddhism he saw around him. The Yeats of 'The Mandukya Upanishad', or of *The Holy Mountain* is almost wistful as he describes the bump on the swami's forehead; Hearn observes, explains, but never envies. The region in which Hearn and Yeats converge yet markedly diverge is that of Japanese art and artefacts, dance and drama: that is where they use the same symbol laden material but look for and find something quite different in it.

Hearn's studies of folk legends, dream traditions, stories and ballads can be likened to those of the affectionate early Yeats of *The Celtic Twilight* who shows a world where peasant and ghost mingle familiarly:

> The house ghost is usually a harmless and well-meaning creature . . . these spirits have a gloomy, matter-of-fact way with them. They come to announce a death, to fulfil some obligation, to revenge a wrong, to pay their bills even – as did a fisherman's daughter the other day – and then hasten to their rest. All things they do decently and in order. It is demons, not ghosts, that transform themselves into white cats or black dogs.[18]

Hearn's demons and *gaki* of Buddhist belief have much in common with Yeats's fairies and *sidhe*; they are like the beautiful 'gentry' of 'Kidnappers' or 'Dust hath closed Helen's eye', who need humans, who desire and spirit away husbands, babies and brides, thus imparting a value to the humanity of the poor peasant.

In many essays Hearn systematically retails folk legends, often beautiful, often grisly. Many have to do with the dead returning, as Yeats's do, to finish the business of their earthly lives. 'A Promise Kept' tells of a man whose only way to keep a promise to return is to kill himself so that his spirit can keep the appointment. 'Of a Promise Broken' tells of a husband who breaks his promise to his first wife by marrying another when she dies, with horrible consequences for the new bride, whose head is torn off. A Buddhist invocation demolishes the avenging spirit, 'but the fleshless right hand, though parted from the wrist, still writhed; – and its fingers still gripped at the bleeding head, – and tore, and mangled, – as the claws of the yellow crab cling fast to a fallen fruit'.[19] Not all revenants are so bloodthirsty: a mysterious pale woman begs for food and is found in the cemetery feeding a living infant; the child was born in the tomb, and the ghost of the mother had thus provided for it, – love being stronger than death'.[20]

Hearn notes numerous variations of such comings and goings between this world and the next, including the macabre joke of a woman who apparently eats corpses, thus frightening away all her suitors until one is brave enough to eat the proffered arm fresh from the coffin and it turns out to be made of the best Kwashi confectionery.

Many legends tell of spirit transference, the spirit of one girl transferred to the body of another and leading an everyday life while her original dead or comatose body is watched over by her family (as in 'Before the Supreme Court'). Not only humans change magically: 'The Story of Kwashin Koji' tells of a wonderfully painted kakemono or religious painting whose scroll goes blank when the artist is cheated and killed; his headless body comes to life (and drinks a good many bowls of wine) and the painting comes back to more than life:

> . . . all saw the boat suddenly turn, and begin to move toward the foreground of the picture. It grew rapidly larger and larger . . . And, all of a sudden, the water of the lake seemed to overflow, – out of the picture into the room, – and the room was flooded; and the spectators girded up their robes in haste, as the water rose above their knees. In the same moment the boat appeared to glide out of the screen, – a real fishing-boat; and the creaking of the single oar could be heard.[21]

But it is difficult to separate legend from all other kinds of Japanese folk belief, nor did Hearn wish to do so. 'Of Ghosts and Goblins', like many other pieces, is partly folklore but partly religion. 'Folklore Gleanings' in *A Japanese Miscellany* include 'Songs of Japanese Children' and 'Buddhist Names of Plants and Animals', which encompass natural history and religion: 'Many names of plants or living creatures refer to Buddhist customs, legends, rites, or beliefs . . . '. 'Dragonflies' considers Japan as 'The Island of the Dragon-fly' and describes the names, etymology and entomology of dragonflies, children's dragonfly games, and dragonfly literature including sixty dragonfly 'picture poems'. These are subdivided into 'Dragonflies and Sunshine', 'Flight of Dragonflies', 'Lightness of Dragon-flies' and glossed as follows:

> In the form *hokku* – limited to seventeen syllables – . . . almost the only rule . . . not at all a rigid one, – is that the poem shall be a little word-picture, – that it shall appeal to some experience of sense . . . the reader will find that they are really pictures, - tiny colour-prints in the manner of the Ukiyo-ye schools.

> Nagare-yuku
> Awa ni yume miru
> Tombo kana!

Lo! the dragon-fly dreams a dream above the flowing of the foam-bubbles.[22]

This translation brings irresistibly (and I suppose coincidentally) to mind Yeats's seventeen syllables:

> Like a long legged fly upon the stream
> His mind moves upon silence.

Folklore and legend are part of Japan's life, its scenery, its nature, its literature; both are imbued with Buddhism and inseparable from visionary belief. Folklore for Hearn, as for Yeats, was a stage in a journey away from Christianity. In 'An Indian Monk', Yeats describes Shri Purohit Swami's book as 'something I have waited for since I was seventeen years old. About that age, bored by an Irish Protestant point of view that suggested by its blank abstraction chloride of lime, I began to question the country people about apparitions'.[23]

Hearn, too, moves from his boyhood religion, this time Catholicism, towards Buddhist belief; the following passage from the essay 'Of Moon Desire' also seems to express his successfully achieved yearning to become part of Japan:

> I remember when I was a boy lying on my back in the grass, gazing into the summer blue above me, and wishing that I could melt into it – become a part of it. For these fancies I believe that a religious tutor was innocently responsible: he had tried to explain to me, because of certain dreamy questions, what he termed 'the folly and the wickedness of pantheism' – with the result that I immediately became a pantheist, at the tender age of fifteen. And my imaginings presently led me not only to want the sky for a playground, but also to become the sky. Now I think that in those days I was really close to a great truth – touching it, in fact without the faintest suspicion of its existence. I mean the truth that the wish *to become* is reasonable in direct ratio to its largeness – or, in other words, that the more you wish to be, the wiser you are; while the wish *to have* is apt to be foolish in proportion to its largeness.[24]

Like Yeats, Hearn starts from 'the country people'. In 'Otokichi's Daruma', the little clay household god, which is blind until an offering is made, is treated with sympathy and humour: 'The blind Daruma can be expected to do wonderful things, because he has to work for his eyes. There are many such funny little deities in Japan.... Faith in very small gods – toy gods - belongs to that simplicity of heart which, in this wicked world, makes the nearest possible approach to pure goodness'.[25] In 'Gaki' we see gods that come from hell but can take part in human life, and Hearn, with typical thoroughness, classifies the thirty-six kinds of Gaki recognised by Japanese Buddhism, which form two divisions, the 'Gaki-World-Dwellers (Gaki-Sekai-Ju)', that is , 'all Hungry Spirits who remain in the Gakido proper, and are, therefore, never seen by mankind'. The other division contains 'Nin-chu-Ju (Dwellers-among-men)', who 'remain always in this world, and are sometimes seen'.

There is yet another classification of gaki, according to the character of their penitential torment. All gaki suffer hunger and thirst; but there are three degrees of this suffering. The Muzai-gaki represent the first degree: they must hunger and thirst uninterruptedly, without obtaining any nourishment whatever. The Shozai-gaki suffer only in the second degree: they are able to feed occasionally upon impure substances. The Usai-gaki are more fortunate: they can eat such remains of food as are thrown away by men, and also the offerings of food set before the images of the gods, or before the tablets of the ancestors. The last two classes of gaki are especially interesting because they are supposed to meddle with human affairs.[26]

He examines Buddhism as it affects the common people: in 'Dust', children playing at funerals with cicadas bring him to a neo-Buddhist understanding:

These little boys and girls, being Japanese and Buddhists, will never, in any event, feel about death just as you or I do . . . In the strangely penetrant light of their creed, teaching the ghostliness of all substance, granite or gossamer . . . this their present world, with its bigger mountains and rivers and rice-fields, will not appear to them much more real than the mud landscapes which they made in childhood. And much more real it probably is not. At which thought I am conscious of a sudden soft shock, a familiar shock, and know myself seized by the idea of substance as Non-Reality.[27]

In 'The Stone Buddha' he fuses the higher Buddhism and simple faith, illustrating the result by a typical ghost story of a haunted house. 'Anger, secretly indulged, can have ghostly consequences,' he observes. This is a Yeatsian, purgatorial notion which he debates throughout the essay, concluding:

We may have to learn that the infinite whirl of death and birth, out of which we cannot escape, is of our own creation, of our own seeking; that the forces integrating worlds are the errors of the Past; that the eternal sorrow is but the eternal hunger of insatiable desire; and that the burnt-out suns are rekindled only by the inextinguishable passions of vanished lives.[28]

But he also examines the less 'popular' essence of Buddhism in 'The Higher Buddhism', to which he relates his own Oriental-Occidental Spencerianism: 'I venture to call myself a student of Herbert Spencer and it was because of my acquaintance with the Synthetic Philosophy that I came to find in Buddhist philosophy a more than romantic interest. For Buddhism is also a theory of evolution'. Spencer's highest point of development, 'Equilibration', corresponds with the supreme point of development in Buddhist evolution, except that in Buddhism 'this supreme point vanishes into Nirvana'.[29] The universe of Matter and the universe of 'conditioned Mind ... represent in their evolution a strictly moral order'. The 'most remarkable teachings of the Higher Buddhism' are:

> That there is but one Reality: That the consciousness is not the real Self: That matter is an aggregate of phenomena created by the force of acts and thoughts: That all objective and subjective existence is made by Karma – the present being the creation of the past, and the actions of the present and the past, in combination, determining the conditions of the future ... All things having form or name – Buddhas, gods, men, and all living creatures – suns, worlds, moons, the whole visible cosmos – are transitory phenomena ... Assuming, with Herbert Spencer, that the test of reality is permanence, one can scarcely question this position.[30]

He tackles the complex notion, alien to Westerners but much dwelt on by Yeats, of Nirvana. As always, his aim is to help Westerners overcome their misunderstandings of Eastern thought. There is an idea, he writes,

> that still widely prevails in Europe and America, the idea that Nirvana signifies, to Buddhist minds, neither more nor less than absolute nothingness – complete annihilation. Nirvana, indeed, signifies an extinction. But if by this extinction of individual being we understand soul-death, our conception of Nirvana is wrong. Or if we take Nirvana to mean such re-absorption of the finite into the infinite as that predicted by Indian pantheism, again our idea is foreign to Buddhism. Nevertheless, if we declare that Nirvana means the extinction of individual sensation, emotion, thought – the final disintegration of conscious personality – the annihilation of everything that can be included under the term 'I' – then we rightly express one side of the Buddhist teaching.[31]

In religious matters he sees himself as a guide, not a guru. Yeats on the other hand sees himself as the guided, the disciple.

Whatever the veneration Hearn felt for religion, his heart was always with the worshippers, the people. In religion Yeats wishes to de-personalize, to see the symbol. Hearn is moved at the shrines he visits by their religious symbolism, but also by the people he finds there: bereaved women hanging up tiny kimonos in memory of dead children, or sending little paper boats out for them. He sees too the poor priest beneath the holy garment, and is sensitive to his human feelings, as when he visits a very poor shrine and is overwhelmed at his own vulgarity in assuming that the priest's offered gift of hot water is a begging bowl.

What Yeats admired in Buddhism was its mystical and contemplative elements. As Alex Zwerdling points out in *Yeats and the Heroic Ideal*: 'what attracted Yeats was the idea of the eternal return, the cyclical view of history, which stressed the recurrence of life in perpetual reincarnation ... Nirvana is the release from the cycles', which Yeats does not want, desiring 'Conflict, more conflict'.[32] He does admire those qualities that Hearn ascribes to Shinto, the indigenous religion of Japan, a mixture of nature-worship and loyalty to the reigning dynasty as descendants of the sun-goddess:

> For Shinto signifies character in the higher sense, - courage, courtesy, honour, and above all things, loyalty. The spirit of Shinto is the spirit of filial piety, the zest of duty, the readiness to surrender life for a principle without a thought of where-fore. It is the docility of the child; it is the sweetness of the Japanese woman. It is conservatism likewise; the wholesome check upon the national tendency to cast away the worth of the entire past in rash eagerness to assimilate too much of the foreign present. It is religion, – but religion transformed into hereditary moral impulse, – religion transmuted into ethical instinct. It is the whole emotional life of the race.
> – The Soul of Japan.[33]

In writing about Sato's sword Yeats stresses what the gift symbolized: continuity, hereditary impulses, loyalty:

> The consecrated blade upon my knees Is Sato's ancient blade, still as it was, Still razor-keen, still like a looking-glass Unspotted by the centuries; That flowering, silken, old embroidery, torn From some court-lady's dress and round The wooden scabbard bound and wound, Can, tattered, still protect, faded adorn. ('A Dialogue of Self and Soul')

The sword that Hearn receives from his pupils (in 'Sayonara'), 'that beautiful sword with the silver karashishi ramping upon its sheath, or crawling through the silken cording of its wonderful hilt', is a symbol both of duty, ritual sacrifice and military dedication ('The sword is the Soul of the Samurai') and of the friendship, affection and loyalty of those who gave it to him.[34] Hearn stresses the personal background to the gift.

This different perspective affects the way in which the two writers approach art. Yeats was obsessed with the dance as a means of abstracting the performer from humanity. His dancer fuses with and is lost in the dance. Art takes over until we can no longer tell the dancer from the dance. Hearn, too, is responsive to classic art, admires it and is moved by it. In 'Kitsuki' he describes the 'Dance of the Miko, the Divineress' performed with what sounds like Yeats's bell-branch, 'a queer instrument . . . somewhat like a branch with the twigs bent downward, from each of which hangs a bell':

> Her every movement is a poem, because she is very graceful; and yet her performance could scarcely be called a dance, as we understand the word; it is rather a light swift walk within a circle, during which she shakes the instrument at regular intervals, making all the little bells ring. Her face remains impassive as a beautiful mask, placid and sweet as the face of a dreaming Kwannon; and her white feet are pure of line as the feet of a marble nymph. Altogether, with her snowy raiment and white flesh and passionless face, she seems rather a beautiful living statue than a Japanese maiden.[35]

Hearn always looks at the dancer beneath the costume and ceremony. In 'Of a Dancing-girl' he describes the geisha's role, her training, the rigours she endures to achieve her elegant accomplishments. He sees the ironic contrast between the beauty and decorum of her dances, songs and music-making and the cruel discipline behind it:

> Her voice may be flexible enough, but lacks the requisite strength. In the iciest hours of winter nights, she must ascend to the roof of her dwelling-house, and there sing and play till the blood oozes from her fingers and the voice dies in her throat. The desired result is an atrocious cold. After a period of hoarse whispering, her voice changes its tone and strengthens. She is ready to become a public singer and dancer.[36]

In 'Bon-Odori' he describes a dance that 'suggests some fancy of Somnambulism, – dreamers, who dream themselves flying, dreaming upon their feet':

> And always the white hands sinuously wave together, as if weaving spells, alternately without and within the round, now with palms upward, now with palms downward; and all the elfish sleeves hover duskily together, with a shadowing as of wings; and all the feet poise together with such a rhythm of complex motion, that, in watching it, one feels a sensation of hypnotism – as while striving to watch a flowing and shimmering of water.[37]

There comes to him 'the thought that I am looking at something immemorially old, something belonging to the unrecorded beginnings of this Oriental life, perhaps to the crepuscular Kamiyo itself, to the magical Age of the Gods; a symbolism of motion whereof the meaning has been forgotten for innumerable years'. This 'Dance of Souls' is reminiscent of the mystic dance in Yeats's 'Rosa Alchemica':

> The dance wound in and out, tracing upon the floor the shapes of petals that copied the petals in the rose overhead, and to the sound of hidden instruments which were perhaps of an antique pattern, for I have never heard the like; and every moment the dance was more passionate, until all the winds of the world seemed to have awakened under our feet.[38]

To yield to the 'immortal august woman' with whom he dances this supernatural dance would be fatal:

> Suddenly I remembered that her eyelids had never quivered, and that her lilies had not dropped a black petal, nor shaken from their places, and understood with a great horror that I danced with one who was more or less than human, and who was drinking up my soul as an ox drinks up a wayside pool; and I fell, and darkness passed over me.[39]

But the rejection cannot dispel the terror.

After their Dance of Souls, on the other hand, Hearn's supernatural dancers turn into ordinary girls:

> Instantly the witchcraft ends, like the wonder of some dream broken by a sound; the chanting ceases; the round dissolves in an outburst of happy laughter, and chatting, and softly-vowelled callings of flower names which are names of girls, and farewell cries of 'Sayonara!' as dancers and spectators alike betake themselves homeward, with a great koro-koro of getas. And I, moving with the throng, in the bewildered manner of one suddenly roused from sleep, know myself ungrateful. These silvery-laughing folk who now toddle along beside me upon their noisy little clogs, stepping very fast to get a peep at my foreign face, these but a moment ago were visions of archaic grace, illusions of necromancy, delightful phantoms; and I feel a vague resentment against them for thus materializing into simple country-girls.[40]

If, then, Hearn always sees the dancer beneath the robe, the country girl beneath the witchcraft, the actor beneath the mask, Yeats does not. The elements of the Noh plays as 'translated by Ernest Fenollosa and finished by Ezra Pound' that attracted him were precisely those that eliminate actor and public as far as is humanly possible. The Noh plays suggested to Yeats 'a form of drama, distinguished, indirect and symbolic, and having no need of mob or Press to pay its way – an aristocratic form'. For Yeats, 'all imaginative art remains at a distance and this distance, once chosen, must be firmly held against a pushing world'. In 'Certain Noble Plays of Japan', he expounds the necessity for art to detach itself from life and by stylization to free itself from suspect realism. The mask is the perfection of this freedom – not only from realism but from the unworthy actor:

> A mask will enable me to substitute for the face of some commonplace player, or for that face repainted to suit his own vulgar fancy, the fine invention of a sculptor and to bring the audience close enough to the play to hear every inflection of the voice. A mask never seems but a dirty face, and no matter how close you go is yet a work of art; nor shall we lose by stilling the movement of the features, for deep feeling is expressed by a movement of the whole body. In poetical painting and in sculpture the face seems the nobler for lacking curiosity, alert attention, all that we sum up under the famous word of the realists, 'vitality'. It is even possible that being is only possessed completely by the dead, and that it is some knowledge of this that makes us gaze with so much emotion upon the face of the Sphinx or of Buddha.[41]

It is in this inhuman dimension that the outreaching Yeats is magnificent. His unachieved and unachievable notion of Japan is only one of the ideas to which he reached out in his determination not to let life substitute itself for art. For Yeats, Japan, like Sato's sword, was emblematic:

> . . . Sato's gift, a changeless sword,
> By pen and paper lies,
> That it may moralise
> My days out of their aimlessness.
> A bit of an embroidered dress
> Covers its wooden sheath.
> . . . In Sato's house
> Curved like new moon, moon-luminous,
> It lay five hundred years.
> Yet if no change appears
> No moon; only an aching heart
> Conceives a changeless work of art.
>   ('My Table', 'Meditations in Time of Civil War')

The sword's permanence is not consoling: individual father and son are lost; art remains. It is in reaching out to this abstraction from the human that Yeats is magnificent.

Hearn's Japan, in contrast, is one in which the abstract, the artistic and the mythological are encompassed by the human:

> To have studied and loved an ancient faith only through the labours of palaeographers and archaeologists, and as something astronomically remote from one's own existence, and then suddenly in after years to find the same faith as a part of one's human environment, – to feel that its mythology, though senescent, is alive all around you, – is almost to realize the dream of the Romantics, to have the sensation of returning through twenty centuries into the life of a happier world.[42]

If there is grandeur in Yeats's unfulfilled reaching is there not also a magnificence in Hearn's sense of arrival?

14

Opening of the Lafcadio Hearn Library in the Embassy of Ireland Tokyo[1]

ANTHONY J.F. O'REILLY

---------- oOo ----------

The objective of this Library is to honour the connection between Ireland and Lafcadio Hearn whose Japanese name was Koizumi Yakumo. Because Hearn also lived in the United States and became one of the principal interpreters of Japan to the Western world, this project celebrates the international friendship between Ireland, Japan and the United States. This friendship is also reinforced by the Ireland Funds around the world which support peace, culture and charity in Ireland.

It is my fervent hope that the Lafcadio Hearn Library will function as a bridge for cultural exchange linking three countries: Ireland, where Hearn came from, Japan, his dearly beloved second homeland; and the United States, which provided the foundation for his success.

Lafcadio Hearn was reared in my native city of Dublin. At the age of 19 he left Europe for the United States where he engaged in journalism. After journalistic assignments in New Orleans, Martinique and New York he came to Japan in April 1890 on an assignment for *Harper's Magazine*. He took up a teaching post in Matsue where he married the daughter of a samurai family. He remained in Japan until his death in 1904.

Lafcadio Hearn was among the first and the best to interpret Japan for the Western world in the Meiji era and also to interpret the West for Japan. Although he wrote particularly for American audiences, his works were also well-known in Europe.

Through his short stories and ghost stories he is known universally in Japan until this day among both older and younger people. His work was undoubtedly influenced by Irish folklore, writings and stories that he heard and read in his formative years in Ireland. He also admired the work of the Anglo-Irish Literary Renaissance and especially the interest of Ferguson and Yeats in the old Celtic sagas.

This Library is one of a number of projects undertaken to honour the memory of Lafcadio Hearn. I must pay tribute to the Ambassador of Ireland, His Excellency Sean G. Ronan, whose personal enthusiasm and leadership have inspired many of these projects. During the 1988 Dublin Millennium celebrations, plaques were unveiled on the two main houses in which Lafcadio Hearn lived as a boy in Dublin. One was unveiled by the Mayor of Matsue, Mr Yoshijiro Nakamura, and the other by the Minister for Home Affairs, Mr Seiroku Kajiyama. The Irish Ambassador's Perpetual Prize is given at the annual recitation contest of Hearn's work among high school students in Matsue.

In view of the continuing interest in Hearn in Japan, there

is need of an accessible library in Tokyo of his works, biographies, papers, books, memoirs and articles about him. Apart from his own writings, many of the books, memoirs and articles about him are very scarce and exist only in first or limited editions.

As Hearn is a major connection in Irish-Japanese relations the Lafcadio Hearn Library at the Embassy of Ireland in Tokyo will be a notable asset for teachers, students and all in official, business, academic and cultural circles interested in Hearn and in his focal position in the wider Europe-Japan-United States trilateral relationship. Further gifts of books, memoirs, letters and articles about Lafcadio Hearn will be especially welcomed and prized. Former owners might place their bookplates in the volumes donated to make the association more intimate. In any event the Embassy will insert a bookplate in each presentation.

The H. J. Heinz Company is very happy to sponsor this library. Heinz has invested in Japan since 1961 and is proud of its association with this country.

Heinz, a company with over 50 affiliates in 22 countries throughout the world, is a food products maker with over a century of history behind it. Our products are sold in 200 countries around the world and are esteemed in Ireland as well as Japan. We are strengthening our commitment to the Japanese market by producing an increasing range of products at our Utsunomiya plant and we are grateful for the dedication and commitment of our Japanese President, Mr Masahira Ogawa.

It is hoped that all who are interested in Lafcadio Hearn will utilize this new Library and notify others of the accessible collection.

15

An Irishwoman's Diary:
A Visit to Matsue

LORNA SIGGINS

———————————— oOo ————————————

'Do not fail to write down your first impressions as soon as possible.' Sound advice this was from a kind English professor to Lafcadio Hearn, soon after the writer's arrival in Japan 100 years ago.

The Greek-born son of an Anglo-Irish doctor in the British Army did just that and more, earning the eternal gratitude of the Japanese. Unlike many Western writers and scholars, Hearn did not try to impose his own Western 'civilized' values on interpreting life in an archipelago that had just emerged from two centuries of isolation.

'I want to die here,' he is reported to have said when he set foot in Yokohama in 1890, having been sent from the US

An Irishwoman's Diary: A Visit to Matsue

to write for *Harper's Magazine*. And die he did, though disillusioned and discontented, after 14 years of trying to capture the spirit of a unique culture.

FIRST IMPRESSIONS

Narrow streets enlivened with a profusion of Chinese and Japanese characters on gilded and lacquered signboards; the delicate, exquisite beauty of the most ordinary items, like a pair of wooden chopsticks in paper packaging; the Hokusai figures in straw raincoats, hats and sandals; the *kring* and *krang* of the getas (Japanese wooden clogs); the illusion of an elfish fairyland which is only broken by the passing of a taller foreigner; the 'sacred and matchless mountain, Fujiyama' – these were some of the impressions that Hearn recorded on his first day in the Orient.

Were he to return today, he would still find much of what he loved about the only place he knew as home. There are the lush forests and dramatic mountain ranges; the adaptation of nature in carefully manicured gardens, ceramic art and ikebana (flower-arranging); the attention to cleanliness; the exquisite packaging; the houses that still look like 'great wicker-work pigeon-cages'; the tatami mats and futons hung out on balconies; the happy mixture of Shinto and Buddhist in a country with a low crime rate, no drug problem and full employment . . .

But the streets signs are now neon, career women wear smart suits and one million yen faces 'Westernized' by cosmetic surgery, young Tokyo kids are let loose as Elvis and James Dean lookalikes on Sundays in Harajuku and the Shinkansen (bullet train) line has torn its way across the landscape.

ADOPTED NAME

One of the Shinkansen routes has taken Hearn's adopted Japanese name, Koizumi Yakumo. It carried me to Matsue, on the Japan Sea, where Hearn was at his happiest. 'Landscape reflecting the changing light of Sligo' was how Ciaran Murray, former *Irish Times* journalist and authority on Hearn, described it before I left Tokyo. 'That's why they say he loved it, why some of his Japanese ghost stories have a strong Celtic influence, and why he is compared to Yeats.'

Hearn first met his wife, Setsuko Koizumi, only daughter of a poor samurai family, in Matsue, when he took up a job as English teacher in a secondary school. He only lived 14 months there, deciding to move because of the 'Siberian cold'. Still, the 'Chief City of the Province of the Gods', as he called it, left an indelible impression on him. Writing about its remarkable sunsets, he prayed that glass would never become universally adopted in Japan. Without paper windows, there would be no more 'delicious shadows'.

MEMORIAL MUSEUM

It is to Matsue, formerly a fishing village and now a bustling city, that Japanese flock to visit the Lafcadio Hearn Memorial Museum, adjoining Hearn's former residence below the citadel. His house, with its tiny stream running under a magnolia tree in a beautiful garden, is also maintained in his honour. There is a small assortment of Irish books in the cultural centre's library.

But Matsue has gone one step further. The city council has wooed Hearn's great-grandson, young Bon Koizumi, back there to live by offering him a teaching job in the local high school. Bon had only been to Matsue once before, he told me when we met in his great-grandfather's house. He was brought up outside Tokyo and studied Japanese history and folklore at university. He does not envisage moving away too quickly. Like his great-grandfather, he got married shortly after arriving in Matsue.

Bon's father, Toki, still lives outside Tokyo. He has retired after 30 years' service with the US military in Japan and keeps

An Irishwoman's Diary: A Visit to Matsue

close links with the Irish Embassy in Tokyo, where a Lafcadio Hearn library was opened in September, 1988. The Embassy has been keen to stress the Irish-Japanese link, even though Hearn's years in Ireland were unhappy ones.

So unhappy that Paddy Hearn changed his name to Lafcadio – from Levkas, the name of the Ionian island where he was born – when he emigrated to America in 1869 at the age of 19. In case anyone has forgotten about this, Greece has been fighting back. A visit by Toki and Bon to Levkas four years ago has been reciprocated. 'Irish visitors say that Matsue reminds them of their west coast,' Toki told me. 'But the mayor of Levkas thought that Matsue was just like Greece!'

A number of events have been planned to mark the centenary of Hearn's arrival in Japan, which falls on 4 April. Here, there has already been the announcement of a Hearn library in the Japanese-Ireland Sundai School in Co Kildare. Matsue has planned a festival from 30 August to 3 September, with an interesting symposium and a meeting of the Japan Comparative Literature Association. And the city has decided to fund two literary awards.

16

Lafcadio Hearn and Japanese Poetry

GERRY O'MALLEY

———————————— oOo ————————————

> *Oh, East is East and West is West,*
> *And never the twain shall meet*

So said Rudyard Kipling in 'The Ballad of East and West'. At the very time Kipling was writing that – the last decade of the last century – an Irishman, Lafcadio Hearn, was studying all aspects of Japanese life and attempting to explain Japan to the West.

I say Irish because in Japan he is known and remembered as an Irish writer and folklorist, although he spent only fourteen of his fifty-four years in this country. He was born Patricio Lafcadio Hearn on 27 June 1850, on the Greek island of Leukas, son of an Irish father and a Greek mother.

One of his seventeenth-century ancestors was the Rev.

Daniel Hearn, Archdeacon of Cashel and Rector of St Anne's, Dublin.

When his parents separated Lafcadio was looked after by a great-aunt who was kindly disposed to him but, nonetheless, imposed a strict discipline on her grand-nephew. She sent him, when he was thirteen, to St Cuthbert's College in Durham. Unfortunately, his time in Ireland and England had been a disappointment to him.

In 1869, he emigrated to America and went to work in a newspaper office as a typesetter, later going on to become a journalist. When he was forty years of age he went on an assignment for *Harper's Magazine* to Japan and as soon as he set foot in that country he knew he had found his spiritual home.

One of the aspects of Japanese life which Hearn had to describe and try to explain to the West was the Japanese attitude to poetry. This is so different from ours as to be a source of bafflement to Westerners. His essay 'Bits of Poetry' in his book *In Ghostly Japan* explains it all.

A poem aims at being the quintessence of aesthetic or mystical experience . . . that, at least, is true in the East as well as in the West. But that is about as far as the similarity goes. In Japan, lyric poetry is read by all, understood by all and written by nearly all. To improvise a poem for one's own satisfaction is almost an automatic response to an emotion. And a Japanese on his death-bed would be following a centuries-old tradition if he were to occupy his last moments in expressing his view of the world in a *jisei*, or farewell poem. In the West, this would be regarded as very strange behaviour indeed.

The Japanese poem operates on the echo principle . . . it is an unfinished creation that only achieves completeness in the mind of the reader. It is not just the impression that is important but the reflection afterwards. The subjects are usually slight and unsubstantial: a breath, a smile, a sigh of pain or joy, a landscape mirrored in a drop of water.

A Japanese poem has neither rhyme nor metre. The sing-song Japanese accent takes the place of metre and rhyme is rendered impossible in a language where not only each word but each syllable ends in a vowel.

The best-known poem types are the *haiku* and the *tanka*, the only difference being the number of lines and the number of syllables per line. Since the seventh century the *tanka* is the most common form. A *tanka* has only 31 syllables, arranged in five lines as follows: 5 – 7 – 5 – 7 – 7. So, it is very brief. Some people might say mercifully so. The poem has hardly started when it is finished and that is the whole point: completion of the idea contained in the few lines occurs – or, at any rate, is supposed to occur – in the mind of the reader.

To illustrate the point, here are a few examples:

FIRST LOVE

Although I try hard
to keep my love a secret
it is reflected
in my face and people ask
the reason for my sadness

– That's it! That's all there is! Here's another one:

UNREQUITED LOVE

Although my sad heart
cries out to yours without hope
on a night like this
perhaps the moon fills us both
with the same melancholy

Unrequited love is a common theme.

Alas! cold and hard
as granite one day I found
my love's heart. I sighed

> and the unfeeling echo
> returned the sound from afar.

A final expression of unhappiness in love:

PERFIDY

> Of course the moon shines
> as usual; and of course
> Spring will come this year
> but I cannot feel the same
> since my lover's perfidy

Lafcadio Hearn became Professor of English Literature at the Imperial University of Tokyo, wrote thirteen books, married a Japanese woman and, like John Lennon, took her name. He had four children, one of them an artist. To this day he is highly respected in Japan and is studied as a writer of English and a folklorist. His lectures at the University have been collected and published, an honour given to very few Professors. He never left Japan and died there in 1904. In those last fourteen years of his life, he did more than anybody else before or since to establish a bridge of understanding between East and West.

17

The Literary Criticism of Lafcadio Hearn

PETER MCMILLAN

———————— 000 ————————

At the age of forty-five Lafcadio Hearn, having already had considerable experience teaching in Matsue and Kumamoto, was offered a position at Tokyo Imperial University. Hearn was known to members of the faculty especially Dr Toyama, who had studied in Michigan and had read Hearn in the *Atlantic Monthly*, and was aware of Hearn's fame in the United States and England. Toyama offered the chair of English language and literature to Hearn as a means of strengthening his department. Hearn accepted, but he was always very shy about using the accompanying title, and forbade his students from using it too. He occupied the chair from September 1896 to March 1903 and divided his lectures into three courses: The first course was five hours a week and consisted of textual readings from poets such as Tennyson and Rossetti; the second course was three hours a week and consisted of lectures in the history of English literature; the third course was five hours on miscellaneous themes in English literature.

Hearn does not seem to have been particularly pleased with teaching. At times he found the students difficult; at times he felt a lack of confidence in his own knowledge of English literature. At the end of his first year in Tokyo he wrote to his friend Sentaro Nishida:

> I teach only twelve hours. I have no textbooks except for two classes – one of which studies Milton's 'Paradise Lost' and the other Tennyson's 'Princess' (at my suggestion). I did not suggest 'Paradise Lost' but as the students wanted in different divisions of the class to study different books, [I] made them vote, and out of seventy-eight, sixty-three voted for 'Paradise Lost'! Curious! (Just because it was hard for them, I suppose.)[1]

Hearn had no formal training as a literary critic and was obviously daunted at the prospect of teaching Milton. However, Hearn did have a refined literary sensibility and well-developed sense of taste which combined with his strong sense of honesty and idealism made for stimulating lectures.

Hearn's students wrote the following account of Hearn's delivery style:

> In dictating Hearn gave the punctuation, and sometimes even the spelling of unfamiliar names, so that we, his students, could take down his lectures word for word. He lectured *extempore*, not from any fully prepared notes. He brought with him a tiny memorandum containing only names and dates, and a few volumes of poetical works or anthologies wrapped in a purple *furoshiki*. Undoing this and placing the contents carelessly upon his desk before him, he would slowly begin dictating. When quoting any line or verses, he used to refer to these books, bringing his right eye very close to the pages, and if the line-arrangement of a stanza chanced to be irregular, he would show the irregularity on the

blackboard. Being exceptionally skilled at drawing, he used to make sketches on the board, should a description of anything exotic or unfamiliar to us occur in quotations. Sometimes a faint shy smile would lighten up in his face when he seemed satisfied with the effect of his drawing. Apart from this, the lecture went on uninterruptedly. Like the music of running waters the sentences flowed from his lips. We, his students, listened eagerly, busily taking down his words. Gradually the subject under discussion held us enthralled. Lafcadio Hearn took into account the mentality of his students and entered into it himself. His incomparable power of paraphrasing clarified passages difficult for us to understand, revealing often to us hidden conceptions and unsuspected charms. It often seemed to us as if we were actually leaning out from the bar of Heaven beside the Blessed Damozel, or walking along the corridors of the Palace of Art, till the bell for the fifteen minutes recess broke the spell.[2]

Another student, Prof. Uchigasaki, later of Waseda University, wrote of the lectures:

He lectured between nine and twelve hours a week and not one of us ever felt that his hours were ever too long. On the contrary we always grieved that they could not be longer. It was universally known that he hated to see anyone at his home, but he was another person in his lecture room, being most exceedingly kind and diligent. He never missed in his duties as a professor at the university, attending every day and never being late for even one hour. He usually carried a small note-book in the class room, which had in it, however, some name of a book or author, the date and a few other simple things, and he gave us the lectures – such remarkable lectures that we will not easily forget – entirely from his memory. His memory was indeed wonderful. Sometimes there were a few written lectures, criticism on poetry, the history of English literature, the outline of European literature and others, most beautifully written in themselves and full of interest and charming with a grace of style. He taught us to see the creation of Almighty God.[3]

Few teachers can look forward to such high accolades on their passing, but I imagine that Hearn's strong sense of idealism, honesty, and protection of the weak must have made a strong impression on his students and that his reputation amongst the students is a deserved one. Yet despite the students' high praise of the lectures, Hearn himself remained to the end unconfident in his ability as a lecturer in English literature. When his friend and literary executor, Paymaster Mitchell McDonald, suggested that he publish the lectures, Hearn wrote back to him:

> Thanks for your interest in my lecture-work; but you would be wrong in thinking the lectures worth printing. They are only lectures dictated out of my head, not from notes even: so the form of them cannot be good. Were I to rewrite each of them ten or fifteen times, I might print them. But that would not be worth while. I am not a scholar nor a competent critic of the best; there are scores of men able to do the same thing incomparably better. The lectures are good for Tokyo University, however, – because they have been adapted, by long experience, to the Japanese student's way of thinking and feeling, and are put in the simplest possible language.[4]

It is clear then that Hearn never had any intention of his lectures being published. However, after his death one of his students, R. Tanabe, suggested to Mitchell McDonald that the lectures be published and placed the students' note-books at his disposal. Amongst the students were Sejiro Ibaraki, Masanobu Otani, Ryuji Tanabe, Sakusaburo Uchigasaki, Motoi Kurihara, Sadjiro Kobinata, Teisaburo Ochiai, Riushiro Ishikawa, and Shigetsu Kishi. McDonald willingly agreed to undertake the project and, in his room in the Grand Hotel in Yokohama, typed up the lectures into several volumes before bringing them to Professor Erskine of Columbia University.

The entire mass of notes amounted to some 400,000 to 500,000 words. Erskine made a selection of forty-four lectures and published them in two volumes entitled *Interpretations of Literature* (Dodd, Mead & Co., New York) in 1915. They were well received and other volumes soon followed: *Appreciations of Poetry*, 1916; *Life and Literature*, 1917; *Talks to Writers*, 1920; *Pre-Raphaelites and Other Poets*,

1922; *Books and Habits*, 1921. Others of the type-written folios were left unused and published later.

Taking into account that the author never had any intention of publishing, and that the manuscripts were made up entirely from students' notes, and the extraordinary contribution of MacDonald, one cannot help but be surprised at the success of the venture. *The Daily Telegraph* wrote: 'It is extraordinary how simple these lectures are without being bald or dull. Only a fine scholar who was also a writer of real distinction could have given them.'[5] This was echoed by later comments including that of *The Observer* who wrote: 'A word of praise must be given to the excellent work of the Hokuseido Press which is doing so much to popularize the works of Lafcadio Hearn.'[6] But no comments equalled those of the editor, Erskine who wrote: 'In substance if not in form they [the lectures] are criticism of the finest kind, unmatched in English unless we return to the best of Coleridge, and in some ways unequalled by anything in Coleridge.' And he continues:

> It is hardly too severe to say that most critics talk around a poem or a play without risking a judgement on the centre of their subject; or else, like even Coleridge at times, they tell you what you ought to read into a given work, instead of showing you what is waiting there to be seen. Lafcadio Hearn is remarkable amongst critics for throwing a clear light on the genuine literary experience – on the emotions which the books under discussion actually give us.[7]

An analysis of the criticism will show that Erskine considerably over-estimated the importance of Hearn's criticism. Nevertheless, his comments are interesting in that they reflect typical, if slightly extreme, praise at the time of publication.

It is quite natural to doubt the authenticity of these lectures as they were dictated by students, excellent students but non-native speakers. Furthermore, Hearn himself never had the chance even to see the manuscripts, let alone re-write or correct them. However, the spirit of the lectures is amply captured. One reason for this is that Hearn was very conscious of his audience and spoke slowly and deliberately, so it seems that the students had no problems in carefully transcribing the content of the lectures. Furthermore, Erskine professes to have interfered very little in the editing of the lectures. He wrote:

> In editing these lectures for the volumes in which they first appeared, I tried to make as few alternatives as possible. Only those manuscripts have been published which were fairly clear; all passages which were so mangled as to call for a reconstruction of the text, I omitted, and if the omission seems to affect in any essential way what remained, I rejected the whole lecture. No additions whatever were made to the text; only the punctuation was made uniform, and the numerous quotations verified. . . .
> Allowing, therefore, for such mistakes as are incident to proofreading, the reader will find here a close record of Hearn's daily instruction to his Japanese class in English literature. The record is unique.[8]

So much for the way in which these lectures came to be printed. It is a remarkable story especially in light of the emphasis that is often made on Hearn's difficulty as a person. It is often claimed that he had no friends for any period of time and many enemies. The story of the publication of his lectures reveals on the contrary that Hearn was capable of attracting devotion and loyalty to an extraordinary degree.

Turning to the development of Hearn's thought, the most important influence was the Social-Darwinist, Herbert Spencer (1820-1903). Before Darwin, Herbert Spencer had worked out his own theory of evolution, most clearly illustrated in his *First Principles* (1862) and *Principles of Ethics* (six parts 1879-93). For Spencer, philosophy, unlike other sciences, could claim complete generality so that its characteristic theories are true of everything. However, it is only in terms of an evolutionary theory that this claim can be empirically verifiable. Thus Spencer set out to show how his principle of evolution, of progress from an 'indefinite incoherent homogeneity to a definite coherent heterogeneity' is exemplified throughout nature and in the individual, social, and even moral life of humanity. Furthermore – as in Social-Darwinism – the development and structure of human societies can be explained in terms of the evolutionary forces that shape non-human biology, and especially in terms of the survival of the fittest. Figures as diverse as Marx, Theodore Roosevelt, and Hitler have been attracted to this theory, but the principal objection to it remains in the difficulty of claiming that that which is at once an inexorable descriptive law of nature can at the same time be morally or politically mandatory.

The all-encompassing nature of the theory, its ability to reconcile and explain inner and outer reality is what attracted Hearn and thereafter his thought was strongly influenced by Spencer. However, Hearn did not simply accept the theory as it was, but rather adapted it to his own view of reality, which ultimately became a kind of Spencerian Buddhism. Hearn had studied Oriental religions before coming to Japan and had come to the conclusion that Buddhist metaphysics were similar to the metaphysics of Herbert Spencer. The correspondence between the two was enough evidence for him that Buddhism was the only faith that could be reconciled with science, since he believed implicitly in the scientific accuracy of Spencer's synthetic philosophy.

Spencerianism figures largely in the work of Hearn from then on and the central tenets of his literary criticism can all be explained by recourse to Spencerianism.

In 'The Question of the Highest Art' Hearn acknowledges his debt to Spencer:

> ... we may fairly assume that the intellectual life represents something higher than physical life, and that ethical life represents something higher still. In short, the position of Spencer that moral beauty is far superior to intellectual beauty, ought to be a satisfactory guide to the answer of this question. If moral beauty be

the highest possible form of beauty, then the highest possible form of art should be that which expresses it . . . I do not think that anyone would deny these premises from a philosophical point of view. (p.7) . . . I should say the highest form of art must necessarily be such art as produces upon the beholder the same moral effect that the passion of love produces in a generous lover. Such art would be a revelation of moral beauty for which it were worth while to sacrifice self, – of moral ideas for which it were a beautiful thing to die. Such an art ought to fill men even with a passionate desire to give up life, pleasure, everything, for the sake of some grand and noble purpose. (p.9)[9]

Great art, he continues, should inspire us to be noble and if it fails to do so it is not great art. As for the highest possible art it has not existed in the past. Furthermore, sculpture, music, and painting cannot be the highest art, a title which is reserved for drama, poetry and great romance, all of which can produce 'purely moral enthusiasm'.

For Hearn life is the art of emotional expression and the business of the writer is to record an emotion and reproduce it in writing. The first act of writing is the art of observing one's relation to life, one's emotions, one's memories, one's mature judgements. Secondly, writing involves the art of recording these memories, emotions and judgements. Yet Hearn opposed strictly moralistic literature. Rather the morality came from the sense of beauty of the actions described which in turn inspires the reader to moral action. When one reads a beautiful book, one is training one's character and reaching a stage in one's development whereby it becomes more difficult to feel or think or do an unworthy thing. The greater the beauty of the book, the more profound the moral reaction. The case of Madame Bovary is a good example. Hearn argues that we do not want to become like Madame Bovary herself, but rather like the author who created such a splendid work. The beauty of this and other works inspires men to act unselfishly and so morally.

Hearn resolutely set himself against the doctrine of art for art's sake, and was likewise opposed to the admiration of language for its own intrinsic beauty. His analysis of Sir Thomas Browne, for example, praises the beauty of Browne's prose, but warns the reader not to seek after anything in language beyond faithful service to the subject matter. Hearn, however, forgave the excesses of Browne's style stating that in Browne's particular case the subject matter was 'properly served'.

That Hearn's literary criticism is largely affective, largely based on the effect the work has on the reader rather than centred on the way in which an artist composes is abundantly clear. However, Hearn does not entirely neglect the subject of how the author composes. His distinction between sensation and emotion, for example, points the way towards a theory of creativity, one heavily influenced by Wordsworth. Sensation, he writes is feeling without judgement, and emotion is the instinctive judgement passed upon sensation. Hearn illustrates the concept with the example of a man who stubs his toe and may feel any of a variety of emotions, such as anger or embarrassment. But regardless of which emotion, it is the emotion itself rather than the sensation which interests the reader, and the writer would create a very meaningless passage if he tried to present the sensation only and ignored the emotion. In ghost stories, for example, what is fascinating is the recognition of emotions we have in dreams and therefore a great ghost story must follow closely the essential characteristics of dream experience.

Feeling and experience are the two most important tenets in Hearn's literary criticism, and they come to operate in the overall appraisal of both new and old books. For Hearn no book which is entirely bad could become famous, so that in the case of books long published we may simply respect the judgement of previous generations. Furthermore, the study of these books with established reputations helps the reader to recognize life itself by developing a more sensitive memory and a livelier imagination, so that eventually the reader can recognize truth to experience even in unknown works. As the value of the book lies not in its conformity to outward tradition but rather in its reflection of the reader's experience, the art of reading is ultimately nothing more than the discrimination amongst one's experiences. This is also of course the role of the writer who then transforms these intimate experiences into writing:

> In all my lectures I have never failed, when I had the opportunity, to remind you that literature is not the art of writing books, but the art of expressing feeling – feeling, which means everything common in human life.[10]

Hearn's literary criticism is in the end an integrated part of his overall philosophy. From the time he was a child Hearn was always a passionate defender of the weak and the frail, from the over-worked horse and trapped insects in the natural world to the abused black woman and exploited factory workers in the human world. Hearn's instinct for justice was probably so keen because he himself had suffered so many injustices and throughout his manhood he was in a perpetual search for a just society, a society that would be kind to both the weak and the frail and also embrace the strange, the unusual, and the exotic. With his synthesis of Spencerian metaphysics and the tenets of Buddhism he came to believe – at least temporarily – that the East was a spiritually superior universe and moving in the direction of perfection.

Hearn evaluates writers in the same way. Writers are ever improving in the pseudo-social-Darwinian cosmology and the greatest writers up to now are those who create the greatest sense of beauty which in turn inspires the necessary sense of morality. Because of Hearn's predilection for the magical and the supernatural, William Blake is ranked very highly, as is Coleridge, but not Wordsworth or Byron who are relegated to inferior positions. One of the main reasons for the praise of Blake is that Blake, too, was a great champion and proponent of justice, especially in such works as *The Songs of Innocence and Experience*. Blake's 'A Little Girl Lost', about the hypocrisy of blaming only the girl for getting pregnant; 'A Little Boy Lost', about the horrors of the Inquisition; and 'The Fly' all express a sympathy that both writers had for small, neglected and unjustly treated members of the natural and human worlds. Both writers, too, had a strong sense of the injustices perpetuated upon children, and in Hearn's analyses of both Cowper and Crabbe, for example, he chooses poems about boyhood and boarding school life. He then uses the poems as an occasion to lecture on the horrors of boarding school, based, of course, on his own experiences at Ushaw.

Thus, Hearn, by making a direct application of his literary theory to his own personal experience, simultaneously illustrates the strengths and weaknesses of his theory. Hearn shows, for example, how literature cans serve as a comfort and a light in the discovery and assimilation of one's own subjectivity. The coming across of Cowper's and Crabbe's poems must have been like small treasures in the growth of Hearn's personality, because of his ability to so strongly identify with the depicted experience, but it is excessive to conclude from this that boarding as an institution is unjust and thereby everyone is guaranteed to have a terrible experience there. Hearn failed to discriminate sharply enough between personal experience and experience in general, and as the concept of personal response forms the basis of his literary theory, he unwittingly highlights the dangers of applying this theory to an examination of individual literary works by failing to limit his inferences to the confines of his own experience. The average reader would find, for example, that a disproportionately high number of the poems deal with subjects such as the injustice perpetuated upon children and other such topics, thus revealing Hearn's rather extreme and even unbalanced view of the world. Furthermore, his implicit belief that he had already found the perfect society and that man is continually evolving towards perfectibility are concepts that few could accept these days.

Yet despite the problems of the literary theory, these writings reveal and help to clarify further the ever-complex personality of Hearn. Operating throughout his writing, whether it be on Japan, or America, Byron or Blake is his implicit sense of an ideal and just world – which he briefly thought he had discovered in Japan – where true justice and harmony coincide and the spirit of Hearn is thus liberated. Precisely because of the highly selective nature of Hearn's analyses, his literary criticism on the one hand exposes the flaws of the theory itself, and on the other magnifies and sharpens our understanding of the range and preoccupations of Hearn's personality.

Finally, it is only fair to Hearn to keep in mind his original intention in these lectures which was to communicate a difficult subject to students who previously would have had little exposure to it. The students were for the most part having their first real exposure to English literature taught by a Westerner and from a Western perspective and as such they are exemplary. Even though the contemporary reader may find Hearn's evaluations of individual authors at times misconstrued, his analyses of the works, especially the poems, are both incisive and sympathetic; Hearn brought to his lectures a keen and sensitive literary intelligence and a familiarity with a huge body of literature. According to contemporary accounts he was also a first-rate teacher. One good example of Hearn's pedagogical acumen was his decision to shift the focus of the lectures from the intellectual plane to the emotional one as it demonstrates clearly that he understood very well the psychology of his students and the best way to make English literature accessible to them. His letter to Mr Ellwood Hendrick about the possibility of a lecture tour in America illustrates how aware he was of the problems his students faced:

Under these circumstances you might well ask how I could fill my chair. The fact is that I never made any false pretenses, and never applied for the post. I realise my deficiencies; but I soon felt where I might become strong, and *I taught literature as the expression of emotion and sentiment, – as the representation of life. In considering a poet I tried to explain the quality and the powers of the emotion that he produces. In short, I based my teaching altogether upon appeals to the imagination and the emotions of my pupils,* – and they have been satisfied.[11]

Whatever misgivings we may finally have about Hearn's slightly quirky literary theory, one hundred years later the individual analyses still serve as an excellent introduction to non-native speakers of English who are approaching the subject of English literature for the first time.

18

Lafcadio Hearn and Early Irish and Japanese Mythology and Literature

PETER MCMILLAN

———— oOo ————

My topic is certain patterns of feeling and expression common to Japanese and Irish literature and mythology, especially early literature where these parallels are often most explicit. A broad topic indeed, so please be kind enough to regard this as a kind of personal essay which does not from the beginning make any claims towards scholarship. I first became interested in the wonders of Japanese mythology and sensibility through reading Lafcadio Hearn and as he provides such an important cultural link between Ireland and Japan, I would like to make a few remarks about his Irishness and how that may have oriented him towards his rich understanding of Japanese culture.

Hearn was born to an Irish father and Greek mother and he spent his formative years in Dublin where he was brought up by his great-aunt Sarah Brenane. These days, however, many Hearnians either ignore Hearn's Irish background or see it as unimportant, and there are a variety of reasons for this lacuna in Hearn's biography. One of these reasons is that Hearn is of such a mixed background – born on the Greek island of Lefkas, raised in Ireland, educated in England, and then having spent twenty years in the States – that he is claimed to have various nationalities by scholars from the respective countries. To the English his days at Ushaw in Durham are the most important, to the Americans he is an American writer, and in Japan both the Greek and the Irish Ambassadors regularly attend commemorations of both his Greek and Irish heritage. In the future, biographical work on Hearn will have to appraise the relative importance of all these claims, but that does not appear likely for some time.

Another important reason for the neglect of Hearn's Irishness is the result of the author's own insistent recreation of himself and the ensuing obliteration of his Irish childhood from his past. Hearn was abandoned by his mother shortly after their arrival in Ireland, and later by his father. Hearn blamed his father's cruelty towards his mother as the reason for her return to her homeland, and when he grew up he seemed to retain forever an association with Ireland as the source of the unhappiness that sent him into exile. Yet by Hearn's same attempt to eliminate his childhood from his past, we can infer its importance to him. The negative aspect of this was his continual quest for a just and loving society which could embrace the strange, the weak and the frail which Hearn believed he had discovered in Japan. A more positive aspect of his Irish background was that he grew up implicitly believing that the supernatural was part of the natural world. And the stories and fairy tales that he heard growing up in Ireland left him wonderfully open and receptive to the similar sense of the magical that he discovered in Japan. It is some of these common patterns of feeling and expression that I would like to address here.

From the time he was a child Hearn was always a passionate defender of the weak and the frail, from the overworked horse and trapped insects in the natural world to the abused black woman in the human world. Hearn's instinct for justice was probably so keen because he himself had suffered so many injustices and throughout his manhood he was in perpetual search for the just society, a society that would be kind to both the weak and the frail and also embrace the strange, the unusual, and the exotic. With his synthesis of Spencerian metaphysics and the tenets of Buddhism he came to believe – at least temporarily – that the East was a spiritually superior universe and moving in the direction of perfection. Thus Hearn's Japanese sojourn was much better for him. He was fascinated by the mysteriousness of Japan and its sense of the supernatural and magical in everyday life. Of course Hearn had been exposed to a similar sense of the magical during his upbringing in Ireland and it was precisely this aspect of his childhood which left him so open to Japanese culture. Living in Japan Hearn relished a kind of pleasure that he had first experienced as a child, but in Japan this experience was not associated with feelings of unhappiness, guilt or alienation. His Irishness allowed him to accept the Japanese experience as just and right and so he was never critical or patronizing of Japan itself, even though he disliked some of the changes caused by the growth of industry.

So much for Hearn, who stands as one model of an appropriate, if complicated, way to respond to another culture. Let us now look at the two societies of Ireland and Japan. These days the differences between the two countries are much more apparent. Yet if one examines the cultural roots of both countries, one can find patterns of feeling and many similarities in our outlook and response to the world. I would just like to briefly point out some of those parallels in the hope that they provide the basis for further study.

Both Ireland and Japan are island nations, and in the beginning anyway the island status acted as a barrier against invasion. Both are embodied as a female persona and both have a dual religious habitat. In Japan the more orthodox Buddhism coexists with the native Shintoism, and in Ireland Catholicism has until recently incorporated folk mythology and superstition into its practice. In the literature of both countries there is a sense of the love of economy and simplicity of expression where one grasps by intuition rather than by reason and where a large part of the expression is left up to the reader. Both nations, too, share a love of the spontaneous, the romantic, the natural and the magical. There are, too, similarities in our natural surroundings, our temperament and our aesthetic sense.

Many people have pointed out, for example, that *haiku* is a uniquely Japanese form of poetic expression. However, medieval Ireland also has a very splendid body of short lyrical verse similar in subject-matter and expression to Japanese haiku and in some cases *waka*. Here is a charming Irish haiku on winter:

> Cold has seized the birds' wings,
> season of ice,
> here is my news.

We can see clearly from this one example that for both Japanese and Irish there is the same love of nature and belief in the importance of the unsaid. In terms of other literary forms, motifs and imagery there are many other parallels too. And both literatures rely on the interplay of a mixture of both verse and prose. In Japanese one could mention such works as the *Tale of Genjii* the *Ise Monogatari* and the *Kojiki*. In Irish we have such works as the *Táin Bó Cuailgne* and *Buile Suibhne*.

Another common element of early Japanese and Irish sensibility is a deep sense of topography and place naming.

An important Irish document in this context is the *Dinnsenchas* or the history of Irish places. The word actually means topography and especially the names of famous places. The book is a collection of Old Irish legends each set against the backdrop of a particular place. *Leabhar Gabhála Eireann* (The Book of Invasions) also includes many etymologies including that of the naming of Ireland. In the Ulster Cycle Cuchulain's journey is minutely described citing more than fifty place names. A similar kind of obsession with place is seen in the lyrical poems. Rutherford in his study *Celtic Mythology* claims that in this respect Celtic mythology and Hindu Shamanism bear many similarities. The main characteristics of Shamanism are present in the Celtic myths and the only way they could have come there is through druidism. Hence Rutherford claims Celtic mythology is a topography of the supernatural reality, a topography that goes back 3000 years.

Classical Japanese literature and society show a similar fascination with topography, especially evident in such works as the *Kojiki* which is full of folk etymologies. In the *Kojiki* as the Emperor Jimmu approaches Yamago, the political centre, his brother wounds his hand and dips it into the sea and so the sea becomes known as the sea of blood – *chi no umi*. In another episode, the river where Opo-yama-mori dies is called Kawara which is intended as an onomatopoeia for the sound his clanking armour makes as it sinks through the water.

At the beginning of the eighth century the Japanese government ordered the 60-odd Japanese provinces which composed the country to make up a topographical record of each prefecture, outlining the origin of place names and ancient tales associated with them. The collection came to be known as the *Fudoki* or topographical records. Only one of these remains complete – that of the *Izumo Fudoki*. All four *Fudoki* lay the highest stress on the origin of place names or ancient legends associated with these. To know the origin of the place is to be able to control the spirit of the place, and this was of the utmost importance and it is a custom which in part is still carried on to the present day. The *Manyōshū* and other classical Japanese works show a similar obsession with the names of places.

Both ancient cultures believed in the power of poetry and verse as a means of fulfilling prophecy and or causing disaster, though the expression of such belief is quite different. In Ireland it was the exclusive power of the *file* or druid to make utterances come true. The Irish druids were lawgivers, and interpreters of religious questions. They were responsible for the regulation of religious worship and sacrifice. The *file* could declaim and he could prophesize. Most dreaded was his power to sing *glam Dicin* – a form of lampoon with the potency of a spell which at one extreme could be used to drive out rats and at the other to disable or to kill a human victim. The *glam* was feared as much as or more than the weapons of an enemy and even the greatest heroes avoided falling victim to it. When Ferdia is ordered by his Queen Mebh to do mortal combat with Cuchulain, his fellow student in arms, he tries to refuse only to be warned that he will be satirized. So he chooses to do the Queen's bidding and dies for his efforts. The *glam* has a mythological origin. When the divine bard Coirpre visits the Fomorian tyrant Bress, offended by his shabby treatment, he leaves the palace without taking leave of his host and instead of the customary panegyric, he sings the first *glam* recorded in Ireland:

> No meat on plates
> No milk from kine
> No welcome for the late
> No reward for the bards
> May Bress's cheer be what he gives to others.

The King comes out in red blotches as a result and as the monarch must remain unblemished the King has no option but to abdicate. Later, Coirpre again uses his satirical skill to take away the honour of the Fomorian warriors thereby incapacitating them even before the battle. Other cases record the poet's power to kill by means of his verse. In the *Annals of Connacht* the cause of the Lord Lieutenant, John Stanley's death is a poet's spell (*firt file*). However, the poet was not only a power of destruction, but also protected the king from sorcery, and had the power to prophesy.

As Fergus Kelly points out in *A Guide to Early Irish Law*, the poet had the highest status amongst the professionals. He was the only one who could claim the full *nemed* status. His function was to satirize and to praise. 'His high status thus reflects early Irish society's deep preoccupation with honour (enech lit. "face"): it is damaged through satire and increased through praise.' Kelly goes on to point out that this characteristic was noted by the sixteenth century chronicler Stanihurst and even in the twentieth century Tomás O Criomhthain records in his autobiography *An t-Oileánach* how he gave up his work for a day to listen to the Island poet (*file*) rather than risk being satirized. Given the high sense in which honour was held in Irish society it is no surprise that the law should hold verbal assaults as a most serious crime. 'The words for "to satirize" (*aerad* and *rindad*) have the basic meanings "to strike" and "to cut", which indicates the destructive power which satire was believed to hold.' Many kinds of satire required full payment of the victim's honour price.

The Japanese held similar beliefs in the great power of language and its spiritual force. The spiritual forces moving through language were called *kotodama*, which may be translated as language spirit. Jin'ichi Konishi in his *A History of Japanese Literature* points out that the Japanese treated language with great caution:

> The reason for such caution is found in the nature of the *kotodama*. If its formidable power were directed toward the creation of an inauspicious event, it might result in the unleashing of a wholly unanticipated magic force that would sow evil through the world.

Moreover, if the *kotodama* was overworked at its task of bringing about felicitous events, its power ran the risk of debilitation. Whether invoked for good fortune or calamity, then the *kotodama* was not to be unleashed frivolously.

Konishi cites the example from the *Kojiki* whereby Prince Yamato Takeru meets disaster by mistaking his adversary. The prince is on his way towards Mount Ibuki whose god he is intent on subjugating. In the foothills he meets a white boar and, not realizing that he is actually the god dressed in disguise, he utters a *kotoage* to the effect that the boar must be the god's messenger and so it is not necessary to kill him now as he can kill him later. The mountain god is enraged and causes a hail-storm to fall, damaging the prince's health and eventually leading to his death.

Again, the *kotodama* was not only agent of destruction but also could function in the creation and protection of fortuitous circumstances. In 813 the Emperor Saga made a progress to the southern lake and commanded the literati to compose poems. Fujinara Sunohito (756-818) composed the following: 'On this very day/ As we gather by the lake,/ the cuckoo sings/ "A peaceful rule forevermore!" – / Did this reach our sovereign's ear?' The Emperor composed the following verse in reply: 'The cuckoo – as I listened to its song/ I heard this as well/ May the poet's line sustain/ the sovereign's rule forever.' As Konishi points out, their witty exchange is based on a belief in the power of *kotodama*. Auspicious events once voiced have the power of becoming efficacious.

Moving on to another similarity between the early culture of the two countries, one might mention the importance in respective mythologies of birds. However, this belief in the spirituality of birds is very widespread and I do not want it to be misunderstood as a phenomenon limited to the two countries. In Irish mythology there are many examples of birds and of the human taking bird form, especially that of the swan. Indeed, one of the great works of medieval Ireland is *Buile Suibhne*, recently translated by Seamus Heaney as *Sweeney Astray*. It is the story of Sweeney who cursed the church and so is turned by a cleric's curse into a bird and condemned to fly all over Ireland. During his trips around Ireland Sweeney celebrates the natural beauty of Ireland and so transforms his hardships into poetry. One of the places he loved the most was Alternan in Tireragh about which he composed:

> Sainted cliff at Alternon
> Nut grove, hazel-wood!
> Cold quick sweeps of water
> fall down the cliff-side.
>
> Ivies green and thicken there,
> its oak-mast is precious.
> Fruited branches nod and bend
> from heavy-headed apple trees.

Another famous story employs the bird as a central metaphor is the 'Children of Lir'. Jealous of the love of her husband for his four children, the stepmother turns them into swans and orders them to remain in that shape for nine hundred years. Likewise in the 'Wooing of Etain' both the heroine and Mider are transformed into swans and Caer, the dream-girl in 'Aengus' alternates between human and swan forms. When Aengus sees her in her avian manifestation with her 'thrice fifty' companions about her all but Caer are paired together with silver chains. So he takes the shape of a swan and joins her.

Japanese mythology is also full of the sense of the mysteriousness of the bird and its connection with the otherworld. There are so many examples in the *Kojiki* that I will limit my discussion to that work alone, but even from these following examples the importance of the bird will be abundantly clear. The *Kojiki* is a mythological account of the founding of Japan, the equivalent in Ireland being *The Book* of *Invasions* or *Leabhar Gabhála Eireann*. Both works are unreliable as historical documents, but both give us a fascinating account of the preoccupations and mentalities of our forefathers. In early Japan, for example, the crow seems to have been regarded as a messenger of the sun-deity or as a sacred bird sent to guide travellers. This folk belief has persisted even to recent times in Wakayama prefecture where there was a taboo against driving crows away. In the *Kojiki* a similar role is played by a giant crow (*yata-garasu*) which descends to guide Emperor Jimmu to Yamato, a divine intervention to aid the chosen.

In another tale Prince Po-Muti-Wake is unable to speak, but once when he hears the cry of a high flying swan he utters childish babblings for the first time. Opo-Taka is sent to capture the bird in the belief that the bird is the external soul or soul-substitute of the prince and by capturing it the power of speech would be returned. In the *Kojiki* version the prince does not regain speech after the bird is captured, but in the *Nihon Shoki* version the prince's power of speech is returned.

Another whole chapter of the *Kojiki* is devoted to celebratory songs sung on the auspicious occasion of a wild goose laying an egg within the borders of Japan. Takesi-Uti-No-Sukune sings: 'As a sign that my lord/ Should rule with long life – / The wild goose, it seems, has laid an egg.' The song reflects the belief that when a bird came flying its spirit entered the human body and revitalized the person. The wild goose's laying of a golden egg thus had extraordinary potency in revitalizing the spirit of the Emperor and the song quoted above and the other two songs of this chapter which praise the Emperor and call for his longevity were called *poki-uta* (blessing songs). Incidentally, in an earlier story the Emperor and his courtiers are all allegorised as birds. The Emperor Nintoku is called Opo-sazaki (Great Wagtail); Paya-busa-wake means Falcon Lad and Me-dori means 'Woman Bird'.

Similarly, in early Japan there seems to have been a custom

of dressing up as birds for funerals. As the soul of the dead was believed to assume the form of a bird, the wearing of bird-costumes was seen as an indispensable aid in helping the deceased fly to the other world. Thus when Ame-no-waka-piko dies a funeral house is built, and mourners dressed as birds perform the funeral rites:

> They made a wild goose of the river the bearer of the burial offerings; heron the broom-bearer; a kingfisher the bearer of the food offerings; a sparrow the grinding woman; and a pheasant the weeping-woman.

The most poignant and lovely passage of the *Kojiki* employs a similar use of this idea. It is the scene where upon his death the soul of Yamato Takeru is transformed into a huge white bird and takes to the sky. There is an extraordinary pathos in the scene of the bird flying across the rocky terrain followed by his wife and children whose feet are cut by the bamboo reeds, but forgetting their pain continue after the bird, weeping and singing to him: 'The plover of the beach/ Does not go by the beaches,/ But follows along the rocky shores.' This tale is still revived in present-day Japanese works most notably in Ennosuke Ichikawa's wonderful kabuki version, where Ichikawa actually flies through the auditorium at the end of the performance (suspended on a rope of course).

Time will not permit an elaborate discussion of other topics, but I would like to mention in passing a few other parallels. One of these is the abundance of stories connected with water representing another world. Celtic legend abounds in folk-tales of underwater cities and palaces – possibly the origin of the Atlantis legend. In one tale, for example, the beautiful Eithne is brought up in the court of the sea god, Manannán Mac Lir. She loses her veil of invisibility after bathing with her human friends, and as she is unshielded from mortal gaze she cannot return to the 'sidh' and wanders sadly until she eventually arrives in a monastery.

She is befriended by the monk and received into the church and the company of humans; a devout Christian she nevertheless is still lonely and one day hears voices from the other world calling sadly to her. Soon after she dies in the arms of St Patrick.

Japan's 'Urashima Tarō' is a typical Japanese tale which employs the metaphor of the sea as the other world. Urashimatarō is a young man who saves a turtle from cruel treatment by boys and in return is taken on the turtle's back to an underwater palace where he lives happily with a princess. Like Tír na nÓg one never ages in this other world, and when the hero finally returns to earth he opens a box which he was told not to and becomes a very old man.

The folk legends of both countries also contain many legends of the fear of the sea. There is the famous story of Heike crabs of Danatsu Bay called after the warriors killed there and the victor Minamoto who is later killed in a storm at the same location. Hearn has written about the phantom ship which is common to both Ireland and Japan. According to Hearn if the ship comes from behind one will not be harmed, but if it approaches in front of one it means death. Thomas Mason in his book *Islands of Ireland* reports that sighting a phantom ship meant instant death. A phantom ship appeared before the Blasket drowning that took the lives of an island visitor and the son of Thomas O'Croghan (Tomás O Criomhthain), the great Irish story-teller.

A further parallel between the two cultures is the abundance of tales about beautiful women who are really goddesses or fish or foxes or birds, but who temporarily assume human form to live with a man as the ideal wife. In both cultures the woman almost invariably puts the man under some condition – or *geis* – and invariably the man breaks his promise and the woman returns to the other world. In Japan the most famous of these tales is 'Yuki Onna', made famous by Hearn. It is the story of a man who is saved in a snowstorm by the woman of snow who makes him promise he will tell no one. The next day a beautiful woman arrives, marries him and is an ideal wife and mother. They live together happily for many years, but one day the husband lapses and tells his wife the story. Of course, his wife is the woman of snow who has taken human form, and on realizing that he has betrayed her, she returns to the other world forever.

Another similar story is 'Tsuru Nyobo' (Crane Wife) which tells of a hunter who saves a wounded crane which then flies away. The next day a lovely lady arrives and weaves him an exquisite white cloth. The hunter sells the fabric in the village and soon becomes a rich man. Again he makes a promise never to watch her weaving. They live happily together, but gradually the man becomes greedier and demands she weaves more and more cloth. The lady becomes weaker and weaker and one day when the hunter decides to look at her weaving he discovers that she is a crane and weaving from her own body. She says goodbye and flies away forever.

Irish mythology and tales are also full of similar tales. Macha, for example, in the *Táin Bo Cuailgne* turns up at the home of Crunniac Mac Agnomain of Ulster. Because of her beauty she is given a great welcome, and before fulfilling her duties as his wife she provides food and clothing for the children. Likewise, she makes her husband promise that he will never ask her to demonstrate her skill as a runner, even though she can run like the wind. However, one day while at the races Crunniac boasts that she can outrun any horse and, to save his honour, forces Macha to compete even though she is pregnant. She wins the race but collapses on the track and bears twins, the Emain Macha, on the spot. Before returning to the other world she curses the men of Ulster that they may experience the pains of labour at the time of their greatest need. Similarly, there is the story of Inisquin who marries a mermaid. She warns him not to let any of the O'Briens of Coloan into the house. Typically, one of the O'Briens does enter the house after the races and the mermaid returns to the lake with the children.

In short Celtic mythology has influenced writers from Chaucer to Shakespeare, especially in the latter's *The Tempest* and *As You Like It*. There are Celtic influences in Corneille and Moliere, Scott, Tennyson, Swinburne, Arnold and Hardy. In Ireland W.B. Yeats, Lady Gregory, J.M. Synge and many other writers made extensive use of mythology. Even on the popular level movies such as *Excalibur* and *Conan the Great* employ Celtic ideas throughout. In Japan, too, mythological material is often re-shaped for contemporary audiences. Just two examples are Junji Kinoshita's dramatic version of 'Tsurunyobo' (The Crane Wife) called *Yuuzuru* and Michio Katoh's version of the 'Taketori monogatari' – Kaguyahime – called *Nayotake*.

I have been attempting to highlight similarities not only in the mythologies and their literary manifestations, but also shared patterns of feeling of the two cultures. The starting point for future studies will be a recognition of the traditional propensity of both cultures to allow for the supernatural to reside in the natural. An examination of the life and work of Lafcadio Hearn makes us aware of the similarities of the parallel traditions, even if such a result was not Hearn's intention. There is no doubt that Hearn's Irish upbringing informed him with a literary, mythological and imaginative background which made him intuitively receptive to the splendours of the Japanese tradition. Indeed, perhaps the greatest part of Hearn's achievement rests in his understanding that by going to Japan he was in a sense going home. And in the sense that he was going home, Hearn was able to make clear to the Japanese where their true home lay.

19

Hearn's Japan: A Visit to the Oki Islands

JAMES A. SHARKEY

──────── oOo ────────

In the summer of 1992, Ambassador Sharkey visited the Oki Islands in the footsteps of his fellow-countryman Lafcadio Hearn. He found in them the same sense of an older civilization as Hearn's relative, Synge, did in the Aran Islands.

In Japan, visitors are never far away from the beautiful and the unexpected. Here in Tokyo, I have been suddenly surprised and uplifted by the sight of something lovely breaking down the barrier of my busy working day: the great autumn sun of evening spilling red across the sky over the skyscrapers of Shinjuku; cherry blossom couples on the Chidorigafuchi; the silence of a morning fall of snow in the old shrine near my home in Roppongi.

But often it has been on journeys outside this bustling capital that I have sensed most clearly the coaxing warm-hearted spirit of Japan and where I have heard the sound of its heartbeat, loud and strong.

Far from Tokyo, something special happened to me and my family this summer. We went to the Oki islands, a cluster of volcanic islands some 70km north of Shimane and Tottori prefectures in Western Honshu, and I was welcomed there as the first ambassador to visit 'since the Age of the Gods'.

I was following humbly in the footsteps of the writer Lafcadio Hearn who a century ago visited this lonely archipelago. Hearn informs us that before him 'not even a missionary had ever been to Oki and its shores had never been seen by European eyes', except on very rare occasions.

Even for the Japanese, Oki was then one of the least-known parts of Japan, and this excited Hearn's curiosity and had a natural appeal to his romantic, restless, searching soul. Today, Oki remains safely off the main tourist track, splendid and secure in its overwhelming beauty and in its comparative though ever-diminishing isolation.

Hearn made the short trip to Oki in a coastal steamer overflowing with passengers, personal belongings, baskets of squirming eels and squawking chickens. Eventually, on the cabin rooftop amid a cargo of rolling, pitching watermelons, he found space to rest, smoke his pipe, admire the famed pine trees of Mionoseki and watch the 'ghostly peak' of Daisen fade behind the clouds.

My journey to Oki was speedier and less daunting. I travelled from Izumo by plane, rising high over the great shrine, circling the clear calm waters of Lake Shinji and the pine-lined craggy shore of Shimane Prefecture before heading outwards across the Japan Sea. But though I was the beneficiary of all the contemporary comforts, I shared Hearn's sense of exhilaration, and like him I found my visit inspiring, invigorating, unforgettable.

Hearn had been told to expect in Oki a people who were

civilized yet simple, honest beyond belief and kind to strangers. He was not disappointed. In this little-visited island chain, he also found a people who were courageous and gentle, stately and handsome, virtuous and hospitable, hardworking, good-humoured and generous beyond anticipation. These enviable characteristics, shaped as the islands are shaped by the winds and waves of time, are the inheritance of all who live in Oki today.

These same traits also belong to the islanders of a different ocean and a different tradition: the Aran Islands off Ireland's western seaboard. By coincidence, the Aran Islands were also observed, admired and brought to the attention of the world by a relative through marriage of Hearn, the Irish dramatist John Millington Synge.

Like Synge, Hearn spent his boyhood and his youth in Dublin and like Synge he found in the folklore, the haunting beauty, the intimacy and the special fortitude of island communities a welcome escape from the pressures of modernism and change.

Synge discovered in the Aran Islands the exposed seam of a timeless Gaelic civilization, rich in music, story-telling, poetry and song. Hearn found in Oki a respect for learning and tradition and a strong sense of the civilization of an older Japan. How could it have been otherwise among these hardy islanders whose 'only boast' he tells us 'was that of having kept their race unchanged since the time the Japanese first came to Japan'.

Although in 1892 when Hearn went there these islands were the domain of everyday fisher-folk, they had also been home in the Middle Ages to golden exiles from the great centres of Japan's Kansai region.

The people of Oki sheltered these wondrous strangers and took them to their hearts; they listened to their tales of distant deeds; they admired their learning and their eloquence and they passed the memory of their presence and their ways from generation to generation. That respect for tradition and reverence for learning has remained very much part of island life down to the present time.

On our visit to Oki, my family and I saw marvels we will always remember; sacred places where emperors walked and where the mighty Gotoba once called the pine tree and the pond to silence; towering cliffs trailing streamers of white waterfall; the silver blue flame of flying fish rising from the rolling seas; sheltered clearwater inlets with crowded fishing boats impatient for the night's catch; strong snorting bulls bred for the clash of battle, and horses, shy with strangers, grazing at the tall cliffs' perilous edge. Hearn told of all these things and much more besides, and he wrote with affection and good humour, with keen perception and a reverence which he could scarcely conceal.

Hearn's first major Japanese anthology, *Glimpses of Unfamiliar Japan*, was completed and published while he was living in Kumamoto where he had gone after Matsue to conserve his health and seek a measure of financial security. The detailed account of his visit, contained in that anthology under the title 'From Hoki to Oki', is among his finest writing, vital and vivid to this day.

No writer before Hearn or of his generation succeeded so sensitively and so effectively in communicating a sense of Japanese tradition and civilization during a period of profound transition. And perhaps no foreign writer has won such a place of honour and distinction in the imagination of the people of Japan.

What an inspiring thing it is to learn from Japanese friends that their earliest encounters with their own folklore – the marvellous tale of Mimi-Nashi-Hoichi or of Yuki-Onna/The Snow Woman – were in a book written by Hearn almost a century ago recounting tales told to him, sometimes in flickering lamplight, by his loving wife, Setsu, or by strangers on dusty highways or in sleepy country inns.

In Shimane, where Hearn first came in 1890, there was on the mainland and on the islands, in the houses of farmers, fishermen and merchants, a close familiarity with the stories and the ways of old Japan, stretching back in time, back even beyond the building of the magic Izumo Taisha.

When Hearn travelled to Oki in1892 he came to restore himself at the well of that living tradition. As a pilgrim he came in search of the comforting reassurance and the strength of the old Japan which he loved and which he pined for.

Like Hearn, visitors to Oki today will also leave refreshed, reassured and restored by the privilege and the memory of their experience.

20

The Horror and Ghostly Writings of Lafcadio Hearn

SEAN G. RONAN

———————— oOo ————————

A century after his time, Hearn is not quite so well known on this side of the Atlantic. In view of his Irish background and his valuable permanent contributions to English literature, it is desirable and appropriate that more attention should be accorded to his fascinating career and literary achievements.

The post-war years have seen a substantial revival of interest in Hearn and his work. A number of important anthologies and books about him have been published in recent years. In his lifetime and into the 1930s Hearn was quite famous inside and outside Japan but, understandably, interest in him waned during World War II.

The term 'Wandering Ghost' is the title of a recent book on the Odyssey of Lafcadio Hearn,[1] but my treatment will concentrate on his Irish connections, his wanderlust and his place in the supernatural literary tradition.

I should mention a Hearn connection with Clontarf which will be of interest to members of the Bram Stoker Society. It is the house at 17 Fairview Avenue. In the *Tithe Allotment Book* (1827) 'Daniel J. Hearn Esq., Mrs Hearn, Fairview Avenue' appeared as owners of land in townlands Correagh and Moycashel in Co. Westmeath. In the *General Valuation of Rateable Property in Ireland* (1854) Elizabeth Hearn, Daniel's wife was noted as an immediate lessor of the whole land in the townland of Correagh comprising 344 acres. According to *Thom's Directory*, these Hearns who were Lafcadio's grandparents, lived at 17 Fairview Avenue in Dublin until 1849. The valuation of the house was £26.[2]

It is a fine double-fronted house which would be well worth seeing and there are plenty of facilities for slaking the thirst nearby. From 17 Fairview Avenue the Hearns moved to 48 Lower Gardiner Street where Lafcadio and his mother stayed with his grandmother when he came to Dublin aged two in 1852. So he just missed staying at 17 Fairview Avenue by a few years.

Patricio Lafcadio Hearn was born in 1850 in the Ionian island of Lefkas, close to the Homeric island of Ithaca. His father Charles Bush Hearn, a graduate of Trinity College, Dublin, was a surgeon in the British Army stationed there and his mother was a pretty local lady. His father was transferred to the West Indies so he sent his wife and young son to stay with his mother in Dublin. They moved to live with Lafcadio's grandaunt Mrs Sarah Brenane at 21 Leinster Square. His father returned from the West Indies and had the marriage annulled. His mother being desperately unhappy returned to Greece never to see her son again. His father remarried and was assigned to the Crimea and later to India.

He died of malaria in the Gulf of Suez on his way back to Ireland in 1866.

Lafcadio, therefore, involuntarily lost his parents by the time he was seven years of age. Mrs Brenane took good care of him and moved to 73 Upper Leeson Street. Being a serious convert to Catholicism she was very strict with Lafcadio. At times he was locked in his bedroom developing great fears of ghosts and goblins. He spent happy summer holidays with Mrs Brenane in Tramore and in Co. Wexford and also with his aunt Catherine Elwood in Cong, Co. Mayo on the shores of Lough Corrib. From contact with relatives, tutors, servants, fishermen and farming people he became familiar with Irish ghost stories, folklore and strange tales. Thus was born one of the great interests that he so talentedly developed in Japan.

His grandson Toki Koizumi was in Ireland recently and visited all the places associated with Hearn and also met his cousins. He discovered from reading a book entitled 'Irish Folk Tales and Legends' that quite a few of the stories that Lafcadio told to his father Kazuo, apart from those of Hans Andersen and the Brothers Grimm, were in fact Irish.

Incidentally, there is a relationship between Lafcadio Hearn and John Millington Synge, whose older sister married Henry Francis Stephens, a first cousin of Lafcadio.

Mrs Brenane sent him to St Cuthbert's College in Ushaw, Durham, where he lost an eye in a sporting game, an affliction that affected him for the rest of his life. Mrs Brenane's fortunes declined when she came under the influence of a distant relative Henry Molyneux. Lafcadio was withdrawn from St Cuthbert's and apparently went to a Catholic college at Yvetot near Rouen for a short period. Then he stayed with a former maid of Mrs Brenane, Catherine Delaney née Ronane, in London. In 1869 at the age of 19 he was given his fare to America and told to go to a brother-in-law of Henry Molyneux in Cincinnati, Thomas Cullinane, who told him to go to the devil and look after himself. Lafcadio says he did both.

In Cincinnati, after a difficult start, he became famous as a journalist specializing in gruesome and bizarre reporting and translations from contemporary French writers and poets. After eight years he went to New Orleans, and again after hard times established a good reputation as a super journalist and translator from French and Spanish literature. He was particularly interested in Creole language, customs and folklore and indeed in voodoo. Following a two-year stay in Martinique he produced a novel and an attractive book of sketches about the French West Indies.

In 1890, when he was 40 years old, he came to Japan on an assignment for the publishers Harpers, where he spent the remaining 14 years of his life, during which he wrote 13 enduring books on Japan, married a Japanese lady of a samurai family, became a Japanese citizen taking the name of Koizumi Yakumo, and became Professor of English Literature in the Imperial University of Tokyo.[3]

Hearn is best known and honoured in Japan as an adopted son. To thousands of Japanese and Americans his name spells magic, represented by his Japanese tales of long ago, delicate, transparent, ghostly sketches of a world unreal but with a haunting sense of spiritual beauty.

His genius grasped better than anyone else the very essence of Japan. A century later he is still acknowledged as the best interpreter of the inner life of Japan for the West and his contribution to Western knowledge of Japan has been enormous.

His output is substantial as a super journalist, novelist, essayist, folklorist, literary critic, translator from the French, educator, travel and letter writer. His fascination with strange happenings and stories of spirits, fairies and ghosts grew out of a life-long interest in the supernatural and the ways that human experience intersects with a complex realm of indefinable forces.[4]

The word 'ghost' appears a thousand times in Hearn's

books in endless association with all his thoughts. Even in his youth he began puzzling over those blind instincts and tendencies, those strange impulses, desires and memories that well up from the unknown depths within us. He began even to ponder over what psychologists attempt to probe as the subliminal self.

He said of himself: 'I have the double sensation of being myself a ghost and of being haunted, – haunted by the prodigious luminous Spectre of the World.'[5]

Defining his own life and the consequences of its nomadic course, he sees a kind of affinity between a wanderer like himself and ghosts he will meet:

> Perhaps the man who never wanders away from the place of his birth may pass all his life without knowing ghosts; but the nomad is more likely to make their acquaintance. I refer to the civilized nomad, whose wanderings are not prompted by the hope of gain, nor determined by pleasure, but simply controlled by certain necessities of his being, – the man whose inner secret nature is totally at variance with the stable conditions of a society to which he belongs only by accident.[6]

In his lecture 'The Value of the Supernatural in Fiction' he gave a good explanation of the importance of ghost stories. He said that the universe is a mystery, a ghostly one: all great art reminds us of the universal riddle; all great art has something ghostly in it. It touches something within us which relates to infinity. The thrill we get from a work of art is akin to that which the ancients got when they thought they saw a ghost. The ghostly always represents some shadow of truth. The ghost story has always happened in our dreams and reminds us of forgotten experiences, imaginative and emotional, and hence thrills us. It has charm because a dream experience is used. For the dream furnishes us with the qualities of ghostly tenderness literature contains. In visions of the dead we have unselfish affection; everything else is gentle.[7]

Hearn defines nightmare as the supernatural or collective

psychical basis of legend, folk-tale and myth. After tracing the etymology of the word 'nightmare' as far as its origin 'Night-Mara', he reminds us of the Scandinavian belief that this Mara was a female spectre, not hideous or fantastic of aspect, like the hollow Ell-women or witch-wives, but fascinatingly beautiful. After he has explored the meaning of nightmare in the terms of the Mara motif or spectral lover theme, Hearn finds the psychic horror of ghost stories changed into something entirely different. It comes to assume a 'weird beauty'. For him terror, interchangeable with beauty, is universal; but it is also tied down to a specific locality.[8]

In an article on the horror of Gothic architecture written much later in 1900, he speaks as a child looking with fear at the power of Gothic forms but it is his own controlled terror that he reveals:

> To his startled imagination, the building stretches itself like a phantasm of sleep, – makes itself tall and taller with intent to frighten. Even though built by hands of men, it has ceased to be a mass of dead stone; it is infused with Something that thinks and threatens; – it has become a shadowing malevolence, a multiple goblinry, a monstrous fetish![9]

His long infatuation with Edgar Allen Poe, the master who portrayed the depths of human perversity, whom he regarded as an older brother in misfortune, influenced his writing in many ways. Indeed, where would the Gothic novel, be without the good old Edgar Allen Poe! Hearn accepted with pleasure the nickname 'The Raven' given to him by his first and closest friend in America, the printer Henry Watkin.

The early nineteenth century in which Poe lived was an era when pseudo-Orientalism was in fashion. It was an age beguiled by things Gothic – quaint folklore, macabre legends, preternatural events, medieval history, forgotten tombs, ruined abbeys. He specialized in horror and terror because he discovered that they were popular and he needed to make a living. Hearn had to make a living as well. Apart from his journalistic work he turned in his spare time to translation of the French writers who had been influenced by Poe – Baudelaire, Gautier, Flaubert, Loti, Anatole France, Zola and Maupassant.[10] He was also influenced by the works of Horace Walpole and Edward Bulmer-Lytton.

In Lafcadio Hearn's personal library now located in the University of Toyama north-west of Tokyo there is according to the Catalogue a four-volume set of *Melmoth the Wanderer* by Charles Robert Maturin, 2nd edition, Edinburgh 1821, also works of W.B. Yeats and James Clarence Mangan.

Like W.B. Yeats, Hearn's approach to literature was much influenced by folk beliefs and superstitions. He was acquainted with Yeats' early work and considered him to be the representative poet of fairy literature. In his essay 'Some Fairy Literature' he praised Yeats' poem 'The Host of the Air' (1899), his play 'Land of Hearts Desire' (1894) and Samuel Ferguson's (1810-1886) 'The Fairy Thorn'[11] for their power to communicate pleasurable fear and weird beauty. He wrote that Ferguson was a poet of very considerable ability, some of whose work would live long in English literature.[12]

He had a very special regard for the writings of J. Sheridan Le Fanu, and refers to him several times in his writings. In a letter to Basil Hall Chamberlain in February 1894 he says:

> By the way, you have read Mérimée's 'Carmen', of course – matchless story! – but would you not like to read the sweetest and tenderest gypsy-story ever written? If you have not yet read it, let me most humbly pray and beseech you to read J. Sheridan Le Fanu's 'Bird of Passage: A Love-Story'. You will thank me if you read it. It is very short. Sheridan Le Fanu is a very great artist at his best. His 'My Uncle Silas' is a terrible but tremendously powerful novel.[13]

There is no reference to Bram Stoker in Hearn's writings or letters, so it is not clear whether before he died in 1904 he ever read 'Dracula' which was published with an international edition in 1897. The possibility cannot be excluded seeing that he was familiar with the works of Yeats published later than 1897.

Between 1872 and 1877 when he lived in Cincinnati Hearn wrote more than 400 newspaper articles and began translations from leading contemporary French writers. The reportage in *The Cincinnati Enquirer* and *The Cincinnati Commercial* is graphic in detail and often horrifying in content, not for the squeamish. His best stories described the misfits, the outcasts and those on the fringe of society, the worlds of criminals, immigrants, indigents, con-artists, prostitutes and ex-slaves. It has been called Hearn's period of the gruesome.[14]

In November 1874 he created a sensation in the newspaper world by a series of articles on what is known as the Tanyard Murder case. In the opening article 'Violent Cremation' he gives a gruesome description of the charred corpse of a murder victim stuffed into a furnace:

> The fragments of the burned body on the clean white coffin lining rather resembled great shapeless lumps of half-burnt bituminous coal than aught else at the first hurried glance; and only a closer investigation could enable a strong-stomached observer to detect their ghastly character – masses of crumbling human bones, strung together by half-burnt sinews, or glued one upon another by a hideous adhesion of half-molten flesh, boiled brains and jellied blood mingled with coal. The skull had burst like a shell in the fierce furnace-heat; and the whole upper portion seemed as though it had been blown out by the steam from the boiling and bubbling brains. . . .

and then

> . . . through all the grim murderers, demoniacally pitiless, devilishly desperate, gasping with their exertions to destroy a poor human life, looking on in silent triumph, peering into the furnace until the skull exploded and the steaming body burst, and the fiery flue hissed like a hundred snakes![15]

There is an undeniable gift for the prose of horror here which might be an inspiration to the modern media!

The following are headlines of some other horror articles written by Hearn in this period:

THE ELIXIR OF LOVE. The tomahawker tries suicide. He searches for the juggler, but failing in that tries an artery. He would die 'all for love'.

THE HAUNTED AND THE HAUNTERS. Ghostly minstrelsy in the city stables. A goblin in a gas-pipe.

THE DANCE OF DEATH. Enquirer reporter in a dissecting room. The skeleton of Cunny – odors of the charnel house – student buzzards and stinking stiffs.

THE CHARNEL HOUSE. Ghastly groping in the decay of graves.

GOLGOTHA. A Pilgrimage to Potter's Field. The sexton-guardian of nameless graves. His secret alliance with ghouls. Extraordinary facilities afforded to resurrectionists. Grave-robbing gravely winked at.

ASSASSINATION. A woman's throat cut near her own door in a dark alley. She rushes speechless and bleeding into her house and dies.

HACELDAMA. Humanity and inhumanity in the shambles. Hebrew slaughterers, Gentile butchers, and consumptive blood-drinkers.

A SLAUGHTER HOUSE STORY. About one who drank three glasses of blood, and went blind.

GIBBETED. Execution of a youthful murderer. Shocking tragedy at Dayton. A broken rope and a double hanging. Sickening scenes behind the scaffold-screen.[16]

Hearn never really cultivated his sense of humour, which is rather a pity.

His earliest ghost story was 'The Cedar Closet' written in 1874. It tells of a recurring ghostly apparition of a love-hungry ancestress of the narrator's husband. The setting, atmosphere, plot progression and denouement are unmistakably Gothic.[17]

His book *Stray Leaves from Strange Literature*[18] published a decade later marks his departure from conventional Gothicism for the realms of folklore, legend and myths. The collection includes Egyptian, Polynesian and Eskimoan legends, tales from Indian Buddhist Literature, such as 'The Corpse-Demon', stories from Moslem lands and traditions retold from *The Talmud*. The central theme is the perennial human dichotomy between passion and wisdom with the emphasis more on the former. Everyone here is a slave of his passion whether for power, knowledge, immortality or woman. Love, the ultimate passion, can be destructive as well as a life-giving source. It triumphs when it ceases to be mere infatuation or passion. It assumes a more peculiar aspect in the form of love for supernatural beings or the spectral love theme as in the stories 'The Book of Thoth', 'The Fountain Maiden' and the 'Bird Wife'.[19]

Hearn's next book *Some Chinese Ghosts* (1887)[20] is far superior to its predecessor. In this collection of six Chinese legends he set out as he said in the preface to seek 'especially weird beauty' and recreate his own versions. He was artist as well as translator.

In 'The Soul of the Great Bell' he deals with the theme of filial pity. The metals for making the Great Bell will not fuse until according to an astrologer the flesh of a maiden be melted in the crucible. Ko-Ngai, the embodiment of heavenly grace, sacrifices herself to ensure her father's success. When leaping into the molten metal, her maid clutches her 'tiny dainty shoe'. Whenever the bell now perfectly blended rings the name Ko-Ngai, Chinese mothers whisper to their children, 'Listen! that is Ko-Ngai crying for her shoe.'

In 'The Story of Ming-Y', Hearn takes up his favourite themes of spectral love between Ming-Y a young poet-scholar and a lady who is actually the ghost of a favourite mistress of a famous ancient poet. Ming-Y as she predicted obtains high dignities and honours but can never forget her even after his marriage into an illustrious house.

The sacrifices the artist must make for his art is the motif of 'The Tale of the Porcelain-God'. To meet the imperial command of producing an impossible vase with the tint and aspect of living flesh, the master-artisan Pu gave his own soul for the soul of his vase. Thus the vase is created not only seeming to be flesh but also uttering whenever tapped the name of its creator, Pu.

However, it is by his Japanese legends that Hearn the story-teller is best remembered. Numbering more than fifty they constitute a quarter of his total output in Japan. Beginning with *In Ghostly Japan* (1899), they increase with *Shadowings* (1900), *A Japanese Miscellany* (1901) and *Kottō* (1902) until they take up most of *Kwaidan* (1904) and the posthumous *Romance of the Milky Way* (1905).[21]

Living in a world that accepts the supernatural as an integral part of its daily life and having explored the Buddhist theory of Karma in terms of Spencerian evolution, Hearn was convinced that the ghostly is at the very centre and not just at the periphery of human existence. His concern now is with the domain of ghosts. Everything he sets out to recreate is weird or ghostly whether it be horror, beauty or laughter.[22]

He gives us a large number of stories romantic, heroic and horrible, all of them with a fascination of strangeness yet perfectly intelligible to Western readers. They read like the most delicate and modest of translations whether he is translating or not. The tales scattered through his books and almost filling *Kwaidan*, which means strange or weird tales, make up one of the greatest treasures ever found by a translator in an entirely foreign land. Their beauty, splendour, tenderness or horror is not to be denied. His great achievement is harmony of tone with a plain lucid style leaving the reader free to listen to the characters and watch events.

Among the best known of his Japanese tales is 'The Story of Mimi-Nashi-Hoichi' or 'Hoichi-the Earless', the opening piece in *Kwaidan*, which was Hearn's own favourite. A blind biwa player is a renowned reciter of a medieval battle between famous clans. His chanting is so magnificent that even the goblins weep. Trouble begins when Hoichi is led away nightly by a ghostly voice to appease the souls of the ancient warriors. The patron-priest writes down the holy sutra text all over the body of Hoichi – except his ears. That night Hoichi is for the first time free from the ghostly power, but the angry spirit tears off his ears, which boosts his professional success all the more!

The artist theme appears again in 'The Boy Who Drew Cats',[23] one of Hearn's few fairy-tales. It is about an acolyte of a village temple who is dismissed because of his excessive fondness for drawing cats on walls, screens and holy scriptures. That night, when he takes shelter at a deserted temple, he cannot resist drawing cats before falling asleep. Ironically, the cats he has drawn save his life from 'a goblin rat bigger than a cow'.

A very beautiful tale with a Tír na nÓg or sort of Rip Van Winkle theme is 'The Dream of a Summer Day' (*Out of the East*). It is the story of Urashima, perhaps the most famous of all Japanese legends. For releasing a turtle sacred to the Dragon God of the Sea, a fisher-boy was brought by the Sea God's daughter to an enchanted island where summer never dies. They married and eventually he insisted on returning to see his parents but it was four hundred years later. Recklessly he broke a promise he made to his flower-wife by opening a lacquered box she gave him. Suddenly, he began to change and fell down lifeless on the sand like Óisín.

This tale relates to another one 'Hi-Mawari' (*Kwaidan*) meaning 'sunflower' which has an Irish setting. 'The dearest and fairest being in his little world' referred to in both stories was his aunt Mrs Catherine Elwood.

The young samurai in 'The Story of Ito Norisuke' (*The Romance of the Milky Way*) represents the archetype of all Hearn's ideal lovers. He is led to wed a beautiful ghost but they are destined to meet only once in ten years. When morning dawns they exchange gifts in remembrance – a little *suzuri* or ink-stone for the *kogai* of his sword. He departs from the ghostly region, dreaming of their reunion ten years ahead. His health gradually fails and he dies just as the tenth year comes around asking that the ink-stone be placed in his coffin.

Other famous tales are 'The Story of O-Tei' (*Kwaidan*) about a girl who is reborn in another human being to be finally wedded to her lonely betrothed, thanks to their mutual pledge; 'Of a Promise Broken' (*A Japanese Miscellany*) where the dead wife's ghost returns as soon as her samurai husband breaks his promise to remain faithful to her memory and tears off the new bride's head; 'The Story of Chūgorō' (*Kottō*) about a poor retainer who dies in love with a beautiful woman at the bridge, actually a great and ugly frog; 'Yuki-Onna', (*Kwaidan*) the Snow Woman who melts into a bright white mist as soon as her human husband reveals their secret; 'The Story of Aoyagi' (*Kwaidan*) about the spirit of a tree which marries a young samurai only to return to its own world; 'Jikininki' (*Kwaidan*) the man-eating goblin who in awful Shape entered the death chamber to devour the corpse and indeed the offerings possibly for dessert! and so forth.

Professor Basil Hall Chamberlain has said that none could understand Hearn who did not take into account his belief in ghosts.[24] His ghostly tales and legends have indeed earned him an honoured place in the supernatural literary tradition.

Apart from that he stands out not merely as a writer who has revealed an idealized Japan to the Western world but one whose thought and wide range of interests have rendered him universally appealing. His nomadic and mental destinies have been followed with both joy and anguish. A century after his time his aesthetic standards and the charm of his art survive. This shows him to be a man of genius and a very great writer. Here in Ireland he has been included in the Junior Certificate English curriculum which will help to stimulate interest in his life and work among the younger generation in his 'Fatherland'.

21

Lafcadio Hearn's Interpretation of Japan

PAUL MURRAY

———————————— oOo ————————————

Lafcadio Hearn was profoundly influenced by religion, morality and scholarship. These factors, together with certain convictions and/or prejudices, informed his vision of Japan. Among these convictions was an unshakable belief in the virtue of the common man; in Japan he believed that this was in inverse proportion to his degree of Westernization. Another important factor was Lafcadio's failure to master the Japanese language and so his contribution was of a different order to that made by his great scholarly contemporaries – Satow, Aston, Chamberlain – although it could be claimed that his extensive field-work in the area of Meiji customs and folklore constitute a considerable body of scholarship, albeit in a different nature to that of the men just mentioned.

Many people will be surprised that I describe Hearn as a man deeply concerned with religion. Because he abandoned Christianity in his youth, he is generally thought of as anti-religious; in fact, he was deeply concerned with – one might say obsessed by – religion, philosophy and the supernatural in his life and writing. In the decade prior to his arrival in Japan, Lafcadio had immersed himself in Buddhism as well as in Herbert Spencer's 'synthetic philosophy'; his attempt to reconcile the two was an important impulse in bringing him to Japan. When he got there, the experience of encountering a living Buddhism enthralled him.

His scholarship preconditioned him, however, not just to delight in Buddhism, but to accept a second and to him new religion in Japan, Shinto. He had absorbed the work of the French historian, Fustel de Coulanges, whose book, *La Cité Antique*, linked the religious practices of ancient Greece and Rome with the religion of the hearth. Hearn believed that in Shinto he had found the Japanese equivalent, a means of relating Japan to the classical world as well as of differentiating it from contemporary Western culture.

He also believed that an understanding of its religion was essential to the comprehension of any society and, in *Japan: an Attempt at Interpretation*, his late attempt to codify his views, he set out, overtly, to interpret Japan through religion. However, the majority of chapters in his first book on the country, *Glimpses of Unfamiliar Japan*, published ten years earlier in 1894, were also concerned with religion and the supernatural. So, too, was much of the writing sandwiched in between: for example, *In Ghostly Japan*, which appeared in 1899, could just as easily have been called 'In Buddhist Japan'.

Hearn's moral outlook permeated all his work on Japan. Stated simply, he did not believe, unlike Basil Hall Chamberlain for example, that might was right; on the contrary, he distinguished between the West's material superiority, then overwhelming, and what he saw as its moral inadequacy. He had been sceptical about the civilizing mission of Western imperial expansion from his earliest Cincinnati journalism and this turned into downright hostility in his Japanese work.

If we turn from his outlook to examine Hearn's life in Japan we can see that it falls into four main sections, reflected in his books, even if there is not an exact chronological match. Firstly, there was the initial period spent in Yokohama and Matsue, 1890-91, mirrored in *Glimpses of Unfamiliar Japan*; then three years in Kumamoto, 1891-94, represented by *Out of the East*; two years in Kobe, 1894-96, which produced two books, *Kokorō* and *Gleanings in Buddha Fields*; the remainder of his life, 1896-1904, was spent, reluctantly, in Tokyo where he wrote a further eight books.

In my view, Hearn's early interpretative Japanese work, done between his arrival in 1890 and his move to Tokyo in 1896, was generally his best. It was distinguished by an insistence on seeing Japan from a Japanese perspective and explaining it to his Western audience in these terms. This differentiated him from most of his contemporaries – and I include here such notable scholars as Basil Hall Chamberlain, Ernest Satow and William George Aston – as well as many who have written of Japan since. Furthermore, I see his vision as double-edged, illuminating Japanese culture on the one hand and, on the other, providing a critique of what he perceived to be the West's shortcomings.

Many will see him as a one-dimensional malcontent, a man who despised his own civilization, perhaps because of the unhappy circumstances of his childhood, when he fell between the stools of various cultures, Greek, Irish, and English. Certainly, his childhood was traumatic, and he never had a sense of belonging, to the Greek world of his mother, to the Protestant Irish world of his father, or to the Roman Catholic world of the great-aunt who brought him up. While this may have helped generate the undeniably neurotic — and artistic — elements in his personality, Hearn's upbringing left him without that sense of the righteousness in his own culture which characterized many of his contemporaries, and this in turn preconditioned his approach to Japan. It resulted in the paradox that Hearn, the life-long prototypical and determined outsider, should have attempted to see Japan with an insider's eye.

One could discern elements of his alienation from mainstream Western culture in his early American work: the portrayal of Tahiti, for example, as a paradise destroyed by the intrusion of Western capital and religion. In Cincinnati, he identified with suffering and the underdog, from dumb beasts in the slaughterhouses to the condemned at he end of a rope, from the outcasts of Bucktown, the city's vice quarter, to the negro culture of the riverside levee. Much the same pattern could be seen in his focus on the Creole cultures of New Orleans and the West Indies and his immersion in the world of French culture when he was in the United States.

The interpretation of Hearn as an iconoclastic misfit leaves out of account, however, Hearn's rapid progress from youthful radicalism to a trenchant conservatism while still a young man. In New Orleans he came to see political developments from the old slave-owners' perspective; in the West Indies this led him to adopt occasionally condescending attitudes towards the region's negro population.

Looked at, therefore, in terms of the dynamics of his own development, it might not have been a great surprise if Hearn had adopted patronising attitudes towards Japan, similar perhaps to those evident in *Madame Chrysanthème*, that novel of 1880's Nagasaki by Pierre Loti, a literary icon and correspondent of Hearn's. The fact that he did not was primarily due, I think, to his belief that he had found there a traditional society, at the same point in the evolutionary scale as classical Greece and Rome, morally and spiritually superior to the world from which he had come. In other words, his conservatism, which produced one reaction in the West Indies, produced a fundamentally different one in Japan.

Hearn's political views could occupy a lecture in themselves but I would summarize them by saying that he rejected contemporary Western notions of *laissez-faire*, not from the viewpoint of socialism, which he abominated, but from the perspective of a traditionalist who believed that the collectivism of pre-capitalist societies could provide a morally superior form of existence. He also saw that the Japanese bureaucracy was shaping a new world power, a process which clearly was not in train in the West Indies. Finally, there was an elusive emotional chemistry between a man for whom the supernatural seemed to weave in and out of everyday life and a culture which gave him the sensation of being in a world of mysteries and living gods, with a 'delicious ghostliness' closer and more real than the mortals around him.

'The Japanese Smile', an outstanding essay in his first book, *Glimpses of Unfamiliar Japan*, provides in microcosm the essence of Hearn's reaction to Japan; the views he formed at that stage did not change over the years in their essentials. The inspiration lay in a visit paid by Lafcadio to the open port of Kobe after spending three years in a Japanese environment. By living in the interior for the bulk of his first four years in Japan he had developed a triangular perspective, balanced between the traditional society of the interior, the West, and the Westernized world of the Treaty Ports. Viewed through this prism, he was now able to view the reactions, and the interaction, of Japanese and foreigners with a fresh eye. Struck by their mutual incomprehension, he took the differing nature and purposes of the smile in the cultures of East and West to illustrate the gulf between them:

> If the Japanese are puzzled by English gravity, the English are, to say the least, equally puzzled by Japanese levity. The Japanese speak of the 'angry faces' of the foreigners. The foreigners speak with strong contempt of the Japanese smile. . .[1]

The Japanese smile was often taken as a sign of heartlessness by Westerners who do not understand that it was, in fact, the outward aspect of the regulation of the expression of feeling in Japanese society; by contrast, Western facial expressions seemed unnaturally grave to Japanese, who did not comprehend the role of the smile in disguising emotions, especially aggression, among Occidentals. To Hearn, the differing nature and purposes of the smile illustrated the mutual misunderstanding which arises from mistaken assumptions of the universality of cultural norms.

Surveying the process of modernization, and accepting its necessity – Japan, he said, could have attempted no less – Hearn still felt that many of the fine traditional qualities of the Japanese race were being lost or coarsened. At the same time, he believed that the Japanese could distinguish between Western material superiority and Western morals and he was optimistic that Japan would be able to assimilate Western civilization while preserving its 'peculiar modes of thought and feeling'.[2] On the other hand, he was critical of what he saw as a lack of originality and metaphysical speculation in the Japanese character and admitted missing aspects of Western life while living in the interior.

We can see in this essay that Lafcadio had not, as some have imagined, turned away from the modernizing world of Meiji Japan to shut himself off in an arcane purity in the interior. He was in fact concerned with the dynamics of change in Meiji society from the beginning. Even that wonderful literary confection, 'My First Day in the Orient', also in *Glimpses of Unfamiliar Japan*, achieves much of its effect from the juxtaposition of the wonders of this new civilization with the disagreeable symbols of Westernization; you may have Hokusai's own figures walking about but they are passing ugly new European buildings; the shop of Buddhist images is next to the shop selling American sewing-machines; the exotic streets are lined with telegraph poles; there may be infinite hand-built variety in crafts but there are also machine-made products to meet the vulgar foreign demand; Japanese trees may be lovely but they have to be protected against the vandalism of foreign tourists; he may have been describing Japanese Yokohama but he had come from the European quarter. In other words, right from his first essay on Japan, Hearn was dealing with the process of modernization and, indeed, much of the effect of his description of the traditional derives from this consciousness on the part of the reader.

In the wider context, he was concerned with Japan's relationship with the West and was in a sense interpreting the two worlds to each other. This is true of 'The Japanese Smile', to which I have already referred, as well as of a number of important essays in his early books, especially 'Jiujutsu' and 'Of the Eternal Feminine' on *Out of the East*; 'The Genius of Japanese Civilization' in *Kokoro*; and, 'About Faces in Japanese Art', in *Gleanings in Buddha Fields*.

In 'Jiujutsu' the martial art was used as a metaphor for the manner in which Japan dealt with the outside world, of using an opponent's superior weight and strength against him. He formulated a distinction in the Japanese approach between imitation and assimilation; Japan had taken only what she needed from the West and nothing was borrowed for purely imitative reasons:

> Those who imagine the Japanese to be merely imitative also imagine them to be savages. As a fact, they are assimilative and adoptive only, and that to a degree of genius.[3]

By taking only what she needed materially from the West and rejecting those aspects of Western culture not of practical use in building up her strength, Japan was practising a form of national jiujutsu on the Western powers. Hearn contradicted Sir Harry Parkes' prediction that Japan would become a 'South American republic'; 'the fierce heart of Old Japan' was beating too soundly for that.[4] For a man allegedly living in a fairyland, this essay seems to me to be a superb analysis of Japanese *realpolitik*.

Lafcadio Hearn photographed in Kobe, Japan, 7 April 1895

2. Leinster Square, Dublin, c.1850.

3. No.48 Lower Gardiner Street, Dublin.

4. Strandhill House, Cong, Co. Mayo.

5. Belair House, Tramore, Co. Waterford.

6. Lafcadio Hearn memorial plaque on 73 Upper Leeson Street, Dublin.

7

Henry Hearn Molyneux, 1837-1906, distantly related to the Hearns

8

Richard Holmes, father of Lafcadio's grandmother, Elizabeth Hearn née Holmes

9

Richard Hearn, d.1890, unmarried, brother of Charles Bush Hearn and uncle of Lafcadio

10. The Rt.Revd. Alexander Arbuthnot, Bishop of Killaloe. A great-uncle of Lafcadio's grandmother Elizabeth Hearn.

11. Major Robert Thomas Hearn, 1823-62, brother of Charles Bush Hearn, and uncle of Lafcadio.

12. Lafcadio's aunt Jane, 1832-1906, daughter of Lt.Col.Daniel James Hearn and Elizabeth Holmes.

13. The Rt.Revd Robert Thomas Hearn, Bishop of Cork, and grandson of Lafcadio's uncle, Major Robert Thomas Hearn

14. Mrs Catherine Frances Elwood, d.1861, sister of Charles Bush Hearn and aunt of Lafcadio.

16. Elizabeth Hearn, nee Holmes, Lafcadio's paternal grandmother.

18. Lafcadio's half-sister Posey Gertrude Brown.

15. James Daniel Hearn, 1854–1935, Lafcadio's younger brother.

17. Lafcadio's half-sister Minnie Charlotte Atkinson.

19. Lafcadio's half-sister Elizabeth Sarah Maud.

20

Robert James Hearn, Lafcadio's
great grandfather, 1734-92

21

Daniel James Hearn, Lafcadio's
grandfather, 1768-1837

22

Surgeon-Major Charles Bush
Hearn, Lafcadio's father, 1818-66

23

Lafcadio Hearn in the 1870s

24. Lafcadio Hearn aged about eight with his 'adopted mother', great-aunt Sarah Brenane.

25. Portrait of Sarah Brenane.

26. Lafcadio Hearn aged about 16 at Ushaw College, Durham

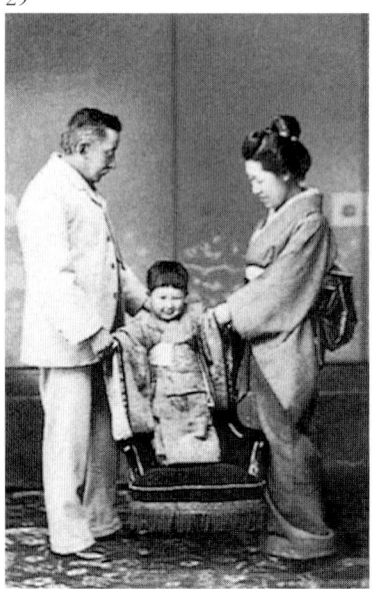

27. Lafcadio Hearn Museum and Library, Sundai Ireland International School, Curragh, Co. Kildare.

28. Tramore, Co. Waterford.

29 Lafcadio Hearn and his wife Setsu with their eldest son Kazuo at the age of two, Kobe 1895.

Also published in *Out of the East*, 'Of the Eternal Feminine' took as its theme the contrasting sexual attitudes of East and West and how these could lead to mutual misapprehension; this is of especial interest given Hearn's belief in – and practise of! – sexual freedom when he lived in the West. Now he took the view that much of Western literature, based on the idea of romantic love, was incomprehensible to a Japanese imbued with filial piety, the basis of society; in the Orient, affection had to be subordinated to duty, especially to the parents. Not alone did he try to make his Western readership see Japan from a Japanese point of view, he told them that if they wished to understand the Orient, they must study the Occident's life and thought from the Oriental perspective. By deconstructing the certainties of their own culture, in particular the ideal of the Eternal Feminine, all pervasive in the West but unknown in the ancient East, the Westerner could come to appreciate the values of the East. Basil Hall Chamberlain wrote that it was 'quite the best thing ever written on Japan'.[5]

Hearn's double vision of East and West was, if anything, even more in evidence in 'The Genius of Japanese Civilization' in *Kokoro*, the first of his two Kobe books. Here he perpetrates a type of jiujutsu by luring his Western reader into a false sense of security with an outline of the two cultures with which he would be comfortable: Japan could not match the epic scale of the ultimate expressions of European culture, from medieval cathedrals to Verdi and Wagner. Having made this concession, Hearn then denounces the 'hard, grim, dumb' utilitarianism of a Western city, and opposes it with the suppleness and polymorphic malleability of Japanese life. The West built for permanence, Japan for impermanence; he challenged the Western assumption that stability is necessary for progress; Japan had demonstrated that enormous development was possible without any stability at all:

> Uniformly mobile, and thus uniformly impressionable, the nation has moved unitedly in the direction of great ends.[6]

It was the absence of 'egotistical individualism' and the teachings of Shinto and Buddhism which had enabled Japan to act as a collective whole and thus 'preserve its independence against prodigious odds'.[7]

The common worker in the West was, he said, less free than his Japanese counterpart, a fascinating concept even today. He linked the ancient civilization of Japan with its 'capacity to threaten Western manufacturers'.[8] Building on this social vision in another essay, Hearn predicted that the future competitiveness of Japanese industry would be based on the aesthetic superiority of her culture, rather than on cheap labour; in fact he saw an essential truth which has been vindicated in our own generation: 'The art-genius of a people may have a special value against which all competition is in vain.'[9]

He even predicted what has in fact happened since the Second World War, that Japan's place in the world would be established by commercial rather than military means.[10] I note that a key claim made for Sir George Sansom by Gordon Daniels was that, in the 1930s, he saw that Japan was 'rapidly passing out of the imitative phase and is developing into a powerful industrial and commercial state';[11] without disrespect to Sansom, it can be said that Hearn had foreseen this four decades earlier. By contrast, Basil Hall Chamberlain was confident in 1904 that the West had little reason to fear Japanese economic competition.[12]

The theme of art was continued in 'About Faces in Japanese Art', published in his second Kobe book, *Gleanings in Buddha Fields*. The last in the series of great essays which completed Hearn's early, interpretative, phase in Japan, it was, incidentally, inspired by a paper to be presented to the Japan Society in London. Rebuking the Japanese Minister there for comments made on that occasion, when he drew attention away from Japanese art to the triumphs of the Sino-Japanese War, Hearn warned that Japan's future industrial prosperity would depend on the 'conservation and cultivation of the national art sense'. Indeed, the ability to supply the armaments for the war in China was due to 'the commercial results of that very art sense'. Japan would have to rely on her 'aesthetic faculty, even in so commonplace a field of industry as the manufacture of mattings; for in mere cheap production she will never be able to undersell China'.[13]

More generally, while the essay was essentially a comparison of popular Japanese and Western art, it also explored Lafcadio's long-standing interest in the ways in which the respective cultures expressed their aspirations. The detailed realism of a contemporary Western engraving was compared unfavourably with the suggestiveness of popular Japanese art:

> A common Japanese drawing leaves much to the imagination, – nay, irresistibly stimulates it, – and never betrays effort. Everything in a common European engraving is detailed and individualized. Everything in a Japanese drawing is impersonal and suggestive. The former reveals no law: it is a study of particularities. The latter invariably teaches something of law, and suppresses particularities except in their relation to law.[14]

Hearn made the imaginative leap of trying to study Western facial expressions through Oriental eyes; the result, as might be imagined, was distinctly unflattering.[15]

I should say at this point that Hearn's relationship with Japan, while always respectful, was also ambiguous; indeed, it was so complex that it caused the Japanese writer, K.K. Kawakami, to wonder if Hearn was a lover or hater of Japan.[16] However, the underlying unity of vision which united the five great essays I have mentioned was a determination to make his Western audience see Japan from a Japanese perspective and a willingness to juxtapose Western norms with their Japanese counterparts in a way which deflated an automatic assumption of superiority on the part of the Westerner. In the 1905 edition of *Things Japanese*, Basil Hall Chamberlain said of Hearn's earlier work:

> Never perhaps was scientific accuracy of detail married to such tender and exquisite brilliancy of style ... Lafcadio Hearn understands contemporary Japan better, and makes us understand it better, than any other writer, because he loves it better.[17]

Despite an almost Oriental tendency toward self-deprecation, Hearn had a very clear vision of his own position in the contemporary field of Japanology:

> The difference between myself and other writers on Japan is simply that I have become practically a Japanese – in all but knowledge of the language; while other writers remain foreigners, looking from outside at riddles which cannot be read except from the inside.[18]

Hearn's Tokyo period may have given him the material for eight further books but, with the exception of *Japan: an Attempt at Interpretation*, his focus turned away from the overtly interpretative. Having explored Shinto in considerable depth in his early books, the balance now swung back to Buddhism and his long-standing interest in reconciling it with Western science.

A second great preoccupation of these later years was the supernatural. All his life, his mind and consciousness had been permeated by horror but now it steadily increased until it became the predominant ingredient in the books which he published at the rate of about one a year. His mature, simplified, prose style admirably suited these translations of *kwaidan*, or traditional ghost stories, and it is for these that he is primarily remembered in Japan today. A third significant element in the later books was the autobiographical, the public laying bare of childhood experiences so traumatic that they remained vivid in his consciousness.

This is not to assert that Hearn had nothing further to say about Japan. Quite the contrary but, with one great exception, he was now content to illuminate specific aspects of Japanese life without the interpretative purpose which had marked his finest earlier work.

That exception was, of course, *Japan: an Attempt at Interpretation*. A view has grown up that having been written just before his death in 1904, it represented a kind of late flowering, a welcome infusion of realism into the work of a writer who hitherto had been wholly unrealistic; to some it was even a form of *mea culpa*. This was expressed by the British diplomat, Frank Ashton-Gwatkin, in his novel, *Kimono*, written under the pseudonym, John Paris: Hearn's books were opium visions of a fairyland which had never existed and he had learned nothing about Japan until, in a state of disillusionment, he wrote *Japan: an Attempt at Interpretation* at the end of his life.

It will be obvious from what I have said so far that I do not agree with this rubbishing of Hearn's work prior to the *Attempt at Interpretation*. Indeed, I see the *Attempt* as organically linked with the earlier Japanese work although in some vital respects it actually represents a regression in the accuracy of his analysis.

The organic link to his earlier work was, of course, Shinto which he had early come to see as the embodiment of the Japanese spirit. In *Japan: an Attempt at Interpretation*, Shinto is again seen as the bedrock of Japanese society, the religion of respect for the ancestors now shading into the concept of the rule of the dead, blending with the growing hold which the *kwaidan* had on his mind.

The structure and coherence of *Japan: an Attempt at Interpretation* is especially impressive coming from an author whose previous work had been seriously lacking in architectonic ability. It has also the superficial attraction that, rather than having to search through a dozen books of disparate material where even the individual essays often lack cohesion, the *Attempt at Interpretation* seems like manna from heaven, a neat summary in one structured volume.

Contrary to appearances, however, Hearn had not

suddenly been graced with architectonic ability out of the blue; the structure of *Japan: an Attempt at Interpretation* was largely borrowed: about half the chapter headings come from Fustel de Coulanges' *La Cité Antique*.[19] Furthermore, the fundamental objective of de Coulanges' book, to show that the institutions of ancient Greece and Rome were based on popular religious beliefs, stemming specifically from the cult of the dead, was applied to Japan by Hearn. One needs, however, to exercise caution in entering this rather arcane area of scholarship: his influence on Hearn is controversial among de Coulanges scholars, with the modern view being more sceptical of the extent of that influence.[20]

Another scholarly input came from the familiar figure of Herbert Spencer. Between his all-embracing evolutionary structure and Hearn's adaptation of de Coulanges to fit into it, Lafcadio developed a theory that Japanese civilization was at the same stage of development as the West had been at in the millennium before Christ. The result was to some extent a negation of Hearn's earlier view that Japan was *sui generis* and should not be evaluated in relation to the norms of the West. Under Spencer's influence, Hearn had become deeply pessimistic about the future, developing Orwellian visions of universal subjection under the sway of industrial combines and socialism. He now decided that the group structure of Japanese society rendered it incapable of democracy and that its future competitiveness would depend on the expansion of Western-style individualism. Not that he had changed his views on the baleful influence of the West; he reiterated at great length the destructive potential of Christianity for Japanese society and the need to keep Western capital at bay.

While one could say that Hearn may have departed somewhat from his earlier insistence on seeing Japan from a Japanese perspective and was now instead imposing the straitjacket of Western philosophical orthodoxy, this is only half the story; paradoxically enough, many of the ideas infusing the *Attempt at Interpretation*, as well as some of his earlier work, had been in circulation in Japan for some time before. The Confucian scholar, Yasui Sokken had, in his 1875 book, *Bemmō* or *Exposure of Falsehood* expounded the view that Christianity was incompatible with the ethical notions of ancestor worship, filial piety, and loyalty to superiors which were fundamental to the Japanese polity. Similarly, the Buddhist scholar, Inouye Tetsujirō, a colleague of Hearn's at Tokyo University, had written of a conflict between the state and Christianity. Certain Buddhist sects had been teaching the compatibility of Buddhism with modern science. And if Hearn declared that he worshipped Spencer, he was not alone: in the words of Sir George Sansom, 'the gospel of most intellectuals in Japan was the gospel of Herbert Spencer'.[21] While therefore the *Attempt at Interpretation* was in some respects the least accurate of Hearn's major interpretative statements on his adopted country – it has been called his worst book on Japan[22] – it did represent a unique fusion of contemporary Western and Japanese ideas.

Having looked at Hearn's interpretation of Japan, it might now be useful to see how it is regarded today. Professor Hirakawa of Tokyo University has commented:

> Hearn's writings are today so discredited among American Japanese specialists that if a young student quotes Hearn sympathetically, he is almost certain to be criticized by his academic advisers and considered a belated romanticist unfit for serious scholarship. There is, however, no problem at all with quoting the authoritative Chamberlain.[23]

It might be interesting, therefore, to look briefly at Basil Hall Chamberlain and see how this figure, who seems to be carved out of a scholarly Mount Rushmore, really does compare with Hearn. This is particularly appropriate as, his scholarly achievements notwithstanding, it is as an interpreter of Japan, through his book *Things Japanese*, that Chamberlain is now primarily remembered. Also, the two men were exact contemporaries..

Their views on Japan had points of similarity as well as difference. Both accepted the necessity of Meiji modernization to ward off what they saw as predatory Western powers and both were contemptuous of Christian missionary activity when used as an agency of imperial expansion. Hearn, however, accepted the validity of indigenous Japanese culture and, accordingly, regretted the process of change. Chamberlain, by contrast, saw 'civilized white men on the one hand' opposed by a Japan emerging from 'Asiatic semi-barbarism' on the other, needing to prove her fitness to be brought into the 'family of Christian nations'[24] and he had no doubt that 'European ways' were superior 'materially and intellectually'.[25] To Hearn, the Westernization of Japan represented a moral and societal regression; in Chamberlain's view it became more civilized as it became more Westernized. He was blunt in his dismissal of Japanese philosophy,[26] literature[27] and music.[28] The fundamental dividing line between the two men was therefore Hearn's insistence on seeing Japan in its own terms and Chamberlain's equal insistence on a Western perspective.

◻

It is inconceivable that Hearn would have written much of Chamberlain's *Things Japanese*: for example, the chapter on 'English as She is Japped', with its extended mockery of Japanese malapropisms in English, sounds very like an anthology of anecdotes swapped over dinner in a foreigners' club, an environment frequented by Chamberlain but shunned by Hearn.[29] These differences of viewpoint are to be expected: Chamberlain remained essentially within a Western environment in Japan; Hearn, by contrast, was seen by his fellow Westerners as having 'gone native', living a mainly Japanese lifestyle, avoiding them as much as he could.

Chamberlain was fiercely loyal to the Treaty Ports' Western inhabitants; his fury at the British Government for what he regarded as a diplomatic humiliation over the Anglo-Japanese agreement of 1894 was due mainly to his indignation at the prospect of foreign residents having to submit to the rule of Japanese law.[30]

It was this issue more than any other which revealed the incompatibility of Hearn's and Chamberlain's views on Japan. Hearn's insistence on seeing the treaty revision from Japan's point of view infuriated Chamberlain, who wrote:

> But surely these are not the lines on which to judge a treaty between a great Western state and that two penny half-penny Brummagem imitation of one which these frock-coated officials have made of Japan.[31]

In other sections of *Things Japanese*, Chamberlain underlined these sentiments by emphatic approval of 'gunboat policy' to be administered by Western powers to a Japanese Government which, if it showed 'dread and dislike' of 'high-handed policy' would quickly come to see that it was 'founded in reason'.[32]

The two men were also fundamentally opposed on the merits of Shinto, a highly political subject in the context of the time. Chamberlain, a sturdy rationalist in the nineteenth-century tradition, believed that Shinto was being fraudulently re-invented as a new religion of loyalty and patriotism by an illiberal and obscurantist Japanese bureaucracy which dared not allow the light of freedom and scientific thought to be shed on their furtive enterprise.[33]

The differences between the two men continued posthumously. Within a few years of Hearn's death, his reputation was engulfed in the most acrimonious controversy, with former friends prominent on both sides. Among other things, he paid a heavy price for having ignored the taboos of his time, particularly on the coloured question in the United States.

Chamberlain played a particularly destructive role in undermining Hearn's reputation as an interpreter of Japan. Professor Hirakawa has documented the progressively more negative entries on Hearn in the later editions of *Things Japanese* and related them to Chamberlain's unhappy personal circumstances, particularly the shame of having his brother, Neville Stewart Chamberlain, achieve notoriety as a Nazi theorist.[34] By the 1939 edition he was writing that Hearn's life had been a succession of dreams which had turned into nightmares; that, awakening from his dream of Japan, he realized he had taken a false step; the Japan he had described could only have existed in his own imagination, and so on.[35] At this stage, Chamberlain's language had taken on echoes of *Concerning Lafcadio Hearn*, the attempted comprehensive demolition job which another erstwhile friend, George Gould, had written a few years after Hearn's death in an effort to salvage his own reputation.[36] There were echoes also of Frank Ashton-Gwatkin's negative views.

As well as his unhappy personal circumstances, I think that Chamberlain may have been responding to the darkening international mood as the world prepared for war. Hearn was then out of tune with the times; the man who had extolled the charms of a new ally and rising world power at the end of the nineteenth century was not the man for the Manchurian crisis, the Second World War, or its aftermath. Indeed, Arthur Kunst has written that

> ... the Great Pacific war with Japan in the 1940s seemed for a time to have obliterated Hearn from the American consciousness, a kind of guilt over a youthful infatuation. The misleading notion of Hearn as a spokesman for Japan left him without literary defences when Japan and things Japanese became enemy.[37]

Yet it was at this time that Hearn may have exercised his greatest influence. In 1945, General MacArthur accepted the argument of a memorandum prepared by Brigadier General Bonner Fellers that the Showa Emperor should not be prosecuted for war crimes. As a young college undergraduate, Fellers had been persuaded to study the writings of Lafcadio Hearn by a Japanese Quaker woman, Yuri Isshiki. When Fellers arrived in Japan in 1945, both Isshiki and her friend, Michiko Kawai, a leader of the anti-war movement, presented him with arguments against prosecution of the Emperor. Within a few weeks, Fellers submitted his memorandum to MacArthur. Quite what influence Hearn's writings exercised on Feller's decision may never be precisely disentangled, but it seems fair to assume that Hearn's interpretation of Japan, with its emphasis on Shinto, and the importance of the Emperor in that system, at least played a role in conditioning Fellers to accept the logic of the arguments put to him in 1945.[38] The fact that Fellers became a close personal friend of Kazuo Koizumi, Lafcadio's eldest son, and was photographed with him at Hearn's grave, underlines the connection.

Now that the memory of international antagonisms earlier in the century are fading in history, we can, I hope, see dispassionately the merits as well as the failings of a man who, in addition to being an artist of enduring merit, was arguably the finest of a talented generation of early interpreters of Japan. Indeed, the tide may already be turning: reviewing my book, Francis King, novelist and Hearn anthologist, claimed in *The Spectator* to have learned more from Hearn's *Attempt at Interpretation* than anything else on Japan[39] and the Tokyo Bureau Chief of the *Financial Times* commented that Hearn's 'Jiujutsu', 'invites an obvious moral for anyone negotiating with Japanese business or government'.[40] Few people of his era tried harder to promote mutual understanding between East and West and he remains worth reading for his penetrating analysis of Japan, as enduring as the magic of his prose.

22

Lafcadio Hearn and the Irish Tradition

PAUL MURRAY

―――――――――― oOo ――――――――――

Although Lafcadio Hearn's relationship with Irish literature has generally been overlooked, I have not set out to cast him in the straightjacket of a particular tradition: he was far too elusive and his genius too malleable for that. If ever a man achieved Goldsmith's ideal of being a citizen of the world, it was Patrick Lafcadio Hearn. He was not exclusively Greek, Irish, American, or Japanese but was a unique amalgam of a variety of influences. His relationship with Ireland, like his feelings for the United States and Japan, was ambiguous, although he came to terms with it in a series of remarkable essays towards the end of his life. We might also bear in mind that ambiguity is not necessarily a wholly negative phenomenon: in his *Redress of Poetry*, Seamus Heaney defends what he terms 'two-mindedness' in the context of what some would regard as conflicting cultural imperatives.

So, I am not claiming Hearn exclusively for the Irish tradition, though he did spend his most formative years in Ireland and no biographer can afford to ignore their impact, and while I do not believe that he should be seen exclusively in an Irish context, he certainly does have an Irish dimension. Here, I want to look at three interrelated aspects of Hearn's relationship with the Irish tradition: background, subject matter and language. I should make it clear that I am a biographer who aims to apply historiographical rather than literary critical analysis, and that my aim in examining Hearn's writing is to try to illuminate both his life and his meaning, rather than to enter the realm of academic literary criticism *per se*.

Hearn was one of an extraordinary quartet of writers who grew up in Dublin in the decades just after the middle of the nineteenth century. Bram Stoker, author of *Dracula*, was just a few years older, born in 1847, his family home was in Clontarf, a similar suburb on the north side of Dublin to the township of Rathmines on the south side where Hearn grew up. Oscar Wilde and George Bernard Shaw were, respectively, four and six years younger than Hearn. Their families all lived within a short distance of each other: the Wilde residence in Merrion Square and the Shaw home in Synge Street are no more than a short walk from 73 Upper Leeson Street where Hearn spent some of his most formative years.

'Church of Ireland middle class' would describe all their backgrounds, although there were, of course, gradations of individual family circumstance. While championship of the common man would later be a feature of the work of Hearn and Shaw, and folklore a basis for the literary output of Hearn, Wilde and Stoker, they were all the products of what might now be termed 'drawing-room culture'. The cradle of genius in the Dublin of their era was one of gatherings around the piano to sing the often maudlin songs and ballads of the time. James Joyce would later preserve this world in aspic in his *Dubliners* and John McCormack would immortalize its torch songs on shellac. Shaw, of course, was immersed in it from an early age, courtesy of his mother and her music teacher, George Vandeleur Lee, but Hearn, too, remembered those gatherings around the piano in Mrs Brenane's plush drawing-room, with standards of the time, such as Father Prout's *The Bells of Shandon*, being performed. Indeed, it was memories of his beautiful aunt, Catherine Elwood, singing Thomas Moore's *Believe me, if all those endearing young charms* [*Irish Melodies* (1808-34)] which inspired one of Lafcadio's late Japanese pieces, 'Hi-mawari' (1904).

Oscar Wilde proposed to, but Bram Stoker married, Florence Balcombe, daughter of a Lieutenant Colonel in the British army. Both Stoker's and Hearn's grandfathers had served in the same regiment; Hearn's grandfather was a Lieutenant Colonel, as was Florence Balcombe's. Stoker was friendly with the Wildes, especially Oscar's mother, a famous collector of Irish folklore. Hearn was one of the first critics to see the sterling worth beneath the young Wilde's foppery and, as writers, they shared a common interest in fairy tales, both men publishing books of them within a decade of each other later in the century. The Wildes were solidly comfortable materially, but they were tainted by the whiff of scandal well before Oscar's downfall when Sir William Wilde was sued by a female patient for alleged sexual indiscretion. Indeed, beneath the Victorian decorum of these four writers's families, sex wreaked havoc in various forms. Oscar Wilde was imprisoned for homosexuality, and his biographer, Richard Ellmann, believed that he died of syphilis. Similarly, Daniel Farson, Bram Stoker's great-nephew and biographer, states that he too died of the same disease. Given his sexual waywardness prior to his marriage in Japan, Hearn was perhaps lucky to escape that fate.

Lafcadio was the product of a passionate union between his officer-surgeon father and his Greek mother. Their first child was born out of wedlock and Lafcadio was in gestation when they married. Shaw's parentage and background contained similar complications. The de facto *ménage à trois* in which Shaw's mother lived with her husband and music teacher has given rise to speculation about his parentage. Both the Hearns and Shaws were downwardly-mobile minor gentry, attempting to maintain a semblance of respectability while the economic basis of their position was slipping away. Indebtedness was a feature common to both families, as it was to the Stokers: indeed, Lafcadio's father, who borrowed heavily from his great-aunt, was ruined, as was Lafcadio, when she became bankrupt. Both Shaw and Hearn experienced the grind of poverty in London in their youth.

Thus, Hearn grew up in a small, tightly-knit, and intensely literary world in Dublin. If we look outside Lafcadio's immediate contemporaries, we find that Dion Boucicault, a popular dramatist of the mid-century was born in 47 Lower Gardiner Street while young Patrick Lafcadio spent his first period in Dublin at number 48 in the same street. J.M. Synge attended school in Upper Leeson Street, where Lafcadio lived with Mrs Brenane for some years. W.B. Yeats was born in Sandymount, a nearby suburb, shortly after Hearn left for England. On the other side of the country, George Moore, just two years younger than Hearn, grew up on his family's estate on the shores of Lough Cara in County Mayo; Lafcadio spent a good deal of his youth, vividly recalled in some of his best Japanese work, on the estate of his Elwood relations, on the shores of Lough Corrib, also in County Mayo. Moore grew up listening to his father's tales of the East and went to Paris to study painting, as Lafcadio's uncle, Richard Hearn, had done a generation previously.

Hearn's work throughout his life was permeated by

horror, and in this respect he has a great deal in common with the older writers of the Irish Gothic tradition, Charles Maturin and Sheridan Le Fanu. Maturin was a Church of Ireland clergyman and Le Fanu the son of one; Hearn was the great-grandson of an eminent Archdeacon of Cashel, and Church of Ireland clergymen abound in his family tree. Maturin's father, like Bram Stoker's, was a civil servant in the British administration in Ireland. Hearn's father was an officer-surgeon in the British army. All previous three generations of the Hearn family had been educated at Trinity College, Dublin, as were Stoker, Le Fanu and Maturin. All of their families occupied comfortable middle-class niches, being employed by the state either through the Church of Ireland or the armed forces. Yeats too was a product of a similar background.

Hearn, however, can be sharply differentiated from the other Irish Gothic writers by the fact that he had been brought up as a Roman Catholic, although important elements of his consciousness-forming were Protestant. We know that his great-aunt, Mrs Brenane, made little effort to inculcate Catholic, or even Christian, beliefs into him; the only attempt at that was a rather ham-fisted effort by a religiously-obsessed young relative. When she died, she left her considerable collection of books to Lafcadio which, strangely, included nothing overtly religious, certainly nothing of a Roman Catholic or pietistic nature. Indeed, the authors listed by Hearn were generally Protestant: Locke, Byron, Scott, Edgeworth and so on. The other writers whom we know had influenced him were also outside the Roman Catholic tradition: Milton, whose *Paradise Lost* impressed him both for its imagination and its other-world vocabulary; Defoe; and, most potently, the rabidly anti-Catholic Matthew Lewis, whose *Tales of Wonder* gave him nightmares.

Lewis's *The Monk* (1796) was in some respects the prototype for Charles Maturin's *Melmoth the Wanderer*

(1820), arguably the first great classic in the Irish Gothic tradition and one with which Hearn was familiar. While one might discern Gothic elements in earlier Irish writers like Maria Edgeworth, whom Hearn had also read, Maturin's work shares Lewis's blazing, paranoiac anti-Catholicism. His language and the cadences of his style seem to me to anticipate uncannily Hearn's early journalism. Take, for example, this passage describing a mad-house in *Melmoth*:

> Then your hours of solitude, deliciously diversified by the yell of famine, the howl of madness, the crash of whips, and the broken-hearted sob of those who, like you, are supposed, or *driven* mad by the crimes of others.[1]

and compare it with a Cincinnati tenement as seen by Hearn:

> ... the moans of the poor sufferer, the agonized scream of the tortured child, the savage whipping and violent cursing, the broken floor pried up in drunken fury, – all seemed the sights and sounds of a hideous dream, rather than the closing scene of a poor life's melodrama.[2]

In his personality, Lafcadio embodied the wild anti-Popery of Maturin, extravagantly claiming that he would be pursued to the grave by the Jesuits, who had supposedly educated him, although he had never attended a Jesuit school. At the same time, his ambiguity towards Roman Catholicism mirrored that of Le Fanu – whom he particularly admired as a writer – and Stoker, who, as Protestant writers, in 'Carmilla' and *Dracula* respectively, accord a positive power to Roman Catholic ritual in subduing the forces of darkness. In his personal life, Hearn was friendly with a number of Catholic priests. In the West Indies his imagination was impressed by the achievements of the Dominican priest Père Labat, and in Japan he was defensive of the Catholic missionaries *vis-à-vis* their Protestant counterparts. Part of the answer to this riddle might be that Hearn's background was essentially Protestant despite his upbringing as a Catholic, so he was able to embody in himself the full ambiguity of the Irish Gothic tradition.

Hearn landed in Japan in 1890, the year that Bram Stoker is believed to have started work on *Dracula*. The similarities between the two men run much deeper than the coincidences of birth and geography: horror pervaded the work of both. It is fascinating that Stoker should have begun *Dracula*, in its early pages overtly a journey to the Orient – Jonathan Harker in the very first paragraph states that he feels he is entering the East at Budapest – just as Hearn was beginning his Oriental sojourn in Japan. Hearn translated vampire material from the French, and in his person, by drinking blood and eating bugs, he reflected the proclivities of Dracula and his assistant, Renfeld. Similarly, Stoker based his story 'The Burial of the Rats' among the *chiffoniers*, the rag-pickers of the Paris dumps, and one of Hearn's best Cincinnati pieces was 'Les Chiffoniers' (1874) set in the dumps of that city. The declaration of Stoker's narrator, that he 'determined to investigate philosophically the chiffonier – his habitat, his life, and his means of life', was very similar to Hearn's approach. Lafcadio's translation of Gautier's 'Arria Marcella', in *One of Cleopatra's Nights* (1882), could be straight from the pages of writers in the Irish tradition of literary horror. As well as the crumbling of the ghoul into dust, there is the same mingling of the non-Christian world of ghosts, vampires and prehistoric religion which is controlled by Christian ritual. Later, in Japan, Hearn would also write of vampires: 'The Story of Chugoro', in *Kotto* (1902), for example, concerns a great and ugly frog who appears as a beautiful woman to drain young men of their blood. The theme of the interrelationship of the devil with the human world recurs in a number of Hearn's other translations from the French, most notably in Flaubert's *The Temptation of Saint Anthony*.

Lafcadio's translations from French were part of his complex relationship with French culture, the importance of which extended far beyond the translations themselves and which profoundly influenced his interpretation of Japan. This relationship should be viewed in the context not only of his family background but of the wider cultural links between Ireland and France. These were symbolized by the Napoleonic vogue for the ancient figure of Oisin or Ossian, and the influence of Thomas Moore, whom Hearn admired, on such French cultural luminaries as Berlioz. Bram Stoker's father moved to France as a result of his debts, as Oscar Wilde would flee there after his release from prison. Hearn also took refuge there mentally, by claiming a French education and immersing himself in French literature. Indeed, Wilde took the name 'Sebastian Melmoth' when he went in disgrace to France in 1897, emblematic of his outcast role, knowing that the French would understand a reference to Charles Maturin's Irish exile who had so influenced Baudelaire and Balzac. Hearn's grandfather, a hero of the Napoleonic wars, prided himself on his fluent French. His uncle, Richard, was one of the first Irish artists to go to France to study art, blazing a trail which many others would follow in the mid-nineteenth century. Wilde composed original works in French, as Samuel Beckett would do in our own century, while Lafcadio translated extensively from it. Even if there is no evidence to substantiate Lafcadio's claim to have been educated in France, the fact that he *wanted* to have been there is significant, as was his very deliberate immersion in French language and culture during his years in America.

We know from his correspondence with Yeats, that, as a child in Dublin he had had a Connaught nurse who told him Irish fairy-tales and ghost stories. Thus began a lifelong interest in folk material which would manifest itself in his journalistic writings on black culture in Cincinnati, and find its first sustained outlet in book form in his New Orleans work. I suspect that when many of us think of fairy-tales, we think of the bowdlerized Victorian versions of the dark originals. In fact, the fairy stories common to much of the pre-industrial world, including Ireland, constitute a netherworld, living parallel to, and sometimes interacting with, the living, similar in some respects to the ancient Japanese religion of Shinto which Hearn would later make central to his analysis of Japan. There are clear parallels here in the interaction of the otherworld beings with the living in Irish lore; for example, in their women becoming lovers of mortal men, and some of the marvellous *Kwaidan*, those weird tales which Hearn translated from the Japanese folk tradition. There are also parallels between fairy-tales and vampirism – the notion of the dead continuing to live in their burial chambers, sometimes seeking to lure unwary mortals to their doom by assuming enchanting shapes or presenting enticing spectacles. Thus Lafcadio's devotion to folk material links him both to his contemporaries, and to the younger figures of the Irish literary revival – Yeats, Lady Gregory, Synge – as well as backwards to the earlier Irish poets of the nineteenth century.

In tracing the line of Irish Protestant supernatural fiction through Maturin, Le Fanu, Stoker, Yeats and Elizabeth Bowen, Roy Foster has linked an interest in the occult with folklore. Hearn believed that folk tales were of priceless value to the true artist, which the uneducated peasant was fully capable of being; indeed, education was likely to destroy the source of his poetry. His view of peasant life in Ireland was remarkably similar to the Shinto-based ethos of pre-Meiji Japan and, in a sense, provides a bridge from his Irish youth to his mature Japanese work:

> Anciently woods and streams were peopled for him [the peasant] with invisible beings; angels and demons walked at his side; the woods had their fairies, the mountains their goblins, the marshes their flitting spirits, and the dead came back to him at times to bear a message or to rebuke a fault. Also the ground that he trod upon, the plants growing in the field, the cloud above him, the lights of heaven all were full of mystery and ghostliness.[3]

Compare this with Yeats's vision of the survival of the supernatural in the Irish countryside:

> Once every people in the world believed that trees were divine, and could take a human or grotesque shape and dance among the shadows of the woods; and deer, and ravens and foxes, and wolves and bears, and clouds and pools, almost all things under the sun and moon, and the sun and the moon, not less divine and changeable; they saw in the rainbow the still bent bow of a god thrown down in his negligence; they heard in the thunder the sound of the beaten water-jar, or the tumult of his chariot wheels; and when a sudden flight of wild duck, or of crows, passed over their heads, they thought they were gazing at the dead hastening to their rest; while they dreamed of so great a mystery in little things that they believed the waving of a hand, or of a sacred bough, enough to trouble far-off hearts, or hood the moon with darkness.[4]

Here, the same concept is being expressed in such similar language that the authors could almost be interchangeable. Both men believed in the fundamental importance of folk material to their art. In Yeats's case, it was some of the greatest poetry in the English language; in Hearn's a great body of work, culminating in the masterly *Kwaidan* (1904) or Japanese ghost stories of his later years. Hearn posited the fundamental importance to art of the supernatural in his lecture 'The Value of the Supernatural in Fiction' and a phrase in it, 'there is something ghostly in all great art' was considered by Yeats as possibly a definitive definition of poetry.[5]

Hearn understood the grounding of Yeats's poetry in the myths and legends of Ireland. He connected romanticism, folklore and horror and maintained that the Celtic belief in fairies had created an imagination that was 'romantic, poetic and also terrible'.[6] He believed that Yeats, 'who himself collected a great number of stories and legends about fairies from the peasantry of Southern Ireland', was the most 'representative' poet of the folklore-based genre.[7] Yeats's poem, 'The Host of the Air', he regarded as the outstanding contemporary fairy poem, unsurpassable in its field, especially in its ability to communicate 'the pleasure of fear', an art Hearn greatly admired. Not only did he appreciate the 'rare excellence' of the early Yeats – the poet was thirty-nine when Lafcadio died in 1904 – he also understood that ancient Celtic literature had inspired much of his poetry.

So passionate did Hearn feel about this excellence that he wrote a letter of violent protest to Yeats in June 1901 when 'The Host of the Air' appeared in *The Wind Among the Reeds*, revised from its earlier form, telling the poet that 'this wonderful thing . . . must have been blown into you and through you as by the Wind of the Holy Ghost'.[8] Quite what impact this connection with Lafcadio had on Yeats is hard to determine but he did give the name 'Hearne' to the hero of an unfinished novel; he also wrote of a 'witch doctor' called Hearne who lived on the border of counties Clare and Galway.[9]

Both men were attracted by similar material. It is clear from a satire which he wrote in his Cincinnati days that Lafcadio was familiar, to some extent at least, with the Fianna Cycle of early Irish legend and, more specifically, that he was aware of the story of Oisín in this lore. Oisín was said to have accompanied a beautiful woman to the Land of Youth. After what seemed like a short time, he asks to go back to his homeland; the lady allows him but enjoins him not to set foot on the soil of Ireland. He finds when he gets back that he has actually been away for three hundred years and that the Fianna are long dead and gone. Unthinkingly, he comes into contact with the ground and is instantly changed into an old man. This story parallels the Japanese legend of Urashima Taro that Hearn uses as the backbone for 'The Dream of a Summer Day', where he entwines it with glorious memories of his youth in Ireland. Yeats too was attracted by the Oisín theme: his dramatic dialogue *The Wanderings of Oisín* was published in 1889 (the year before Hearn went to Japan), and in its language and subject matter it mirrored many of Hearn's preoccupations.

Hearn's awareness of Irish myth and legend also found an outlet in New Orleans, where he wrote the story of 'St Brandan's Christmas' for the *Times-Democrat* (24 December 1884). It ends with the 'horrid and frightful deformity' alone upon an ice cliff: the vision of Judas, on day-release from hell, seen by the ancient Irish saint, Brendan, on a Christmas morning. There is, incidentally, a passage in this tale which anticipates a vision of rural Ireland which found expression in Irish literature and politics earlier this century:

> But now and again an Irish fisherboy, gentle and loving to an old mother spinning by the peat fire at home, pure of heart and careful of his duty, rocked as ever on the great waves that dash high up the iron-bound coast of Western Ireland, and dreaming of the lost glories of the green land, has seen the gold and purple curtains of the sunset lift for a moment over the shining sea . . . [10]

There are other links between Hearn and the Irish literary tradition. for example, he appreciated the work of the older nineteenth-century Irish poets who influenced the Celtic revival, particularly William Allingham and Sir Samuel Ferguson. He particularly admired the latter's 'extraordinary power in arousing the sensation of the weird'.[11] Ferguson had, of course, used ancient Irish saga material, and it is noticeable that it was the elements of the ghostly and the weird in this tradition to which Hearn related. His use of the phrase, 'terrible beauty',[12] later immortalized by Yeats, is an indication of his probable familiarity with the work of Standish O'Grady, who is credited by Roy Foster with having originated it. We know from his lectures that he was also familiar with the work of Burke, Congreve, Farquhar, Goldsmith, Lever, Sheridan and Swift.

As a young journalist in Cincinnati in the 1870s, Hearn's main local interest was in the music and lore of the black inhabitants of the levee quarter on the banks of the Ohio. I believe that the traditional music he would have heard in Ireland, and the value placed on folk culture in general by the

Anglo-Irish élite, may well have conditioned Hearn to accept African-American culture without the prejudice which clouded the approach of so many of his contemporaries. He embodied in himself therefore two of the fundamental impulses in Irish nineteenth-century culture, the aristocratic and the popular. Both of these were evident in his American and West Indian work on the coloured races, at once enlightening if sometimes condescending. It was only when he got to Japan that both elements fused into a coherent, unified vision of another culture with which he could comfortably identify.

In addition to common subject matter, Hearn shared some fundamental intellectual and philosophical influences with his Irish contemporaries. Both Hearn and Shaw went through youthful periods of anarchism before converting to one of the grand, all-encompassing, evolutionary philosophical structures of the time. Together with Wilde, both were profoundly influenced by the philosophy of Herbert Spencer, who, if largely forgotten nowadays, nevertheless wielded enormous influence on intellectuals both in the West and in Japan around the end of the last century. All three were concerned with socialism, albeit in different ways: Hearn and Wilde as critics, while Shaw adhered to Fabianism. Indeed, Hearn was deeply concerned with political issues all his life, as evidenced by his private correspondence and his newspaper editorials, including those in the *Kobe Chronicle* (1894). He saw Japan's wars with China and Russia from a wider, geo-political historical perspective. One finds evidence of a political engagement also in the work of Yeats and, currently, Seamus Heaney. Another important intellectual influence on Hearn was the work of the Irish philosopher George Berkeley, whose core argument that the material would exist only in the subjective consciousness of the observer also interested Joyce and Beckett.

Hearn's use of language is another area where traces of Irish influence can be discerned. He set out his philosophy in his correspondence with Basil Hall Chamberlain, in which he pointed out that his approach to language was entirely different to that of his friend: 'For me words have colour, form, character; they have faces, ports, manners, eccentricities; – they have tints, tones, personalities. That they are unintelligible makes no difference at all'.[13] On another occasion, when Chamberlain admonished Hearn over the correct use of 'shall' and 'will', Lafcadio responded that tone was everything; the word nothing. He was guided by euphony and felt:

> ... angry with conventional forms of language of which I cannot understand the real spirit. ... I am 'colour-blind' to the values you assert; and I suspect that the majority of the English-speaking races – the raw people – are also blind thereunto. It is the people, after all, who make the language in the end, and in the direction of least resistance,[14]

The fact that the technically correct use of 'shall' and 'will' is part of the linguistic divide between Ireland and England is, I think, relevant here. So, too, was his rejection of Chamberlain's plea that he write with 'justice and temperateness'; he was far too passionate and anarchic in his approach to language for that.

Chamberlain may, somewhat unintentionally, have penetrated to the core of their difference when he suggested that Lafcadio's linguistic waywardness could be attributed to the 'Irish invasion' of the United States, a mass movement of which Lafcadio had been a part. Indeed, when Lafcadio had lived in the United States he had maintained that he 'hated' English and hoped to re-shape it to serve his specific literary ends. He continued doing this to some extent for the rest of his life. Just run a modern spell-check through Hearn's writings and you will realize by its rejections how much Hearn manipulated the language out of the rules and regulations beloved of Chamberlain.

In his anarchic, creative, individualistic use of language

Hearn is clearly related to the Irish tradition, Joyce in particular. His disregard for the grammatical correctness which the Victorian English raised to such a fine art is representative of the process which Joyce brings to a triumphant culmination in *Ulysses* and *Finnegans Wake*. There are, of course, other parallels with Joyce. As a young man in New Orleans in correspondence with an American friend on the subject of the Irish keening wail (part of the 'wake' for the dead which is celebrated in the title of Joyce's last work), Lafcadio wrote of the strong similarities between the Mongolian and certain Irish faces. Joyce in *Stephen Hero* describes the Irish peasantry as 'Mongolian types'. In his draft autobiography, Hearn describes an outburst from a sombre young girl of strong religious bent who had taken it upon herself to instruct him in morality, and this is similar to the celebrated sermon on hell which Joyce would later pen in *A Portrait of the Artist as a Young Man*. While Lafcadio's autobiography was never finished or published, its picture of an unwilling young intellectual being force-fed with muscular Catholicism anticipates not just Joyce, but later writers such as Patrick Kavanagh, John McGahern and Colm Tóibín.

The final rubric under which I would like to consider Lafcadio's relationship with the Irish tradition is that of Orientalism. I referred earlier to the Gothic component of Maria Edgeworth's writing: it also contained elements of Orientalism as did the work of the earlier eighteenth-century Irish writer, Frances Sheridan, whose *The History of Nourjahad* has Gothic as well as Oriental aspects to it. A recent critic, Robert L. Mack, has described the character of Nourjahad as 'a kind of Faustus figure' – the Faustian legend being, of course, central to the Gothic genre – stating that his 'misplaced desire for immortality, too, recalls Gulliver's account of the Struldbrugs in Swift's *Gulliver's Travels*.[15] It also recalls Maturin's Melmoth and the vampires of Le Fanu and Stoker. The same critic states the '*Nourjahad* possesses a lush physicality — a delight in the voluptuous descriptions of sensuous excess' and places it in a genre of English-language fiction which is able to 'present readers with a range of alternative cultural possibilities'.[16] The parallels here with Hearn's American and Japanese work are too striking to be missed. The subject-matter and language of Hearn's *Stray Leaves from Strange Literature* (1884) and *Some Chinese Ghosts* (1887), as well as his translations from the French in his American period, possess lush physicality and delight in voluptuous descriptions of sensuous excess, and his Japanese work, above all, presents readers with alternative cultural possibilities. Maria Edgeworth's *Murad the Unlucky* has been described by the same critic as 'a corrective oriental tale', the clear implication of which 'is that the spoils of colonialism . . . are the results of misguided avarice and ambition' and 'exposing beneath the lush romanticism of eighteenth-century orientalism the harsh realities of life in the "gorgeous East" . . . Edgeworth tells us that we shall have to rethink the *Arabian Nights* if we are ever to understand the East'.[17] Hearn's Japanese work, with its rejection of colonialism and its insistence that Japan and even the Occident be viewed from a Japanese perspective has therefore much the same message for the Occidental reader as his Irish literary predecessor.

In dealing with the work of Frances Sheridan and Maria Edgeworth we have come full circle, linking some of the earliest Irish literary influences with the final phase of Lafcadio's life. I should like to leave the last word to Hearn himself, writing to Yeats of his Dublin childhood towards the end of his life in Japan: 'But I hope you will not think me unsympathetic in regard to Irish matters . . . forty-five years ago, I was a horrid little boy, "with never a crack in his heart", who lived in Upper Leeson Street, Dublin. . . . So I *ought* to love Irish Things, and do'.[18]

23

W. B. Yeats and Lafcadio Hearn: Negotiating with Ghosts

GEORGE HUGHES

———————————— oOo ————————————

In early January 1874, at 16 Barr Street, Cincinnati, in the home of a certain Mr and Mrs Smith, the young Lafcadio Hearn encountered his father's ghost. Or, to put it more precisely, he *spoke* to his father's ghost: the ghostly voice came, rather indistinctly, he says, out of a trumpet. Ghosts speaking out of trumpets may seem a little improbable to us now, but Hearn's experience was not uncommon at the time. W. B. Yeats also spoke to ghosts through trumpets, in his case to the ghost of Leo Africanus, probably in 1912, at a seance arranged by a Mrs Wriedt of Detroit on her visit to London (Cott 73-80: Goldman 108-29).

The question of whether one can actually speak to ghosts

was of interest, indeed of very strong interest, to both these writers. But they were also concerned in a wider way to establish their standpoint in relation to ghosts – or, in other words, to negotiate a position in relation to them. If I cannot pretend to know how much they succeeded in their negotiations, I hope I can indicate how such negotiations could prove important and productive in their writings. There are significant differences as well as convergences in their attitudes, which emerge particularly when they turn towards Japan.

☐

Before I try to show in more detail what I mean, it would perhaps be as well to provide some justification for putting Hearn and Yeats together–other than their experiences with speaking trumpets. There are some obvious points in common: both had Anglo-Irish parents, both were important members of the fin de siècle literary scene, both were interested in Japan and both were interested in ghosts.

There are also some delicate, but nonetheless direct links between the two. Yeats is said to have particularly liked, as a definition of poetry, Hearn's phrase 'There is something ghostly in all great art' (*Collected Letters* III, 101 n. 1). He seems to have been familiar with some of Hearn's work, as he refers to Hearn in the Introduction to his play *The Resurrection* (1931) (*Explorations* 396). The reference concerns 'the re-birth of the soul', for which Yeats says Hearn had found 'empirical evidence' among the Japanese. Yeats does not say what work of Hearn's he has in mind, and the comment is rather misleading in relation to Hearn. It usefully points up a difference in fundamental ideas between the two writers, though they do share an interest in the idea of rebirth.

Hearn undoubtedly admired the work of Yeats. He gave what must be some of the first university lectures anywhere on Yeats, certainly the first in Japan, sometime between 1896 and 1903. (One of the student transcripts of these lectures, from which the published versions have been taken, has some difficulty with the name, and settles finally on 'Samuel Batler Yeats' [Kobinata ms.]) Hearn also wrote a letter to Yeats, about the poem 'The Host of the Air' from *The Wind Among the Reeds*, which he goes through in one of these lectures. He objected, in strong terms, to changes that Yeats had made from an earlier printed version. (The complaints are quite understandable from a teacher's point of view, since Yeats had left out some of the lines and phrases he focused on in his lecture.) Yeats replied promising a partial restoration, though he did not in fact change later versions (*Collected Letters* III, 101-2).

Hearn's letter to Yeats suggests that he has been attracted by their common Irish background and interest in Irish folklore; but the lectures indicate that he has also (as we might perhaps expect from a fin de siècle figure like Hearn) been particularly impressed to read of Yeats's reputation in France. Hearn talks about Yeats in three lectures: 'Some Fairy Literature', 'Some Symbolic Poetry' and 'Two Mystical Rose Poems'. (*Life and Literature* 324-39: On Poetry 141-70, 729). In the lecture on fairy literature he discusses *The Land of Heart's Desire* (1894), which he says shows supernatural events, although 'the play of emotions is purely and intensely human'. He likes this because 'an impossible situation is made to become intensely interesting'. It is typical of Hearn that he should enjoy work with supernatural themes, but (unlike Yeats) find a non-supernatural justification for his enjoyment.

□

My concern here, however, is not particularly to develop these biographical connections, but to place Yeats and Hearn together in regard to ghosts. And my real excuse for considering them in this way is that I want to put their interest in the context of Japan. This is not the only context in which their ghostly concerns could be discussed, but by focusing on the topic of ghosts I think we can gain some new insight into the way Yeats developed what he called his Nō plays, just as we can gain some insight into the way in which Hearn made himself such an important commentator on Japan and Japanese culture.

Hearn leaves us only one account of a successful seance (though he wrote several articles on the subject of spiritualism in Cincinnati); Yeats, on the other hand, left many. His first, and rather unsatisfactory experience was in 1885. Then from 1911, after an encounter with a medium (Mrs Chenoweth) in Boston, he began to attend seances actively. And in London in 1912, with Mrs Wriedt he was lucky enough to have the experience of hearing 'an exceedingly loud voice' which came through a long tin trumpet 'standing on its broad end in the middle of the room'. Mrs Wriedt said the voice had come for Mr Gates. Yeats, who was always happy to cooperate in such matters, said 'this was evidently me' (Goldman 116).

Yeats visited other mediums around England, and seriously studied the automatic writing of Elizabeth Radcliffe—work that probably stimulated Georgie Hyde-Lees to try automatic writing after their marriage. And it was automatic writing by spirit controls that lay behind Yeats's two versions of *A Vision* and some of his most famous poetry. He also lectured in enthusiastic vein to the London Spiritualist Alliance in 1914 (Kutch 114-35).

The ghosts which appear in late nineteenth and early twentieth century writing are no doubt within traditions that go back to Hamlet or Banquo, Alcestis or the Witch of Endor. But they were also a distinctive new phenomenon of an age worried by the death of the past. Although they were unreal in terms of common sense, they seemed to speak of a greater reality. Ghosts verified people's roots in various places, in the houses or the countryside they loved, and yet their modern popularity was also connected with growing internationalism (since the ghost craze was trans-Atlantic), and the fashion for mediums and spiritualist societies was bound up with many of the techniques of modern publicity. There were so many ghosts–they were so active then–where, one wonders, have they all gone now?

The spiritualist craze started, according to Janet Oppenheim, in 1848 in America, in Hydesville, New York, when ghosts began to give messages to the young Fox sisters, Margaret and Kate, by banging on a wall. America remained important as a source of mediums, but they spread their activities fairly rapidly to England. Tricks were exposed, but many people were not entirely convinced by the exposures. 'Because mediumship is dramatisation,' Yeats later said, 'even honest mediums cheat at times . . . and almost always truth and lies are mixed together. But what shall we say of [the spirits'] . . . knowledge of events, their assumption of forms and names beyond the medium's knowledge or ours? What of the arm photographed [by Dr Ochorowicz] in a bottle?' (*Explorations* 365-6). Lafcadio Hearn would not have believed in Dr Ochorowicz's arm, since he wrote an article in *The Cincinnati Commercial* in 1875, in which he systematically discussed the kind of tricks that spirit photographers could play: over-printing on used negatives, holes in the developing tanks and the like ('Spirit Photography'). But Yeats liked spirit photographs: he even had his own photograph taken with a spirit aura. He is looking serious and contemplative, in a creased jacket and wearing a bow-tie, with a large round, rather surprised-looking, ghostly face coming out of the top of his head (Goldman plate 1).

☐

For Hearn and Yeats, however, it was not just a question of visiting spirit mediums for a joke, they had what amounts almost to an obsession with the subject of ghosts. B. H. Chamberlain says 'No one could understand Lafcadio Hearn who did not take into account his belief in Ghosts' (*Japanese Letters* lv). It is certainly true that in the United States, in the West Indies, in Japan, Hearn is constantly writing about ghosts. Some of his work on ghosts is in the form of exotic folk-tales translated or edited from other sources (like *Stray Leaves from Strange Literature*, 1884); some consist of anecdotes recounted by informants in New Orleans or in the West Indies. Yeats is similarly involved in collecting and publishing Irish fairy tales and ghost stories. He insisted that the 'mystical life' was the centre of all he did, and that his aim as a writer was to reconcile 'spiritist fact with credible philosophy' (Ellmann 97, 294).

In Hearn's work the term 'ghost' does not just come up in stories of the supernatural. He uses it widely to refer to people, mountains, the 'world-Ghost', ' the supreme ghost', the Blue Ghost', the 'ghostly facts' of the universe. Elizabeth Bisland, his editor and friend (whom Hearn refers to as 'my dear, sweet, ghostly sister') says 'the word "ghost" appears a thousand times in Hearn's books, in endless association with all his thoughts'. Nonetheless Hearn is prepared to accept (unlike Yeats) that most modern spiritualism is 'humbug'. He thinks the ghosts of spiritualists are too domesticated and probably fakes. What he means by 'ghost', on the whole, is that which gives us a deep sense of emotional unity. Personal ghosts are an illusion (*Japanese Letters* I, 475; II, 379, 382, 265).

Writers, however, Hearn thinks ' must seek their material in those parts of the world where ghosts still linger'. They should be in pursuit of ghost stories because, although such stories are illusory, they reveal to us what we have in common with others, and something of our own 'primeval fears'. Hearn is extremely interested in the way supernatural fiction works, and comes to the conclusion that it is fundamentally based on 'dream-experience'. And within that dream experience he thinks the most common fear is '*the fear of being touched by ghosts*' (*Japanese Letters* 215; *On Art* 115-28; 'Nightmare Touch', *Shadowings*)

Ghost stories, then, must not be dismissed, because they are based on dream-experience. Modern scientific theory can find an explanation for them in terms of our common unconscious lives. Ideas of reincarnation, Hearn thinks, can also be related to scientific theories of heredity, or in Herbert Spencer's phrase, to 'organic memory'. For Hearn this is a 'dim inherited memory of experience in other lives' – though he stresses that the term 'memory' is used only in a symbolic sense: 'instinct' or 'intuition' might also be used. Since there is some kind of organic memory, the old ideas of metempsychosis, transmigration or resurrection were not simply false, 'they were rather foreshadowings of a truth vaster than all myths and deeper than all religions'. Behind everything is a nameless and unnamable force: 'we are, each and all, infinite compounds of fragments of anterior lives' (*Lectures* 8-9; *Oriental Articles* 110; *Gleanings* 89-90). The basic theory is perhaps a little confusing and confused, but it is a theory that attempts to use modern science to account for ancient ideas. It does not imply (as Yeats's comment on Hearn suggests) that he had found any *empirical* evidence for reincarnation in Japan.

Yeats himself is more determined to believe in ghosts and spirits of a personal type: 'We may come to think that nothing exists but a stream of souls.' Memory, however, is also a focus for him, and he says that in trying to explain modern theories of 'forgotten personal memory' he came on the theory of a 'Great Memory [containing images] passing on from generation to generation.' But this concept alone was not enough for him, because he found intention and choice within the organisation of the images in the memory. (Hearn, by contrast, found only a 'dim inherited memory'. He does not see it as organized.) Yeats concluded that some of the memories in our great sea of memory were actually the memories of dead people. who were still 'living in their memories'. In his view the dead were able to organize their own memories and, since we draw on these organized memories, they were 'the source [in us] of all that we call instinct'. The memories of the dead are, in a rather confusing way, *within* us – but shadows and materializations may also seem to take place *outside* us 'among walls, or by rocks and trees' (*Mythologies* 343-66).

There are obviously profound differences between these two theories, particularly in their view of persons or individuals; but they move within similar terminology, and both writers conclude for their own reasons that accounts of ghosts and spirit-experiences are worth taking seriously.

Hearn and Yeats also found that the topic of ghosts could easily be linked to folklore, when it was happily mixed with matters of more general concern, and could even gain a respectable proximity to academic or scientific studies. When this topic was in turn linked to Japan – as Yeats said he had attempted to 'annex Japan to Ireland' (*Letters* 807)–then ghosts were given the added support of the prestige that surrounded Japanese art in the late nineteenth and early twentieth century. Ghosts in Japanese form were exotic: audiences would not be tempted to dismiss them as comic frauds.

Japan is far more obviously important in the work of Hearn than in Yeats, but ghosts-plus-Japan have a productive effect on the work of both these writers. In Yeats's drama in particular, and in Hearn's travel writings, the conjunction allows a kind of creative freedom that was difficult to obtain otherwise. We can put together what we might call a productive triangle of ghosts, folklore and Japan – within which Yeats and Hearn are able to give their obsessive interest an artistic life.

□

We can trace the emergence of this productive triangle in Yeats's work through his association with Ezra Pound and their commentaries on the Fenollosa translations of Nō drama. Pound says:

> All through the winter of 1914-15 I watched Mr Yeats correlating folk- lore. . . . and data of the occult writers, with the habits of charlatans of Bond Street [i.e. spirit mediums]. If the Japanese authors had not combined the psychology of such matter with what is to me a very fine sort of poetry, I would not bother about it (*Classic Noh* 26).

In the introduction he wrote for Lady Gregory's collection of folk-lore, Yeats also brought in Swedenborg and other authorities on the supernatural; but the correlation Pound speaks of between Japanese drama and spirit mediums of Bond Street (or in Yeats's version, Soho and Holloway,) still figures importantly. In Yeats's 1914 lecture to the Spiritualist Alliance, he had insisted that Japanese Shintoism was 'nothing but simple Spiritism. There was no doctrine in Spiritism today that was not in Shintoism. It was in the beautiful philosophy of the Noh drama of Japan' (*Kutch* 127). (Hearn, by the way, also suggested that in the doctrines of Shinto 'We have . . . a conception resembling very strongly the Spiritualistic notion of ghosts' [*Kokoro* 268]).

Yeats found further support in his ideas from the experiments in automatic writing he performed with his wife. The recent publication of the *'Vision' Papers* shows him being strongly encouraged by 'spirit controls' – communicating through Georgie Yeats – to write Nō plays. 'You *must* write poetry', the spirit tells him, and 'I have also given you material for a Noh play'. (2.387) Part of the slightly comic sub-text of these papers stems from the feeling Georgie Yeats obviously had that he was wasting his time and ought to be getting on with his work. At one point Yeats is told: '. . . simplify your life nothing else. Don't look for work outside your own'. 'What do you mean. . . .' he asks.

'Lectures? plays?' The spirit firmly answers: 'Lectures'. Yeats then asks about Nō plays, and is told: 'Noh all right–lectures if settled & not done at random from restlessness.' (1. 208)

□

If we examine the plays that Yeats actually wrote, and which he refers to as his own Nō plays (*Letters* 615), however, we may be surprised to find that in the first of them, and perhaps the most important – *At the Hawk's Well* (1917) – ghosts or mediums do not seem to appear at all. At least they do not appear in a guise that we can connect directly with the spirit mediums of Bond Street or Soho. The play is set in Ireland, and the story that Yeats uses is of Cuchulain's attempt to find a well of miraculous water.[1]

All the same, it will not do to play down, as Denis Donoghue or Helen Vendler have done, the relation between *At the Hawk's Well* and Japan. Yeats follows the Nō both in terms of what he sees as its poetic technique, and in the importance he gives to the climactic dance of the hawk. The old man describes her dance:

> Look at her shivering now, the terrible life
> Is slipping through her veins. She is possessed (*Variorum* 408).

As Katharine Worth points out, Yeats had been interesting in putting dance into drama for some time, but it is in *At the Hawk's Well* that we finally and clearly find a dance which represents a form of spirit possession. And there is no doubt that it was Yeats's idea of specifically Japanese dance that led to this. In Fenollosa's essay on the Nō he emphasizes that the 'most certainly Japanese element of the drama was the sacred dance in the Shinto temples'. He goes on to say: 'The ancient Shinto dance or pantomime was probably, at first, a story enacted by the local spirit... Shintoism is spiritism' (*Classic Noh* 63). Fenollosa does not, I think, mean modern spiritualism here, his reference is to ancient Greek religious practices. Yeats, on the other hand, had grasped at a connection that suited his own interests: and thus he could base the convergence of Nō and Western ideas on the figure of the spirit medium. The drama of the medium's possession, ritualized in a dance, provides for him a link between East and West.

Yeats's use of the dance, and its significance for him, can be related to Hearn's writings on Japan. Hearn was also profoundly impressed by a dance, the Bon-odori, that he saw in a mountain village when he was living in Matsue. He describes it in *Glimpses of Unfamiliar Japan* (1894):

> Out of the shadow of the temple a processional line of dancers files into the moonlight and as suddenly halts. . . figures lightly poised as birds. . . and so slowly, weirdly, the processional movement changes into a great round, circling about the moonlit court and around the voiceless crowd of spectators. . . Unto what, I ask myself, may this be likened? Unto nothing; yet it suggests some fancy of somnambulism, – dreamers, who dream themselves flying, dreaming upon their feet.
>
> And there comes to me the thought that I am looking at something immemorially old, something belonging to the unrecorded beginnings of this Oriental life. . . a symbolism of motion whereof the meaning has been forgotten for innumerable years. . . there creeps upon me a nameless, tingling sense of being haunted. . . what is it? I know not; yet I feel it to be something infinitely more old than I, – something not only of one place or time, but vibrant to all common joy or pain of being, under the universal sun (132-8).

This is deservedly one of Hearn's most famous descriptions of Japan – one of the moments when Japan becomes all he wants it to be: ghostly, beautiful, remote from the modern Western world, exotic and yet somehow speaking of deeps of the mind. The dance is birdlike, somnambulistic (Yeats also talks of 'somnambulistic' journeys in association with ghosts [*Explorations* 47]) and it makes Hearn feel haunted. It is perhaps ironic that in the case of both Yeats and Hearn a Japanese version of ritual dance is necessary for the Western writer to convince himself that a sacred universal 'communitas,' a living world of myth, is still possible.

□

Yeats and Hearn come together in their view of Japanese dance, but for Hearn the dancers are only one example of an experience of what he calls 'Ghostly Japan'. These dancers are not actually ghosts, they only seem to be ghostly to him.

In most cases, in Hearn's Japanese work, real communication with personal ghosts is imagined as something for other people, not for Hearn himself. In particular, seeing ghosts is possible for unselfconscious members of the kind of closed community of the old Japan he so lovingly observed at Matsue and so longed to enter. Hearn is constantly aware of how far he is from the mental world which contains Japanese ghosts, his 'incapacity to enter into the soul-life of this ancient East'. A trained sociologist coming to the few remaining traditional areas of Japan would find, he said 'the rule of the dead'. But he would also recognize that 'between those minds and the minds of his own epoch no kinship of thought, no community of sentiment, no sympathy whatever could exist' (*Japan* 460,383).

This kind of distance is not something Yeats emphasizes; though of course he does not have personal experience of Japan and he selects only a very limited area for his attention. When Hearn describes Japan for Western readers, however, he is always performing a balancing act for them: he has special insight and sympathy, but he is still an outsider. Between inside and outside he has somehow to try to keep his foothold, while still entertaining his non-Japanese audience. 'I ask nobody,' he says to his readers 'to take for granted the possibility of the Iki-ryo [living ghosts], except as a strong form of conscience.' If he can place these ghosts firmly within the mental world of Japan, however, he can then abandon the need for logic, consistency or verifiability that are demanded in the West; and he is extremely happy with such a position. 'The house now occupied by one of my friends used to be haunted,' he tells us. It is not his own house of course; and, once he has made plain that this is not his own account he is giving, he can go on to suggest that 'the Iki-ryo, which are the ghosts of the living, may come at all hours; and they are much more to be feared [than the Shi-ryo, ghosts of the dead], because they have power to kill' (*Out of the East* 172-6). Does Hearn believe in all these vengeful spirits? Certainly not in a straightforward way. But since his friend believes in them, he can assure himself that they do have some kind of effect, some undeniable place, in a real world of somebody's experience.

Hearn's admirers have often preferred to ignore his reservations and surround him with the aura of the ghostly. Nobushige Amenomori, for example, describes Hearn working at one o'clock at night alone in his study:

> It was not the Hearn I was familiar with: it was another Hearn. His face was mysteriously white; his large eye gleamed. He appeared like one touched with some unearthly presence (*Atlantic Monthly* 524).

Obviously Hearn is here presented as a kind of spirit medium of the arts: but for Hearn himself inspired figures who can communicate directly with ghosts exist most comfortably within the setting of re-told folk tales. It is within a distant and legendary world 'Some centuries ago' that he frames the figure of Mimi-nashi-Hōïchi, the blind biwa player who chants the story of the Heike battles to the ghosts of the Heike clan. Hōïchi hears his ghostly audience 'murmuring praise': "How marvellous an artist!– Never in our own province was playing heard like this!" (*Kwaidan* 10). He represents an ideal artist for Hearn, someone in tune with the ghostly in several senses; but he is placed away from the reader's world, within a framework of literary effects, cultural explanations and footnotes. There is a marked difference between this and Yeats's introduction to *The Celtic Twilight*, where Yeats tells us 'I have... been at no pains to separate my own beliefs from those of the peasantry'.[1] Unlike Yeats, Hearn *did* separate his beliefs from those of the peasantry; though he also enjoyed pointing out how they might shadow one another at times.

☐

Yeats would like to enter into negotiations with ghosts first and then sort out the implication afterwards. Japan, the Nō, folklore, ghosts and fairies can all be used by him: he is determined to ignore conventional barriers and categories of knowledge. He would also like to bring the question of how negotiations take place firmly back to his own contemporary world, as we see in *The Words upon the Window-Pane* (1934).

In this play Mrs Henderson, a modern spirit medium who has travelled from England to Dublin to give seances, is interrupted by the ghosts of Jonathan Swift, Vanessa and Stella. They speak through Mrs Henderson, performing again the tragic struggles of their relationships–though she herself claims not to know who Swift is.

It has been pointed out that in some respects Yeats draws here on the Nō tradition: I would not disagree. I would like to point out that Yeats's dramatic ghosts have become, in this play, the ghosts of ancestors. Swift and Stella are not literally Yeats's ancestors, but at the time he wrote the play he was busy constructing a Protestant ancestral tradition for himself with figures like Swift. Negotiating with ghosts in this play has become not just a glimpse of deep reality perceived through a trancelike dance, but a kind of Yeatsian ancestor-worship.

If Yeats was involved in a nostalgic search for ancestors in his later career, so of course was Hearn. In Hearn's case this meant looking more and more towards Greece, which he associated with his mother. His feeling for his own ancestors, however, also goes with a deepening sense of the significance of Shinto and ancestor-worship in Japan. Hearn had always given Shinto more respectful treatment than writers like B. H. Chamberlain, and in his final work *Japan: An Attempt at Interpretation* (1904), he insists that from the ancestor-cult 'almost everything in Japanese society, derives'. Understanding the treatment of ghosts, is for him the key to understanding Japan. He compares the 'ideas of the old Greeks regarding the dead' and 'the ideas of the old Japanese'.

No doubt because Hearn himself came from a broken home, he was deeply impressed by what he calls the 'domestic worship [of Japan], which regards the dead as continuing to form a part of the household life, and needing still the affection and the respect of their children'. The bond with ancestral ghosts was originally one of fear, he suggests, but it has been replaced by a 'religion of affection'. '[The ghosts of the ancestors] are not thought of as dead. ... Unseen they guard the home, and watch over the welfare of its inmates: they hover nightly in the glow of the shrine-lamp; and the stirring of its flame is the motion of them. ... They were the givers of life, the givers of wealth, the makers and teachers of the present: they represent the past of the race, and all its sacrifices;–whatever the living possess is from them' (28-9, 44-5). He sees Japanese ancestor-worship not as superstition, but as something the West might profitably learn. In his own household in Japan, he recounted reverently in a letter to Chamberlain, 'Some of the prayers are said for me' (*Japanese Letters* 182).

Despite radical differences in their personal concepts of ghosts, then, there is an interesting convergence here between these two writers: for both of them Japan (or at least their idea of Shinto in Japan) legitimizes reference to ghostly ancestors. They both deplore the neglect of their forbears – and are drawn in their writings to the Japanese rituals that embody respect for the dead.

□

It is clear, I hope, from these comparisons I have sketched out, that the topic of ghosts for both Yeats and Hearn is not a minor one in relation to their work. It is one that touches on their ideas of creativity, inspiration, the universality of emotions, and it is deeply involved with their creation of a tradition to which they would like to belong. As I have been attempting to show, they are both involved in a *series* of negotiations throughout their lives, and for both of them those negotiations touch at important points on Japan.

And yet we must admit that their negotiations with ghosts are not entirely happy. They want to negotiate, they take up their different positions from which to do so, but the ghosts do not, on the whole, want to respond. Even when they perform their dreaming act, like Swift in *The Words upon the Window-Pane*, communication is somehow blocked: Swift simply repeats again his terrible decline. In Hearn's world the ghosts may come, but they come to the Japanese, and not to Hearn. The kindly ancestral ghosts are not those of his ancestors. The circle which they look over and guard is one from which Hearn is excluded by his birth.

But in one important respect of course things have turned out rather better. These attempts at negotiation, or this fascination with the prospect of negotiation, leaves behind it some of the most interesting, if some of the more problematic work, of the two writers. The triangle of ghosts, folklore and Japan – whatever its difficulties – has been a productive one from a literary point of view. The writers finally speak louder than the ghosts – even when the ghosts speak through trumpets.

24

Hearn, Yeats and the Problem of Edmund Burke

GEORGE HUGHES

―――――― oOo ――――――

Reading Lafcadio Hearn, we are confronted at once with someone who was himself a voracious consumer of other people's books. What remains of Hearn's personal library at Toyama provides us with a fascinating index of a *fin de siècle* mind at work; but everywhere in Hearn's letters, journalism and university lectures we find evidence of his eager auto-didacticism, his constant search for theoretical explanations, and his ability to incorporate his reading into various personal projects.

We catch Hearn at a particularly interesting angle, however, when we find him reading and discussing Irish writers. What does he make, for example, of Edmund Burke, when he is living and teaching in Japan? And how does this compare with the famous reading of Burke by W. B. Yeats – a reading which directly confronts the Irish politics of his own day?[1] These questions seem particularly interesting at a time when Burke's own reputation is fiercely in question. What exactly, we might ask, do Hearn and Yeats find in this Irish author? And how do they use what they have read?

☐

Burke's image among modern critics of Romanticism is often fairly simple: he has become the arch-reactionary. Marilyn Butler is more generous than many, but her comments may be taken as representative. One gathers that she neither agrees with, nor likes him. Burke is 'the great apologist for the counter-revolution', 'anti-individualist', 'anti-rationalist', the author of 'polemic against intellectuals'. He is accused of inciting fear of radicals, and 'Fear makes men cruel' (65, 180, 55). From an Irish perspective, however, Burke appears more sympathetic. Seamus Deane, it is true, sees him as an imperialist; but Deane also thinks that 'the main planks of British liberalism in the nineteenth century' came from Burke's writings (24). And Conor Cruise O'Brien, in his massive and densely argued defence of Burke, *The Great Melody*, has read him as a critic of empire, shaped definitively by early experience of discrimination against Irish Catholics.

Lafcadio Hearn and W. B. Yeats, both writing in the early years of the twentieth century, also saw Burke in relation to his Irish context. They saw him, it is true, rather differently; but what they saw is more complex than could be summarized in the phrase 'counter-revolutionary'. Burke was a writer, for both of them, who had an important role in arguments about tradition. He took his place (to use Foucault's terms) in a 'body of knowledge' that could be linked to 'other forms of power'. He was not beyond criticism, but he was an exemplary figure in modern politics.

The forms of power these writers were interested in, are of course not the same. Yeats claimed Burke as a precursor in public life, but wrote in his notebooks that Burke was 'only tolerable in his impassioned moments' (*Explorations* 293). Hearn was more directly concerned with Burke's ethical integrity. He was faced with the problem of Burke when he was employed as a teacher in Japan, and he insisted that Burke's writing was not a good model for Japanese students; but he had to find a way of explaining nonetheless why Burke was 'one of the greatest masters of language who belonged to English literature', and the founder of a new prose style (*History* I 440).

☐

Hearn's relation to Ireland is of course quite different from that of Yeats, and this must determine to some extent a difference in their engagement with Burke. Yeats was born in Ireland, spent his early years there and was involved for most of his life in fights over one Irish cause or another. His concern with Irish matters is of fundamental significance in reading all his work. Hearn by contrast was only partly of Anglo-Irish origin (his mother was Greek). He lived in Dublin from the age of 2 to 13, and then was sent to a Catholic school in England. But this did not (as O'Brien thinks Burke's experience at a Catholic hedge-school in Ireland did) leave Hearn with deep sympathy for Catholics; rather it left him with a loathing for any form of institutionalized Christianity. For most of Hearn's life his cultural interests–at least as they are reflected in his writings– were to be found in France, the United States and (after 1890) Japan. Hirakawa Sukehiro has suggested that Hearn repressed his feelings about Ireland because he felt he had been abandoned by his father, and that seems a possible explanation, though not finally provable (*Introduction*, Murray 2). Hearn's interest may possibly have revived in Ireland at some period of his life, since he did announce in one of his late letters 'I am Irish rather than English', and in his last years he 'half-hope[d] to go, for a time at least, to Ireland'.[2]

In one part of his life, however, we can draw certainly on evidence that Hearn had Irish matters in mind: as a teacher of English and of English literature in Japan, Hearn felt it necessary to read over the classics of prose in English again, and his attention did focus from time to time on Irish writers. He lectured on Burke to students at Tokyo University; and since his lecture notes have been preserved in remarkable detail, and published as a *History of English Literature*, we know what he thought about Burke—or at least what he thought it worth communicating to Japanese students about Burke.

Hearn gave Burke a prominent place in the course he taught on the history of English Literature. Among the essayists of the eighteenth century he said 'the greatest figure of the later period was certainly Edmund Burke'. And he emphasized the Irishness of Burke with a firmness that we might not expect: Burke, he says, 'was one of the great Irishmen, not Englishman [sic], of the 18th century' (*History* I 437). (Swift, on the other hand, he decided had been born in Ireland but was truly English.) Burke, we are told, had a personality of great charm and force, and part of the charm was Irish. He immediately placed Burke within the famous triumvirate of writers born in Ireland: Burke, Swift and Berkeley:

> ... in point of personal charm, there is only one other Irishman of the age to be compared with him—that was Bishop Berkley [sic]. But Berkley with all his lovableness, did not possess the dominating power, this personal force of Burke. In his power to dominate, Burke rather resembled Swift; but he has none of Swift's cruelty. (*History* I 438)

In fact, of these three writers Hearn obviously found Berkeley the most immediately sympathetic, partly because he thought his anti-materialist philosophy looked forward to the insights of modern science, and partly because he thought his ideas were compatible with Buddhism and Eastern philosophy.[3] He was enthusiastic enough about Berkeley to devote a full separate lecture to him. About Burke he had strong and obvious reservations.

When we turn to Yeats, we find that the conjunction of the three great Irish writers is a matter of course, and stems from his attempt to give shape and dignity to an Anglo-Irish Protestant tradition. In a letter to Joseph Hone he wrote: 'I want Protestant Ireland to base some vital part of its culture upon Burke, Swift and Berkeley' (qutd. Torchiana xii). He also adds Goldsmith to his list: in the Introduction to *The Words upon the Window Pane* he writes: ' I read Swift for months together, Burke and Berkeley less often but always with excitement, and Goldsmith lures and waits' (*Variorum* 957). These writers represent for Yeats a tradition of Irishness which is distinguished from Englishness and England:

> Born in such a community, Berkeley with his belief in perception, that abstract ideas are mere words, Swift with his love of perfect nature, of the Houyhnhnms, his disbelief in Newton's system and every sort of machine, Goldsmith and his delight in the particulars of common life that shocked his contemporaries, Burke with his conviction that all States not grown slowly like a forest tree are tyrannies, found in England the opposite that stung their own thought into expression and made it lucid. (*Essays* 402)

Seamus Deane suggests that this, as a version of eighteenth-century literary and intellectual history, is 'manifestly absurd' (29). In the case of Burke, Deane claims, Yeats has confused his reaction to England with his reaction to France. Whether we accept Deane's point or not (and it seems in the light of O'Brien's book rather a one-dimensional view of Yeats) the interest here must lie in the way that Yeats has created the idea of an intellectual and oppositional tradition, rising from the community in which these writers were born.

In his youth it seems that Yeats did not find Burke

sympathetic at all. He rejected him, he tells us, because he saw Burke as part of an English system and as part of the eighteenth-century world, while he saw himself (as Hearn also did) as a Romantic. Burke does appear quite early in Yeats's speeches, however, and even gets a favourable mention in 1898. (Ellmann 115). But much of the time he seems more interested in the figure of Burke as a politician than in a close reading of his ideas. Hearn, too, thought that Burke was 'greater as a personality than as a writer–greater as an orator and statesman than as a mere man of letters'; but this stems from his sense that Burke has a 'faulty style' (*History* I 439). Yeats does not discuss the style in detail, and is impressed by Burke as a figure in a tradition of administration and political thought. Burke appears, for example, in a letter Yeats wrote to describe a Dublin sculptor visiting Coole Park after Lady Gregory's death, to 'pay his respects':

> [The sculptor] walked from room to room then stopped at the mezzotints and engravings of those under or with whom. . . the Gregorys have served, Fox, Burke and so on, and after standing silent said 'all the nobility of earth'. (qutd. Hone 428)

Burke represents here a figure in a tradition of a peculiarly aristocratic kind. But Yeats also makes a fascinating conjunction of ideas in a diary entry around 1926, when he writes:

> Preserve that which is living, help the two Irelands, Gaelic Ireland and Anglo-Ireland, so to unite that neither shall shed its pride. Study the great problems of the world, as they have been lived in our own scenery, the rebirth of European spirituality in the mind of Berkeley, the restoration of European order in the mind of Burke. (qutd. Hone 379-80)

It is of particular interest here that Burke is seen in the context of *uniting* the two Irelands, because one of the most famous references to Burke by Yeats is in his Senate speech on divorce in 1925, when he spoke in a way that many immediately felt (and still feel) was deliberately divisive. Yeats claimed Burke here for an Irish tradition of liberal, non-Catholic, thought, and suggested that the inheritors of this tradition faced the threat of extinction:

> I think it is tragic that within three years of this country gaining its independence we should be discussing a measure which a minority of this nation considers to be grossly oppressive. I am proud to consider myself a typical man of that minority. We against whom you have done this thing are no petty people. We are one of the great stocks of Europe. We are the people of Burke; we are the people of Grattan; we are the people of Swift, the people of Emmet, the people of Parnell. We have created the most of the modern literature of this country. We have created the best of its political intelligence. (*Senate Speeches* 99)

It is a deeply felt statement for the rights of what had become a powerless minority in Ireland. And the use of Burke's name ties in with Yeats's conception of Burke's career, notably summed up in the lines that O'Brien takes as the epigraph to his book:

> American colonies, Ireland, France and India
> Harried, and Burke's great melody against it.
>   'The Seven Sages'

Burke has a 'great melody' of political argument, and he fights for those who are 'harried'.

Hearn had no direct connection with political legislation in the way Yeats did – neither in Ireland nor anywhere else – though he was certainly interested in politics, and not slow to take sides in his years a journalist. But when he talks about Burke it is to emphasize the ethical integrity of Burke, and not his relation to a liberal tradition. 'About political, social and even literary matters,' he informed his students, 'Burke thought only from the standpoint of ethics.' Burke's work, he says, was intended to stir the moral sympathies of his audience 'their sense of justice or their capacities of honest indignation'. 'All his policies, all his ethics, all his notions and opinions were solved for him by such simple moral questions as "Is this right?" – "Is this honest? Is this good for the country and for the people?"' (*History* I 441).

This view of Burke, we may note, depended just as much as Yeats's on Hearn's sense of the political context in which he was speaking. He was not as it happened very sympathetic to Burke's view of the French Revolution; he admired early Romantic writing and thought Tom Paine much underestimated: but he was unusually sensitive as a lecturer to the fact that he was addressing a Japanese audience, and that their reactions to Western political ideas would be different from those of student audiences in the West. It is one of the most important aspects of his years in Japan that he established himself as a teacher who was (for all that he had to teach English literature for a living) keenly interested in the development of modern Japanese culture, and eager to try and see things from his Japanese students' point of view. This aspect of his work obviously struck his first students deeply, and it remains important – if sometimes contested – today.[4] In the case of Burke, Hearn knew how his audience was predisposed to the view that Western politics were unethical. Burke, he thought, could show them that it was possible to be ethical within the Western tradition – without being a Christian missionary.[5] And this, given his intense dislike of missionaries, made Burke rather useful.

□

If Yeats found Burke intolerable to read except in his impassioned moments, he suggests that this was because Burke was used to addressing an assembly. Hearn also thought Burke wrote as an orator, though he developed the idea into a serious argument about Burke's style. His concern obviously stems from the fact that Burke was being used in textbooks in Japan as a model of English style, and Hearn had very positive views about the kind of English that should be recommended to Japanese students. He was annoyed when the models he had suggested for texts were rejected, and Burke was used instead.[6]

Hearn described Burke's prose as the start of a new style in English – though it was a 'faulty style':

> . . . there is a strange and splendid beauty, – a disordered beauty, – in this faulty style; – it is immensely powerful;–it astonishes and delights by its rapid succession of discordant but most effective imagery; it has the charm and the color of some tremendous panorama. The chief fault of taste is in the direction of violence. . . . He would compare his antagonists or their measures to insects, to reptiles, to tape-worms, to whales, to mythological monsters or to tropical amphibians, when it suited him. (*History* I 439)

Hearn decided that this style 'laid the foundation to what we call the Coloured Prose' of the nineteenth century. He thought it lay behind the 'richly florid' work of De Quincey, Carlyle, Ruskin and even Macaulay. But he added:

> Burke is a dangerous, a very dangerous master. One is much more tempted to imitate his form than to go to the trouble of analyzing his merits. He is not a good model for the Japanese student of style–quite the reverse. (*History* I 440)

Hearn's views here are shaped by several considerations. If Japanese students were to imitate English styles he thought they should imitate clear simple styles: elsewhere he strongly recommended Defoe as a model, or 'a simple northern style' (like that used in translations of Norse writers.) But although Hearn talked to his students about English style at length, his deepest concern was that they should go on to write well in Japanese–to create a modern intellectual and literary forum in Japan. He pointed to the way in which the written and spoken language were separated at that time in Japan, and quite rightly argued that the important step for Japanese, as for other modern languages, must be to increase the use of spoken forms in writing. The modern writing in English that Hearn recommended to his students was thus a more simple, popular, colloquial style (like Kipling's, for example.)

Anyone who looks at Hearn's own writings in his early career, however, will rapidly see that he had not always favoured simplicity. He had once been keenly interested in producing a kind of French decadent effect in English, and even in his later career, as a writer of the nineties—an exoticist—he had a lingering fondness for the kind of 'richly florid' English prose he had once imitated closely: for De Quincey, Carlyle, Poe and Pater. Burke, he decided, was in fact 'the father and founder' of this style, and of what could be called 'modern Coloured Prose'. If Burke was not to be imitated, he was also not entirely to be rejected. What gave Burke's work its real power he concluded was that it was based on oratory: 'political and religious oratory'. 'He wrote his addresses only thinking how they would sound as delivered with all the art of a well trained voice.' He is finally, then, 'the best example of 18th century Oratorical Prose'. (*History* I 441)

☐

If Yeats used Burke in defence of a 'harried' tradition, and Hearn used Burke in his attempt to encourage a new tradition of writing in Japan, both of them selected very heavily to gain the Burke they wanted. Yeats famously picked up Burke's image of the state as a tree, and although Burke was talking about the British oak, applied it where he could. Torchiana has shown in detail how important this image became to Yeats, and how it ties in with the series of tree images throughout his work (no doubt connected in some way with the famous tree of life images discussed by F. A. C. Wilson and de Man). Hearn, on the other hand, shaped his view of the state on his reading of social evolutionists, and he was much more concerned with the struggle for existence between states than the organic growth of states.

Hearn did recommend to his students that they read Burke

on the Sublime and Beautiful – since this was 'from a literary point of view, . . . his least faulty production'. There is also a slight link between Hearn's own interest in supernatural fiction and Burke on the sublime. Hearn's retold ghost stories (which remain some of his most famous writings in Japan) were highly successful, and he tried to elaborate a theory of writing on the supernatural which could apply to all literatures, including Japanese. To do this he went back to the *Book of Job* for an important example. 'The poet speaks of feeling intense cold, and feeling the hairs of his head stand up with fear. These experiences are absolutely true, and they belong to waking life' ('The supernatural' 123). What Hearn is referring to here is the passage in the *Book of Job* which runs: 'Then a spirit passed before my face. The hair of my flesh stood up.' Hearn makes no mention of Burke, but the same passage is chosen by Burke in his explanation of the sublime. Burke continues: '. . . when this grand cause of terror makes its appearance, what is it? is it not wrapt up in the shades of its own incomprehensible darkness, more awful, more striking, more terrible than the liveliest description, than the clearest painting, could possibly represent it?'[7] Hearn's approach to the supernatural is again evolutionary, but Burke on the sublime is undoubtedly in the same literary tradition.

☐

The meaning of Burke for both Hearn and Yeats, then, goes well beyond the notion that Burke is a counter-revolutionary or an imperialist. In both cases, as we have seen, these writers are using Burke to further programmes of their own; and they rely on highly selective reading. Burke is in many ways quite simply not sympathetic to them, but they appropriate him nonetheless for the bodies of knowledge which concern them. Their appropriations are part of different social negotiations in which they are involved – Yeats in Ireland

and Hearn in Japan. Foucault says that 'No body of knowledge can be formed without a system of communications, records, accumulation and displacement which is in itself a form of power and which is linked, in its existence and functioning to the other forms of power' (qutd. Connor, 11). This may be right, but what we see when we read Yeats or Hearn on Burke is above all the way in which bodies of knowledge shift and re-form. Interpretation of a figure like Burke depends heavily on the position from which we start and the context within which we write: there is not one right reading, or one right use of Burke. His writings can have different functions, can slip into different systems of communication, even from an Irish point of view. We can see clearly now how a writer like Hearn uses Burke–though of course it must be added that we cannot yet see the full implications of the way in which writers of our own generation have come to use the figure of Lafcadio Hearn.

25

Lafcadio Hearn's First Day in the Orient

PETER McIVOR

———————— 000 ————————

It is Yokohama, 4 April 1890, a perfect spring morning as Lafcadio Hearn (1850-1904) disembarks from the steamship *Abyssinia* at the end of a long voyage from Vancouver. He had been on deck since dawn, eager to catch a first glimpse of Mount Fuji. He was later to record his initial impressions in a language as lyrical and emotionally charged as anything he would ever write about Japan:

> Unimaginably beautiful this first vision of the harbour, as we anchor a mile from shore: the softness of the light, the limpidity of distances, the delicacy of the blue tones in which everything is steeped, – create a charm totally new and indescribable. Nothing is intense, though all is clear; nothing is forceful, though all is pleasing and strange: this is the vividness, this is the softness of dreams! And

the idea is enhanced by the wonderful spectral loveliness of the white shape shining above the town, above the blue volcanic ridges beyond it . . . it appears suspended above the horizon like a mirage.
(Lafcadio Hearn, 'A Winter's Journey to Japan'. In Kenneth P. Kirkwood, *Unfamiliar Lafcadio Hearn* [Tokyo: Hokuseidō Press, 1936], 27-28)

He could not have known it at the time, but Hearn's arrival in Japan marked an important turning point in his life, closing the years of nomadic travel begun in Dublin in 1863 on departure for school in England and which, in the intervening decades, had taken him to France (possibly), the United States and the West Indies. As he approached the age of 40, Japan was his final destination:

A sampan takes me and my baggage to the *Hatoba* – the landing place. . . . A very little suffices to cross the harbour; and I stand on earth again. . . . I am in Japan. (ibid., 28)

Although already a well-known journalist and author in the United States, Hearn was certainly glad to leave the trials of Philadelphia and New York – his final homes there – behind him. Money was just one of his problems. One biographer describes him at this time as broken in health mentally and physically following a year marked 'tragically by quarrels, broken friendships, disputes with his publishers and everyone else, and a most pathetic misjudgment of everyone about him' (ibid., 20). His arrival in Yokohama in 1890 was a more than adequate tonic, the memory of which was to sustain him for the rest of his life. He wrote of it:

My own first impressions of Japan, – Japan as seen in the white sunshine of a perfect spring day, – had doubtless much in common with the average of such experiences. I remember especially the wonder and the delight of the vision. The wonder and delight have never passed away: they are often revived for me even now, by some chance happening, after fourteen years of sojourn.
(*Japan: An Attempt at Interpretation* [New York: Macmillan, 1905], 9)

The 'wonder and delight of the vision' were to become

the special subject of Hearn's discourse on Japan. His 13 books on Japanese subjects, together with extensive personal correspondence and newspaper articles, represent a remarkable achievement.

To appreciate this achievement, it is necessary to understand the historical context of the Japan in which Hearn had arrived in 1890. He had, in fact, sailed into Yokohama just three decades after the nation, under the threat of an American armada led by Commodore Matthew Perry (1794-1858), had been opened to the West after three centuries of self-imposed isolation. It was the age of the Meiji emperor (1868-1912); the age of foreign intrusion; the age of the treaty ports and foreign settlements.

Hearn's presentation of Japan can best be understood within the context of this foreign trespass. His topic was the 'Old Japan' threatened by external intervention. If his 13-volume work was a protest against the powerful currents of Western life affecting Japan in the mid-Meiji era, it was a protest conducted largely in celebratory terms, weighted with 'the wonder and the delight' of Japan, and of everything that distinguished East from West.

There are, of course, other sides to Hearn's interpretation of Japan – his interest in the macabre and the supernatural, as in *Kwaidan*, first published in 1904, or his structured analysis of Japanese history and society, as in *Japan: An Attempt at Interpretation* – but he largely withheld these aspects of his exploration until later years or registered them privately in personal correspondence. It is his experience of Japan as recorded in earlier books such as *Glimpses of Unfamiliar Japan* (1894) and *Out of the East* (1895), which has ensured the popularity of his work down to our own time. Among the essays in those early books, perhaps none is more characteristic of his approach to Japan than 'My First Day in the Orient', the opening essay of his first book on Japan, *Glimpses of Unfamiliar Japan*.

'My First Day in the Orient' is an account of the

wonderful spring day Hearn spent dashing from temple to temple by rickshaw in the Japanese quarter of Yokohama shortly after his arrival. In itself, the subject of the essay is unremarkable: in the 1890s a first-day rickshaw ride through Yokohama was a popular tourist activity. Nor was the idea of writing about the experience unusual: a contemporary travel writer, Douglas Sladen (1856-1947), had also described a first-day rickshaw ride through Yokohama in the opening two chapters of his 1892 travel journal, *The Japs At Home*.

Given the rural orientation of Hearn's later work, however, 'My First Day in the Orient' is of particular interest because it deals with the life of an eastern Japanese city which, as a treaty port, offered perhaps the greatest concentration of Western intervention in Japan at that time. What is surprising about Hearn's account of his first day is that it offers little indication that no city in Japan at that time had played a greater role in the nation's Westernization.

Yokohama had been, in fact, the scene of some of the most traumatic events in Japan's modern relationship with the West. It was here that Commodore Perry landed in 1854 to await the shogun's reply to a letter presented a year earlier, seeking the opening of the country. Here, too, the Treaty of Kanagawa was signed, ending the isolationist policies of the Tokugawa Shogunate. Foreign influence on Yokohama continued long after Hearn's time. In September 1945, just off the Yokohama coastline, General Douglas MacArthur accepted the surrender of Japan upon the battleship *Missouri*.

When Hearn arrived in Japan midway through the 90-year period between the Treaty of Kanagawa and Japan's surrender, the process of Westernization was well under way. After just one day in Yokohama in May 1878, the English traveller, Isabella Bird (1831-1904), could write that the city was '. . . not imposing in any way . . . its Bluff represents the suburbs of Boston; its Bund, the suburbs of Birkenhead, with a semi-tropical hallucination' (*Unbeaten Tracks in Japan* [London: John Murray, 1880], 15). She added that she longed 'to get away into real Japan' (ibid., 20).

This response was not unusual. Yokohama had, after all, been established in 1859 as a settlement specifically built for foreigners and, at least until the demise of the treaty port system in 1899, had remained separate from the rest of the nation. It had its own foreign language press; it had its own system of justice – under extraterritoriality provisions – and its own social life. Picture postcards from the period show the strange mixture of Western and Japanese street scenes that made up the city, with great continental and Victorian buildings side by side with flimsy Japanese wooden structures. Yokohama remained the chief place of residence for foreigners throughout the treaty period. In 1870, the expatriate population was about 1,200. By 1894, it had increased to about 5,000. While more than half were Chinese, Westerners numbered 2,400, a figure that would remain constant until the Great Kantō Earthquake in 1923.[1]

Sympathetic biographies written shortly after Hearn's death have sustained the popular image of the author as an isolated foreigner allowed uniquely privileged access to aspects of Japanese life and culture denied to everyone else. Nina H. Kennard, for example, wrote that Hearn '. . . elected to live the everyday life, and enter into the ordinary interests and occupations of this strange people, as no Occidental ever had before' (*Lafcadio Hearn*, [Port Washington: Kennikat, 1967], 203). But this is just part of the story.

Lafcadio Hearn's arrival in Yokohama was very much a part of a wider influx of foreign merchants, scholars, engineers, doctors, missionaries, diplomats and tourists that had been increasing year by year since the time of Commodore Perry. Even when seen within the context of the small Irish presence in Meiji Japan, Lafcadio Hearn was not alone as an interpreter of Japan. In his entry on books on Japan in his miscellany *Japanese Things* (1905), Basil Hall Chamberlain, then professor of Japanese literature at the Imperial

University in Tokyo, selected a dozen works 'as probably the most generally useful that are accessible to English readers', which included contemporary works not only by Hearn but those by other Irish writers, such as *History of Japanese Literature* by W.G. Aston (1841-1911) and a 12-volume study entitled *Japan and China* by Captain Frank Brinkley (1841-1912). English-language journalism in Japan, prior to the turn of the century, also showed a strong Irish influence. The same Frank Brinkley had been the owner and editor of the main newspaper in Yokohama, *The Japan Mail*, since 1881; a rival newspaper, *The Japan Gazette*, was owned, until his death in 1891, by another Irish newspaperman, J.R. Anglin.

Although Hearn took his place in the Western life of the city — he wrote to Basil Hall Chamberlain on the day of his arrival seeking the professor's assistance in helping him to find a job — very little of Western Yokohama is communicated in 'My First Day in the Orient'. By the first page Hearn has left the Western quarter and it is entirely the Japanese city which engages him. References to the West are minimal: an English professor, a street with telegraph poles, an electric bell, a shop selling American sewing machines, a tall foreigner. Where the artifacts of the West are in evidence, they are not, Hearn tells us, incongruous: '. . . for each sample of Occidental innovation is set into an Oriental frame that seems adaptable to any picture' (*Glimpses of Unfamiliar Japan* ([Tokyo: Charles E. Tuttle, 1976], 8).

If these references suggest that Hearn seeks to inject into his essay a sense of the intrusion of the West, they do not undermine its primary focus on the Eastern city. 'My First Day in the Orient' is essentially a wide-eyed record of wonder and delight that communicates an atmosphere of make-believe, sustained by the use of a lyrical and highly adjectival language. What is strikingly apparent, in comparison with other travelogues of this kind, is Hearn's sympathy with the new civilization he has discovered. This sympathy is most apparent in references to the Japanese people with whom he comes into contact and whose trials he immediately understands: the physical exhaustion of his rickshaw man; the poor health of the Buddhist priest before whom he makes his first mistake – he drops coins into a cup of water which the priest offers him to drink; the blindness of the *amma* (masseuse), whose whistle he hears on returning to his hotel in the evening. If the structure of the essay characteristically allows Hearn to branch out from his central theme to explore all kinds of incidental curiosities (the use of *kanji* ideographs, *geta*, Japanese feet, Shinto *torii* gates), nothing of the history or experience of Yokohama as a treaty port is included.

'My First Day in the Orient' is a modest essay, but is important in understanding Hearn's early work because it establishes from the outset the specific nature of his interest in Japan. This was directed less towards interpretation of the impact of Western intrusion on Meiji Japan as to the recovery of what was being lost in the transformation. The essay itself begins with the idea of recovery:

> 'Do not fail to write down your first impressions as soon as possible', said a kind English professor . . . 'they are evanescent, you know; they will never come to you again, once they have faded out. . . .'
> (*Glimpses of Unfamiliar Japan*, 1)

The reflection prompts Hearn to consider the kind of narrative he is creating and the process of its creation: a recollection of a 'first kuruma-ride out of the European quarter of Yokohama into the Japanese town', based on notes he had taken at the time and which, he concedes, could not reflect 'all the lost sensations of those first experiences' (ibid., 1).

Inevitably, the most important element in a recollection of this kind is the powerful visual impact of what he sees, from 'Hokusai's own figures walking about in straw rain-coats, and immense mushroom-shaped hats of straw' (ibid., 10) to a 'grove of cherry trees covered with something unutterably beautiful, – a dazzling mist of snowy blossoms clinging like summer cloud-fleece about every branch and twig' (ibid., 20-21). The most memorable visual image of the essay reveals Hearn's preoccupation with Japanese religions and religious practices. It is the image of a young woman in the twilight worshipping before a tiny shrine guarded by two statues of crimson monsters. It is this contrast between the delicacy of the woman and the two grotesque statutes that really engages Hearn.

☐

The novelist Ōe Kenzaburō, in his Nobel lecture in Stockholm in December 1994, spoke of Japan 120 years after its modernization, as split between what he calls 'two opposite poles of ambiguity', one the orientation towards learning from and imitating the West, the other the maintenance of traditional culture. In a sense, the cultural and social implications of the opening of these poles of ambiguity in the Meiji period were the special province of Hearn's work, just as they were that of contemporary Japanologists such as Chamberlain. It is reasonable to consider how Hearn's work reflects these tensions and whether it offers a real interpretation of the modernization process or whether, in largely rejecting the inevitable direction taken by Japan following the opening of the country, Hearn was a nostalgist charting the end of an era with a note of regret sometimes seeming to border on fantasy.

'My First Day in the Orient' suggests that Hearn's interest, from his first day in Yokohama, lay primarily in Japan as a historical civilization that somehow survived the march of time. We know from his later work and from his correspondence that he fully understood the nature of the transformation taking place during the Meiji Era. In *Japan: An Attempt at Interpretation*, he lists the measures taken to modernize Japan from 1871-1891: the abolition of the daimyo class, the withdrawal of edicts against Christianity, the prohibition of wearing swords, suppression of the samurai as a military body, and the organization of a new army and navy and an educational system. Yet, in the same book, he can write of his own life in Japan in terms of a return to an ancient civilization, such as that of Greece or Rome:

> And yet, to witness the revival of some perished Greek civilization, – to walk about the very Crotona of Pythagoras, – to wander through the Syracuse of Theocritus, – were not any more of a privilege than is the opportunity actually afforded us to study Japanese life. Indeed, from the evolutional point of view, it were less of a privilege, – since Japan offers us the living spectacle of conditions older, and psychologically much further away from us, than those of any Greek period with which art and literature have made us closely acquainted.
> (*Japan: An Attempt at Interpretation*, 20-21)

Hearn's texts are sprinkled liberally with references to Greece and Rome and his emphasis on Japan as an ancient civilization which, unlike the classical civilizations of Europe, had been largely ignored by Western scholarship, defines his purpose in Japan and the context in which his narrative is written. 'Old Japan survives,' he said, 'in art, in faith, in customs and habits, and in the hearts and homes of the people: it may be found everywhere by those who know how to look for it' (*Gleanings in Buddha Fields* [Tokyo: Charles E. Tuttle, 1971], 152).

Although 'My first Day in the Orient' is set in the East of Japan rather than in its West, in Yokohama rather than Izumo (present Shimane Prefecture), in the city rather than in the country, we can nonetheless identify in it the preoccupations that were to engage Hearn throughout his life in Japan, even though the 'Old Japan', at least in Yokohama was slowly playing itself out. It is thus not surprising that his work emphasizes the ancient and the unfamiliar, visits to temples and shrines, subjects such as religion, folklore, history and mythology, rural customs and practices, nor that the locations he chooses as settings for his essays are often in parts of Japan least touched by the West, the interior provinces such as Izumo, cities such as Matsue where Hearn later lived. This was his special provenance from the start. Despite the opening essay, *Glimpses of Unfamiliar Japan* is very much a book about Western Japan. 'Even yet,' Hearn was later to write, 'in those remoter districts where alien influence has wrought but little change, the charm of the old existence lingers and amazes; and the ordinary traveller can little understand what it means' (*Japan: An Attempt at Interpretation*, 418).

Although Hearn did not return to live in Yokohama, the memory of his first day in the Orient, he conceded, 'never passed away'. He allowed it occasionally to colour his later work and in an essay called 'A Conservative', in *Kokoro* (1896), he chose to narrate anew the events of his arrival on the *Abyssinia*. The retelling is appropriate because 'A Conservative' is, in a sense, a brief history of Japan from the closing years of the Tokugawa Shogunate to the middle of the Meiji Era as seen, not through the eyes of a foreigner, but through those of a dispossessed samurai whose way of life has been wholly undermined by Western intervention. In describing the samurai's return to Japan after a journey to Europe and America where he has been trying to understand how the West became so powerful, Hearn allows himself to recreate, in loving detail, the circumstances of his own arrival as a penniless writer six years before. Like Hearn, the samurai returns to Japan at the port of Yokohama on a cloudless April morning. Like Hearn, he joins the foreigners on deck to get a first glimpse of Mount Fuji before disembarking. Like Hearn, the samurai, looking out at the coastline, sees nothing of 'the modern Japan; he saw the Old' (*Kokoro: Hints and Echoes of Japanese Inner Life* [Tokyo: Charles E. Tuttle, 1972], 208).

26

Kokoro – A Century Later

SEAN G. RONAN

――――――――― oOo ―――――――――

I am very pleased to have been invited by the Ireland Japan Association and to give the Inaugural Lafcadio Hearn Lecture here in the James Joyce Centre this evening. I wish to thank both the IJA and the Centre for the honour and the opportunity so extended to me. I hope I can do justice to the occasion and that all of you who were good enough to come will find the subject matter of worthwhile interest.

The idea of an annual lecture on Lafcadio Hearn, proposed by Dr Thomas P. Hardiman, which might concentrate on his writings is timely, as the centenary period of Hearn and his writings on Japan has already commenced.

It will be recalled that Lafcadio Hearn arrived in Yokohama in April 1890, aged 40, as a correspondent of *Harper's Magazine*. He married the daughter of a *samurai* and they had a family of three sons and a daughter. He took Japanese citizenship in the interests of his family, adopting his wife's family name Koizumi and as a first name Yakumo. He became a Professor of English at the University of Tokyo and later at Waseda University. He died in Tokyo at the age of 54 due to a heart attack in 1904.

During his fourteen years in Japan Hearn produced thirteen books, commencing with *Glimpses of Unfamiliar Japan* in 1894 and ending with *Japan: An Attempt at Interpretation* published posthumously in 1905. *Out of the East* was published in 1895 and *Kokoro*, the subject of our analysis this evening, in 1896 – just one hundred years ago, and so we celebrate its centenary here this evening. The decade 1894-1904 was a productive period in Hearn's writings on Japan. He produced on average one book per year which provides much scope for memorial lectures in the years to come leading up to the centenary of his death in 1904.

It is a tribute to Hearn's particular genius and personality that his works are read, analysed and appreciated a century after his time. In fact, no writer on Japan is receiving more attention these days than Hearn. In his lifetime and into the 1930s he was quite famous inside and outside Japan. Understandably, interest in him waned during World War II when his writing was perceived to have been resolutely pro-Japan. Consequently, his influence was stifled by the sentiments of prominent American critics. In Japan, too, he was dropped after its defeat in 1945.

In the early 1960s interest in him surfaced again with the publication of Elizabeth Stevenson's biography[1] and Beong-sheon Yu's critical study of Hearn's art and thought.[2] An anthology of his writings, edited by Francis King, was published by Penguin in 1984.[3] It was, however, during the centenary of his arrival in Japan in 1990 that both Japanese and foreign scholars began to re-evaluate the life and work of the man who for over half a century was the principal interpreter of Japan for the West. That centenary was celebrated in Matsue on the Japan Sea where Hearn taught English after his arrival in Japan. The centennial essays on the occasion, edited by Professor Kenji Zenimoto, have been published by the Hearn Society of Japan.[4]

Now the pendulum has swung the other way and Hearn is being recognized as a complex and fascinating personality whose life and work demand serious reconsideration. In the past ten years a dozen or so important books and innumerable articles on Hearn have been published in the United States, Japan, Britain and Ireland, culminating with *A Fantastic Journey* which is a definitive study of Hearn's life and literature by Paul Murray[5] and *Koizumo Yakumo, The Folklorist* by his great grandson, Bon Koizumi.[6]

It is now becoming clear that Hearn is a multi-dimensional figure whose career is by no means limited to his writings on Japan. Evaluations are taking into consideration his Irish background, his American and West Indian periods, his fiction, folklore and literary criticisms, his philosophical ideas and his translations from nineteenth century French literature.

Professor George Hughes of the University of Tokyo says: 'Critical interest (in Hearn) has shifted dramatically in its focus; the branch line of Hearn studies now looks much nearer the centre than anyone had thought and is suddenly busy with traffic'.[7]

Coming to the East, following his successful career as a journalist in the United States, Hearn was enchanted with all aspects of Japanese life. His sketches of what he saw or heard, hundreds of them, are, like the prints of Utamaro and Hiroshige, priceless artistic representations of the Old Japan. Most notable are his renderings of the rich and varied Japanese folklore and *kwaidan* or stories of ghostly and strange things.

Unlike most foreigners, Hearn became fully integrated into Japanese society, marrying, as I said, the daughter of a *samurai* and adopting Japanese citizenship. Critical of Western materialism, he did not have a colonialist reformist attitude or a sense of the Orientalism described by Edward Said. His outlook was rather that of a visionary as regards his own identity and that of Japan.

Not only did Hearn eloquently interpret Japan for the West and the West for Japan but he helped the Japanese to identify and appreciate their own cultural values. His love of Japan was an active participation in the *kokoro* or heart and inner life of the country.

As an example of Hearn's topicality in Japan, a play about him entitled *Nippon no Omokage* or *Features of Japan* is showing in Kinokunia Hall, Shinjuku, Tokyo, from 19 June, which is today, to 30 June. It is adapted from an NHK TV programme written by Taichi Yamada, playwright and novelist. I hope it is successful. Maybe we shall hear more about it.

An emerging theme in the re-evaluation of Hearn is the importance of his Irish background. His contacts during his formative years with relatives, tutors, peasant maids, country-folk and fishermen in Dublin, Cong and Tramore familiarized him with Irish folk-tales, ghost stories, legends and songs, which enabled him to enter easily into the world of Japanese fantasy.

He grew up in Dublin, the city of Charles Maturin, Sheridan Le Fanu and Bram Stoker – who was a contemporary, He was interested in the Irish literary revival and the old Celtic tales and fairy literature of W. B. Yeats and Samuel Ferguson. These traditions and the strong sense of the supernatural in everyday life were of great significance for Hearn when he came to Japan.

Professor Kenji Zenimoto, President of the Hearn Society of Japan, has said: 'The more I read Hearn, the more I am convinced how important his Irish background is.'[8]

Professor Sukehiro Hiragawa, a leading Hearn scholar, finds it satisfying to see Yeats and Hearn together in the same perspective. It is almost certain, he says, that Hearn is going to be redefined and revived with an Irish dimension.[9] His forthcoming book *Rediscovering Lafcadio Hearn*,[9(a)] is eagerly awaited and will undoubtedly provide a balanced and just appraisal of Hearn's work.

The fifteen stories and essays comprised in Hearn's bewitching book *Kokoro*,[10] which was inspired by his time as a journalist in Kobe, treat of the inner rather than the outer life of Japan, for which reason, as Hearn himself says, they have been grouped under the title *Kokoro* meaning 'heart'. The word also signifies mind, in the emotional sense; spirit; courage; resolve; sentiment; affection; and inner meaning – just as we would say in English 'the heart of things'. 'Soul' would also be an analogous concept.

The stories and essays in the book fall into four categories dealing with:

(1) The Japanese character and civilization such as 'The Genius of Japanese Civilization', 'After the War', 'A Glimpse of Tendencies' dealing with the future of Japan and 'A Conservative' dealing with the training of a *samurai*.

(2) Stories about the customs and folklore of the common people of Japan such as 'At a Railway Station', 'A Street Singer', 'By Force of Karma', 'The Nun of the Temple of Amida', 'Haru', 'In Cholera-Time' and 'Kimiko'.

(3) Philosophical thoughts on 'The Idea of Preexistence', 'Ancestor-Worship', the greatness of Japanese art 'From a Travelling Diary' and 'In the Twilight of the Gods'.

(4) An Appendix with Three Popular Ballads which he read before the Asiatic Society of Japan on 17 October 1894.

In all the book runs to 388 pages including 61 pages for the ballads.

Hearn's move from teaching at Kumamoto to journalism, again in the mixed Western and Japanese society of Kobe, led him to reflect on the relative merits and future developments of the two cultures. His thoughts are set out in the major *Kokoro* essay, 'The Genius of Japanese Civilization'. Astonishing as the Japanese victory in the Sino-Japanese War of 1894/5 seemed politically, it was much more astonishing psychologically; for it represented the result of a vast play of capacities with which the race had never been credited abroad, capacities of a very high order. He finds it wonderful that the 'Occidentalization' of Japan showed that the race brain could bear so heavy a shock.

Compared with the West, Hearn thought that Japan's intellectual or emotional life was dainty but small but between the two he found an incalculable difference in emotional volume, in imaginative power, in artistic synthesis. He marvels at the lack of outward material signs of that immense new force Japan has been showing both in productivity and in war. The strength of Japan, like the strength of her ancient faith, needs little material display: both exist where the deepest real power of any great people exists − in the Race Ghost.

Generally speaking, the West constructs for endurance, the Japanese for impermanency. Few things for common use are made in Japan with a view to durability. All the small things used in daily life illustrate the national contentment with impermanency. The dearest spot to all is, not the place of birth, but the place of burial; and there is little that is permanent save the resting-places of the dead and the sites of the ancient shrines.

Buddhism, with its vast doctrine of impermanency, that the universe is an illusion, that only through suppression of every desire can humanity reach the eternal peace, certainly harmonized with the older racial feeling. Though the people never much occupied themselves with the profounder philosophy of the foreign faith, its doctrine of impermanency must, in the course of time, have profoundly influenced the national character.

Hearn is attracted to the simplicity and lack of materialism in everyday life and also the standard of cleanliness, very nice manners and faultless though simple attire.

Critics have tried to make fun of Sir Edwin Arnold's remark that a Japanese crowd smells like geranium-flower. Yet the simile is exact! The perfume is called *jako*, which when sparingly used, might easily be taken for the odour of a musk-geranium. In almost any Japanese assembly including women a slight perfume of *jako* is discernible; for the robes worn have been laid in drawers containing a few grains of *jako*. Except for this delicate scent, Hearn points out that a Japanese crowd is absolutely odourless.[11] Indeed, there should be a good market for *jako* in Ireland!

Japan has given irrefutable proof that enormous development is possible without that stability which we consider necessary in the West. The explanation, he says, is in the race character: 'The relative absence from the national character of egotistical individualism has been the saving of an empire; has enabled a great people to preserve its independence against prodigious odds. Wherefore Japan may well be grateful to her two great religions, the creators and the preservers of her moral power: to Shinto, which taught the individual to think of his Emperor and of his country before thinking either of his own family or of himself; and to Buddhism, which trained him to master regret, to endure pain, and to accept as eternal law the vanishing of things loved and the tyranny of things hated.'[12]

In his essay 'After the War' Hearn says that the military revival of the Empire began with the conquest of China. The future, though clouded, seemed big with promise; and, however grim the obstacles to loftier and more enduring achievements, Japan had neither fears nor doubts. He warned that the future danger was just perhaps in this immense self-confidence. It was not a new feeling created by victory. It was a race feeling which repeated triumphs served only to strengthen.

But as soon as the terms of peace with China had been announced, Russia interfered, securing the help of France and Germany to bully Japan. But the Russian action was suddenly checked by the sinister declaration of British sympathy for Japan. Peace was however secured in a dangerous situation by the return to China of the Liao-Tung Peninsula, in exchange for a compensatory increase of the war indemnity previously exacted. But Japan's national pride had been deeply wounded and the country could scarcely forgive its rulers.

Even then, in 1896, the Russo-Japanese War of 1904-5 was anticipated. Speaking of fallen comrades, Hearn quotes an old man as saying: 'Perhaps by Western people it is thought that the dead never return. But we cannot so think. There are no Japanese dead who do not return. There are none who do not know the way. From China and from Chosen, and out of the bitter sea, all our dead have come back, – all! They are with us now. In every dusk they gather to hear the bugles that called them home and they will hear them also in that day when the armies of the Son of Heaven shall be summoned against Russia.'[13]

In 'A Glimpse of Tendencies' Hearn shows the Japanese resentment to the foreign settlements which controlled foreign trade and exploited Japan in the process. In the beginning, Hearn says that the mutual dislike of Oriental and Occidental was racial, and therefore natural. The irrational violence of prejudice and malignity which developed at a later date was inevitable with the ever-increasing conflict of interests. The barriers of racial feeling, of emotional differentiation, of language, of manners and beliefs, were likely to remain insurmountable for centuries. Though instances of warm friendship, due to the mutual attraction of exceptional natures able to divine each other intuitively, might be cited, the foreigner, as a general rule, understands the Japanese quite as little as the Japanese understands him.

Hearn predicts that with further organizational improvement the Japanese could reasonably expect to get foreign trade under control as the next great step towards the realization of the national desire, *Japan only for the Japanese*. But the foreign settlements remain constant sources of irritation; and their commercial conquest by untiring national effort would alone satisfy the country, and prove even better than the war with China, Japan's real place among the nations. That conquest, he thinks, will certainly be achieved, as indeed it was, in the new century.

Hearn also points out that even Christian mission-work must be left to native missionaries; for just as Buddhism never took definite form in Japan until the teaching of its doctrines was left entirely to Japanese priests, – so Christianity would never take any fixed shape till it has been so remodelled as to harmonize with the emotional and social life of the race. Even thus remodelled it can scarcely hope to exist except in the form of a few small sects.

On the future of Japan Hearn predicts great changes both for better and for worse without dwelling on the grim probabilities of war, or internal disorder leading to a resurrected Shogunate in modern uniform. But Hearn ventures qualified predictions based on the reasonable supposition that the race will continue to assimilate its new-found knowledge with the best relative consequences.

Physically, he thinks that the Japanese will become, before the close of the twentieth century, much superior to what they are now, but moral improvement is hardly to be expected – rather the reverse.

Untruthfulness, dishonesty and brutal crime would steadily increase. Hearn feels that it cannot be maintained that the standard of chastity and moral conditions in Japan were worse than in the West. In one respect they were certainly better; for the virtue of Japanese wives was generally in all ages above suspicion.

The statement has been made that there is no word for chastity in the Japanese language. Hearn says this is true in the same sense only that we might say there is no word for chastity in the English language, – because such words as honour, virtue, purity, chastity have been adopted into English from other languages. Open any good Japanese-English dictionary and you will find many words for chastity. Just as it would be ridiculous to deny that the word 'chastity' is modern English, because it came to us through the French from the Latin, so it is ridiculous to deny that Chinese moral terms, adopted in the Japanese tongue more than a thousand years ago, are Japanese today. The statement, like a majority of missionary statements on these subjects, is otherwise misleading; for the reader is left to infer the absence of an adjective as well as a noun, – and the purely Japanese adjectives signifying chaste are numerous. The word most commonly used applies to both sexes, – and has the old Japanese sense of firm, strict, resisting, honourable. The deficiency of abstract terms in a language by no means implies the deficiency of concrete moral ideas, a fact which has been vainly pointed out to missionaries more than once.[14] It should be noted that these were, of course, English and American missionaries, not Irish. Irish priests, in fact, did not go to Japan until after World War II.

Hearn also predicted that intellectually there would doubtless be great progress but that in other respects, some temporary retrogression is to be looked for. Just so certainly as Japan has attempted that which is above the normal limit of her powers, so certainly she must fall back to that limit, or rather, below it. Such retrogression will be natural as well as necessary. But Japan must develop her own soul; she cannot borrow another.

Finally, Hearn considers that Japan will remember her foreign teachers more kindly in the twentieth century:

But she will never feel towards the Occident, as she felt towards

China before the Meiji era, the reverential respect due by ancient custom to a beloved instructor; for the wisdom of China was voluntarily sought, while that of the West was thrust upon her by violence. She will have some Christian sects of her own; but she will not remember our American and English missionaries as she remembers even now those great Chinese priests who once educated her youth, and she will not preserve relics of our sojourn, carefully wrapped in septuple coverings of silk, and packed away in dainty whitewood boxes, because we had no new lesson of beauty to teach her – nothing by which to appeal to her emotions.[15]

The essay 'A Conservative' is a long study of the effects of history and foreign intrusion on a young dispossessed *samurai* who was trained to be fearless, courteous, self-denying, despising pleasure and ready at an instant's notice to give his life for love, loyalty, or honour.

Both at home, and in wanderings in Europe and America his way of life was undermined by exposure to Western life and achievements. But its wastefulness impressed him more than its greed of pleasure and its capacity for pain. Western civilization and religious teaching taught him to understand the worth and beauty of his own. When he returned to Japan, eventually through the port of Yokohama glimpsing Mount Fuji, as Hearn himself had six years previously on his first arrival in Japan, what attracted the young *samurai* most was not anything of the modern Japan, he saw the Old.[16]

It is perhaps by his Japanese folk-tales that Hearn is best remembered and those in *Kokoro* rate among the best he wrote. Professor Hirakawa has singled out 'At a Railway Station' as one that appeals particularly to Japanese, exemplifying Hearn's stylistic artistry and capacity for cultural interpretation. The text of the story is as follows:-

KOKORO
I
AT A RAILWAY STATION
Seventh day of the sixth Month;-
twenty-sixth of Meiji (*i.e. 7 June 1893*)

Yesterday a telegram from Fukuoka announced that a desperate criminal captured there would be brought for trial to Kumamoto to-day, on the train due at noon. A Kumamoto policeman had gone to Fukuoka to take the prisoner in charge.

Four years ago a strong thief entered some house by night in the Street of the Wrestlers, terrified and bound the inmates, and carried away a number of valuable things. Tracked skilfully by police, he was captured within twenty-four hours – even before he could dispose of his plunder. But as he was being taken to the police station he burst his bonds, snatched the sword of his captor, killed him and escaped. Nothing more was heard of him until last week.

Then a Kumamoto detective, happening to visit the Fukuoka prison, saw among the toilers a face that had been four years photographed upon his brain.

"Who is that man?" he asked the guard.

"A thief," was the reply – "registered here as Kusabé."

The detective walked up to the prisoner and said:

"Kusabé is not your name. Nomura Teïchi, you are needed in Kumamoto for murder."

The felon confessed all.

I went with a great throng of people to witness the arrival at the station. I expected to hear and see anger; I even feared possibilities of violence. The murdered officer had been much liked; his relatives would certainly be among the spectators; and a Kumamoto crowd is not very gentle. I also though to find many police on duty. My anticipations were wrong.

The train halted in the usual scene of hurry and noise – scurry and clatter of passengers wearing geta – screaming of boys wanted to sell Japanese newspapers and Kumamoto lemonade. Outside the barrier we waited for nearly five minutes. Then, pushed through the wicket by a police sergeant, the prisoner appeared – a large, wild-looking man, with head bowed down, and arms fastened behind his back. Prisoner and guard both halted in front of the wicket; and the people pressed forward to see – but in silence. The the officer called out:

"Sugihara San! Sugihara O-Kibi! Is she present?"

A slight, small woman standing near me, with a child on her back, answered, "Hai!" and advanced through the press. This was the widow of the murdered man; the child she carried was his son. At a wave of the officer's hand the crowd fell back, so as to leave a clear space about the prisoner and his escort. In that space the woman with the child stood facing the murderer. The hush was of death.

Not to the woman at all, but to the child only, did the officer then speak. He spoke low, but so clearly that I could catch every syllable:

"Little one, this is the man who killed your father four years ago. You had not yet been born; you were in your mother's womb. That you have no father to love you now is the doing of this man. Look at him – [here the officer, putting a hand to the prisoner's chin, sternly forced him to lift his eyes]- look well at him, little boy! Do not be afraid. It is painful; but it is your duty. Look at him!"

Over the mother's shoulder the boy gazed with eyes widely open, as in fear, then he began to sob; then tears came; but steadily and obediently he still looked–looked–looked – straight into the cringing face.

The crowd seemed to have stopped breathing.

I saw the prisoner's features distort; I saw him suddenly dash himself down upon his knees despite his fetters, and beat his face into the dust, crying out the while in a passion of hoarse remorse that made one's heart shake:

"Pardon! Pardon! Pardon me, little one! That I did – not for hate was it done, but mad fear only, in my desire to escape. Very, very wicked I have been; great unspeakable wrong have I done you! But now for my sin I go to die. I wish to die; I am glad to die! Therefore, O little one, be pitiful! – forgive me!"

The child still cried silently. The officer raised the shaking criminal; the dumb crowd parted left and right to let them by. Then, quite suddenly, the whole multitude began to sob. And as the bronzed guardian passed, I saw what I had never seen before – what few men ever see – what I shall probably never see again – the tears of a Japanese policeman.

The crowd ebbed, and left me musing on the strange morality of the spectacle. Here was justice unswerving yet compassionate – forcing knowledge of a crime by the pathetic witness of its simplest result. Here was the desperate remorse, praying only for pardon before death. And here was a populace – perhaps the most dangerous in the Empire when angered – comprehending all, touched by all, satisfied with the contrition and the shame, and filled, not with wrath, but only with the great sorrow of the sin – through simple deep experience of the difficulties of life and the weaknesses of human nature.

But the most significant, because the most Oriental, fact of the episode was that the appeal to remorse had been made through the criminal's sense of fatherhood – that potential love of children which is so large a part of the soul of every Japanese.

There is a story that the most famous of all Japanese robbers, Ishikawa Goëmon, once by night entering a house to kill and steal, was charmed by the smile of a baby which reached out hands to him, and that he remained playing with the little creature until all chance of carrying out his purpose was lost.

It is not hard to believe this story. Every year the police records tell of compassion shown to children by professional criminals: Some months ago a terrible murder case was reported in the local papers – the slaughter of a household by robbers. Seven persons had been literally hewn to pieces while asleep; but the police discovered a little boy quite unharmed, crying alone in a pool of blood; and they found evidence unmistakable that the men who slew must have taken great care not to hurt the child.[17]

The tale typifies Hearn's skill as a reporter and his technique as a story-teller, appealing strongly to the reader's sensitivities and strengthened by use of the first person. It is also a remarkable penetration of the Japanese mind. What Hearn wanted to convey to Western readers, according to Professor Hirakawa, was the Japanese heart, *kokoro*, the Japanese mind in the emotional sense. Hearn's intellectual approach was complemented by an emotional approach.

'At a Railway Station' appears to have been based on an article in the *Kyushu Nichinichi Shimbun* of 22 April 1893. A literal translation of the relevant part reads as follows:-

> The policeman in charge stopped the prisoner, took off the prisoner's hat, and turned to the family of the dead Miyazaki, saying:
>
> 'Look at this man. It is he who killed Mr Miyazaki seven years ago. This man is the criminal who killed your husband; this man is the criminal who killed your father. Your heart must be burning with resentment, but it is now time for you to resign yourselves to the fate.'
>
> The widow and the mother, recalling the days past, could not look at the prisoner's face any more, knelt down on the spot and shamelessly cried in the presence of others. Touched by the sight, spectators also wiped tears from their eyes. The son of Miyazaki

(who had been in his mother's womb when his father was killed, is now seven years old) did not know what the problem was. A look of wonderment appeared on his face, as he watched his mother and his grandmother weep. Then the policeman addressed the child:

'Because you were in your mother's womb, you did not know it. But this is the burglar who ran away, killing Mr Miyazaki, your father. Look at his face. Take a good look at his face.'

Though he was young, the child, hearing that this was the bad man, murderer of his father, raised his eyes and gazed with indignation at the face of the criminal, and shed tears in spite of himself. A hush fell over the crowd as they viewed the scene, and the usually tearless policeman coughed to conceal his emotion. The criminal blinked his eyes and said: 'You are the bereaved family of Mr Miyazaki. Although I put him to the sword in my desire to escape, I had no grudge or hatred against him. I was able to flee from this city, Kumamoto, at that time, but the Way of Heaven could not be challenged. I am now arrested to my great shame, and am soon to be hanged at the gallows. You may think that I am a hateful, loathsome wretch; but talk is of no use now. I am going to be fairly punished and justice will be done, so please don't be worried anymore.'

The policeman then placed the hat on the prisoner and took him away to the prison.[18]

The modifications made by Hearn to the original report will be apparent and indicate his literary skill.

The Austrian poet and dramatist, Hugo von Hofmannsthal, in a critical appreciation, says:

> 'At a Railway Station' is an anecdote, almost a trivial anecdote, not exempt from sentimentalism. But it was written by one who knew how to write, and what is more, it was felt beforehand by one who knew how to feel.[19]

Hearn also penetrates to the heart of things Japanese in stories such as 'Kimiko', the name of a beautiful geisha who learned about the power of beauty and weakness of passion, the craft of promises and the worth of indifference; and all the folly and evil in the hearts of men. Fulfilling the Japanese idea of beauty, Kimiko became a fashionable mania – one of the great sights and sensations of the time. But she allowed no one to imagine himself a special favourite. Then a 'fool' tried to kill himself because of her and she nursed him back to 'foolishness'.

Kimiko loved this youth but between her and other geishas there was a difference of gentle blood and she refused to marry him, saying: 'In the knowing of wrong, I am very, very much wiser than you. . . Never shall I be your wife to become your shame.' In the period of the tenth month, Kimiko disappeared, never to be seen again.[20]

A handsome young Buddhist priest has a similar problem in 'By Force of Karma'. He was. . . extremely handsome. . . much too handsome for a priest, the women said. He looked like one of those beautiful figures of Amida made by the great Buddhist statuaries of other days. . .

> The women did not think about his virtue or his learning only: he possessed the unfortunate power to attract them, independently of his own will, as a mere man. He was admired by them in ways not holy. . . And the more he shrank from the admiration of the time, or the adulation of the unabashed, the more the persecution increased, till it became the torment of his life.

Eventually, he received a letter 'written in that woman-language in which every syllable is a little caress of humility'. It was more than he could bear:

> The hour was early; the night windy and dark. . . he hurried out into the blackness, and reached the railway exactly in time to kneel down in the middle of the track, facing the roar and rush of the express from Kobe.[21]

In 'A Street Singer' Hearn describes a peasant woman who was ugly and blind but had a miracle of a voice, unutterably touching in its penetrating sweetness. Her husband was paralyzed but she supported him and her little son, because whenever she sang the people cried and gave her coppers and food. Hearn finds in her voice qualities able to make appeal to something larger than the sum of the experience of one race, – to something wide as human life, and ancient as the knowledge of good and evil.[22]

In his philosophical essays in *Kokoro* Hearn discusses his continuing preoccupations with the concepts of pre-existence and ancestor-worship. It is the idea of pre-existence, he says, more than any other which permeates the whole mental being of the Far East. The interpretative power of Buddhism and the singular accord of its theories with the facts of modern science, appear especially in that domain of psychology whereof Herbert Spencer has been the greatest of all explorers. No small part of our psychological life is composed of feelings which Western theology could never explain.[23]

The validity of a union of Spencerian evolutionism and Buddhism, which Hearn sought to establish in *Kokoro*, and in other writings such as *Exotics and Retrospectives* (1898),[24] has not been accepted but his theoretical treatises show that he was far more than just a writer of folktales and travel sketches.

On ancestor-worship Hearn maintains that the doctrines of Shinto,

> . . . are not in the least degree more irreconcilable with modern science than are the doctrines of Orthodox Christianity. . . . They conflict less with our human ideas of justice; and, like the Buddhist doctrine of karma, they offer some very striking analogies with the scientific facts of heredity – analogies which prove Shinto to contain an element of truth as profound as any element of truth in any of the world's great religions. Stated in the simplest possible form, the peculiar element of truth in Shinto is the belief that the world of the living is directly governed by the world of the dead. . . . This hypothesis no modern thinker can declare irrational, since it can claim justification from the scientific doctrine of psychological evolution, according to which each living brain represents the structural work of innumerable dead lives, – each character a more or less imperfectly balanced sum of countless dead experiences with good and evil.[25]

Hearn points out that in the West we have no common faith in the existence of an active spiritual relation between our ancestors and ourselves. Even on All Souls Night the dead are not considered as related to the living by any stronger bond than memory and they are thought of rather with fear than love.[26]

In Japan, the feeling towards the dead is utterly different. It is a feeling of grateful and reverential love. It is probably the most profound and powerful of the emotions of the race, that which especially directs national life and shapes national character. Patriotism belongs to it. Filial piety depends upon it. Family love is rooted in it. Loyalty is based upon it. . . . Even among the sceptical students of a new generation the old sentiments are still uttered: 'Never must we cause shame to our ancestors;' 'It is our duty to give honour to our ancestors'. The Japanese never think of an ancestor as having become 'only a memory': their dead are alive.[27]

Hearn's treatment of Japanese civilization and the role of ancestor-worship were pursued in greater depth in his final synthesis *Japan: An Attempt at Interpretation* published posthumously in 1904.[28] While perhaps being somewhat uneven in structure, *Kokoro* a century later still ranks as one of Hearn's finest works comparable with *Glimpses of Unfamiliar Japan* (1894),[29] *Kwaidan* (1904)[30] and *Japan: An Attempt at Interpretation*.[31] It is a wide panorama of touching stories and folk-tales, shrewd comments on the Japanese character and civilization and studies of Far Eastern philosophical concepts.

Kokoro was a timely publication coming just after Japan's victory over China in 1895 when the West was increasingly interested in Japan and the Japanese mentality. Exemplifying Hearn's artistic style and the gem-like quality of his stories, it is, in my opinion, as fine a piece of writing as will be found anywhere in the English language. It was translated into ten European languages. *Kokoro* shows how Hearn was able to identify with the common people of Japan and think their thoughts and how he qualifies as a shrewd interpreter of the inner life of Japan. Professor Hirakawa says that 'Objectively Hearn is, in Japan, the best known of foreign writers who have ever come to Japan. To many Japanese Hearn is a symbol of true appreciation of the Japanese character. You may say that Hearn's writings have dated. But compared to others who came to Japan from the middle of the nineteenth century through the middle of the twentieth century, Hearn's position is distinctly high... Hearn is still very popular in Japan'.[32]

Although much has changed in Japan since the days when Hearn fell in love with the country, the 'hints and echoes of Japanese inner life' portrayed in *Kokoro* still have a remarkable truth about them, for the Japanese spirit has changed considerably less than the material conditions of Japanese life.

In conclusion, I should like to read a poem entitled *A Shrine for Lafcadio Hearn (1850-1904)*, composed by Sean Dunne, who passed away to tragically and untimely at the age of 39 in August 1995 just as he was beginning to realize his great literary potential. This is in memory of them both (see pp. 5-6).

27

The Achievement of Lafcadio Hearn

ALLEN E. TUTTLE

———————————— oOo ————————————

Lafcadio Hearn's literary reputation has been marked, not only by the adoration of small cults, but by the scramble of book collectors, angry words and recriminations, a miasma of legend and lore, and a bibliographical nightmare of editions from the world's publishing centres. In the confusion, Lafcadio Hearn has come perilously close to being remembered more for his life than for his work. He has been variously classified as aesthete, decadent, folk-lorist, economic rebel, moralist, and even as the Lord Byron of Japan. Admired for his sensitive, impressionistic prose and his avoidance of hard, ugly realism, he has also been condemned for a lack of form and for overwriting.

In the 1890s and the early part of this century his essays and tales from Japan stirred the imaginations of thousands of readers, engendering poetic conceptions of Japan that linger even today, in spite of the fulminations of some critics on both sides of the world that Hearn was reporting, not on Japan, but on his own private utopia. In America, during the last war, he was blamed for having set up in the public mind unrealistic stereotypes of the Japanese, thereby contributing to the difficulties in assessing the character of the enemy. It might seem that this present decade, bewildered by two world wars, the H-bomb, and a torrent of technological wonders would find Hearn's little world hopelessly quaint; but in Japan new editions, as well as books and articles about him continue to come from the presses, and in America since the last war there have been likewise numerous articles, some reprinting of his work, a good biography, and a novel based on his life. In America this interest has been stimulated in part by the war and the consequent occupation of Japan. Most of the blind adulation, the fierce partisanship, and the rancours of old quarrels have subsided now to permit us to see the work of this strange literary figure in some perspective.

Hearn still perplexes the makers of anthologies and literary histories. His hybrid and exotic character, together with the coincidence of his mature literary period with pivotal years in literary history, poses special problems for scholars with an urge for classification, for Hearn fits a literary niche as awkwardly as he once fitted his bourgeois social niche in Cincinnati and New Orleans. He did not spring from the native American soil that nurtured Whitman, Howells, and Twain; nor from the Brahmin tradition that endowed the names of Longfellow, Holmes, and Lowell with social and literary standing. His was a name derived from a root meaning to wander, stray, become outlaw. If there are such things as race ghosts – and Hearn believed there were – he was multiply haunted by the intermingling of Irish, English, Greek, and perhaps Gypsy ancestors. Born in 1850 on Santa Maura in the Ionian Isles, he referred to himself variously throughout his life as Greek, Latin, and Oriental. Through the lack of a more fitting and generally recognized international classification, he is sometimes included in English and sometimes in American literary histories.

His boyhood was spent in Ireland and England. After an erratic two years in France, he came to America at the age of nineteen and remained twenty-one years without acquiring citizenship. Not until he was over forty years old did the problem of national attachment assume any importance with him, and then he relinquished British citizenship to become a subject of the Mikado. To the youth of nineteen years who had proved intractable to his Irish grand-aunt and to the French Jesuits alike, America in 1869 was land of fresh beginnings. He symbolized his break with the past by dropping his first name, Patrick, and taking a second and very un-American-sounding name, to become euphoniously 'Lafcadio Hearn'.

Fleeing to a new country, the rebellious young Hearn could not escape completely from the past. He could not escape the gnawing insecurity of an orphan cut off from his family and caste. From childhood he carried the idealization of his dark-skinned mother, whom he never saw after he was six years old. It was her race-soul in him, he believed, that responded in a ghostly way to the beautiful and artistic in life. He could not escape the hypersensitivity and shyness accompanying the consciousness of his short stature and limited eyesight. He could not elude the ghosts who had first visited him in early childhood, striking terror in his heart and making permanently real for him the supernatural. Later, they whispered through the palm trees in the tropical moonlight on Martinique and haunted the rational superstructure of Herbert Spencer's Synthetic Philosophy. No one can understand Hearn, his friend Chamberlain said, without taking into account his belief in ghosts. A shy dreamer devoted to the goddess of beauty, he was 'tormented by grim realities' and ill-equipped to begin life in his new surroundings. His first years there, filled with suffering, were to incubate a life-long aversion to competitive Western civilization.

The young Hearn did not achieve a sense of security in America until 1873, when he became a regular contributor to the *Cincinnati Enquirer*. Through his journalistic career in Cincinnati and later in New Orleans, he retained considerable freedom in the choice of subject and treatment. Though sheer necessity forced him to conform to the exigencies of practical journalism, many times he seemed to be scarcely naturalized intellectually. He was most at home when some trifle of the day provided him with the pretext for digressing on an exotic theme. Then he could lead his readers down recondite paths into little-known corners of history or lift them away into an imaginative world far removed from Cincinnati and New Orleans. At such times he could draw upon his wide acquaintance with books, particularly his own strange library. His literary ideal was French, and his literary enthusiasms were alien to bourgeois America of the 1870s and 80s. He found his most congenial subjects, not on Main Street, but in Negro sections and along the levee; in the back rooms of Chinese laundries, where the children of Tien Hia sang to him songs of their native land; and in the proud Creole district, where old-world customs were undergoing decay; and in the dimly-lighted police stations, into which were brought muscular men and mysterious women with vague backgrounds of lust and murder; and in the backways of Louisiana swamp land, with its primitive settlements of Tagalog-speaking Filipinos.

One of the most characteristic aspects of his work was a gothic element. In Cincinnati he wrote articles on the advantages of cremation, the work of body-snatchers, dealers in second-hand tombstones, the technique of animal slaughter, grisly murders, and the like. Hearn was never to abandon completely this strain. It lost much of its early crudity in the 1880s, when he was falling increasingly under the spell of the French Impressionists; then the gothic was touched with verbal delicacy and a ghostly shudder. The strain recurred, saturated with Japanese antiquity, in some of his later folk tales from Japan. Closely related to the gothic in Hearn's early American work were exotic and erudite elements. A glimpse at the bibliography in his first published volume, *Stray Leaves from Strange Literature*, reveals the range of his exoticism: translations from the Arabic, Persian, Hindustani, Chinese and Icelandic; an *Anthologie Erotique*; a French work on Esquimaux mythology; a collection of legends from the South Seas; the Talmud. He wrote to a friend: 'I have pledged me to the worship of the Odd, the Queer, the Strange, the Exotic, the Monstrous. It quite suits my temperament.'

Whatever his subject, he expressed himself with a fastidiousness comparable to Flaubert's, worrying over just the right word here and a semicolon there. He worked for warmth of colour, richness of imagery, and a poetic suggestiveness of word and phrase. His lush, introverted, impressionistic, sensuous English was unique in American journalism of the 1880s. This heightened style is found in perhaps its most polished form in his collection of weirdly exotic tales entitled *Some Chinese Ghosts* (1887). Rejecting the realism of Zola, he declared that 'the law of true art . . . is to seek beauty wherever it is to be found and separate it from the dross of life as gold from ore'. Whatever emotional, intellectual, and spiritual centre Lafcadio Hearn possessed up to the time he became a convert to Spencer's Synthetic Philosophy was that of beauty, beauty for its own sake.

In the early 1880s his newspaper writing revealed a marked interest in science. In 1883 he wrote that he was doing nearly all the scientific editorials for the newspaper. He was reading Darwin, Fiske, Romanes, Vignole, Haeckel, a little Spencer, and others. His scientific knowledge, however, was sketchy and often diluted by his own fancy. His reading of Spencer's *First Principles* was an electrifying experience, and from the time he completed it, probably early in 1886, to the end of his life, he was an avowed disciple of its author. The enthusiasm he had for Spencer did not, as with many of his other enthusiasms, grow dim with the passing years. Old friends dropped out of his affection, new idols supplanted old ones in his literary pantheon, and his creative work took on a succession of scenic backgrounds, but Spencer survived all change. An admirer of the heightened style of the French Romanticists, Hearn nevertheless applied himself to the flat, colourless prose of the Synthetic Philosophy, finding it 'puissant, compact, and melodious'; a sceptic by temperament, he accepted with childlike faith the teachings of his philosophical master.

That part of *First Principles* which made the strongest initial impact on him was the exposition of 'the Unknowable', which gave him a faith in something beyond phenomena and deepened his sense of mystery in the universe. The Unknowable became for Hearn both god and the permeating power behind man and nature. He tried to express a sense of this mystery behind the evolutionary process in *Chita*, which appeared in book form in 1889. Based on an after-dinner tale of George W. Cable, it deals with the destruction by hurricane of a resort and most of its pleasure-seekers. It embodies an estimate of the terrible expense of existence. Over all the destruction and death, life and love, broods the mysterious Unknowable. Related to *Chita* in its expression of the power of nature is *Two Years in the French West Indies* (1890), with its thrill and awe of beauty, which is the 'inexplicable communication of the mind with the Unknowable'. This account of his two-year respite from the higher civilization is saved from mere journalism by the depth and sensitivity of his perception and his attempt to understand the people rather than be satisfied with the usual curiosities of a globe-trotter.

In the spring of 1890 Hearn set off for Japan. He had intended staying only a few months to gather literary materials, but he lived on there until his death in 1904.

Thirteen volumes of impressions, analyses, and folk-tales came from his pen during his fourteen years there, not to mention the posthumously published lectures, translations, and journalistic pieces. Avoiding the Western port cities, he first settled in the isolated province of Izumo, where he absorbed those naive and strangely beautiful impressions of people and scenes which appeared in print among *Glimpses of Unfamiliar Japan*. There at the provincial capital he experienced a sense of security in the respect of the governor, the devotion of fellow teachers and students in the school at which he was teaching, and the love and comfort of a samurai woman he married. 'I am thinking,' he wrote to an American friend, 'that the East will keep me bespelled forever as Merlin was kept in Broceliande.'

With his second publication on Japan, *Out of the East* (1895), Hearn established a loose, congenial literary pattern. Aware that his talent was not of the kind to sustain long, integrated pieces of work, he produced a succession of anthologies containing bits of legend and lore; observations on the Japanese character, illustrated by story, verses, proverbs, or a contemporary event; reveries and speculations, often on some psychological curiosity, and often combining science and fancy. Such is the composition of *Kokoro, Gleanings in Buddha-Fields, Exotics and Retrospectives*, and the remainder of the authorized volumes except the last, *Japan – an Attempt at Interpretation*.

These miscellanies are likely to be deceptive, suggesting to the casual reader merely literary gossamer spun by a dilettante out of random raw materials. Fragile and ghostly many of the pieces are (often Hearn laboured hardest over the slightest ones), but they belie the strength of convictions that flow through his work and give it a kind of integration. For Hearn the immemorial customs, the superstitions, the popular art, and religion were inextricably bound up with the race-spirit, Shinto and Buddhism being especially valuable keys to the soul of Japan. Buddhism, he believed, embraced a theory of spiritual evolution reconcilable with physical evolution as taught in the West. Never did he forget the power – biological, psychological, and sociological – of the dead over the living and the mysterious power of inherited memory. Spencer's philosophy pushed back intellectual and emotional horizons for him, increasing and deepening the mysteries of life, and yet offering, as in the *Sociology*, the best rationalization of life's phenomena. The focus of his interest, however, was not on any scholarly or artistic aspects of his adopted land, nor even on the charming externals of life there, but on the heart of the people. An alien could never hope to understand it thoroughly; only by indirections, by patience, long study, observation, and sympathy could he divine something of its ghostly composition.

The people in backwoods Japan were, he felt, the happiest in the world. Unspoiled by competitive Western civilization, their lives were characterized by simplicity, aesthetic sensitivity, kindness, cheerfulness, courtesy, and self-effacement. As he moved among these people he felt that somehow time had turned back for him, that he was witnessing a culture older than that of ancient Greece. Evolution had virtually ceased for them. During more than two hundred and fifty years of the Tokugawa Shogunate the isolated nation had reached what Spencer would call an equilibrium; changes had been slight, and life had settled down into a fixed pattern including an ethical system superior to anything known in the West. Hearn knew, however, that he was at the deathwatch of Old Japan; he knew also that he would never like the young Japan that was already showing considerable vitality in the larger cities, where he had to live most of the time as a teacher. He hastened to record his insights into the soul of the old order.

As an avowed evolutionist, he admitted that Japan would have to change if she were to survive; she would have to step into the flow of evolution and make adjustments quickly. she would have to develop her industry, train scientists, prepare for armed aggression against her, and even discard some of the amiable facets of her character. These changes he discusses in *Japan – an Attempt at Interpretation* (1904), his most ambitious analysis of the factors operating in the national life. There was an ambivalence in Hearn between what he loved and what he knew, intellectually, must be. He went to Spencer for the latter, but his heart was not in it. He could not turn affectionately to New Japan, with its vulgar scepticism, vanity, aggressiveness, and embarrassment for having risen so lately from its old-fashioned past. 'Now to my poor mind,' he wrote to a Japanese friend, 'all that was good and noble and true was Old Japan. . . .'

A casual reader coming upon one of Hearn's essays in praise of the ethical and artistic values nurtured by the old order might well wonder how, with such conservatism, Hearn could ever be called a bohemian. It was as a young man that he earned the epithet, but even in America he was never the merry madcap given over to the carefree life of the senses; his bohemianism, though it exalted the sensuous experiences of the moment, possessed a vein of deepening seriousness that prevented him from becoming a mere dabbler in sensation. The New Orleans bohemian came to understand in Japan that ethical beauty is superior to sensuous beauty; and as his thinking matured, his literary style, pruned of its extravagances, became firmer, more direct. He could look back to his American days and deprecate his 'Period of Gush'.

Much has been made of Hearn as restless literary adventurer, and yet his spirit was not adventurous in the usual sense of the word; nor was his restlessness simply a reaction to humdrum security. In America he felt he had not been properly endowed by nature to take his place in a world of broad shoulders and strong wills; temperamentally he was an alien there. A basic insecurity drove him to seek not risks, but security: that is what he sought all his life. Without personal qualities for success in the struggle for existence he sought security in some accomplishment removed from commercial competition. Without the background of a solid education he turned to the security of the odd and the exotic. Uneasy in his successive environments he longed for a refuge that would both stimulate and comfort him.

Sometimes Hearn created his own world out of whatever was strangely beautiful and far away. His admirers still mine the American work, including many posthumously published volumes of his journalistic writing, for these highly-coloured pieces that stand out strangely against the homespun American background of the 1870s and 80s. But if Hearn was an exotic, he was also a Victorian, stimulated from the beginning of his career by current scientific ideas. During his soul-struggle in Japan over the impact of evolutionary science and industrialism on traditional spiritual values (for Eastern as well as Western culture was being shaken), he emerges as an intellectual and spiritual first cousin of the great English Victorians. Today's reader finds much in the Japanese work that is quaint, but he finds, too, some strikingly prophetic insights and modern judgements: realistic assessments of the struggle for power in the Orient, notice of an awakened China, a distrust of Russian imperialism. Much of Hearn's interpretive work is so attached to the Synthetic Philosophy – the inheritance of acquired characteristics, for instance – that it is subject to the same objections made against Spencerism, though many a reader may discover that there is more vitality in the Hearn-Spencer concepts than he had realized. The reader with historical imagination may marvel that with limited scholarly materials and without professional training in sociology, Hearn accomplished the interpretation he did, combining science and sensibility. Most readers, however, probably prefer Hearn's early impressions of Old Japan – ghostly, delicate, seemingly spontaneous, and partly compounded of their author's idealism. Japan may never again seem so beautiful.

28

Some New Hearn Primary Source Material

PAUL MURRAY

———————— oOo ————————

Following the publication of my biography, *A Fantastic Journey: The Life and Literature of Lafcadio Hearn*, late in 1993, I was contacted by Sir Derek Oulton, a Hearn descendant and former distinguished public servant now at Cambridge University, who very kindly provided me with a list of names, addresses and telephone numbers of other surviving members of the family with material of possible interest.

Through this means I came into possession of copies of collections of primary source material which had been inherited by various Hearn family members and which had not been available to scholars when I wrote my biography.

The material, most of which remains in private collections, is presented in categories rather than reflecting the various collections — letters, diary, memoranda, and illustrative material, following a rough, but not invariable, chronological order in the various categories.

The material is intended to be a resource for scholars and serious students of Hearn and I have not therefore explained the context of individual items (this would inflate an already extensive piece to an impossible length), although I do attempt to draw attention to certain elements of significance.

I owe a particular debt of gratitude to all those who have helped me in this endeavour and who have placed their collections at my disposal, especially Sir Derek Oulton, Basil Hearn, Denis Stephens, Joan Murphy, Daniel Hearn, Shane Hearn and Christopher Oulton.

I am especially grateful to Toki Koizumi, Lafcadio's grandson, for his permission to quote from hitherto unpublished material written by his grandfather, and for his unstinting help and encouragement.

I should also say that only new Hearn family material is covered here; I do not attempt to deal with other new primary sources which have become available elsewhere.

Some New Hearn Primary Source Material

LETTERS

Letter from Susan Maria Hearn (Lafcadio's great-aunt on his father's side) to 'My Dearest Robert' [Hearn] (Lafcadio's uncle), Lower Gardiner Street, Dublin 12 June [1850],* Wednesday.

This letter reveals a very religious streak in Susan as she tells Robert to pray to and to trust God. She refers to an acquaintance having recently received a letter from Charles [Bush Hearn, Lafcadio's father]:

> She had a letter from Charles yesterday, he does not yet know when he will be in Ireland or in what post he will be stationed.

[* The letter is attributed to 1850 as 12 June 1850 fell on a Wednesday; it seems strange that Charles was in Limerick later in the month and all was settled so soon; see following letter.]

Letter from Susan Maria Hearn to Robert [Thomas Hearn], 26/6/1850

This letter begins as follows:

> We have been in a great state of excitement all the last week – Sir Robert in town and [?] dear Charles arrived on Monday 17th – and left us on Saturday 22nd – and on Friday 21st just as we were going to bed who should knock at the door but our dear Richard [Hearn, Lafcadio's painter uncle] who is with us now looking uncommonly well and in good spirits – he left Paris to spend some time with Charles in Chatham but Charles was ordered off before he got there and was obliged to leave this the very day Richard came – Charles is most happily placed in Limerick – and I believe Richard will proceed there and stop some time with him before he returns to Paris.

Considering that this was written the day before Lafcadio was born, it describes his father caught up in a whirl of military and family activity while his aunt gives no hint of being aware that he had left behind in Greece a wife, Rosa, who was about to bear his second child. In my opinion, it offers powerful reinforcement for the view put forward in my book that Charles Bush Hearn had abandoned her and his children, had not told his family or his military superiors of his marriage and was not the moving spirit behind their eventual turning up in Dublin[1]

LETTERS FROM LAFCADIO HEARN TO MINNIE ATKINSON

This collection of Lafcadio's letters to his half-sister, Minnie Atkinson, have not, I believe, been at the disposal of Hearn scholars since Nina Kennard's 1912 biography.[2] Sight of the originals does not radically alter our knowledge derived from Kennard but does add some new information. I propose to comment only on this new information.

Letter 1
No address, Undated

Only a portion of this letter survives and is dealt with in Kennard[3]

Letter 2
No address, Undated

Hearn claims that he was 'sent to a horrid Roman Catholic School, kept by a hateful, venomous-hearted, bigoted old maid. I was very brutally treated there for several years'.

This school must have been before Ushaw, the Roman Catholic boarding school in England which he attended from 1863 to 1867. Whatever its faults, Ushaw was not kept by an old maid of any description! Neither was the Institution Ecclesiastique, near Rouen in France, which previous biographers have speculated he may have attended prior to Ushaw. If he had been at this school for several years, it was most likely to have been in Dublin. He does not say if it was a boarding or day school; most likely it was the latter.

He goes on to say that 'meanwhile' (ie, while he was at the school), Mrs Brenane became acquainted with Henry Molyneux, the Svengali-like figure who gained dominance over Mrs Brenane, the great-aunt who had assumed responsibility for Lafcadio's upbringing: this certainly places the school before Ushaw because Molyneux was well in control of Mrs Brenane's affairs by the time Lafcadio was sent there.

Lafcadio makes no mention of it being in France although later in the letter he says he was withdrawn from school in France at the time of Mrs Brenane's 'ruin' but we know that he was in Ushaw at that stage. This also diminishes the possibility that he might have gone to France, to stay with his Uncle Richard, for example, after he was withdrawn from Ushaw.

This information is in line with my previous reconstruction of Hearn's education[4] that he went to some form of preparatory school in Ireland before Ushaw, and is, I think, a further indication that he was not educated in France for any significant period of his life.

The unreliability of Hearn's claims is, however, underlined by another passage in the letter, where he claims that Henry Molyneux had been brought up by the Jesuits. We know that he was educated by diocesan priests at Old Hall, Ware.[5] Lafcadio's obsession with the Jesuits (we should bear in mind that his half-sister was of staunchly Protestant background) continued with the claim that he was sent to 'Jesuitical friends' of Molyneux in America. The erroneous claim that he himself had been educated by the Jesuits is repeated in later letters.

He alleges that Molyneux's wife, Agnes Keogh, was 'a little Jewess who had become a Roman Catholic Convert' and that her Jewish relatives insisted on a marriage settlement (which led ultimately to Mrs Brenane's bankruptcy). We also know that this is not true: Agnes Keogh was of Roman Catholic stock on both sides of her family.[6]

He does, however, add some useful information about Molyneux which may well be reliable: that he was very tall, handsome but with 'unpleasant' eyes; that Lafcadio 'hated' him (Molyneux may well have decoded these feelings and arranged for his protagonist to be packed off to a distant boarding school). Hearn has him acting as a 'travelling salesman' when he met Mrs Brenane; this is not necessarily discordant with the possibility that he may have had an Admiralty post[7] and a depot for Oriental goods[8] but it would certainly have spurred him to attempt the social position promised by Mrs Brenane's money.

He names his 'first love' as Isabella Molyneux, Henry's daughter:

> I believe she afterwards became a nun. I think she was good. She was the only one of that family who ever spoke kindly to me.

Letter 3
No address, 7 JUNE 1892

This letter is interesting in that Lafcadio is portraying himself as prospering in Japan – making 'a bank account as fast as honest work can produce', not expecting to have children, and speculating about leaving (albeit in fairly playful fashion):

> I have no babies; and don't expect to have any, and may be able to cross the seas one of these days to linger in your country awhile. But really I don't know. I drift with the current of events.

Whether the country in question is England or Ireland is a moot point: he tells her in the next letter that 'you are very happy to be able to live in England' although the available evidence would suggest that she was living in Portadown in what is now Northern Ireland. Indeed, it is apparent from a later letter (21 May 1893) that Lafcadio was not clear either about her address or where Portadown was: he had had to look it up in *Whittaker's Almanac* to be able to reply to her initially.

He tells her that only Occidental marriages are a hindrance on affection between kindred:

> For the Japanese wife is only the shadow of her husband – infinitely unselfish and *naïve* in all things. . .

Whatever about the fine qualities of Setsu Koizumi, his Japanese wife, naïveté was hardly one of them!

Letter 4
No address, 10 JANUARY 1893

Lafcadio is insistent that Mrs Brenane had made a will, saying that he used to go to an aged lawyer (whose name he was, however, unable to remember) with her. He was unusually positive about his father:

> There must have been wonderful rigor in that blood of father's, to have made so strong a resemblance in his children by two different mothers.

Perhaps of greatest interest is a long account of his early days in America:

> Where was I? – in America, wasn't it – in that last letter,- dropped into the enormous machinery of a life I knew nothing about. Friends tried to get me work, after I had been turned out of my first boarding-house for inability to pay. (I lost father's photograph at that time, by seizure of all my small earthly goods and possessions.) It was soon found I never could be an accountant – naturally defective in mathematical capacity, and even in ordinary calculation-power. So I was entered into a telegraph office as telegraph messenger-boy. But I was 19; and the other boys were very young: I looked ridiculously out of place, and was laughed at. I was touchy then,- went off without waiting for my wages. Enraged friends refused to do anything further for me. Boarding-houses turned me out of doors. At last became a boarding-house servant – lighted fires, shovelled coal, etc. in exchange for food and privilege of sleeping on floor of smoking-room. I worked about

1½ year [sic];- finding time to read and to write stories. The stories were published in cheap weekly papers,- long extinct; but I was never paid for them. I tried other occupations also – canvassing, show-card writing, etc. These bought me enough to buy smoking tobacco and second-hand clothes – nothing more. One day, I found my way to the office of an old English printer named Watkin. He took a fancy to me,- told me to come and talk to him whenever I got time. Soon after I was turned out of the boarding house, owing to the change of owner-ship. I slept two nights in the street,- for which the police scolded me: then I found the refuge in a mews where some English coachmen allowed me to sleep in the hayloft at night, and fed me by stealth with victuals stolen from the house. At last even that had to stop. So I went to see Watkin.

The dear old man laughed and said to me:- 'You do not know anything yet: I will teach you. You can sleep in my office, and I'll teach you printing. I can't pay you, because you are no use to me except as a companion, but I can feed you.' He made me a paper bed (paper shavings from the book-trimming machinery): it was nice and warm. I lived two years with him. I was absurdly, morbidly sensitive, and used to quarrel with him; but he understood me, and when I ran away from him in a huff, he would hunt me up and bring me back laughing.

I left him to become a proofreader in a printing house,- then associate editor of a weekly paper,- then clerk in a mailing office,- then assistant editor of a larger weekly,- then a reporter on the daily press,- etc., etc.

This passage is fascinating and infuriating. Fascinating because it is in some ways the most coherent account to date of his early days in America and infuriating because it both harmonizes and conflicts with other evidence.

Firstly, he does not mention New York or any change of city, so my earlier assumption, that he went straight to Cincinnati on his arrival in the United States, stands. However, he repeats that he had a variety of jobs before meeting Henry Watkin, which conflicts with Watkin's account, that Lafcadio came to see him a few days after his arrival in Cincinnati; Watkin's account is less romantic and, to my taste, more credible. Hearn portrays himself as finding Watkin on his own initiative; according to Watkin, Hearn was introduced to him by a Mr McDermott; again, I find Watkin's account more credible.

On the other hand, Hearn does admit to a morbid sensitivity at this stage and to falling out with, and running away from, Watkin during his two years with him: it is possible that he found other menial jobs during these intervals, or even while he was staying with Watkin. Also, he repeats, in more credible detail, the story of sleeping in a hayloft and being fed by stealth, which featured in some draft autobiographical scraps he left behind.

He talks of 'friends' trying to get him work initially: this is consistent with other evidence which would indicate that he was sent to friends or contacts of Henry Molyneux and was provided with some money to get him started in Cincinnati. The fact that he carried his father's picture around with him and was clearly distressed when he lost it underlines the complexity of his feelings towards his errant parent.

Finally, he mentions publishing in cheap weekly papers: this accords with the literary detective work of Albert Mordell who found articles from this period which he attributed to Lafcadio. Hearn does say that they were 'stories' and the articles identified by Mordell were of a different nature but this might just be a careless choice of word by Hearn.

On the subject of his upbringing he had this to say:

> Religion had never had any influence upon me,- except in a literary way. I liked stories of angels and devils – especially devils. I had read as a boy of devils coming in the shape of beautiful girls to tempt various saints. I remember at the age of fourteen praying devoutly that such a sweet devil would come to me – for which I would have sold fifty souls.

The statement that religion had never had any influence on him *except in a literary way* tends to confirm my existing view, that he was not subjected to excessive religiosity by Mrs Brenane but that he was heavily influenced by his reading.

Indeed, I have already put forward the view that the horrors which haunted him most of his life derived from literature, especially Matthew Lewis's *The Monk*.[9] He makes no mention of telling a priest of his desire for an infernal temptress (although accepted by much previous biography, I regarded it as leg-pulling of the pious George Gould).

He then goes on to confess that he spent most of his money on women – quite obviously prostitutes – once he began earning:

> Well, at last I had money to spend. I had long since ceased to believe in devils;- and then the devils I had prayed for came! How much of my soul I gave them I don't know; but I gave them everything I could earn in the shape of money.

Lafcadio provides yet another account of why he left Cincinnati, at variance with previous accounts and the known facts: he suffered a nervous breakdown and failure of his sight through over-work. The doctors gave him three or four months to live; he had to have quiet work; his employers gave him $40 and he went to New Orleans – 'a good place to become a ghost in' – and went 'stone-blind'. With no money and no friend beyond a revolver 'kept to me in case the doctor failed'. He recovered and was able to take advantage of the vacancies created by a yellow fever epidemic to get into journalism. He left New Orleans when he got tired:

> ... tired of the climate,- tired of the sameness of things,- tired of seeing my friends die,- tired of the petty jealousies that buzz around the least success,- threw up my position and went to the West Indies.

He claimed that the climate suited him while we know that he had great difficulty adjusting to it. He gives the impression of having enjoyed good health there by being 'proof against yellow fever', contrasting himself with 'fresh Europeans' to whom the climate was dangerous, whereas he was seriously ill during his time there.

Lafcadio had come to Japan because 'a return to the artificial life of American cities [would have been] very difficult'; now he did not know how long he would stay, making it clear that concern for his wife, Setsu, was the key consideration in this regard.

Letter 5
No address, 21 MAY 1893

This letter continued a dominant theme of his correspondence with Minnie Atkinson, his loneliness in Japan, his desire to return to Europe – he was speculating about staying for half-a-year at least if sufficient literary work could be found to justify it. The obstacle, as ever, was his family:

> I cannot take my wife to Europe: it would be impossible to accustom her to Western life; indeed it would be cruel even to try. But I may have to educate my child abroad,- which would be an all-powerful reason for the voyage. However, I would prefer an Italian, French, or Spanish school-life to an English one.

Considering that his first child, Kazuo, was then only three months in gestation and would not be born for another six, this passage underlines just how early began Lafcadio's obsession with his son and his determination to have him educated abroad. Later in the letter he says that he would return to the tropics if he became 'quite independent'.

In asking Minnie to send him on copies of reviews of his books, he was mildly critical of his old friend, Elizabeth Bisland, for failing to do so (she had merely given him a flavour of the content), but he was essentially positive about her:

> But she well deserved her good fortune; for she was certainly one of the most gifted girls I ever knew, and has succeeded in everything – against immense obstacles – with no luck except that of her own will and genius.

Speaking of the loss of his eye, he says:

> Yes, I have lost an Eye, and look horrible. The operation in Dublin did not cause the disfigurement, but a blow, or rather the indirect results of a blow, received from a playfellow.

One wonders why the operation was in Dublin if the accident happened at Ushaw, in the North East of England, especially as Mrs Brenane was living in Surrey. In the circumstances, an English city, either nearby Durham or London, would have seemed more logical places for the operation to have been carried out. It has been accepted up to now that the accident took place at Ushaw but one wonders if it could have happened earlier, while he was still in Dublin.

His interest in his father continued in this letter, as Hearn reacted positively to Minnie's offer of providing a photograph. He hoped to visit India, to 'find some tradition of him' there and anticipated a repetition of experiencing the ghostly sensation of having seen it all before, as had happened in the West Indies (where his father had also been posted during his army career).

Letter 6
No address, 17 SEPTEMBER 1893

The theme of loneliness continued, with Lafcadio claiming that he was 'living in a really hideous isolation, far away from books, and bookshops, and Europeans'.

His sensitivity to heat was underlined when he told Minnie of visiting Nagasaki which, while being 'very quaint and pretty", was also 'hotter than any West Indian port in the hot season"; he stayed only twelve hours.

His aversion to ordinary middle-class values was apparent in his comment that the benefit of travel was only to be enjoyed by 'keeping away from fashion-resorts and places consecrated by conventionalism. . .Nothing to me is more frightful than a fashionable sea-side resort. . .' He was at his happiest in 'little fishing villages, and little queer old unknown towns, where there are no big vulgar hotels, and where one can dress and do exactly as one pleases'. This extended to the United States as he begged her not to allow her son to go there: 'never let him go to America, and lose all his traditions'. Regretting how 'horribly matter-of-fact' the world was becoming, he suggested that idealism lived on 'in the English Civil Service, in the Army, and in the Navy', in one of which she might seek to place her son:

> The high courage, and the high sense of duty of the old Northern race at least remain to all seeming more active there. From Havelok the Dane to Havelock of the Indian Mutiny, and from the old Norse Sea Kings: to the Drakes, Blakes, and Nelsons, the national character at home has changed nothing for the worse. But in America, where all the old traditions are lost, and public opinion is morally rotten, the race is not the same. So when I think of your little man with the black eyes, I hope that his life will always be in the circle of English traditions. Wherever the English flag flies, these remain.

He contrasted the different construction of the family in Japan, with its strong bonds of filial obedience, with the situation in the West where the family had been 'disintegrated. . . altogether' and told her of his integration into the Japanese style of living.

Letter 7
No address, 8 OCTOBER 1893

In the course of a long analysis of what he perceived to be his half-sister's character, Lafcadio told her that she had avoided his 'extremes of depression and extremes of exaltation' and claimed:

> But of course you have been shaped in certain influences I never had,- so that you must have perfect poise where I would flounder and stumble.

This was somewhat disingenuous as, up to the age of seventeen, Lafcadio had had a privileged upbringing whereas Minnie and her sisters had lost both parents while young and been brought up by relatives. All of them had grown up in the same social milieu. On the other hand, he probably was being genuine when he professed ignorance of his half-sisters' lives, underlining the extent to which he had been cut him off from his father and his second family:

> I do not know where you were born, where you were educated,- anything of your life; and what is much more, infinitely more important, I don't know your emotions and thoughts and feelings and experiences in the past. What you are now, I can guess. But what *were* you,- long ago? What memories most haunt you of places and people you liked?

In sending photographs, Minnie must have expressed fear of being thought sentimental about their father, as Hearn responded, contrasting the filial piety of the East, to which he now subscribed, with the emotional repression of 'English' upbringing:

> And here in this Orient, where the spirit of more ancient faiths enter into one's blood with the sense of doctrine of filial piety, and the meaning of ancestor-worship,- how very, very strange and cruel it seems to me that my little sister should be afraid of being thought *sentimental* about the photograph of her father! What self-repression does all this mean, and what iron influences in Western life – English life that I had almost forgotten!

Letter 8
No address, 20 NOVEMBER 1893

The family theme continues in this letter, with Lafcadio announcing the birth of Kazuo at 1am on 17 November 1893. Much of the letter was reproduced by Kennard,[10] including his comments on Minnie's sister (Lafcadio's half-sister), Posey, but she omitted those on Lilla, the other sister:

> I got also two photographs of Lilla, and a letter. Lilla's face quite puzzles me. She must have quite a different disposition from both you and Posey. She seems to be very positive. I think she must have a handsome figure. Miss B[island] wrote me the most charming letter about her, but I imagined her quite different from

her picture. – Well, I would like to see you all, and chat, and find out wonderful things about each. Perhaps that will happen.

Most of all, however, Kennard omitted Lafcadio's blistering attack on his brother, James, known as 'Jim":

> – Now for an ugly subject. You ask about 'Jim'. I never much liked his letters – so far as one can feel anybody through a letter my feeling of 'Jim' was unsympathetic and unpleasant. I thought also from the first that his motive in writing was not very brotherly. He made some proposal to write once a year, I think. This was followed by a letter asking for a loan of $500.00. Not being so kind a person as your kind husband, I replied by putting the letter in another envelope and returning it to him. This, however, was a much kinder way of replying than that to which my disgust impelled me. – I suppose you can understand why. But suppose you do not, let me assure you that I would rather cut my throat sixty times over than write even to a rich relative for money, or accept a money-gift from one. Much less would I appeal to a half-blind relative, who had never any chances given to him, and had to fight his way through life with nothing but his wits to help him. Of course 'loans' mean 'losses' – no matter who the borrower; but in any case the thing is disgusting, vile. I don't think of 'Jim' as a brother at all, and don't wish to hear of him again. A man is no good that has a wife and children, and has been working for ever so many years, and still needs to borrow from brothers and sisters. Such a man, who is not really in my opinion a man at all, has no right even to live!
>
> You see, dear Minnie, that I am not so kind and good as John Buckby Atkinson. What is more, I know this:- No greater injury can be done a man of small grit than to lend him money to help him out of difficulties. Thus he will never learn to help himself. I was taught this long ago.

With love to you
Lafcadio Hearn
Nov. 20th 93

> P.S. – I don't wish to think I have never borrowed money, or asked help! I have done it many times, under rational circumstances – but only from business men who knew that my capacity to make money exceeded and justified my request. I do not tell a man he is my brother as a security for a loan.

On a minor point, it is clear from this letter that Kennard mis-transcribed the name of Minnie's husband, Buckby Atkinson, as 'Buckley' Atkinson, an error in which subsequent biographers, myself included, have followed her. The correct name has been confirmed to me by Basil Hearn, who has undertaken some useful genealogical research into this area of the family.

Letter 9
No address, Undated

Lafcadio replies to Minnie's questions about 'Kajiwō', whose birth and early progress he chronicles. He declares that he will bring him up as a Buddhist.

He is scathing about a writer, Clement Scott, who had spent two weeks in Japan, in the lowest brothels of Nagasaki and Yokohama, according to Hearn, and then wrote spiteful untruths about the country. Hearn is indignant that the reviews are open to Scott and closed to him (not quite true!).

He indulges in a tirade against American publishers and expresses the hope of getting 'better treatment from an English house,- the Macmillans, if possible'; *Japan: an Attempt at Interpretation* was, in fact, published by Macmillan ten years later.

He claims he had 'almost' fallen in love with the 'type-writer' – 'a pretty girl' – brought in to facilitate his rapid translation of *Sylvestre Bonnard*.

Letter 10
KUMAMOTO, 30/1/1894

Lafcadio showers affection on Minnie from the beginning:

> Your kindest letter is with me and made me love you very much. We should be very happy together, I know; and our long talks would be revelations of each other. I think, if I know the Gods at all, we shall meet,- at the best time for both of us.

But he tells her to dismiss the idea that they might have been happy together growing up: 'We were too much alike to have loved each other properly. . .' On the subject of music, he says that he has never been able to appreciate the superiority of 'the new German music; the Italian still seemed 'divine' to him. He described himself as 'psychologically. . . all Latin and Pagan'.

This letter lays a lot of stress on the role of the Gods in directing human affairs and includes the passage:

> The dead move us;- their ghostly fingers stir the strings of every life in this world's most incomprehensive puppet-show. I wonder often what particular ghost is responsible for the things unaccountable which I have done.

He expresses gratitude that he has no daughter; if he had one, she would be too dear and he would be inclined, if dying, to want to take her to 'Shadowland' with him, an interesting comment given that he died shortly after the birth of his only daughter.

He refers to Minnie having had 'all your disappointments and troubles in girlhood – childhood', a recognition that life must have been tough for Charles Bush Hearn's second family after his death. He wishes that he 'could talk to you more about Father and India'.

Letter 11
KUMAMOTO, *Undated*

There is more about Kazuo's early development: Lafcadio prays that he might be like Minnie or their father. He speculates that he might die soon because he is 44 without referring to any specific illness.

He expresses his views on how the brutality of the great English public schools like Eton and Harrow spoil their pupils by hardening them through too much brutality; they produce the 'conquerors of the world' but seldom great thinkers. He wants Kaji (a pet name for his son, Kazuo) to be a doctor and plans to take him to Europe.

Letter 12
KUMAMOTO, 10/5/1894

Lafcadio thanks Minnie for getting Mrs Wetherall to write; she was a daughter of Alicia Crawford, Lafcadio's stepmother, by her first marriage to George John Crawford.

Lafcadio expresses concern about Minnie: clearly she has not been well having another child: he advises her not to have any more, saying that he was 'very fully resolved never to become a father again', a sentiment which he repeated later in the correspondence. His anxiety about her derived from his feeling that she was 'the only real *fellow-soul* in my world but me'.

He reveals his desire for children and domesticity before coming to Japan:

> You will laugh at me, and perhaps think it very strange that when only thirty-five I began to feel a kind of envy of friends with children. I knew their troubles, anxieties, struggles; but I saw their sons grow up, beautiful and gifted men, and I used to whisper to myself,- 'But I *never* shall have a child.' Then it used to seem to me that no man died so utterly as the man without children: for him I fancied (like some folk still really think in other lands) that death would be utter eternal blackness. When I did, however, hear the first cry of my boy – *my* boy, dreamed about in forgotten years – I had for that instant the ghostly sensation of being *double*. Just then, and only then, I did not think, but *felt*, 'I am TWO'. It was weird, but gave me thoughts that changed preexisting thoughts. My boy's gaze still seems to me a queerly beautiful thing: I still feel I am looking at myself when he looks at me. Only the thought has become infinitely more complicated. For I think of all the dead who live in the little heart of him – races and memories diverse as East and West. But who made his eyes blue and his hair brown? And will he be like you? And will he ever see the little cousin who has just entered the world? The other day, for one moment, he looked just like your boy in the picture.

This is confirmation of the longing for a home, loving wife

and children which I had extrapolated from the 'Fantastics' of his New Orleans days.[11] Kazuo did, in fact, see his cousin, Charlotte Dorothy Atkinson, when she visited Japan with her mother, Minnie Atkinson, in 1909.

He goes on to tell a tale of being humiliated in his childhood in Dublin by a little girl – he cannot remember if it was Mrs Weatherall as a child- which has already been used by Kennard[12]. It includes a section where the little girl made a caged parrot seize his hair, which proves that the Hearns did have a parrot which in turn adds credibility to the tale told by a family descendant that the Hearns had a parrot which they trained to make anti-Roman Catholic comments when Mrs Brenane arrived. I used this in my book to underline Mrs Brenane's lack of religious sensitivity, about her adopted religion at any rate.[13]

Lafcadio suggests that Minnie might

> Ask her [Mrs Weatherall] if the sun was not then much larger, and the sky much bluer, and the moon much more wonderful than now.

This anticipates the language of one of his most poetic autobiographical reminiscences, in 'The Dream of a Summer Day', published in *Out of the East* a few years later:

> I have a memory of a place and a magical time in which the Sun and the Moon were larger and brighter than now. Whether it was of this life or of some life before I cannot tell. But I know the sky was very much more blue, and nearer to the world. . .[14]

Lafcadio's use of the language of 'The Dream of a Summer Day' in this letter helps to locate it in the same period of his life referred to in his unhappy day's play with Mrs Weatherall as a child. Given the fact that she told Kennard that she first saw Lafcadio when he about five years old,[15] we can assume that he was five or older when the experiences referred to in 'The Dream' occurred. His mother had already left him for good at this stage. This letter therefore adds to the existing weight of evidence that the wondrous being central to his most beautiful piece of writing was not his mother.

This is interesting, not just in the context of literary evolution, but also in relation to straightforward biographical fact. An American commentator has mistakenly identified the subject of the 'The Dream' as his mother[16] and this in turn is misleading other students of Hearn.[17]

Letter 13
KUMAMOTO, 2/6/1894

Minnie has been unwell following childbirth and Lafcadio emphasises that:

> He has taken a vow to have no more children, and he is likely to keep it – even against the wishes of somebody who would wish otherwise.

One can only assume that he is referring to Setsu here.
Of Kazuo, he says:

> I must make an Englishman of him, I fear. His hair has turned bright brown. . . Where did he get this strength from – and his blue eyes? Not from me surely.

Later on he says:

> Kaji-wo's soul seems to be so English that I fancy his memory of former births would scarcely refer much to Japan.

Explaining Buddhist doctrine to her, he says:

> The dead are not dead – they live in all of us and move us, and stir faintly in every heart-beat. And there are ghostly interlinkings. Something of *you* must be in *me*, and of both of us in Kajiwo [Kazuo].

Hearn's theory of the living dead is interesting given that he may well have been familiar with Richard Burton's Hindu tale of *Vikram and the Vampire*[18] and Bram Stoker was writing *Dracula* at this time. The linkage between his half-sister and Kazuo is revealing in terms of Hearn's feeling of kinship with his father's second family.

Letter 14
KUMAMOTO, 24/6/1894

Lafcadio predicts that he will soon have to leave Japan, as the era of foreign influence was rapidly drawing to a close:

> But I fear – indeed I am almost certain that the day is not very far away when I must leave Setsu and Kajiwo to the care of the ancient Gods, and go far away and work bravely for them elsewhere, till Kajiwo is old enough to go abroad. . . Happily my folks will be provided for; and I expect to be able, if I must go, to return in a few years.

He looked forward to a future, presumably in Europe (as Mrs Atkinson was living in Portadown):

> I hope to chat with you by the fire when we are both old, and Kaji has shot up into a man,- looking like his aunt a little – with a delicate aquiline face.

He expressed worries about Kazuo's future but revealed that his birth had given Lafcadio with a much more positive self-image than is normally associated with him:

> Besides, I am beginning to think I am really a tolerably good sort of fellow,- for if I had been really such a monster of depravity as the religious fanatics declared, how could I have got such a fine boy. There must be some good in me anyhow.

He was determined that:

> Nobody shall make a 'Christian' of Kajiwo if I can help it – by 'Xn' I mean a believer in absurd and cruel dogmas. The world talks much about Xity, but no one teaches it: the churches teach Hebraism and monstrosities. Among the Japanese peasantry there is more Xity than among Xus. And the faith of the people seems to me much closer to possible ultimate truths than our own.

Letter 15
No address, 29/10/1894

This is a short note telling Minnie that he has moved to Kobe to take up journalism. Lafcadio returns to the theme that they might meet again in a few years. His book [*Glimpses of Unfamiliar Japan*] 'was to be issued' on 29 September.

Letter 16
KOBE, 2/1/1895

This is another short letter, addressed from the *Kobe Chronicle*, telling her of the inflammation of his eyes which had laid him low.

His attitude towards Kumamoto is evident when he speculates that some papers which had not reached him had probably been 'stolen' there.

His new book, *Out of the East*, is to be published soon. He has been offered 'literary work' in Tokyo with promises of sufficient leisure to pursue his own work.

Letter 17
KUMAMOTO, 11/3/1895

Lafcadio has been sending Minnie Japanese fairy tales and suggests that she read 'the Matsuyama Mirror' first: 'There is a ghostly beauty that I think you will feel deeply. After all, the simplest stories are the best.'

Otherwise the letter is mostly concerned with ancestor-worship and Shinto rites for the dead.

It ends on a tender note, given that the correspondence is drawing to an end:

> Tell me, dear little beautiful sister, how you are always,- give me good news of yourself,- and love me a little bit.

Letter 18
No address, Undated

This letter is described, erroneously, by Kennard[19] as Lafcadio's last letter to Minnie. It is reproduced by her as if in full but it has in fact been edited, with some phrases, such as 'All American publishers are cheats' being taken out. The tone is less warm than the previous – she is now addressed as 'My dear little Sis' rather than the 'My sweet little beautiful Sister' used in the previous letter.

Letter 19
TOKYO, 1/9/1901

Kennard was either unaware of this letter or treated it as if it did not exist. The latter might be suggested by the fact that Minnie was obviously going through a great personal crisis, possibly of a marital nature, to which Kennard may not have wished to allude in print:

> You appear to be very strong: what has befallen you is a terrible strain upon every nerve of one's mental and emotional life; and you needed to be more than brave to bear it. . . the best thing. . . is to think only. . . of the children, and a future to make for them.

It is clear from the letter that Minnie had moved from Portadown in Northern Ireland, possibly as a result of a change in her marital situation, to Bedford in England. Hearn contrasts the positive aspects of her situation there with his position in Japan:

> You are at all events in England,- in Europe,- among your own race and people, with some friends and kindred: that is lucky for the little ones. (Were I to die tomorrow no mortal acquaintance of the old days would extend – or dream of extending – so much as the tip of a finger to help my household. In fact, a number might try to do exactly the reverse.)

This, of course, did not prove to be the case: after his death, Western friends like Mitchell McDonald and Elizabeth Bisland did rally around to support his Japanese family, while Minnie Atkinson went to Japan with Kennard to see if she could assist in carrying out his wishes with regard to Kazuo's education.

This passage supports the Kennard's conjecture in her biography as to why Hearn broke off the correspondence with his half-sister in 1895; she talks of his longing 'to return

277

to his native land, to hold communion with those of his own race', which is very similar to the language of the passage quoted above.[20] This might indicate that Kennard had seen the letter but did not refer overtly to its existence.

On the other hand, she may have been genuinely unaware of it – perhaps it was withheld by Minnie because of its personal nature – as he provided an explanation of his suspension of the correspondence that she did not use and which would surely have altered her treatment of the break had she known of the following passage in the letter:

> Let me tell you now that you are quite mistaken in imagining that you wrote anything to offend or pain me: I cannot imagine you writing that way under any circumstances. I simply felt disinclined to write,- and I very seldom now write letters.

This theme of educating Kazuo abroad recurs in the letter: he says that he had half-expected to go abroad the previous summer and it was not impossible that she would see him the next summer or the one after that. He wanted to take Kazuo to Europe or America for a couple of years:

> Perhaps you could tell me about a nice little country-town in England or Ireland, where I could take him – not far from the sea. I keep him in the sea most of the summer here. England or Ireland is a country where there is no chance for the stranger of earning anything by literature – unless he be a genius; but it is less expensive than the United States, and a better place for a boy to learn the language. On the other hand, for a practical scientific education America offers better chances,- for a later time.

This is further confirmation of the evidence presented in my book that Hearn actively considered returning to Ireland, England and the United States in his last years. It also underlines that fact that he did not distinguish between England and Ireland, important in terms of his transmogrification of elements of his childhood from one country to the other. The countries were, of course, then a single state, the United Kingdom of Great Britain and Ireland, to the service of which most of his ancestors had devoted themselves.

He also made clear that the memory of his public school education in England had not abated:

> English schools are mostly little hells of cruelty; foreign schools in Japan are in the hands of Jesuits or religious fanatics. . .

James Ellacott Beale to Minnie Atkinson, Yokohama, 9/7/1896

This letter is quoted in full in Kennard[21]

Setsu Koizumi [to Lilla Hearn ?], 25/11/1904

This letter has no addressee, but opens with 'My dear Sister'; I assume that it was written to Lilla on the evidence of Setsu's letter of 17/3/1905 to Minnie Atkinson (see below).

Clearly written by someone else in good English, it thanks her for her letter of condolence on Lafcadio's death. Setsu says that Lafcadio often mentioned her name.

Interestingly, Setsu claimed that she intended to send Kazuo abroad 'when he will have arrived at the age adequate to be done so' and hoped for assistance when the time came. This statement of intent was repeated in her letter to Minnie Atkinson of 17/3/1905 (see below). However, when Minnie Atkinson and Kennard arrived in Japan in 1909 and attempted to pursue this subject they got a negative response from their Japanese interlocutors and were told that it would break Setsu's heart if the subject were to be broached.[22] These letters give additional significance to the fact that Kennard does not appear to have taken up the subject directly with Setsu; rather, she allowed herself to be warned off by third parties.

Setsu Koizumi [to Minnie Atkinson?], 17/3/1905

This letter also has no addressee and it opens with 'My dear sister'. It was written by someone else (the handwriting is different from the previous letter) in good English. A response to a letter 'full of warm sympathy', presumably on the death of Lafcadio. Lafcadio had often spoken of her. Setsu had not been able to write before because of her lack of English and not having an address. She had received a letter from 'Miss Lilla' to whom she had sent a reply; I assume that this is the letter of 25/11/1904 above.

She thanks Minnie for photos sent and comments on her resemblance to Lafcadio. Two years previously they had received photos of her three children.

She provides interesting confirmation of Lafcadio's intention of 'visiting' England and America and states that she intends sending Kazuo abroad to study in the future. It also provides another, direct, account of Lafcadio's death:

> Lafcadio had an intention of visiting England and America, and he often said that he would see his sisters and let Kazuo see his aunts. By the advice of doctor he stopped the plan as his health was not very good at that time.
>
> He passed away by heart trouble. A few days before his death he suffered achings in heart which however soon left him. On the evening of Sept. 26th, after supper, he conversed with us pleasantly, and as he was going to his room, a sudden aching attacked his heart. The pain lasted only some twenty minutes. He passed away in peace. A faint smile was resting on his dead face. I could not believe that he died; so sudden was his fate. Una[ni]mously by all papers in Japan his death was recorded with profound regret.
>
> I intend to send Kazuo abroad for studies in future.

Elizabeth [Wetmore (née Bisland)] to Lilla (in these letters her name is spelled both with and without a final 'h') [Hearn (Lafcadio's half-sister)], Long Island, New York, Undated [1906]

Possibly written in 1906 as Bisland talks of an unnamed book, to be issued on 10 November, probably her *Life and Letters of Lafcadio Hearn*, which was published in that year. She claims that the advance orders were the largest ever for the publisher, Houghton Mifflin, and that the leading houses in Paris and Berlin had asked for translation rights. She anticipates that Lafcadio's family will make several thousand dollars from it. She describes Lafcadio as one of the great letter writers in the English language and a genius, 'one of the immortals'.

Bisland professes envy of Lilla's way of life, which seems to consist of studying the languages and art of various countries and sends hearty congratulations to Posey (sister to Minnie and Lilla). It is clear that Lilla has visited her home in Long Island.

Minnie Atkinson to Lillah Hearn, Metropole Hotel, Tokio, Sunday, 21 March [1909]; typescript copy of letter; original not seen by me.

Written by Mrs Atkinson on her visit to Japan in 1909, this letter is worth quoting almost in full as it gives a wonderful flavour of the visit and includes useful material not in Kennard or the diary:

> We came on here in the very unexpected way Mrs K. always does things. Yesterday she told me we were going to stay in Yokohama, and only come here for 2 days or 3 perhaps, or we might not come at all! Mr Mason, a friend of Lafcadio's, said she must not dream of rushing the Japanese, and that I must write to Setsue announcing our arrival at Yokohama, and our wish to visit her, and *await* a reply. This I wrote on Wednesday, no reply came on Friday morning as we expected and she was so impatient, she said she would go to Tokio anyway and present letters of introduction to people, Mr Tanabe, an interpreter, etc. I was not fit to travel for I have had such headaches since leaving the quiet shipboard life and rushing around, and also have a persistent attack of diarrhea; anyway, Mr Mason said it would be most inadvisable for *me* to go as Setsue was more than likely to come to me as soon as possible. I was lying down in the afternoon and a boy came to tell me a Japanese lady was in the hall asking for me! So I went down to find Setsue and Kazuo in the hall. They could not speak English (she had written to tell me this, but her letter arrived after she had gone

back to Tokio). She was so glad to see me and hugged me and cried, poor dear. The boy is such a big fellow, and the most comical Japanese likeness of Carleton you could possibly imagine. A nice looking fellow and wears spectacles. The only thing really that gives the Japanese look is the inward slope of the eyes. I got the hotel clerk to come up to my room with them, and we had a halting conversation for a while, when, to my relief, Mr Mason came. I gave her your photo which she was very glad to have, she says we both remind her of Lafcadio but me most because my profile and the shape of my nose is so exactly like his! When I showed them Carleton's photo they both exclaimed at the likeness to Kazuo, who sat quietly gazing at the photo and murmuring things to himself. His hands are so like Carleton's, long slender fingers. He tried to say something to Dot but is so shy he could not get anything out except 'very glad' – that was Setsue's only English too. I forget if I told you I brought a little gold locket to Setsue with a tiny photo of Lafcadio coloured by Webster, she was so pleased but had to turn her face to the wall to have a little weep over it. They laughed very gaily at a little teddy-bear we brought for the little girl – she is only 5½. I brought the other boys a penknife and a book Professor Foxwell recommended, and Kazuo that zodiac ring of father's I always meant Lafcadio to have if he came to England. Poor Lafcadio, he seems to have huffed with every friend who disagreed with him on any subject – it puzzles some to know what the cause of offence had been!

Mr Mason said they used to see a great deal of him (he has also married a Japanese) till Lafcadio came to ask him one day to help him about becoming a naturalised Japanese, which he did by introducing him to the proper lawyer, etc, to manage it. Mr M. in process of discussion happened to say he knew nothing much about it, as British nationality was always good enough for *him*! L. said nothing at the time, but was very silent, and from that day never darkened his doors and cut him if they met!! Mr and Mrs Young, of Kobe, who had the same experience over some other discussion, both admired and loved him and said he could not possibly be judged by any ordinary standards, and they only felt regret, not rancour, against his decision. He also closed his doors to Professor Chamberlain, his *great* friend, because of some small difference of opinion. . .

Prof. C. is the executor of the will and Setsue has been often with him since. Mr Mason and he are the people who compiled Murray's Guide to Japan and are sort of partners – I don't understand in what exactly. Mr Mason used to teach like Lafcadio, but had a nerve [sic] breakdown, and left Tokio to live in Yokohama. He took Dot and me to tea with his wife, after Setsue and Kazuo left. She can speak English a little and is a very sweet woman – he is devoted to her and told me if he could have his 30 years of married life again he would gladly! He brought me her photo the other day, saying 'I bring you the photo of the best woman I ever met'. They have a nice house European style (and only she dresses in Japanese dress) his two sons have married English girls. He has adopted a little Japanese niece of his wife's as a daughter – adoption of course is very common in Japan – Mr Cross, the gentleman we met on board ship adopted two Japanese relations of his wife. They become their children in every way, and their own parents have no further claim or responsibility. Mr Mason said he was so glad to have met Setsue with me, and she gave the prettiest little apology for the way Lafcadio had treated him after his many kindnesses to him. Mrs Mason is a much better looking woman than Setsue, who, one can see, has never been pretty – she has a heavy face but a sensible face – she regrets very much Lafcadio would not teach her any English. We are to go to her house this afternoon with Mr Tanabe. Mrs Kennard saw the house when she came up alone the other day, and she caught sight of the little girl, another Japanese Hearn, she says. I will leave this open and tell you about our expedition. I am sorry we are not staying at the Imperial Hotel, this seems so far from the centre of things, but Mrs K. found it too expensive after taking rooms and came on here being able to make a much cheaper arrangement. It is comfortable enough but people look very second-class! however she does not want to come across people, or any in connection with the Embassy. . .

We are right down beside the river and dockyard apparently, there is a great hammering going on and various noises from very early in the morning. . . Mr Young and Mr Mason both seem to think Setsue is very well off for a Japanese, she has only the children with her, I had an idea her parents lived with her always; she regretted she could not ask us to stay with her, but said they had everything entirely in Japanese style just as when Lafcadio was alive. She did so wish he could have seen me.

I am so glad the awful rain of yesterday has stopped – it never ceased pouring all yesterday and last night – I have always been told that it comes down with a vengeance here and that Tokio becomes a sea of mud ankle deep.

MONDAY. [22/3/1909]

Kazuo came here with a card from his mother to invite us to dinner at 12 o/c, and so we started off with him to the trams and it seemed such a long way and [as] I was still so seedy Mrs Kennard signed to him that we must have rickshaws. It took about an hour to get to the house, such mud and dirt all the way! Finally we got to the house, the little girl was at the entrance to the avenue and, when the sliding shutters of the house were drawn aside Mr Tanabe the interpreter came forward, a very good-looking Japanese, and Setsue. We were invited to take our shoes off before mounting on the raised part of the floor (the height of a good step from the entrance). Then we got into slippers and went through tat (?) little room to a verandah and up a couple of steps to another room, through which we passed to another, Lafcadio's study just as it was when he died. There was one small chair he used when writing at a desk, but for the rest he always sat on the floor on square cushions. Two sides of the room are occupied by the books forming his library, and in one corner is the 'butsudan', I think it is called, the shrine kept in his memory. Two of his photographs are in it, little vases with flowers, his pen (he always kept two in use and one was buried with him). Only the paper screens divide the front of the rooms from the verandah looking into the garden, and the house would be very cold but for the wooden fire boxes filled with charcoal which they keep stirring up and put beside one when sitting down. They implored me to sit on one of the chairs brought from another room (an American rocker and another) but [I] preferred sitting on the cushions. The second son was out at some distance with a friend, but the 3rd boy came in and made his little bows and greeting and ran off again. Setsue spoke to the little girl and Mr Tanabe explained she had told her I was the same as her dead father, being the sister he loved, and she came over and cuddled against me slipping her hand in mine. She was so delighted with the doll and half-frightened of the Teddy-bear though fascinated when Dot showed her how to make it move.

Then a maid came in bowing down touching the floor with her head and hands, and then trotted away and brought tiny cups of weak tea and highly [indecipherable] cakes. Then we were taken to the second apartment for dinner – you cannot imagine the wonderful amount of queer looking things on little china dishes arranged on trays, and each of us been surrounded with them! Little bowls of strange soup, banana shoots, slices of raw fish decorated with bits of carrot, bits of fried lobster, preserved apricots arranged against bits of some wild bird with a row of feathers like a ridge dividing them from some concoction of fish and stewed apple at the other side of the plate, omelets, stewed rice all in separate little dishes and bowls; though they brought in knives and forks we preferred trying to use the chop sticks and got on better than we had expected. To tell you the truth the taste of these things made me feel sick and I could only pretend to eat. I took a little rice and drank the tea and we kept giving Setsue compliments on the intertainment through Mr Tanabe.

Then we went back to Lafcadio's study and a lot of photograph albums were produced, and all the photos we sent to Lafcadio, yours, Posey's, mine and the children's exhibited. In one of them I found an envelope with the little snapshots of my Portadown drawing-room, and the stanhope with Posey and me in it. Setsue kept telling Mr Tanabe to tell me how much like her dead husband I seemed to her every time she looked at me. Finally as we rose to go, I asked if we could go to see Lafcadio's grave, and Kazuo and the little girl came in a 4th rickshaw with us – it took about an hour to get to the Buddhist Cemetery. It seemed a very bare unfinished place compared to our pretty English God's Acres, and the picture in Life and Letters looks prettier than the reality. Each grave has a little gate made of rough slats of wood – there were two little vases with a spray of plum blossom and peach standing in front of the stone pillar with his name Koizumi Yacoumo [sic] in Japanese characters. Two little trees of which I brought away little bunches of leaves; I have one for you and another for Posey. Kazuo and the small girlie left us here, Kazuo saying very quaintly 'Please come again soon', and we started on the long rickshaw ride to the hotel, and very tired and hungry we felt when we got back. To our surprise we beheld Mr Drabble walk in while we were at dinner, he is going to take Dot and me out, he has been hunting for us in one place or another and, as he said, ran us to earth at last. Today he has some business to attend to. Tomorrow we are going to the school where Mr Tanabe teaches – Mrs Kennard says she will not come, she has had enough of Japanese for the present! but I am interested in seeing everything of course, and Mr Tanabe says the Pieresses [sic] school is a thing most people want to see – the high-class Japanese girls all go to it.

Mason's account of the ending of his friendship with Lafcadio is interesting in that the account reported by Minnie Atkinson in this letter is at variance with that in Kennard[23] and one assumes that Kennard's account (that Lafcadio had cut him off after he neglected to take off his shoes entering his house) also derived from a conversation with Mason on this trip. It throws a fresh light on a matter which has puzzled subsequent biographers.[24]

Setsu Koizumi to Minnie Atkinson, Tokyo, 21/3/1909

This letter conveys an invitation to dinner to Minnie and Nina Kennard in the course of their visit to Japan. Short and affectionate (it is addressed to 'My dear sister Minnie') in good English and good handwriting, it was, according to Minnie Atkinson's diary [entry of 20/3/1909] written by a Mr Tanabe, presumably Hearn's former pupil.

Elizabeth [Wetmore (Bisland)] to Lilla [Hearn], Japan, 26 July [no year; 1911?]

Bisland is writing from a bungalow overlooking the Inland Sea. She refers to Humphrey's health being restored, possibly a reference to her husband. She gives an extended portrait of Kazuo at that time:

> Kazuo has just left after a week's visit, and I am missing him sorely – for a more charming, gifted, delightful boy I never saw. Just what I would wish a son of my own to be. He is so full of tact, so lighthearted, so instinct [?] with artless innocence & kind goodness. You would certainly be proud of your nephew if you knew him. It was his first visit in a foreign house, but not even an involuntary blunder did he make. I had waiting for him a full Japanese costume of soft [?] grey silk, Kimono...& haori, with his crest embroidered on the sleeves, & how very smart & handsome he looked in it. He is five feet six & promises to be much taller, & is as fair as I. Iwao, the second son, looks much more like you and Lafcadio & is the sternest little Samurai. Always at the top of his school, & caring only for success in his classes, for wrestling & jiujutsu. But Kazuo is like his father in mind & character; the same gentle modesty, careful scholarly pains taking-ness, & the same astonishing memory, & love of beauty. Kyoshi, the youngest boy, is the artist, but Kazuo's sketch book was full of delicious caricatures. He plays all sorts of folk music on the flute, & his first efforts at

literature are full of real promise. Most boys of 17 would have been bored to death playing around with an old lady, but we were as happy as children all the week, & had endless fun, doing Japanese flower arrangements, making tiny landscapes in dishes, sketching, writing poetry [?], & going for tremendous walks, and he seemed as amused and happy as possible. If we do settle down in England, which we are still hoping to do, I am going to have Kazuo come to me there for a visit, after he finishes at the university, & then I am sure you will grow to love him as much as I do.

Kazuo Koizumi to Lilla Hearn, Tokyo, 20/12/1912

It is a reply to a letter of hers and provides useful material on the visits of Elizabeth Wetmore (née Bisland) and of Minnie Atkinson, as well as on the Koizumi reverence for the Emperor:

> Now the sad year is going to depart, and the most hateful old and cruel Winter is already come. This year was the most unlucky year for Japan. The Great Emperor's death made all the nation full of grief. At that time the Japanese were all like in a bad dream. After that on the day of the great funeral of the late Emperor, our honorable General Nogi [General Maresuke Nogi (1849-1912), Commander of the Japanese Third Army in the Russo-Japanese War; later principal of a school for the Imperial family] and his wife committed suicides [sic] and again all the nation's hearts were touched.
>
> I want very much that you will visit Japan at the coronation ceremony. My dear Mrs. Wetmore will visit Japan again at that time. Won't you come to our country and stay long, and see all the sights and visit historic places? There are many fine places and buildings in Japan. Mrs. Wetmore stayed long in Japan and visited many famous and fine places. So I suppose she can write a very fine big unmistaken book about our country. Dear Aunt Minnie visited Japan, but she stayed in Japan only a few weeks, so she did not see many fine places, she hurried too much to return to England.

Kazuo's reverence for the Emperor and admiration for Nogi's gesture is in line with his father's attitudes but bearing in mind that Kazuo was now nineteen and his father had been dead for eight years, may be evidence of his mother's influence. By extension, it may indicate that Setsu played a major role in shaping Lafcadio's approach to Shinto and its associated cult of the Emperor.

Minnie Atkinson to Ned [Edward M. Stephens, grandson of Lafcadio's aunt, Jane, and Henry Colclough Stephens], Burgess Hill, Sussex, England, 7/8/1931

Minnie disputed a claim (presumably by Kennard) that Lafcadio never learned to speak Japanese:

> The remarks as to Lafcadio never having learned to speak Japanese is nonsense, as his wife told me, and I fancy it was mentioned in one of his books, he used to love getting her to tell him stories & of course I can personally vouch for the fact *she* could not speak one word of English! I know he never managed to *master* Japanese but it is as you know *most* difficult!

She stated that she could remember nothing of her father.

Minnie was irritated by inaccuracies in Kennard's biography of Lafcadio:

> Did you read Mrs Kennard's book? I was surprised by the tales she had picked [?] up in Ireland, & really she was such a liar, it would not be beyond my belief that she embroidered whatever she got out of some one over there – I threatened to write to the papers and deny the truth of some things she meant to publish about our journey to Japan. She had to omit these – Dot probably told you she offered to give me £50 if I would hand over Lafcadio's letters to her, but I refused & we compromised when I said she could have extracts if she would give the £50 to L's eldest boy to help with [?] the expenses of his education – as I could do nothing in that way myself.

On the reason why Lafcadio stopped writing to her she said:

> By the way I forgot to tell you. Lafcadio stopped writing me those long letters when Posey said she was going to Japan to see him – quaint soul!

From Minnie Atkinson to Ned [Edward Stephens], Burgess Hill, Sussex, England, 6/9/1931

This letter contains material on Lafcadio's habit of breaking friendships as well as on her father, Charles Bush Hearn:

> Lafcadio, there is no denying, was an eccentric as well as a most painstaking genius. This quality of painstaking is so evident in his writings, letters and books; he seemed to me to be anxious to convey his meaning clearly to the reader, to search for the words wherewith to make his meaning absolutely clear – I don't think he was willing to change his opinions! – nor to have much patience with even [?] the kindest most well meaning of his friends; he broke friendships relentlessly [?] – I learned this (or rather was confirmed in my theories about him) when I met Mr. Mason in Yokohama – he by the way though he had married a charming Japanese wife himself, tried to persuade Lafcadio not to carry out his intention of becoming a Japanese *subject* & was simply thrown aside after very true and appreciative friendship, but was not at all bitter about it, quiet kindly [?] old man! – he was removed from this world most suddenly; the club house where he and his son happened to be when the great earthquake came, was thrown right down the Bluff and all in it killed instantaneously! There was always a feeling in my mind that Lafcadio & Uncle Dick were alike in disposition, capable of great affection, but very unwilling to forgive real or fancied offences – I was very fond of Uncle Dick & he told me. . . I was absolutely his favorite among all the nieces – Looking back to one's childhood I can remember his skipping into the big Loughgall drawing room, to sit near while I improvised simple tunes and chords on the...old piano – really it was strange we were never really told anything definite about any of father's youth, or that of *any* of the brothers and sister.

On her father and mother, she has this to say:

> . . . As to my youth my dear! I was not even ('in opes' [?]) the time of the mutiny, which broke out in 1857. Father was home & on leave in Dublin, where he married Mother some time that year – Lilla was born in 1858 when they had returned to India – mutiny was quickly quelled. I appeared in 1859. Posey the following year, a dead born babe the next; and poor little Mother the Autumn of that year died suddenly.

On the ending of her correspondence with Lafcadio, she states:

> . . . he had as you saw in one letter determined *only* to write to me[;] Lilla wrote several times & Posey announced she was going to Japan to see him[.] I wrote to tell him that she had insisted on getting his address from me; saying [?] she could get it from the publishers & I felt it childish to hold out. He simply stopped writing to me at once! & in the end Posey being taken ill in New Zealand never went to Japan after all.

There is no reference to envelopes being returned as stated by Nina Kennard: Minnie says that Lafcadio simply stopped writing.

Edward M. Stephens to Kazuo Koizumi, Dublin, 12/2/1936

This was prompted by Kazuo's publication of *Father and I*; Stephens was interested in any further information Kazuo might be able to add:

> My father and yours were first cousins. They met as children when your father was in Dublin. I'm afraid that his recollection of that period was not a happy one.
>
> He seemed a big boy to my father and his sisters who were younger & were a little afraid of him on account of his eye. One of my aunts told me that he remembered visiting 'Patritci' as they called him, at a Roman Catholic school.
>
> I heard something of your family from Mrs Atkinson & her daughter with whom I spent a holiday in Rome in the spring of 1914, just after their return from Japan.
>
> It happened that just before your book came I had been writing down my childhood recollections of J.M. Synge (my mother's brother)[25]. They included an account of rescuing a kitten from a patch of grass by the pier of a bridge in mid-stream. It was interesting to find that you were doing the same thing at the other side of the world about this same date! I wonder if your father ever talked to you of Dublin or his relations here?

The reference to the Stephens children being afraid of Lafcadio on account of his eye is interesting as it again raises the question of when the accident to it happened. If, as has been accepted up to now, it was when he was at Ushaw, it is unlikely that the Stephens children would have seen much of him, if indeed they saw him at all, apart from a rare visit such as that by his cousin (I assume that this was to Ushaw but it could, of course, have been to an earlier school which Lafcadio might have attended, before Ushaw, possibly in Dublin). Mrs Brenane had taken up residence in England and Lafcadio appears have spent many of his holidays in Ushaw. If he did go home, one assumes that it would have been to Redhill in Surrey, where Mrs Brenane lived. The impression given by this letter is that the Stephens children feared Lafcadio's eye when he was still around Dublin (ie, before going to England in 1863) and this would fit in with Lafcadio's statement that the operation on his eye was performed in Dublin.

Alternatively, he may have returned to Dublin for some time between leaving Ushaw in 1867 and emigrating to America in 1869 and seen his cousins at that stage.

Hugh Rudkin to Daisy [?], Guildford, England, 17/7/1940

Rudkin was the author of the article on Lafcadio Hearn and the Hearn Family which has appeared in *Notes & Queries*[26] the previous December.

He mentions in a P.S. that he had seen in *The Times* a death notice of Miss Elizabeth S.M. Hearn, the youngest daughter of Charles Bushe [Lafcadio's father's middle name was variously spelled both with and without a final 'e'], Hearn, who had died in London in 1938, aged 80.

SERIES OF THREE LETTERS BETWEEN [EDWARD] STEPHENS AND MARY DALRYMPLE HEARN OF AYLESBURY, ENGLAND, 1952

Stephens wrote to an address at Enfield, England, on

5/2/1952, following sight of a death notice in the *Daily Telegraph* of Alice Mary Elizabeth Hearn, enquiring if they were related. Her niece, Mary Dalrymple Hearn, replied from her address in Aylesbury, confirming that they shared a mutual great-great grandfather in Major Robert Thomas Hearn (son of the Venerable Daniel Hearn).

She said that a now-dead cousin used to refer in passing in letters to the 'Dan Hearns' and the 'Cullenswoods' from the house in which they lived. It is possible that 'Cullenswood' was therefore the name of the Hearn house in Correagh; if so, this is the first reference that I have come across to that name.

Mary Dalrymple cautions that few of her family records were very reliable: her aunt had jotted down often mutually contradictory notes on odd bits of envelope. She did say, however, that they had one letter from the Venerable Daniel Hearn to his second wife about some property which he was overseeing for her father (Marcus Dowley) who was Secretary to the Irish Treasury.

Among these bits of family lore was a legend that the Venerable Daniel Hearn's name was originally Heron and that he had changed it to Hearn when he migrated from England to Ireland following a terrific quarrel with his brother, possibly called Anthony. However, she had difficulty with this and other elements of family belief about their genealogy: Daniel Hearn had kept the family crest, motto and coat of arms. She had also spotted the contradiction between the ingrained tradition that he had come over from England with the Duke of Dorset as Lord Lieutenant of Ireland and the fact that Dorset had not landed until 1731, whereas the Venerable Daniel Hearn had graduated from Trinity College, Dublin in 1713 and become Archdeacon of Cashel in 1727.

Edward Stephens replied on 13/2/1952, agreeing that the dates refuted the story that the Venerable Daniel Hearn had been brought to Ireland by Lionel Sackville, Duke of Dorset, but speculates that he might have been appointed his Chaplain because of some earlier family association.

He said that Elizabeth Holmes, Lafcadio's grandmother, was a niece of Sir Robert Arbuthnot, a general in the Peninsular war. He ended by asking if she was aware of the 'tradition of second sight which was a marked and extraordinary faculty in our branch of the family'.

[Edward Stephens] to Mrs [Vera] McWilliams (author of a 1946 biography of Hearn[27]), 19/2/1954

This contains genealogical information, including material relating to Sir Robert Arbuthnot, a granduncle of Charles Bush Hearn, and grand-nephew of John Arbuthnot, doctor to Queen Anne, etc.

Vera McWilliams to [Edward] Stephens, Ann Arbor, Michigan, 1/3/1954

McWilliams thanks Stephens for copies of Susan Hearn's letters and says she will preserve them in her Hearn collection which will eventually be passed on to one of the large Hearn collections at an American university, probably Harvard or Tulane.

Edward M. Stephens to Vera McWilliams, 11/3/1954

This letter contains useful information on Charles Bush Hearn's later years, as well as on Susan Hearn's papers, and is worth extensive quotation:

> The story of her [Alicia's] death, as I heard it, was strangely tragic. When she was sitting with Charles on the verandah, very weak, in an armchair, she seemed inclined to sleep, so he left her for a few minutes to stroll round the garden. When he came back to the verandah, she appeared to be still sleeping in the chair where he had left her, and beside her on the table he saw a letter in his mother's handwriting. Charles turned to his wife, but she was dead. He could not himself believe it until a friend came out of the

house, perceived what had happened, and persuaded him of the truth. The letter, which came from his Calvinistic old mother when he was walking in the garden, was one upbraiding his wife for her matrimonial arrangements, of which his mother had never approved.

His devotion to Alicia was never shaken by the vicissitudes of his life. My aunt, Lizzie Stephens, told me that, when he returned to Ireland after his wife's death, he occupied the room next to hers, and that, one night, she thought she heard somebody crying and went in to see what was the matter. She found him with some small personal belongings of his dead wife on the dressing-table. When he heard the door open, he turned to his niece and said, 'That's all I have left, Lizzie, of everything I lived for.' I cannot remember whence I gleaned a story, which may be a legend, of his death. According to it, he was on his last voyage home when, one evening, as he was walking the deck with the captain, he stopped, held out his arms, said, 'is that you, darling,' and fell on the deck never to recover consciousness.

The story I heard in boyhood about Charles' attitude towards his marriage with Rosa Tessima was this. Her brothers had taken exception to his relations with her and had decided to murder him. One of them attacked him with a knife, which stuck in his pocketbook. Afterwards they decided it would be better that he should marry their sister, and had a form of marriage celebrated according to the rites of the Greek Church when they had made Charles so drunk that he could remember nothing of the ceremony. He found himself confronted, the day after, with his signature in the Church register, and decided to accept responsibility for Rosa as his wife. This story may have been invented to appease his mother.

I heard that Richard Hearn's chief Irish friend in Paris was Edward Burke, who was in the wine business, but I never succeeded in tracing any of his family.

So far as I know, Aunt Susan's diary and, perhaps, other papers, came into the possession of Miss Edith Hardy, who died at Newry some years ago. Her affairs were wound up by a local clergy-man, who sent military medals to Mrs. Dorothy Holmes, but seems to have preserved no papers. I hope that Miss Hardy had parted with Aunt Susan's diary before her death and that it may be safe somewhere.

The story of Lafcadio's grandmother writing a venomous

letter about her matrimonial arrangements in this letter adds to the weight of evidence that Lafcadio's parents never actually divorced. It also supports the conjecture that his father was less than enthusiastic about marriage to his mother.

[Edward Stephens] to Mr [O.W.] Frost, (author of the book, *Young Hearn*) 30/3/1954

This letter contains information on Henry Colclough Stephens, who was married to an aunt of Lafcadio's and in whose house Lafcadio and his mother stayed when they first arrived in Ireland. Stephens used to entertain on a considerable scale and it was believed in the family that it was at his house that Lafcadio played under the table with the boots of soldier colleagues of his father.

Edward Stephens takes issue with Frost's claim that the marriage of Charles and Rosa was annulled at Dublin in the autumn of 1856:

> I would be greatly interested to know whether this refers to the result of any legal proceedings as I have always believed that the marriage was simply disregarded by Charles. The story that I heard as a boy about the marriage was that Rosa's brothers made Charles so drunk that he went through the marriage ceremony without knowing what he was doing, and, on the following day, was confronted with his signature in the register. I also heard that Rosa came to Dublin looking for Charles after he had remarried and gone to India and that she called at Leinster Square where a family of Moores, cousins of the Hearns, lived. She was unable to obtain any information and, so far as I know, then left Ireland.

Frost says in his book that, during the autumn of 1854, Charles probably secured an annulment of his marriage to Rosa Cassimati. How he won his freedom could not be definitely ascertained. In the absence of official documents (which Frost attributes to the destruction of records during 'the Irish Rebellion'; they were actually destroyed during the Civil War), he supposed that the Greek Orthodox marriage certificate 'did not in some respect fulfil English legal requirements'.[29]

It is significant that, according to Stephens, Rosa is alleged to have come back to see Charles, not Lafcadio. Both Frost[30] and Elizabeth Stevenson, a later Hearn biographer, quote, without reference to a source, a family story that Rosa returned once to Ireland 'to see her children' but was not allowed to do so.[31] If Frost and Stevenson were basing their accounts on Edward Stephens' story, they made two crucial changes: (1) that Rosa returned to see her children as opposed to Charles; and (2) that she was *not allowed* see them whereas in Stephens's story she is *unable* to glean information from the current occupants of the Dublin house. Altering the story in this way alters Rosa's character and makes her a concerned mother whereas otherwise there is no evidence to suggest that her behaviour towards her children was any less callous than that of her husband.

Stephens gives the full connection between the Hearns and the Arbuthnots:

> The Arbuthnot connection was as follows:- The famous John Arbuthnot, Queen Anne's doctor, had several brothers, among them George, who married a Miss Peggy Robinson. His son, John, who settled in Ireland, married Anne Stone, sister of the [Church of Ireland] Primate, who resided in Henrietta Street, then called 'Primate's Hill', at a house on the site now occupied by King's Inn's Library. Primate Stone was an associate in Government of the Lord Lieutenant, the Duke of Dorset, whose Chaplain, Daniel Hearn, Archdeacon of Cashel, is said to have been. John Arbuthnot and his wife had a number of children, one of whom was Sir Robert and another was Anne, who married Robert Holmes, and was the mother of a number of children including Elizabeth who became Mrs Daniel James Hearn, Lafcadio's grandmother.

The family connection with the Duke of Dorset as Lord Lieutenant of Ireland in the eighteenth century therefore seems to have been through the maternal, Holmes/Arbuthnot, line as well as, possibly, through the paternal, Hearn, line.

At the same time, his great, great grandfather on his paternal side, the Venerable Daniel Hearn, would have moved in the same influential circles as Primate Stone, the senior Church of Ireland clergyman, whose second wife was the daughter of the Secretary to the Irish Treasury. All this underlines my own belief that the Hearn family were well established in Ireland at the time of the Duke of Dorset's arrival and their position in the politico-religious oligarchy of the eighteenth century did not derive from the Venerable Daniel Hearn's accompanying the Duke to Ireland.

Fragment of Typescript letter. Pages two and three only of three-page letter. No addressee or signature. 'Ned Stephens' written in manuscript at top of page 2. Possibly a draft of a letter from Edward Stephens to O.W. Frost.

The letter deals with the contentious issue of the nature of the separation between Lafcadio's parents:

> In a footnote referring to the marriage of Charles Bushe Hearn and Rosa you state – 'The marriage was annulled at Dublin in the autumn of 1856.' I would be greatly interested to know whether this refers to the result of any legal proceedings as I have always believed that the marriage was simply disregarded by Charles. The story that I heard as a boy about the marriage was that Rosa's brothers made Charles so drunk that he went through the marriage ceremony without knowing what he was doing, and, on the following day, was confronted with his signature in the register. I also heard that Rosa came to Dublin looking for Charles after he had remarried and gone to India and that she called at Leinster Square where a family of Moores, cousins of the Hearns, lived. She was unable to obtain any information and, so far as I know, then left Ireland.
>
> In your letter you mention Robert Clements Arbuthnot Elwood; he was given the name of Mrs. Elwood's grandmother, Anne Arbuthnot, sister of Sill Robert. The Arbuthnot connection was as follows: The famous John Arbuthnot, Queen Anne's doctor, had several brothers among them George, who married a Miss Peggy Robinson. His son, John, who settled in Ireland, married Anne Stone, sister of the Primate, who resided in Henrietta Street,

then called Primate's Hill, at a house on the site now occupied by King's Inn's Library. Primate Stone was an associate in Government of the Lord Lieutenant, the Duke of Dorset, whose Chaplain, Daniel Hearn , Archdeacon of Cashel, is said to have been. John Arbuthnot and his wife had a number of children, of whom one was Sir Robert and another was Anne, who married Robert Holmes , and was the mother of a number of children, including Sarah who became Mrs. Brenane, and Elizabeth who became Mrs, Daniel James Hearn, Lafcadio's grandmother.

[Edward Stephens] to Vera McWilliams, 5/4/1954

This letter is interesting regarding second sight in the Hearn family, the importance of which Stephens appreciated for Lafcadio's work:

> I have mentioned one matter which perhaps should be amplified, the fact that members of the Hearn family had 'second sight'. As the ghostliness of experience is one of the main inspirations of Hearn's work, some account of the gift of vision as claimed by his relations should perhaps be published. This curious gift was always regarded in our family as inherited from the Hearns, and was certainly possessed by my father and one at least of his sisters. My great-grandfather, John Stephens, was a Quaker merchant whose connections were not credited with psychic peculiarities.
>
> I could tell a number of stories of visions seen by my father, a busy Solicitor, who disliked anything connected with spiritualism, and saw visions in spite of himself. They were sometimes of quite ordinary events happening at a distance. About these I never knew him mistaken. Others, not so easily verified, he used to recount with, I am sure, perfect accuracy. My aunt, Mrs. Oulton, occasionally told me of visions she had seen. They were Lafcadio's first cousins, and their power of vision may have been in some way similar to his, or at least their development of a common inheritance.

O.W. Frost to [Edward] Stephens, Champaign, Illinois, 30/4/1954

Frost states that:

> I have never been able to prove that Charles [Bush Hearn] did

obtain a 'deed of separation' (as Mrs Kennard calls it), for the Public Record Office near the Four Courts [in Dublin] has almost nothing on marriage cases prior to 1922.

He suggests that a *Legal Diary* in the library of the King's Inns might have something on marriages for 1856.

[Edward Stephens] to Mr Frost, 10/5/1954, 2, Harcourt Terrace, Dublin

Stephens who was, incidentally, a lawyer said in reply:

> I know of no reason for thinking that the marriage of Charles and Rosa was not legal according to English law. If it had been legally set aside, such a decision would, I think, have been generally known as, of course, it would have put the legality of Charles' second marriage beyond dispute.

It is clear from this exchange that the marriage of Lafcadio's parents may not have been legally dissolved and, accordingly, that Charles's second marriage was not legal. One wonders whether Charles and Rosa might have come to some agreement on the issue and whether the loan which Charles had taken out from Mrs Brenane could be connected with this; ie, did he pay Rosa off? Was her later visit to Dublin to see Charles in some way connected with this? One can only conjecture at this point but the possibility casts an even darker shadow over the circumstances of Lafcadio's youth.

O.W. Frost to [Edward] Stephens, Champaign, Illinois, 1/6/1954

Frost responded on the question of Charles's divorce and says that he had relied on two sources:

1. The statement of Charles's sister, Ann Elizabeth Hardy, in a letter to Lafcadio in 1890 that Charles and Rosa 'agreed to have a divorce at deed of separation'.
2. Lafcadio's statement to his brother that their father had got a divorce through a technicality, on the basis that his

marriage, 'though legal abroad in the Orient, was not legal according to English law'.
This evidence looks weak, especially when set against the contrary indications of the results of Stephens' researches and the fact that Charles Bush Hearn's mother, Mrs Elizabeth Hearn, berated her daughter-in-law for allegedly irregular marital arrangements (see below).

[Edward Stephens] to Mr Frost, 15/9/1954

Stephens retorted that his legal researches, including in the King's Inn's Library, had been unable to find 'evidence that Charles Bush Hearn obtained a divorce'.

[Edward Stephens] to Mrs McWilliams, 5/1/1955

Stephens states that the Westmeath property came into the Hearn family from Miss Anne Dowley, the Venerable Daniel Hearn's second wife. The original estate was purchased in 1743 by Daniel Hearn's father-in-law, Marcus Dowley, Secretary to the Irish Treasury, and amounted to upwards of 2,500 acres. The Dowley parents and the Hearns lived next door to each other in Stephen's Green in houses on the site of what was later St Vincent's Hospital. A settlement of the estate 'appears to have been made' by Robert Thomas Hearn, eldest son of the Venerable Daniel, and his eldest son, Daniel James Hearn, on 30 May 1789.

The documents on which I relied in my book indicate that the Westmeath lands came into the family much later, as part of the marriage settlement of Lafcadio's grandfather, Daniel James Hearn. There is also the question as to why the Westmeath estate was not mentioned in official documents relating to the residency of, for example, Daniel James's father, Robert Thomas Hearn. Why was Robert Thomas Hearn described as being of Scarlet in the Isle of Man and Knockballymore in County Fermanagh in official records[28] and no mention made of extensive estates in Westmeath, particularly if more than one address is being listed? It might be that Edward Stephens accepted the family belief that they had obtained the Westmeath lands in the eighteenth century and simply assumed that they were included in the 1789 settlement.

Also, it is curious that Edward Stephens does not appear to have found in the official records any trace of the indisputable fact that Charles Bush Hearn had borrowed heavily from Mrs Brenane and that the lands in Westmeath, the surety for the loan, became forfeit on Mrs Brenane's bankruptcy; he deals with the disposal of the estate but seems ignorant of these facts.

Dorothy Holmes (younger daughter of Minnie Atkinson, born 1894) to Lilo [Stephens, wife of Edward M. Stephens?], 9/3/1965

> When my mother and I went to Japan in 1909 with Mrs. Kennard (I expect you have seen her book – with our photos in it) aunt Setsue was still alive. Kazuo was the eldest of 3 sons. He was about 15 then, + strongly resembled my brother Carleton. There was also a little girl, Suzuko, who died fairly soon after that, + I heard one of the boys died also. Someone told me that Kazuo and the remaining one were for some reason not on speaking terms. About 20 years ago, I heard through Lurgan Council offices that a mysterious Mrs. McClelland of Ames, Iowa had been writing there + to Portadown making enquiries about me. I wrote off to her, thinking that she must be some lost relative, but apparently she had lived in Japan in her youth, + had always been extremely interested in uncle Lafcadio's books. . .

The letter states that a Mrs McClelland of Ames, Iowa, had the letters which Minnie Atkinson had written to Lafcadio in the 1890s, which Kazuo had given her.

It is interesting that she reveals that she kept in touch with Kazuo and visited a grandson of 'Uncle Jim', Lafcadio's brother. Lilla Hearn had gone to see him in Canada (Dorothy did not know the circumstances under which he went there).

Her mother was the only one of Charles Bush Hearn's

daughters brought up in Armagh – Lilla and Posey were with relatives in England.

On the disposal of the paintings of her great-uncle, Richard Hearn, she says:

> We used to have several of Uncle Dick Hearn's enormous pictures, but when we left Burgess Hill, where there was lots of wall space, no one wanted them & wickedly got rid of them. I'm afraid I never admired them much – they were so vast and gloomy! I have kept a smallish one of a road in France which I always liked – quite a different type from the others. A few years ago, I drove through Barbizon with some American cousins & visited Millet's house & felt rather thrilled with the thought that Uncle Dick must have been there.

Posey Hearn, Charles Bush Hearn's youngest daughter, was twice married and had no children – 'she was a most comical person'.

Marjory (Minnie Atkinson's eldest daughter, born in 1888) married Thomas Inglis Hall who was killed in Mesopotamia in the 1914-18 war and then lived in the south of France. She has three children. Her son, John Inglis Hall, born 1911, went to Trinity College, Dublin, and was a writer. Her second husband was Esmond Grattan Thompson who had died a few years previously.

Her son, Carleton (born 1890), was British Consul at Tetuan, Morocco and died unmarried in 1922.

Dorothy had a miniature of Mrs Richard Holmes, née Arbuthnot:

> She is very fascinating with pearls in her hair & an enormous black hat with ostrich feathers. Aunt Lilla said she was supposed to be a friend of Bonnie Prince Charlie!

Dorothy Holmes to Lilo [Stephens ?], 7/11/1965

This letter contains interesting information about Lafcadio's painter uncle, Richard Hearn.

> Now about Uncle 'Dick' Hearn. I don't know when he was born,

but I see in Frost's book 'Young Hearn' that he died in 1890. My mother went to stay with him in Paris before she was engaged or married. She was married in 1886. She stayed with him in his studio in Paris, + people used to make remarks, as in France an uncle can marry his niece! It was at the time when the Pickwick Papers was coming out in Monthly installments and Uncle Dick used to follow her about reading them aloud with tears of merriment running down his cheeks! I never heard that he became a naturalised Frenchman, or any whisper of the mysterious Miss Jones. Mummy never spoke of meeting a lot of French people when she stayed with him.

... Many of Uncle Dick's pictures were in the vicinity of the River Rance, between Dinard and Dinant. When Mummy stayed with him – I suppose about 1883 or 4, or before, he gave her piano lessons with a Mademoiselle Michelle who had been a pupil of Chopin! – I wonder why he never did a portrait of Mummy, she was so pretty. She never mentioned meeting Millet or any of the Barbizon artists.

[Sir] Derek [Oulton] to Brian [Hearn?], London, 6/6/1974

Contains the following anecdote about Charles Bush Hearn:

Of course you must be right about Surgeon Major Charles Bush Hearn. The reason my grandmother (above) [refers to a genealogical table in the letter which identifies her as Susan Charles Stephens, daughter of Jane Hearn and Henry Counsellor. Stephens] was [called] Charles was – according to my father's [Charles Cameron Courtenay Oulton] romanticised version – that he clattered up to the church where she was being christened, on his military charger, (he being both her godfather and her uncle) and announced loudly 'She is to be called Charles!' (When recounting the story – one of his favourites – my father always split the name into two syllables and accented the second one. This hardly accords with his being a Papist!

Toki Koizumi (son of Lafcadio's eldest son, Kazuo) to [Sir] Derek Oulton, 10/11/1984

Toki gives an account of his own life. He had been working in the Public Information Office of the US Forces in Japan since 1952 and was due to retire shortly.

He also gives information about three of Lafcadio Hearn's children, Iwao (a high school teacher who died of cancer in 1937), Kiyoshi (a painter who committed suicide in 1962 after the death of his wife and 'an intimate friend') and Suzuko (remained unmarried; 'suffered from brain fever. . . caused by scarlet fever' and died in 1944).

Some New Hearn Primary Source Material

DIARY

JOURNEY TO JAPAN: MINNIE ATKINSON'S DIARY OF HER 1909 VISIT WITH NINA KENNARD

I used a typescript copy, not the original manuscript of this diary.

In 1909 Minnie Atkinson, accompanied by her youngest daughter, Charlotte Dorothy, and Nina Kennard travelled to Japan by sea and returned via the Trans-Siberian railway. The journey was organized by Kennard who at that stage had undertaken her biography of Hearn (published in 1912), with the object of meeting Setsu and others who could contribute direct knowledge of Hearn. There are hints that Kennard may have paid for the trip: she was married to a wealthy husband while Minnie was now a widow.

They set off on the *SS Maloia* on 29 January 1909 and there are signs of tension between Minnie and Kennard from the beginning. The second entry [30/1/1909] notes that they have been 'sent' to a table on the other side of the saloon from that allocated to Kennard. A further entry [20/2/1909] found that when they changed to the *Macedonia* at Colombo their cabin was 'stifling' and so much smaller than Kennard's, next door.

The entry for 4/3/1909 states that Kennard 'again would not land' at Hong Kong. On 6/3/1909, at Shanghai, Minnie notes:

> Mrs Kennard says that we shall remain on board the 'Macedonia' to everyone's surprise. Mr Cross seems to think it cannot be done; however it is so arranged.

The following day, it is more of the same:

> ... Mrs K. still says we are to stay; Captain and Purser says we may

but it will not be very comfortable.

The next day, 8/3/1909, Kennard discommodes Minnie and her daughter by insisting on an early lunch, which means that they could not go with the others, as they had wished to do. Then they were left to wander about as Kennard said she did not want them.

They arrived at Nagasaki on 12 March. On the 15th, they dined with the Youngs, Lafcadio's employers in Kobe; they told Minnie that Lafcadio had spoken much of her.

They travelled on to Tokyo and, on the 17th, met W.B. Mason, Lafcadio's friend, who she described thus:

> ... a gentle soul, he had a bad nervous breakdown and has the irresolute manner connected with that kind of illness – married to a Japanese for 30 years and says he has been most happy.

On 19 March, while Kennard is off on a trip to Tokyo on her own, Setsu and Kazuo arrive in response to a letter written to Setsu by Minnie on Mason's advice. It is clear from her description that Setsu was unable to speak English to any degree:

> In the afternoon a messenger came to say that a Japanese lady was waiting in the hall and I found Setsue [sic] and Kazuo – they seemed very pleased to see me but unfortunately we could not speak to each other till I got the hotel clerk to interpret for us until Mr Mason appeared. We all found the likeness between Kazuo and Carleton (Minnie's son) most remarkable, and they could see it from the photograph even. Setsue very pleased with the locket I brought and cried, poor thing, when she saw Lafcadio's likeness (Mr Mason brought a photo of Lafcadio and wife where the likeness between L. and me is most remarkable).

There were two visits to Lafcadio's house, on 20 and 26 March, which have been described in much greater detail by Kennard.[32] However, the diary is an interesting variation in perspective and includes some detail omitted by Kennard.

They left Japan on 2 April 1909 and returned to England via Russia, arriving on 18 April.

Some New Hearn Primary Source Material

MEMORANDA

Incomplete 4-page extract from a document by Elizabeth Holmes Hearn (Lafcadio's grandmother), dated 1887 in other handwriting on the top

This gives a lot of genealogical information which emphasises the grand connections of her antecedents.

Manuscript document entitled 'Notes taken down from Mrs Henry Oulton (née Susan Stephens, daughter of Jane Hearn and Henry Colclough Stephens?), 3 February 1936

It gives the background to Lafcadio's step-mother, Alicia Goslin, daughter of Col. Goslin of the Bengal Lancers. She had two sons and a daughter by George Crawford. Crawford died in Australia and his family were shipwrecked in the Indian Ocean on the way back. Both sons died young as a result of exposure to the sun during this incident.

Her daughter, Madaline [sic], married Col. Wetheral [this name has been usually been spelled with a double 'll' at the end in Hearn biography] and had a daughter, possibly the child with whom Lafcadio played and by whom he remembered being beaten up.

As regards the Holmes family background, it states:

> Mrs Holmes of Waterstown Park was the beautiful Ann Arbuthnot daughter of Bishop Arbuthnot and sister of Sir Robert who was a friend of Wellington.

It paints a difficult portrait of the situation between his parents when his father returned to Dublin during Lafcadio's infancy:

> Shortly after his home coming Rosa suffered some very grave upset but before long recovered and continued living as his wife. It is not

307

certain where he was living while he was in Ireland, possibly in Dundrum.

It states that Rosa's companion, Miss Butcher, and possibly Lafcadio, accompanied Rosa back to Greece for the birth of her third child: 'Mrs Brenane paid their way home. It may have been on this journey that Lafcadio saw and remembered Malta.'

Charles returned to Dublin on 23 July 1856 and married Alicia Crawford on 18 July 1857.

Memorandum prepared by [Edward] 'Ned' Stephens for Vera McWilliams, 5/4/1954 (with a covering manuscript letter to Dorothy [Holmes?], Dublin, 7/12/1954)

A number of points are of interest:

Stephens contradicts Kennard's claim[33] that there was a tradition in the Hearn family that they were of gipsy descent:

> I have never heard anyone of Hearn descent claim gipsy blood. Members of the family of Jane Hearn certainly had 'second sight', and could often describe events happening at a distance. It is difficult to imagine circumstances in which a person of gypsy blood acquired armorial bearings.

He claims that Charles Bush Hearn had arrived back in Ireland alone and was stationed in Limerick when Lafcadio was born; he cites 'Aunt Susan's letter of 26th June, 1850' in support of this (see letter above).

Of Charles Bush Hearn's position within the Hearn family, he says:

> I think the position that Charles occupied was due to his connection with an influential army circle. His mother's uncle, General Sir Robert Arbuthnot, was a friend of Wellington.

Stephens recounts a particularly fascinating anecdote from Lafcadio's childhood:

> Of those of my relations whom I remember, only two remembered seeing Lafcadio as a schoolboy. One was aunt Lizzie Franks (née Stephens) and she said that she remembered him as a queer looking dark boy called 'Patrici' and that once she was taken to see him at some Roman Catholic School. He tried, she said, to insist on her making a genuflection as they passed a statue of the Blessed Virgin on the stairs, but she refused.

Elizabeth Bisland[34] tells of an unidentified 'cousin' who remembered visiting Lafcadio at his 'priest's [sic] college' where he became agitated when she refused to 'bow' to a statue of the Virgin Mary. This may well be the same anecdote, but if it is not, if young 'Patrici' was in the habit of trying to get his Protestant relations respect Roman Catholic pieties, then it strengthens the grounds for conjecturing that he may have gone through a period of engagement with Roman Catholicism at Ushaw. The difference between the request to bow in Bisland's version and to genuflect in this one is significant: bowing to the statue would have been less repugnant to a good Protestant than genuflecting and, if Lafcadio did want genuflection, then he really was in the grip of Roman Catholic piety at that time. The staunchness of the Hearns' Protestantism is underlined by Stephen's description of Elizabeth Holmes Hearn, Lafcadio's paternal grandmother, as 'a Calvinistic person with a very strong belief in the devil, very strict in the upbringing of children'.

Typescript Document Entitled '*HEARN*' and dated 2 July 1954. Unsigned but likely to be by Edward Stephens

This document throws an interesting light on supernatural belief in the Hearn family:

Dr. Henry Oulton, who was married to Susan Stephens, daughter of Henry Colclough Stephens and Jane Margaret Hearn, lived for a number of years at No. 6 North Frederick Street, a street parallel to Gardiner Street where Mrs. Oulton's mother had lived when she was first married, and linked to it by Great Denmark Street and Gardiner's Place. It formed part of the 18th century residential district. Round these houses, at that time about a century old, ghost stories tended to centre. There were unaccountable happenings in the Oulton's house which reached a climax when Posey Hearn, Lafcadio's half-sister, came to stay. The family had often noticed that bedroom doors used to be opened unaccountably at night. Posy Hearn was allotted a bedroom at the top of the house with a door facing the door of another bedroom across the lobby. When she went to bed, the door opposite hers opened, someone seemed to cross the lobby, and her door opened. As there was nobody there, she shut her door and tried to go to sleep. Presently, the door burst open, she heard footsteps coming into the room and a person seemed to fall across her bed. She was thought to have become unconscious from fright, but nothing more happened, and she did not tell the family about the incident until they met at breakfast in the morning. The members of the family said everything they could think of to allay her fears and greatly surprised the eldest daughter, Jane, then a schoolgirl, by saying, when she came down, that she had gone into Posy's room in the night. They heard afterwards that a man who had occupied the house, after suffering sometime from mental distress, had hanged himself from the bannisters of the top landing.

Typescript document unsigned, undated, no heading, possibly by Edward Stephens

It states that after Alicia Goslin broke off their engagement, Charles Bush Hearn did not speak to anybody for a long while afterwards.

About the circumstances of the marriage of Lafcadio's parents it says:

> Her [Rosa's] brother tried to murder Hearn but the attempt failed through his knife sticking in Hearn's pocket book. He subsequently arranged that Hearn should marry his sister. He seems only to have got Hearn's consent through the use of drugs.

Hearn went through the marriage service, according to the rights [sic] of the Greek Church, in a drugged condition and brought the lady home to Dublin as his wife. They had two sons, James, who subsequently went to America, and Lafcadio.

The atmosphere of a conventional Protestant house in Dublin did not suit Mrs Hearn and she soon returned to Greece, leaving Charles Hearn to look after the two children. What became of James I do not know, but a relative Mrs Brenan [sic] by name, who happened to be a Roman Catholic, offered to educate Lafcadio if his father would consent to his being brought up in the R. Catholic faith. This his father agreed to do and himself left again for India. Charles Hearn's action in allowing his son to be brought up a Roman Catholic excited violent resentment among the Protestant members of the family, whose subsequent intercourse with Lafcadio was on this account distinctly restricted.

It happened a considerable time afterwards, on his return to Europe, Charles Hearn was asked by a fellow passenger on board the ship to leave a travelling rug at a friend's house in London. He readily agreed to do this and on his arrival at the house was shown into the drawing room; presently the door opened and the lady he had been originally engaged to walked in, wearing widow's weeds There was no divorce possible according to the Greek law but Hearn seems to have known, or at least to have bean fairly sure that his Greek wife was alive. In spite of this he arranged to marry again and was married in London according to the rights [sic] of the Church of England. He had three children Lilla, Minnie and Posey. He subsequently returned to India with his wife who while there had a very severe illness. She had nearly recovered and was sitting on the veranda, Hearn was in the garden and did not happen to see the post man when he arrived and handed Mrs Hearn the letters. One of them was a letter from one of her Dublin relatives stating in no measured terms that she, Mrs Hearn, was living in sin and should leave her husband without delay. When Hearn returned from the garden he found his wife dead, with the letter in her hand.

Years afterwards he was staying in a house with his niece, who told me the story, and happened to occupy a room next to his. She heard someone crying as she was going to bed and went into his room to see what was the matter. He was sitting with a small shoe and a lock of hair on the dressing table in front of him and when she came in he said 'That is all that is left Lizzie, of everything I lived for.'

In the meantime Lafcadio had a most chequered career. He had been sent to a Jesuit School and taught in the Catholic faith. His cousin remembered going, as a small girl, to see him at the school but all she remembered of the surroundings was a staircase with a statue of the Virgin Mary on the way up, as they passed Lafcadio crossed himself and asked her to do the same. She, as she had been brought up in the school of Orange Protestantism, firmly refused to do so. She seemed to have no distinct impressions of Lafcadio after this incident. Some strange person had come on the scenes [sic] and managed to get hold of Mrs Brenan's [sic] money, after which Lafcadio was left penniless.

I note that in this account that drugs, as opposed to other accounts which specify drink, were allegedly used to get Charles Bush Hearn to marry to Rosa.

The strong religious feelings of the Hearn family are underlined by their resentment of Lafcadio's Roman Catholic upbringing and the attitude of Charles's mother towards his relationship with Alicia.

In this account of the incident of Lafcadio attempting to get his cousin to show reverence to a statue of the Virgin Mary, presumably at Ushaw, he crosses himself and asks her to do the same; in other accounts he asks her to bow or genuflect. These variations may indicate that the story was much discussed within the Hearn family, underlining perhaps the impact which it seems to have had on family members.

PUBLIC RECORDS OFFICE DOCUMENTS

Copies of some original documents from the Public Record Office in England, including:

Some New Hearn Primary Source Material

* The baptismal certificate of Daniel James ('Jim') Hearn, Lafcadio's brother, baptized in the parish of St George the Martyr, in the county of Middlesex, on 12 July 1857. One assumes that, as Daniel James was born on 12 August 1854 (i.e., three years earlier), he was being baptized as an Anglican by his guardians, following his abandonment by his parents and, possibly, an earlier Greek Orthodox baptism. This adds a little to our knowledge of Daniel James's early years although it raised new questions: why he was baptized in Middlesex (he seems to have spent most of his youth in England at a boarding school in Alton, Hampshire) and by whom? The possibly tenuous nature of the relationship between his parents and those responsible for the baptism might be deducted from the misspelling of his mother's name ('Cassamata' instead of 'Cassimati') and the crossing out of 'Soldier' and the substitution of 'Surgeon' for his father's occupation in the register.

* The baptismal certificate of Patrick Lafcadio Hearn, dated 13 July 1850. His mother is described as 'the Noble Mrs Rosa Cassimati, Daughter of Antonio of Cerigo'; her illiteracy is confirmed by a declaration that 'she cannot write'. Patrick Lafcadio's godfather is given as Dr Giovanni Cava; no godmother was listed.

* The marriage certificate, dated 2 March 1867, of Charles Bush Hearn and Alicia A. Crawford in the parish church of St Thomas in the city of Dublin; the marriage actually took place on 18 July 1857. Charles Bush's residence is given as the Curragh Camp (a military base in the centre of Ireland) and Alicia's as 81 Lower Gardiner Street. The occupation of her father, Arthur Gossilin [sic], is given as 'Gentleman'. Charles Bush Hearn is described as a 'Bachelor'.

★ The baptismal certificates of the three daughters of Charles Bush and Alicia Hearn: Elizabeth Sarah Maude, born on 31 March 1858; Minnie Charlotte, born 17 April 1859; and, Posey Gertrude, born 6 April 1860. Their parents' residence is given as Secunderabad, India, for the first two and Trimulgberry, India, for the last.

NEWSPAPER CUTTINGS

A number of these, collected by Lafcadio's Irish relations, are of interest:

Daily Mail, 29/9/1904: A short obituary which describes Lafcadio as 'one of the makers of the Anglo-Japanese alliance'.

The Detroit News, 6/8/1933, 'The American Who Became a Jap', by Russell Gore; an account of the controversial relationship between Hearn and the Countess Annetta Halliday-Antona which allegedly gave rise to the *Letters to a Pagan*. This article, and an accompanying reproduction of one of the 'letters', does nothing to allay doubts about their genuineness.[35]

T.P.'s Weekly, 21/10/1904, 'Recollections of Lafcadio Hearn', by Osman Edwards. An obituary of Hearn in the periodical founded by the nationalist Irish MP, T.P. O'Connor, (this journal also reproduced in Setsu Koizumi's 'The Last Days of Lafcadio Hearn' in the issue of 1/3/1907). Similar to a lecture given by Edwards to the Japan Society of London,[36] it repeats a worrying inaccuracy of that lecture (Hearn is remembered as tall and thin) and adds a new one in the form of Lafcadio's alleged early struggles in Chicago and St Louis.

[*Christian Science Monitor?*; the name of the journal is not evident on the cutting but the article is 'Specially for the Christian Science Monitor'], 28/8/1919, 'Lafcadio Hearn – A Recollection'. No byline. An interesting personal but anonymous recollection of a childhood friendship with Lafcadio by an inhabitant of New Orleans whose father was a friend of the writer.

Untitled, undated, newspaper clipping (A reference to the reigns of the Emperor Taisho and the premiership of Count Okuma would place it in the period 1914-16). 'The Coronation at Kyoto. Pagent and Ritual. Honour of the Shade of Lafcadio Hearn'. Includes a reference at the end to 'an interesting recognition of a dead scholar being the bestowal of the junior grade of fourth Court rank upon the shade of Lafcadio Hearn'.

ILLUSTRATIONS

Among the material is an extensive and useful collection of Hearn photographs and portraits of generally excellent quality (including some previously published in poor quality) a number of which appear in the plate section of this book.

I have seen three pictures by Richard Hearn (Lafcadio's painter uncle) in one collection, a portrait of General Arbuthnot; a pastoral scene; and a member of the Stephens family. A landscape of a scene in south County Dublin by Richard Hearn is in another collection.

Notes & References

---------- oOo ----------

Chapter 1 MARY ROBINSON Matsue Tribute to Lafcadio Hearn

1. During her State Visit to Japan, 20-28 February 1995, the President of Ireland Mary Robinson and her husband visited Tokyo, Osaka, Nara, Hiroshima and Shimane Prefecture.

    On Saturday, 25 February 1995, President Robinson and her husband travelled to Matsue, Shimane Prefecture, the small seaside town on the Sea of Japan to honour Lafcadio Hearn who lived there as a writer and teacher in 1890-91. Her Address was given at the Civic Reception hosted by the Governor of Shimane Prefecture at the Ichibata Hotel, Matsue, on the evening of 25 February.

    On the following day, President Robinson was greeted at the Lafcadio Hearn Museum by the writer's great-grandson, Mr Bon Koizumi who is the Curator. She also paid a brief visit to the house nearby where Hearn lived and planted a tree in front of the bronze bust of the writer in a small park.

    President Robinson then climbed to the top of the seventeenth-century Matsue Castle overlooking the town, which Hearn has described as 'a veritable architectural dragon, made up of magnificent monstrosities'. She was shown the castle's collection of samurai armour and regalia.

    President Robinson also visited the famous Izumo Taisha shrine where the local authorities had distributed Irish flags to a large group of boy scouts and girl guides who waved to them enthusiastically as she was escorted to the Eight-Legged Gate. She and her husband were taken to an inner part of the shrine for a discourse on its significance while the rest of the delegation remained outside.

    In addition, the President toured a winery and had a *tepanyaki* lunch. In the afternoon, the Presidential Party flew to Osaka for trade and investment meetings and a reception for the Irish community there.

Notes

2. The Japanese Government's English Teaching Programme (JET) was established in 1978 to recruit graduates from English-speaking countries to teach spoken English in Japan's secondary schools and colleges.
3. The message from President Robinson to the Kumamoto Prefectural Office in Tokyo was given prior to the President's departure from Japan on 28 February 1995.

Chapter 2 SEAN DUNNE A Shrine for Lafcadio Hearn 1850-1904

1. A copy of the above poem on Lafcadio Hearn by Sean Dunne was presented by President Mary Robinson to his great-grandson Bon Koizumi during her visit to Matsue on Sunday, 26 February 1995.

   Sean Dunne passed away tragically at the untimely age of 39 in August 1995 just when he was beginning to realize his great literary potential. The poem is in memory of them both.

Chapter 3 LILO STEPHENS Lafcadio Hearn and His Relations in Dublin

The article was first published in *Eigo-Seinen* (The Rising Generation) Vol. 119, No. 2, 1 May 1973, Tokyo.

1. Mrs Minnie Atkinson, accompanied by her daughter Dorothy and the author Nina H. Kennard, visited Tokyo in March 1909, where they met Lafcadio Hearn's widow, Setsu, and his four children. An account of the visit is given in Nina Kennard's book *Lafcadio Hearn* (313-318), Appleton, New York, 1912, reprinted by the Kennikat Press, Inc., Port Washington, New York, 1967.

   Nina Kennard, née Anne Homan-Mulock (1844-1926), novelist and biographer, was born in Bellair, King's County, Ireland, eleventh of fifteen children of Frances Sophia (Berry) and Thomas Homan-Mulock. In 1866, she married Arthur Challis K. of Eaton Place; she had four children. She wrote a number of novels mainly featuring aristocrats, and contributed volumes on Rachel and on Sarah Siddons to the Eminent Women series. Her biography of Lafcadio Hearn, 1912, arose from her friendship with Hearn's half-sister, Mrs Atkinson.

Chapter 4 CHARLES V. WHELAN A Profile of Lafcadio Hearn

1. This summary of the life and work of Lafcadio Hearn was originally prepared as a lecture to the Greek-Irish Society at a meeting in Athens on 19 October 1985. It has been extended and revised in the light of later published information.

Sources

Hirakawa, Sukehiro (Professor Emeritus, Tokyo University), *General Fellers and Lafcadio Hearn*, PHP Magazine, Tokyo, December 1983.

Irish Writing on Lafcadio Hearn and Japan

Murray, Paul, *A Fantastic Journey: The Life and Literature of Lafcadio Hearn*, Japan Library, Folkestone, Kent CT20 3EE, 1993.
Ronan, Sean G. and Koizumi Toki, *Lafcadio Hearn (Koizumi Yakumo) His Life, Work and Irish Background*, Ireland Japan Association, Dublin, 1991.
Stevenson, Elizabeth, *Lafcadio Hearn*, The Macmillan Company, New York, 1961.

Chapter 5 TOKI KOIZUMI Lafcadio Hearn and I

1. This contribution is a summary of a talk given by Mr Toki Koizumi to the Ireland Japan Association at Confederation Hotel, Kildare Street, Dublin 2, on 1 June 1993.

Chapter 6 SHERLEY McGILL Two Celts in Japan: Enigma of the East

1. Lafcadio's mother's maiden name was Rosa Antonia Kassimati. The article was published in the *Cork Examiner Supplement* of 16 May 1936.
    Timothy Conroy, later O'Conroy, was born in Ovens, County Cork, Ireland, on 20 August 1883. In 1898 he enlisted in the Royal Navy and saw service in South America, Africa and Arabia. In 1905 he was placed on the reserve list.
    From 1905 to 1910 he travelled extensively on the Continent and became fluent in nine languages. He spent the years 1910-13 in Russia as tutor in the Imperial household, returned to London in 1913 but was back in Russia during the war years as an interpreter. On the outbreak of the Revolution in 1917 he left Russia via the Siberian route and visited Japan briefly on the way back to London.
    Japan must have impressed him as he returned there soon afterwards and spent the next 15 years of his life there (1918-1933). He became a teacher in the Imperial Naval Medical School, married a Japanese lady of a prominent family and in 1920 was appointed a professor of English at Keio University, Tokyo.
    He reacted against militarism in Japan and in 1933 published a very critical book entitled *The Menace of Japan*, which was used in the West for propaganda purposes. O'Conroy fled Japan in 1933 leaving his Japanese wife behind. He died in London in 1935. The fate of his wife is unknown. While Hearn's published work on Japan was favourable to his country of adoption, O'Conroy's was critical.

Chapter 7 ULICK O'CONNOR Irish but as Japanese as the Haiku.

1. The article is a review in *The Sunday Independent* (14 April 1985) of *Lafcadio Hearn: Writings from Japan* – an Anthology edited, with an Introduction, by Francis King, Penguin, 1984.
2. Knock is a place of pilgrimage in County Mayo.

Notes

Chapter 8 ULICK O'CONNOR Lafcadio Hearn in New Orleans

This is the article referred to in the previous contribution. The author states: 'I had been at University in New Orleans and was still a student when I wrote it. It contains some errors and much naïveté but I have left it as it was at the time it was published in *The Dublin Magazine* (1953), when there was very little known about Lafcadio Hearn.'

Chapter 9 ROGER McHUGH Lafcadio Hearn and some Irish Writers

Published in *The Yomiuri Shimbun*, 17 March 1971.

Chapter 10 ROGER McHUGH The Loose Foot of Lafcadio Hearn

The article was first published in *The Irish Times* of Friday, 24 April 1981. Its permission to reproduce the article here is acknowledged.

Chapter 11

The article was published in *The Irish Times* of 3 May 1988.

Chapter 12 CIARAN MURRAY Lafcadio Hearn: a Spiritual Odyssey

1. Interview with L.M. Stephens, 2 Harcourt Terrace Dublin, ms. notes 9 August 1969.
2. Elizabeth Stevenson: *Lafcadio Hearn*, New York 1961, ch. ii.
3. 'In Search of Tír na nÓg', *The Irish Times*, 13 September 1972.
4. 'Beyond the Waters – Matsue and Lafcadio Hearn', NHK broadcast 2 March, transcript. A Japanese summary is printed in *NHK Terebi Eigo Kaiwa*, March 1980.
5. 'Beyond the Waters'.
6. Stevenson, ch. ii.
7. 'Gothic Horror', *Shadowings*, Rutland & Tokyo 1971.
8. Stevenson, ch. ii.
9. Peter Gay: *The Enlightenment: the Rise of Modern Paganism*, New York 1968, ch. v.
10. Stevenson, ch. ii, viii.
11. Ch. vi, viii, xii.
12. Ch. xi, xiv.
13. 'My First Day in the Orient', *Glimpses of Unfamiliar Japan*, 1st series, London 1927.
14. Stevenson, ch. xiv.
15. 'Yaegaki-Jinja', *Glimpses of Unfamiliar Japan*, 1st series, London 1927.
16. Malcolm Cowley: Introduction, Hearn: *Selected Writings*, ed. Henry Goodman, New York 1949.

17. *Japan: An Attempt at Interpretation*, ch. ix.
18. 'A Glimpse of Tendencies', *Kokoro*, Rutland & Tokyo 1972; 'The Japanese Smile', *Glimpses of Unfamiliar Japan*, 2nd series, London 1927.
19. *The Garden of Cyrus*, ch. iv.
20. 'Beyond the Waters'.
21. Stevenson, ch. xiv.
22. 'Beyond the Waters'.

Chapter 13 BARBARA HAYLEY Lafcadio Hearn, W.B. Yeats and Japan

The article was first published in *Literature and the Art of Creation, Essays and Poems in honour of A. Norman Jeffares*, edited by Robert Welch and Suheil Badi Bashmi; Colin Smythe, Gerrards Cross, Bucks, 1988. It is gratefully reproduced with the permission of the estate of the late Professor Barbara Hayley and of the publisher.

1. The most easily available brief biography is in the introduction to the Penguin Travel Library *Lafcadio Hearn: Writings from Japan*, edited, with an introduction, by Francis King (Harmondsworth, 1984). The biographical details of this differ in some respects from those of earlier biographers such as Miss Bisland (see note 2 below).
2. *The Life and Letters of Lafcadio Hearn*, edited by Elizabeth Bisland (London, 1911), p.400.
3. 'The Autumn of the Body', *Essays and Introductions*, (New York, 1961), p.191.
4. 'The Cutting of an Agate', *Essays and Introductions*, p.228.
5. Letter to Shotaro Oshima, 19 August 1927, quoted in Shotaro Oshima, *W.B. Yeats and Japan*, (Tokyo, 1965), p.6. This book considers Yeats's Japanese reading and contacts, and Japanese writings on Yeats.
6. *A Vision*, (London and Basingstoke, 1978), p.301.
7. Letter to Kazumi Yano, January 1928, quoted in Shotaro Oshima, *W.B. Yeats and Japan*, p.23. Yeats never went to Japan, despite various plans for lecture tours.
8. 'Intuition', quoted in *The Life and Letters of Lafcadio Hearn*, Vol, I, p.41.
9. Hearn's letters up to 1890 were published in *The Life and Letters of Lafcadio Hearn*, 1911, in two volumes. His letters after 1890 were collected in *The Japanese Letters of Lafcadio Hearn*, edited by Elizabeth Bisland (London, Boston, New York, 1911).
10. The articles quoted from in this section are from the New Orleans *Times-Democrat*, collected in Lafcadio Hearn, *Essays in European and Oriental Literature* (London, 1923).
11. The variety and extent of Hearn's reading can be judged by the *Life and Letters*, *Japanese Letters* and the *Essays in European and Oriental Literature*.
12. Hearn's method of observing Japan is close to that which he praises in Loti: 'On visiting a new country he always used to take notes of every fresh and powerful impression . . . Nor did such exquisite notework as this alone satisfy him; for mere description of external objects alone forms but a small part of the charm of his books; – he subjoined notes of the thoughts and fancies also which such impressions of sight, sound, or smell produced in the mind; and thus his work is as much introspective as it is retrospective.' ('The Most Original of Modern Novelists: Pierre Loti'. *Essays in European and Oriental Literature*, p.137.)

Notes

13. 'In a Japanese Garden', *Glimpses of Unfamiliar Japan*, (Rutland, Vermont and Tokyo, 1976), p.384.
14. 'A Pilgrimage To Enoshima', *Glimpses of Unfamiliar Japan*, pp.94-5.
15. 'Bon-Odori', *Glimpses of Unfamiliar Japan*, p.123.
16. 'In the Cave of the Children's Ghosts', *Glimpses of Unfamiliar Japan*, p.229.
17. 'Kidnappers', *Mythologies*, (London and Basingstoke, 1959), p.74.
18. 'Village Ghosts', *Mythologies*, p.20.
19. 'Of a Promise Broken', *A Japanese Miscellany*, p.29.
20. 'Chief City of the Province of the Gods', *Glimpses of Unfamiliar Japan*, p.166.
21. 'The Story of Kwashin Koji', *A Japanese Miscellany*, p.50.
22. 'Folklore Gleanings', I, Dragon flies', *A Japanese Miscellany*, pp.94-5, 99.
23. 'An Indian Monk', *Mythologies*.
24. 'Of Moon Desire', *The Buddhist Writings of Lafcadio Hearn*, edited by Kenneth Rexroth (London, 1981), pp.149-50.
25. 'Otokichi's Daruma', *Ibid.*, p.234.
26. 'Gaki', *Ibid.*, p.245.
27. 'Dust', *Ibid.*, pp.22-23.
28. 'The Stone Buddha', *Ibid.*, p.20.
29. 'The Higher Buddhism', *Ibid.*, p.281.
30. 'The Higher Buddhism', *Ibid.*, pp.281-2.
31. 'Nirvana', *Ibid.*, p.50.
32. Alex Zwerdling, *Yeats and the Heroic Ideal*, (New York, 1965), p.151.
33. 'The Household Shrine', *Glimpses of Unfamiliar Japan*, pp.388-9.
34. 'Sayonara', *Glimpses of Unfamiliar Japan*, p.686.
35. 'Kitzuki: the Most Ancient Shrine of Japan', *Glimpses of Unfamiliar Japan*, p.202.
36. 'Of a Dancing-girl', *Ibid.*, pp.531-2.
37. 'Bon-Odori', *Ibid.*, p.134.
38. 'Rosa Alchemica', *Mythologies*, p.288.
39. *Ibid.*, p.290.
40. 'Bon-Odori', *Glimpses of Unfamiliar Japan*, p.137.
41. 'Certain Noble plays of Japan', *Essays and Introductions*, p.226.
42. 'A Pilgrimage to Enoshima', *Glimpses of Unfamiliar Japan*, p.102.

Chapter 14 ANTHONY J.F. O'REILLY Opening of the Lafcadio Hearn Library

1. Remarks by Dr A.J.F. O'Reilly, Chairman and Chief Executive Officer, H. J. Heinz Company, on the occasion of Heinz's sponsorship of the Lafcadio Hearn Library in the Embassy of Ireland, Tokyo, 19 September 1988

Chapter 15 LORNA SIGGINS An Irishwoman's Diary A Visit to Matsue

The article is reproduced with the permission of *The Irish Times*, in which it was first published on 7 March 1990.

Irish Writing on Lafcadio Hearn and Japan

Chapter 16 GERRY O'MALLEY Lafcadio Hearn and Japanese Poetry

The article was broadcast on the Sunday Miscellany programme of Radio Telefis Eireann (RTE) on 24 February 1991. It is reproduced here with the permission of the author and RTE.

Chapter 17 PETER McMILLAN The Literary Criticism of Lafcadio Hearn

The lecture was first published in *International Aspects of Irish Literature*, the papers given at the 1990 IASAIL-Japan Conference in Kyoto, Colin Smythe Ltd., Gerrards Cross, Bucks., 1995 and is reproduced with permission.

1. Letter to Sentaro Nishida, quoted in the introduction to *Interpretations of Literature* by Lafcadio Hearn; edited by John Erskine. New York: Dodd, Mead and Company 1972 p.vii.
2. Quoted in the introduction to *On Art, Literature and Philosophy*, edited by R. Tanabe, T. Ochiai, and I. Nishizake. Tokyo: Hokuseido Press 1941 p.iv and v.
3. Quoted in 'Lafcadio Hearn: A Dreamer' by Yone Noguchi. *Current Literature* Vol.38 No.6 June 1905 pp.521-23.
4. Hearn dedicated *Glimpses of Unfamiliar Japan* and *Shadowings* to McDonald, who was a great friend and admirer of Hearn's. The letter was written in February 1899 and is quoted in the preface of *Interpretations of Literature* Volume I by Lafcadio Hearn edited by John Erskine. New York: Dodd, Mead and Company 1922. pp.vii and viii.
5. & 6. Both are quoted in *On Art, Literature and Philosophy* by Lafcadio Hearn Tokyo: The Hokuseido Press 1941.
7. Quoted in the introduction to *Interpretations of Literature* Vol. I p.ix.
8. Quoted in *Pre-Raphaelite and Other Poets* by Lafcadio Hearn; edited by John Erskine. New York: Dodd, Mead and Company 1930 pp.vi and vii.
9. 'The Question of the Highest Art' p.7 and 9 in *Interpretations of Literature* Vol. 1. New York: Dodd, Mead and Company 1922.
10. Hearn, lecture to his students, quoted in *Life and Literature*, edited by John Erskine. New York: Dodd, Mead and Company 1929 p.ix.
11. Letter to Mr Ellwood Hendrick, September 1902, quoted in the introduction to *Interpretations of Literature* Vol. I. p.viii.

Chapter 18 PETER McMILLAN Lafcadio Hearn and the Early Irish and Japanese Mythology and Literature

This paper was first published on *Centennial Essays on Lafcadio Hearn*, ed. Kenji Zenimoto, The Hearn Society, Matsue, 1996. The volume was published in memory of the centenary of Lafcadio Hearn's arrival in Japan in 1890 and contains the essays read at the Centennial Festival held in Matsue 30 August-3 September 1990.

Research for the paper was conducted under a grant provided by Allied Irish Banks (Tokyo). Grateful acknowledgement is made to Mr Dennis Nolan of Allied Irish Banks for AIB's generous funding.

Acknowledgement is also made to Professor Marie Kai of Waseda University who provided much of the information for this paper, and to H.E. Sean G.

Ronan, former Ambassador of Ireland in Tokyo (1984-1989) who first encouraged me to write about Hearn and who has provided unending advice and support, not only to me but to writers on Hearn everywhere.

Furthermore, I am indebted to the following authors and books for much of the information in the paper:

Fergus Kelly *A Guide to Early Irish Law* (Dublin: Dublin Institute for Advanced Studies, 1988)

Jin'ichi Konishi *A History of Japanese Literature* Vol. 1 (Princeton: Princeton University Press, 1986) Translated by Aileen Gatten and Nicholas Teele

Jin'ichi Konishi *A History of Japanese Literature* Vol. 2 (Princeton: Princeton University Press, 1986) Translated by Aileen Gatten

T.F. O'Rahilly *Early Irish History and Mythology* (Dublin: Dublin Institute for Advanced Studies, 1984)

Ward Rutherford *Celtic Mythology* (Wellingborough: The Aquarian Press, 1987)

Donald L. Philippi's superb translation and notes to the *Kojiki* (Tokyo: University of Tokyo Press, 1968)

Chapter 19 JAMES A. SHARKEY Hearn's Japan: A Visit to the Oki Islands

The article was originally published in Japanese in the *Nipon Keizai Shimbun* and in English in *The Nikkei Weekly* of 4 January 1993. It was subsequently published in Kenkyusha's *The Rattle Bag* issue of 20 January 1994. The courtesy of both publications for the inclusion of the article here is acknowledged.

Chapter 20 SEAN G. RONAN The Horror and Ghostly Writings of Lafcadio Hearn

The talk was originally given at the Bram Stoker Summer School, Clontarf, Dublin, on 25 June 1993 and reproduced in *Centennial Essays on Lafcadio Hearn*, ed. Kenji Zenimoto, The Hearn Society, Matsue, 1996. Their permission is acknowledged.

1. *Wandering Ghosts – The Odyssey of Lafcadio Hearn* by Jonathan Cott: Alfred A. Knopf, New York 1991.
2. 'Lafcadio Hearn (1850-1904) – His Irish Background and Appreciation of Japanese Culture' by Taro Matsuo: *The Hōsei University Economic Review*, vol. LI, no. 1, 1983.
3. For a more extensive biographical account vide *Lafcadio Hearn (Koizumi Yakumo) His Life, Work and Irish Background* by Sean G. Ronan and Toki Koizumi: The Ireland Japan Association, Dublin 1991, third revised edition, 1996.
4. *Lafcadio Hearn and the Vision of Japan* by Carl Dawson: The Johns Hopkins University Press, Baltimore and London, 1992, pp. 88-89.
5. *Gleanings in Buddha-Fields* by Lafcadio Hearn: Charles E. Tuttle Company Inc., Rutland, Vermont and Tokyo, Fourth Printing 1987. Dust. p. 87.
6. 'A Ghost' by Lafcadio Hearn: *Harper's Magazine*, 1889.
7. *Interpretation of Literature* by Lafcadio Hearn ed. by John Erskine: vol. II, pp. 90-103. Dodd Mead and Company, New York 1916.
8. *An Ape of Gods – The Art and Thought of Lafcadio Hearn* by Beongcheon Yu: Wayne State University Press, Detroit, 1964. p. 48.

9. *Shadowings* by Lafcadio Hearn: Charles E. Tuttle Paperbacks (vide 5). Fourth Printing 1984, p. 222.
10. 'Literary Influences on Lafcadio Hearn' – an article by David H. Waterbury: *Hearn Journal*, no. 15, Matsue, Japan.
11. *Catalogue of the Lafcadio Hearn Library in Toyama High School*: Toyama High School, Toyama, Japan, 1927, pp. 11 and 17.
12. *Life and Literature* by Lafcadio Hearn, ed. by John Erskine: Dodd Mead and Company, New York, 1917, pp. 325-331.
13. *The Writings of Lafcadio Hearn – Life and Letters* ed. by Elizabeth Bisland: Houghton Mifflin Company, Boston and New York, 1923, vol. IV, p. 132.
14. *Period of Gruesome – Selected Cincinnati Journalism of Lafcadio Hearn*, ed. by Jon Christopher Hughes: University Press of America, Lanham, New York, London, 1990. On p. 4 Professor Hughes points out that it was Hearn's first biographer George M. Gould in *Concerning Lafcadio Hearn* (1909) who called this Hearn's 'period of the gruesome'.
15. *Lafcadio Hearn: Japan's Great Interpreter – A New Anthology of His Writings 1894-1904*, ed. Louis Allen and Jean Wilson: Japan Library Ltd., Folkestone, Kent 1992, pp. 6-7.
16. Op. cit. ed. by Jon Christopher Hughes: pp. vii-xiv.
17. Op. cit. by Beongcheon Yu: p. 48.
18. *The Writings of Lafcadio Hearn* 16 vols: Houghton Mifflin Company, Boston and New York 1923, vol. II.
19. Op. cit. by Beongcheon Yu: pp. 49-51.
20. *The Writings of Lafcadio Hearn*: Op. cit. vol. I.
21. The books listed are published in *The Writings of Lafcadio Hearn* (vide 18) and in the Charles E. Tuttle Company paperbacks (vide 9).
22. Op. cit. by Beongcheon Yu: p. 56.
23. *The Boy Who Drew Cats* by Lafcadio Hearn, printed in colour by hand from Japanese woodblocks: T. Hasegawa, Tokyo, 1898.
24. Op. cit. ed. Elizabeth Bisland (vide 13): 1923, vol. III, p. 313.

Chapter 21 PAUL MURRAY Lafcadio Hearn's Interpretation of Japan

The lecture was presented to the Japan Society of London on 11 October 1994 (*The Proceedings* No. 124 Autumn 1994). The Society's permission to republish it here is gratefully acknowledged.

1. *Glimpses of Unfamiliar Japan*, Lafcadio Hearn, Houghton Mifflin Company, Boston, 1894; reprinted by Charles E Tuttle Company, Inc, Rutland, Vermont, and Tokyo, 1976, 657
2. *Glimpses of Unfamiliar Japan*, 676
3. *Out of the East*, Lafcadio Hearn, (Houghton Mifflin Company, Boston 1897), reprinted by Charles E. Tuttle Company, Inc. Rutland, Vermont, and Tokyo, 1972, 202
4. *Out of the East*, 236 & 225
5. *More Letters from Basil Hall Chamberlain to Lafcadio Hearn*, compiled by Kazuo Koizumi, Hokuseido Press, Tokyo, 1937, 163
6. *Kokoro*, Lafcadio Hearn, (Houghton Mifflin Company, Boston 1896), reprinted by Charles E. Tuttle Company, Inc. Rutland, Vermont, and Tokyo, 1972, 36
7. *Kokoro*, 35-37

8. *Kokoro*, 30
9. *Kokoro*, 54-5
10. *Kokoro*, 145
11. 'Sir George Sansom (1883-1965)', Gordon Daniels, in *Britain and Japan 1859-1991, Themes and Personalities*, Sir Hugh Cortazzi and Gordon Daniels (ed), Routledge, London and New York, 1991, 280
12. *Things Japanese*, Basil Hall Chamberlain, Fifth Revised Edition, London, J Murray; Yokohama, Kelly and Walsh Ltd, 1904; reprinted in paperback as *Japanese Things*, by Charles E. Tuttle Co., Inc. Rutland, Vermont, and Tokyo, 1971, 249. (This edition is hereafter referred to as *Things Japanese*)
13. *Gleanings in Buddha Fields*, Lafcadio Hearn, (Houghton Mifflin Company, Boston 1896), reprinted by Charles E. Tuttle Company, Inc. Rutland, Vermont, and Tokyo, 1971, 100-101
14. *Gleanings in Buddha Fields*, 113-4
15. *Gleanings in Buddha Fields*, 121-3
16. 'Lafcadio Hearn – Lover or Hater of Japan: Concerning Some Newly Discovered Letters', *Japan*, San Francisco, Vol 15, 1926
17. *Things Japanese*, 65
18. MSS Hearn letter to Horace Scudder, 28/8/95, Kobe; Middlebury College, Middlebury, Vermont, USA
19. *La Cité Antique*, Fustel de Coulanges, 17th edition, Librairie Hachette, Paris, 1900; *The Ancient City: A study of Religion, Laws, and Institutions of Greece and Rome*, Fustel de Coulanges, translated from the French by Willard Small, Lee & Shepard, Boston, Lee Shepard, & Dillingham, New York, 1874, 3-7
20. See *Les intellectuels et l'avenement de la troisieme republic, 1871-1875*, Bernard Grasset, Paris, 1931, and *The Historical Thought of Fustel de Coulanges*, Jane Herrick, The Catholic University of America Press, Washington DC, 1954, 117, for contrasting views
21. *The Western World and Japan, A Study in the Interaction of European and Asiatic Cultures*, GB Sansom (1950), Charles E Tuttle Company, Vermont & Tokyo, 1977, 478
22. 'Lafcadio Hearn's "At a Railway Station". A Case of Sympathetic Understanding of the Inner Life of Japan', Professor Hirakawa Sukehiro, paper given at the Woodrow Wilson International Centre for Scholars, Smithsonian Institute, Washington D.C., 19/7/1979; published in *Lafcadio Hearn: Japan's Great Interpreter, A new anthology of his writings 1894-1904*, Louis Allen & Jean Wilson (ed), Japan Library, Sandgate, Kent, 1992, 282-301
23. 'Supplementary Comment on the Lafcadio Hearn Paper', Professor Hirakawa Sukehiro, paper given at the Woodrow Wilson International Centre for Scholars, Smithsonian Institute, Washington D.C., 19/7/1979; published in *Lafcadio Hearn: Japan's Great Interpreter, A new anthology of his writings 1894-1904*, Louis Allen & Jean Wilson (ed), Japan Library, Sandgate, Kent, 1992, 302-8
24. *Things Japanese*, 489
25. *Things Japanese*, 237
26. *Things Japanese*, 368
27. *Things Japanese*, 295
28. *Things Japanese*, 339
29. *Things Japanese*, 137-146
30. *Things Japanese*, 488-497
31. *Letters from Basil Hall Chamberlain to Lafcadio Hearn*, compiled by Kazuo

Koizumi, Hokuseido Press, Tokyo, 1936, BHC to LH, 8/9/1894, Miyanosita, 112-4
32. *Things Japanese*, 361-2
33. 'The Invention of a New Religion', Appendix published in *Things Japanese*, 531-544
34. 'Who Was the Great Japan Interpreter, Chamberlain or Hearn?', Sukehiro Hirakawa, paper read to *Perspectives on Japonisme, The Japanese Influence on America*, An International Conference at Rutgers, May 13-14, 1988
35. *Things Japanese*, Basil Hall Chamberlain, 6th Edition Revised, Kegan Paul, Trench, Trubner & Co, 1939, 295-8
36. *Concerning Lafcadio Hearn*, George M Gould, MD, with a bibliography by Laura Stedman, George W Jacobs and Company, Philadelphia, 1908
37. *Lafcadio Hearn*, Arthur E. Kunst, Twayne Publishers Inc., New York, 1969, 126
38. 'MacArthur Aide May Have Saved Emperor From Trial', Mutsuo Fukushima, *Daily Yomiuri*, 4/1/1993
39. *The Spectator*, 1/1/1994
40. *Financial Times*, The FT Review of Business Books, 15/3/94

Chapter 22 PAUL MURRAY Lafcadio Hearn and the Irish Tradition

The article was first published in *Irish Studies Review* No. 15 1996. Its permission to reproduce it here is gratefully acknowledged.
1. Matthew Lewis, *The Monk* (London, 1820), p. 156.
2. 'Some Pictures of Poverty', *The Selected Writings of Lafcadio Hearn*, ed. Henry Goodman (New York, 1949/1971), p. 257.
3. *On Poetry*, ed. L Hearn, R Tanabe, T Ochiai and I Nishizaki (Tokyo: third revised edition, 1941), p. 13.
4. W B Yeats, *Writings on Irish Folklore, Legends and Myth*, ed. Robert Welsh (London, 1993), pp. 190-1.
5. Reginald Leslie Hine, *Confessions of an Uncommon Attorney* (London, 1945), p. 152.
6. *On Poetry*, p. 253.
7. *On Poetry*, p. 253.
8. MS Hearn letter to W.B. Yeats, 22 June 1901, Tokyo.
9. *Writings on Irish Folklore*, p. 280.
10. New Orleans *Times-Democrat*, 24 Dec. 1889.
11. *On Poetry*, p. 257.
12. L Hearn, *Shadowings* (Boston: Little, Brown, and Co, 1900; reprinted by Charles E Tuttle Company inc. Rutland, Vermont and Tokyo, 1971), p. 218.
13. *The Japanese Letters of Lafcadio Hearn*, ed. Elizabeth Bisland Wetmore (Boston and New York: Houghton Mifflin Company, The Riverside Press, Cambridge, 1910), p. 430.
14. *The Life and Letters of Lafcadio Hearn*, ed. Elizabeth Bisland, vol. XIV of the Koizumi Edition of *The Writings of Lafcadio Hearn* (Boston and New York: Houghton Mifflin Company, The Riverside Press, Cambridge, 1910), pp. 336-7.
15. *Oriental Tales*, ed. Robert L Mack (Oxford, 1992), p. xxx.
16. *Oriental Tales*, ed. Robert L Mack, p. xxxiii.

Notes

17. *Oriental Tales*, ed. Robert L Mack, p. xlviii.
18. MS Hearn letter to W.B. Yeats, 24 Sept. 1901, Tokyo.

Chapter 23 GEORGE HUGHES W. B. Yeats and Lafcadio Hearn: Negotiating with Ghosts

1. As Richard Taylor has suggested, Yeats may have picked up some ideas from the play *Yorō* by Zeami, which was among the unpublished Fenollosa papers. Yet I think we must admit that the relationship is not close. The plot, as has been suggested, could equally have come from William Morris's *The Well at the World's End*. (Incidentally Hearn also uses the story of a Fountain of Youth in the chapter called 'The Dream of Summer's Day' in *Out of the East* (1895)–though I would not suggest there is any connection with Yeats here.)

Works cited

Amenomori, Nobushige. 'Lafcadio Hearn, the Man'. *Atlantic Monthly*. 96. 1906.
Donoghue, Denis. *The Third Voice*. Princeton: Princeton UP, 1959.
Ellmann, Richard. *Yeats: The Man and the Masks*. Harmondsworth: Penguin, 1979.
Goldman, Arnold. 'Yeats, Spiritualism and Psychical Research', *Yeats and the Occult*, ed. G. M. Harper. London: Macmillan, 1976.
Hearn, Lafcadio. 'Among the Spirits', *Cincinnati Enquirer* (25 Jan. 1874). Reptd. in Jonathan Cott, *Wandering Ghost*.
—. *Gleanings in Buddha Fields*. 1897. Rutland: Tuttle, 1971.—. *Glimpses of Unfamiliar Japan*. 1894. Rutland: Tuttle, 1976.
—. *Japan: An Attempt at Interpretation*. 1904. Rutland: Tuttle, 1956.
—. *Japanese Letters of Lafcadio Hearn*, ed. Elizabeth Bisland. London: Constable, 1911.
—. *Kokoro* 1896. Rutland: Tuttle, 1972.
—. *Kwaidan*. 1904 Rutland: Tuttle, 1972.
—. *Lectures on Shakespeare*, ed. I Inagaki. Tokyo: Hokuseido P, 1928.
—. *Life and Letters of Lafcadio Hearn*. ed. Elizabeth Bisland. 2 vols. Boston: Houghton, Mifflin, 1906.
—. *Life and Literature*, ed. John Erskine. New York: Dodd, Mead, 1921.
—. *On Art, Literature and Philosophy*, eds. R. Tanabe et al. Tokyo: Hokuseido P, 1932.
—. *On Poetry*, eds. R. Tanabe et al. Tokyo: Hokuseido P, 1934.
—. *Oriental Articles*, ed. I Nishizaki. Tokyo: Hokuseido P, 1939.
—. *Out of the East*. 1897. Rutland: Tuttle, 1972.
—. *Shadowings*. Boston: Little, Brown, 1900.
—. *Spirit Photography*. ed. P. D. Perkins. Los Angeles: John Murray, 1933.
Kutch, Peter. '"Laying the Ghosts"?–W. B. Yeats's Lecture on Ghosts and Dreams'. *Yeats Annual* 5 (1987).
Oppenheim, Janet. *The Other World: Spiritualism and Psychical Research in England 1850-1914*. Cambridge: Cambridge UP, 1985.
Murray, Paul. *A Fantastic Journey: The Life and Literature of Lafcadio Hearn*. Folkestone, Kent: Japan Library, 1993.
Taylor, Richard. 'Assimilation and Accomplishment: Nō Drama and An Unpublished Source for *At the Hawk's Well*'. *Yeats and the Theatre*, Ed. R. O'Driscoll et al. London: Macmillan, 1975.

Vendler, Helen. *Yeats's Vision and the Later Plays.* Cambridge, Mass: Harvard UP, 1963.
Worth, Katharine. *The Irish Drama of Europe from Yeats to Beckett.* London: Athlone P, 1986.
Yeats, W. B. *Explorations.* London: Macmillan, 1962.
—. *Letters of W. B. Yeats*, ed. Allan Wade. New York: Macmillan, 1955.
—. *Mythologies.* London: Macmillan, 1955.
—. *The Celtic Twilight.* 1893. Bridport: Prism Press, 1990.
—. *The Classic Noh Theatre of Japan.* 1917. New York: New Directions, 1959.
—. *The Collected Letters of W. B. Yeats III*, ed. John Kelly and Ronald Shuchard. Oxford: Clarendon P, 1994.
—. *The Variorum Edition of the Plays of W. B. Yeats.* ed. Russell K. Alspach. London: Macmillan, 1966.
—. *Yeats's 'Vision' Papers.* ed Steve L. Adams et al. 3 vols. Iowa City, U of Iowa Press, 1992.

Chapter 24 GEORGE HUGHES Hearn, Yeats and the Problem of Edmund Burke

1. See for example Torchiana and Whitaker.
2. Quoted in Osman Edwards, 'Some Unpublished Letters of Lafcadio Hearn', *Transactions and Proceedings of the Japan Society* Vol. xvi (1917-8) 29. At the same meeting of the Society in which Edwards' paper was read, Professor Joseph Longford, who had been on the consular staff of the British Embassy in Tokyo, claimed that Hearn was an Irish Nationalist 'in the most extreme sense of the term' (32). But since Longford also explained that he had never been able to strike up any more than an official relationship with Hearn, and since he was misinformed about Hearn's early life, he is not a completely reliable source of information.
3. He got these ideas from Spencer and Huxley.
4. I discuss this aspect of Hearn at length in my article on 'Hearn as a Critic', reprinted in *Centennial Essays on Lafcadio Hearn*. Carl Dawson in his essay 'Lafcadio Hearn: Western Critic in an Eastern World', in the same volume, and in *Lafcadio Hearn and the Vision of Japan*, takes a different and, I think, misguided point of view.
5. He also emphasized that Burke was an extremely kind patron to his juniors, treating them kindly 'as a poor student might be treated by a rich family in Tokyo'. *History* I, 445.
6. See letter to Sentaro Nishida Jan. 1893 in *Life and Letters* II 102. 'several new books I recommended have been adopted, but there were changes made in my list, I think for the worse. . . . Burke's Essays (selected) were adopted instead of a volume of stories I proposed'.
7. *Sublime and Beautiful* 108-9. Interestingly Yeats also uses this quotation from Job 4.15 both in the introduction to 'The Resurrection' *Variorum* 935; and in 'The Words upon the Window-Pane': 'at other times I think as Dr Trench does, and then I feel like Job – you know the quotation – the hair of my head stands up. A Spirit passes before my face.' *Variorum* 945.

Works cited
Burke, Edmund. *A Philosophical Enquiry into the Origin of Our Ideas of the Sublime and Beautiful.* 1757; London: Rivington, 1812.

Notes

Butler, Marilyn. *Romantics, Rebels and Reactionaries: English Literature and its Background 1760-1830*. Oxford: Oxford UP, 1981.
Catalogue of the Lafcadio Hearn Library in the Toyama High School. Toyama: Toyama High School, 1927.
Connor, S. *Postmodernist Culture: An Introduction to Theories of the Contemporary*. Oxford: Basil Blackwell, 1989.
Dawson, Carl. *Lafcadio Hearn and the Vision of Japan*. Johns Hopkins UP, 1992.
Deane, Seamus. *Celtic Revivals: Essays in Modern Irish Literature 1880-1980*. London: Faber and Faber, 1985.
De Man, Paul. *The Rhetoric of Romanticism*. New York: Columbia UP, 1984.
Edwards, Osman. 'Some Unpublished Letters of Lafcadio Hearn', in *Transactions and Proceedings of the Japan Society* Vol. xvi (1917-8).
Ellmann, Richard. *Yeats: The Man and the Masks* (1948) Harmondsworth: Penguin, 1987.
Hearn, Lafcadio. 'The Supernatural in Fiction' in *Complete Lectures: On Art, Literature and Philosophy*, ed. R. Tanabe et al. Tokyo: Hokuseido P, 1932.
—. *A History of English Literature: In a series of lectures* (Tokyo: Hokuseido P, 1927.
—. *Life and Letters of Lafcadio Hearn* ed. Elizabeth Bisland. Boston: Houghton, Mifflin, 1906.
Hone, Joseph. *W. B. Yeats 1865-1939*. (1943) London, Macmillan 1962.
Murray, Paul. *A Fantastic Journey: The Life and Literature of Lafcadio Hearn*. Sandgate, Folkestone: Japan Library, 1993.
O'Brien, Conor Cruise. *The Great Melody: A Thematic Biography of Edmund Burke*. London: Sinclair-Stevenson, 1992.
Torchiana, Donald T. *W. B. Yeats and Georgian Ireland*. Evanston: Northwestern UP, 1966.
Whitaker, Thomas R. *Swan and Shadow: Yeats's Dialogue with History*. 1964; rep. Washington: Catholic Univ of America P, 1989.
Wilson, F. A. C. *Yeats's Iconography*. 1960; London: Methuen, 1968.
Yeats, W. B. *Essays and Introductions*. London: Macmillan, 1961.
—. *Explorations*, London: Macmillan, 1962.
—. *The Senate Speeches of W. B. Yeats*, ed. D. R. Pearce. Bloomington: Indiana UP, 1960.
—. *The Variorum Edition of the Plays*. ed. R. K. Alspach. London: Macmillan, 1966.
Zenimoto, Kenji ed. *Centennial Essays on Lafcadio Hearn*. Matsue: Hearn Society, 1996.

Chapter 25 PETER McIVER Lafcadio Hearn's First Day in the Orient

Acknowledgement is made to the editor of the *Japan Quarterly* for permission to reproduce this article which first appeared in the *Japan Quarterly* April-June edition 1996, published by the *Asahi Shinbun*, Japan.

1. J.E. Hoare, *Japan's Treaty Ports and Foreign Settlements: The Uninvited Guests 1858-99*. Sandgate, Kent: Japan Library, 1994, p.7 & 14.

Irish Writing on Lafcadio Hearn and Japan

Chapter 26 SEAN G. RONAN Kokoro – A Century Later

The Inaugural Lafcadio Hearn Lecture by former Ambassador Sean G. Ronan, was sponsored by the Ireland Japan Asociation in association with the James Joyce Centre and given at the James Joyce Centre on Wednesday 19 June 1996.

1. *Lafcadio Hearn*, Elizabeth Stevenson, The Macmillan Company, New York, 1961.
2. *An Ape of Gods: The Art and Thought of Lafcadio Hearn*, Beongcheon Yu, Wayne State University Press, Detroit, 1964.
3. *Lafcadio Hearn, Writings from Japan*, An Anthology edited, with an Introduction, by Francis King, Penguin, London, 1984.
4. *Centennial Essays on Lafcadio Hearn*, edited by Kenji Zenimoto, The Hearn Society, Matsue, Japan, 1986.
5. *A Fantastic Journey: The Life and Literature of Lafcadio Hearn*, Paul Murray, The Japan Library, Folkestone, Kent, 1993.
6. *The Folklorist, Koizumi Yakumo, from the Works he Produced in Japan* (in Japanese), Koizumi Bon, Kobunsha, Tokyo, 1995.
7. Professor George Hughes in *Studies of Comparative Literature No. 65*, University of Tokyo Press, also article 'Lafcadio Hearn Rediscovered' by Professor Sukehiro Hirakawa, Epic World, Vol. 2, No. 2, March 1995.
8. Panel Discussion on Lafcadio Hearn at IASAIL Conference, Otani University, Kyoto, Friday, 13 July 1990.
9. *Op. Cit.* by Paul Murray, p. 12.
10. *Kokoro*, Lafcadio Hearn, Houghton Mifflin Company, Boston and New York, 1896. Republished by Charles E. Tuttle Company, Inc., Rutland, Vermont and Tokyo, 1972, seventh reprinting 1987.
11. *Ibid.* p. 31.
12. *Ibid.* pp. 36-37.
13. *Ibid.* pp. 107-108.
14. *Ibid.* pp. 147-149.
15. *Ibid.* p. 154.
16. *Ibid.* p. 208.
17. *Ibid.* pp. 1-7.
18. *A Case of Sympathetic Understanding of the Inner Life of Japan: Lafcadio Hearn's 'At a Railway Station'*, Professor Sukehiro Hirakawa, a paper given at the Woodrow Wilson International Centre for Scholars, Smithsonian Institute, Washington DC, 19 July 1978. Offprint from *Japan in Comparative Perspective*, Prof. Sukehiro Hirakawa, University of Tokyo Press, pp. 81-82.
19. *Prosa II*, Hugo von Hofmannsthal, pp. 104-107.
20. *Kokoro, op. cit.* pp. 307-325.
21. *Ibid.* pp. 155-169.
22. *Ibid.* pp. 40-46.
23. *Ibid.* pp. 222-256.
24. *Exotics and Retrospectives*, Lafcadio Hearn, Little Brown and Co., Boston 1898. Republished by Charles E. Tuttle Company, Inc., Rutland, Vermont and Tokyo, 1971, fourth reprinting 1987.
25. *Kokoro, op. cit.* pp. 267-268 and p. 271.
26. *Ibid.* p. 282.
27. *Ibid.* pp. 282-284.
28. *Japan: An Attempt at Interpretation*, Lafcadio Hearn, The Macmillan Company, New York, 1904. Republished by Charles E. Tuttle Company,

Inc., Rutland, Vermont and Tokyo, 1956, fifteenth reprinting 1984.
29. *Glimpses of Unfamiliar Japan*, Lafcadio Hearn, Houghton Mifflin Company, Boston, 1904. Republished by Charles E. Tuttle Company, Inc., Rutland, Vermont and Tokyo, 1976, fifth reprinting 1986.
30. *Kwaidan Stories and Studies of Strange Things*, Lafcadio Hearn, Houghton Mifflin Company, Boston, 1904. Republished by Charles E. Tuttle Company, Inc., Rutland, Vermont and Tokyo, 1971, nineteenth reprinting 1990.
31. *Japan: An Attempt at Interpretation*, Lafcadio Hearn, *op. cit.*
32. 'Supplementary Comment on the Lafcadio Hearn Paper' at the Woodrow Wilson International Centre for Scholars, Smithsonian Institute, Washington DC, 19 July 1978. Offprint from *Japan in Comparative Perspective*, Prof. Sukehiro Hirakawa, University of Tokyo Press, p. 99.

Chapter 27 ALLEN E. TUTTLE The Achievement of Lafcadio Hearn

The article was published in *The Dublin Magazine* issue for April-June 1956. The magazine ceased publication at the end of 1956.

Chapter 28 PAUL MURRAY Some New Hearn Primary Source Material

1. *A Fantastic Journey: The Life and Literature of Lafcadio Hearn*, Japan Library, Folkestone, 1993, 212-214.
2. *Lafcadio Hearn*, Nina H. Kennard, 1912, reprinted by the Kennikat Press, Inc., Port Washington, N.Y., 1967.
3. Kennard, 232-3.
4. *Fantastic Journey*, 252-55.
5. *Fantastic Journey*, 256.
6. *Fantastic Journey*, 251.
7. *Fantastic Journey*, 252.
8. Kennard, 46.
9. *The Irish Post*, London, 20 November 1993, 11-12.
10. Kennard, 248-50.
11. *Fantastic Journey*, 77.
12. Kennard, 33-4.
13. *Fantastic Journey*, 221.
14. *Out of the East*, Lafcadio Hearn, Houghton Mifflin Company, Boston 1897, Reprinted by Charles E. Tuttle Company, Inc. Rutland, Vermont, and Tokyo, 1972, 20.
15. Kennard, 32.
16. *Lafcadio Hearn and the Vision of Japan*, Carl Dawson, Baltimore, 1992, 6.
17. Review of *Fantastic Journey* in *Eigo Seinin*, September 1994.
18. *Vikram and the Vampire or Tales of Hindu Devilry*, Richard F. Burton, Longmans, Green, and Co., London, 1870.
19. Kennard, 289-91.
20. Kennard, 291.
21. Kennard, 292-3.
22. Kennard, 340-1.

23. Kennard, 356.
24. *Lafcadio Hearn*, Elizabeth Stevenson, The Macmillan Company, New York, 1961, 292.
25. *My Uncle John*, Edward M. Stephens, edited by Edward Carpenter, OUP, 1974.
26. 'Lafcadio Hearn', H.E. Rudkin, *Notes and Queries*, 9 December 1939.
27. *Fantastic Journey*, 217.
28. *Lafcadio Hearn*, Vera McWilliams, 1946; reprinted Cooper Square Publishers, New York, 1970.
29. *Young Hearn*, O.W. Frost, Hokuseido Press, Tokyo, 1958, 30.
30. *Young Hearn*, 33.
31. Stevenson, 11.
32. Kennard, 361-383.
33. Kennard, 16.
34. *The Life and Letters of Lafcadio Hearn*, Elizabeth Bisland (ed), Vol XIII, the Koizumi Edition of the Writings of Lafcadio Hearn, Houghton Mifflin Company, The Riverside Press, Cambridge, Boston and New York, 1923, 30.
35. See *Fantastic Journey*, 327-8, footnote 88.
36. See *Fantastic Journey*, 284-5.

APPENDIX I
LAFCADIO HEARN: PRINCIPAL DATES

1850	27 June	Patricio Lafcadio Hearn is born in the Ionian island of Leucadia (now Levkas), as the second child of Charles Bush Hearn (Irish) and Rosa Antonia Kassimati (Greek).
1852		Richard, his father's younger brother, takes Lafcadio and his mother to Dublin.
1854		Rosa leaves Lafcadio under the care of Mrs Brenane (his grand-aunt) and goes back to Greece. The third son James Daniel was born there.
1857		Marriage of Charles and Rosa annulled. He marries Alicia Goslin Crawford.
1863		Lafcadio enters St Cuthbert College at Ushaw near Durham.
1866		Lafcadio accidentally loses his left eye sight at Ushaw while playing the game known as Giant's Stride.
1867		Mrs Brenane's bankruptcy compels Lafcadio to leave his school. Lafcadio studies for a while at the Roman Catholic school at Yvetot near Rouen and then goes to Paris.
1869		Lafcadio goes to Cincinnati in the USA, counting on his relatives to help him get established.
1870		Lafcadio works as a general reporter on the *Cincinnati Enquirer*.
1877		Lafcadio moves to New Orleans.
1887	July	Lafcadio goes to the West Indies.
1889	October	Lafcadio receives a letter from James Hearn for the first time, in which James introduces himself as his younger brother.
1890	March	He leaves America for Japan on board the *SS Abyssinia* as a correspondent of *Harper's Magazine*.
	April	Lafcadio arrives in Yokohama, with a letter of introduction to Basil Hall Chamberlain of the Imperial University of Tokyo.
	July	Lafcadio is appointed to teach English at Matsue Normal School and Matsue Middle School, Shimane Prefecture.
	August	He arrives in Matsue by way of Himeji and Tsuyama.
1891		Lafcadio marries Koizumi Setsu, whose father was a

		high-ranking samurai before the Meiji Restoration.
	November	Lafcadio starts his new post at the 5th Higher School (Dai Go Kotogakko, now the University of Kumamoto).
1893		Birth of eldest son, Kazuo.
1894		Lafcadio resigns the 5th Higher School and enters the service of the *Kobe Chronicle*.
1895		He leaves the *Kobe Chronicle* owing to an eye disease.
1896	January	Lafcadio is naturalized as a Japanese citizen and changes his name to Koizumi Yakumo.
	September	Lafcadio is appointed Professor of English Literature at Imperial University of Tokyo and the Koizumis move to Tokyo.
1897	February	Birth of his second son, Iwao.
1899	December	Birth of his third son, Kiyoshi.
1903	March	Lafcadio leaves the Imperial University of Tokyo.
	September	Birth of his only daughter, Suzuko.
1904	March	Lafcadio accepts a position as lecturer in English literature at Waseda University.
26 September		Lafcadio dies suddenly of a heart attack.

APPENDIX II: HEARN'S TRAVELS IN JAPAN

1890	17 March	Leaves Vancouver, Canada, for Japan
	4 April	Arrives at Yokohama by the steam-boat *Abyssinia*
	8 August	Leaves for new assignment in Matsue, where he remains until 15 November 1891
1891	November	Moves to Kumamoto, where he remains until the beginning of October, 1894
1892	Summer	Travels to Hakata, Kobe, Kyoto, Nara, Mihonoseki and Oki
1893	Spring	Travels to Hakata and Nagasaki
1894	Summer	Travels to Tokyo and Yokohama
1894	October	Moves to Kobe, where he remains until 20 August 1895
1896	Spring	Travels to the Keihanshin Area
	Summer	Travels to Izumo and Matsue
1896	September	Moves to Tokyo.
1897	Summer	Spends summer at Yaidzu and every year after that
1904	26 September	Dies at his home in Okubo, Tokyo

APPENDIX III
CHRONOLOGY OF THE WORKS OF LAFCADIO HEARN

1882	*One of Cleopatra's Nights, and other Fantastic Romances*, Théophile Gautier, translated by Lafcadio Hearn
1884	*Stray Leaves from Strange Literature and Other Stories*
1885	*Gomo Zhèbes-Little Dictionary of Creole Proverbs; La Cuisine Creole; Historical Sketch Book and Guide to New Orleans and Environs*
1887	*Some Chinese Ghosts and Other Stories*
1889	*Chita: A Memory of Last Island*
1890	*The Crime of Sylvestre Bonnard*, Anatole France, translated by Lafcadio Hearn
	Two Years in the French West Indies
	Youma
1894	*Glimpses of Unfamiliar Japan*
1895	*Out of the East*
1896	*Kokoro*
1897	*Gleanings in Buddha-Fields*
1898	*Exotics and Retrospectives*
1899	*In Ghostly Japan*
1900	*Shadowings*
1901	*A Japanese Miscellany*
1902	*Fantastics and Other Fancies*
	Kottō
1904	*Kwaidan*
★ ★ ★	Published posthumously ★ ★ ★
1905	*The Romance of the Milky Way and Other Stories*
	Japan: An Attempt at Interpretation
1910	*The Temptation of St. Anthony*, Gustave Flaubert, translated by Lafcadio Hearn
1911	*Leaves from the Diary of An Impressionist*
1915	*Interpretations of Literature*, 2 vols.
1916	*Appreciations of Poetry*
1917	*Life and Literature*
1918	*Karma*
1924	*An American Miscellany*
1925	*On Art, Literature, and Philosophy*
1926	*On Poets and Poems*
1927	*A History of English Literature*

APPENDIX IV HEARNS' FAMILY TREE

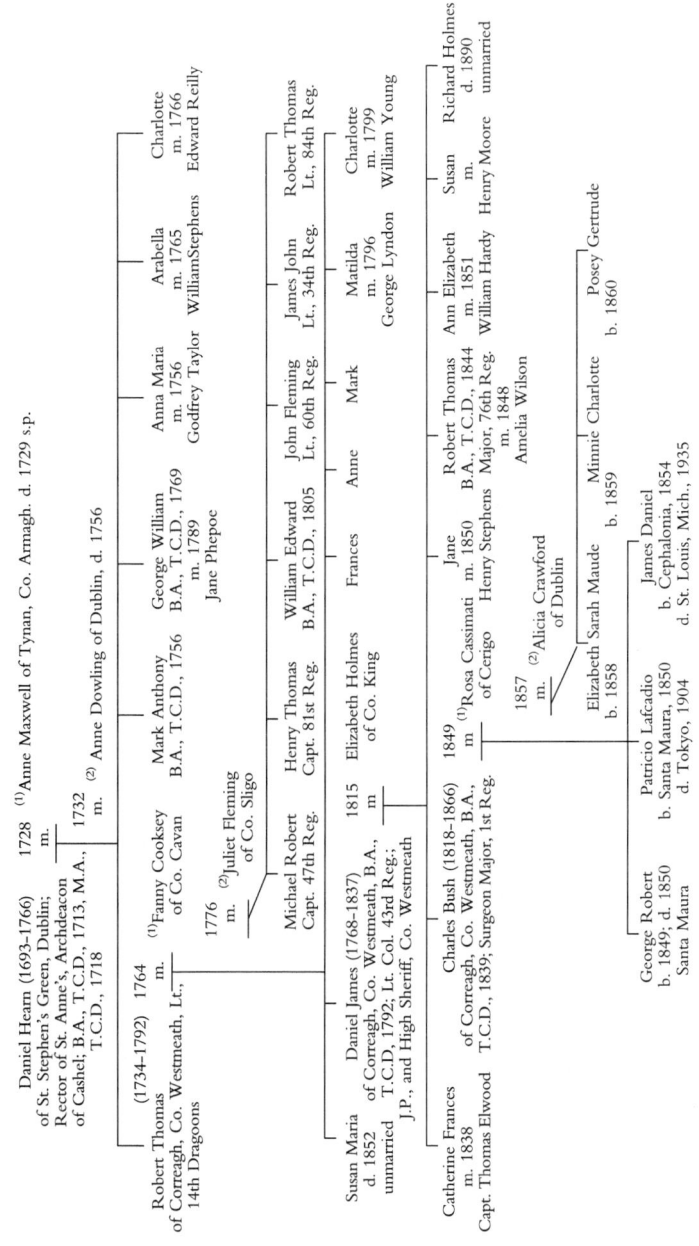

Daniel Hearn (1693–1766) 1728 (1) Anne Maxwell of Tynan, Co. Armagh. d. 1729 s.p.
of St. Stephen's Green, Dublin;   m.
Rector of St. Anne's, Archdeacon   1732 (2) Anne Dowling of Dublin, d. 1756
of Cashel; B.A., T.C.D., 1713, M.A.,
T.C.D., 1718

(1734–1792) 1764
m.

Robert Thomas	Fanny Cooksey (1)	Mark Anthony	George William	Anna Maria	Arabella	Charlotte
of Correagh, Co. Westmeath, Lt.,	of Co. Cavan	B.A., T.C.D., 1756	B.A., T.C.D., 1769	m. 1756	m. 1765	m. 1766
14th Dragoons	1776 m. (2) Juliet Fleming of Co. Sligo		m. 1789 Jane Phepoe	Godfrey Taylor	William Stephens	Edward Reilly

Michael Robert — Henry Thomas — Elizabeth Holmes — William Edward — Frances — Anne — Mark — John Fleming — James John — Matilda — Robert Thomas — Charlotte
Capt. 47th Reg. — Capt. 81st Reg. — of Co. King — B.A., T.C.D., 1805 — — — — Lt., 60th Reg. — Lt., 34th Reg. — m. 1796 George Lyndon — Lt., 84th Reg. — m. 1799 William Young

1815
m.

Susan Maria   Daniel James (1768–1837)   Charles Bush (1818–1866)   1849   Jane   Robert Thomas   Ann Elizabeth   Susan   Richard Holmes
d. 1852   of Correagh, Co. Westmeath, B.A., of Correagh, Co. Westmeath, B.A., m (1) Rosa Cassimati m. 1850   B.A., T.C.D., 1844   m. 1851   m.   d. 1890
unmarried   T.C.D. 1792; Lt. Col. 43rd Reg.; T.C.D., 1839; Surgeon Major, 1st Reg.   of Cerigo   Henry Stephens Major, 76th Reg. William Hardy   Henry Moore   unmarried
              J.P., and High Sheriff, Co. Westmeath   m. 1848
                                                                                        1857   Amelia Wilson
                                                                                        m. (2) Alicia Crawford
Catherine Frances   of Dublin
m. 1838
Capt. Thomas Elwood

George Robert   Patricio Lafcadio   James Daniel   Elizabeth Sarah Maude   Minnie Charlotte   Posey Gertrude
b. 1849; d. 1850   b. Santa Maura, 1850   b. Cephalonia, 1854   b. 1858   b. 1859   b. 1860
Santa Maura   d. Tokyo, 1904   d. St. Louis, Mich., 1935

337

APPENDIX V
PATRICK LAFCADIO HEARN AT USHAW COLLEGE

In Ushaw's records Hearn's first name appears in its Latin form 'Patricius', abbreviated to 'Pat'. His surname is occasionally spelt 'Hearne'. The *Diary* records that he arrived on 9 September 1863, aged thirteen; his birthday was 27 June; his place of origin or home was Redhill, London. He was put into the lowest class, the First Class of Elements. At the end of each term the whole College assembled to hear the examination results read out from a volume known as the *Reading Up Book*. All Hearn's results are listed below: '9/15' means he was placed 9th out of 15 students in the class.

	LATIN	FRENCH	ENGLISH	ARITHMETIC	GREEK	
Christmas 1863	25/31	4/31	1/31	24/31		First class
Easter 1864	29/31	21/31	1/31	22/31		of
Summer 1864	27/32	12/32	3/31	22/32		Elements
Christmas 1864	6/15	5/14	1/15	11/15		Second class
Easter 1865	10/15	8/15	9/15	13/15		of
Summer 1865	8/14	2/14	1/14	10/14		Rudiments
Christmas 1865	6/18	3/18	1/18	16/18	12/15	First class
Easter 1866	9/18	4/18	1/18	18/18	11/16	of
Summer 1866	9/20	12/20	1/20	15/20	16/17	Rudiments
Christmas 1866	15/15	9/15	1/15	13/14	12/16	Fourth class
Easter 1867	9/15		1/15	15/15	12/15	of
Summer 1867	5/15	7/15	2/15	15/15	7/15	Humanity

Hearn entered the Third Class of Humanity in the academic year 1867–68 but left the College on 28 October 1867.

Copyright of Ushaw College Library: reproduced with permission.

APPENDIX VI

English Composition.

I.

Theme for Graduating Class of 1893:—

— Carlyle, having been asked by a student,— "What shall I read?"— made answer,— "Read that which is eternal". Comment upon this incident; and write your own opinion as to what is "eternal" in good books,— considering the word "eternal" as referring only to the whole history of human civilization, and its probable future.

II.

Theme for Fourth-year Class (Eng. II.):—

"The Story of Tithonus,"— as recited by the teacher.

III.

Theme for Preparatory Classes, P.1.A & P.1.B.

"The Story of the Man who Lived for a Thousand Years,"— as recited by the teacher.

IV.

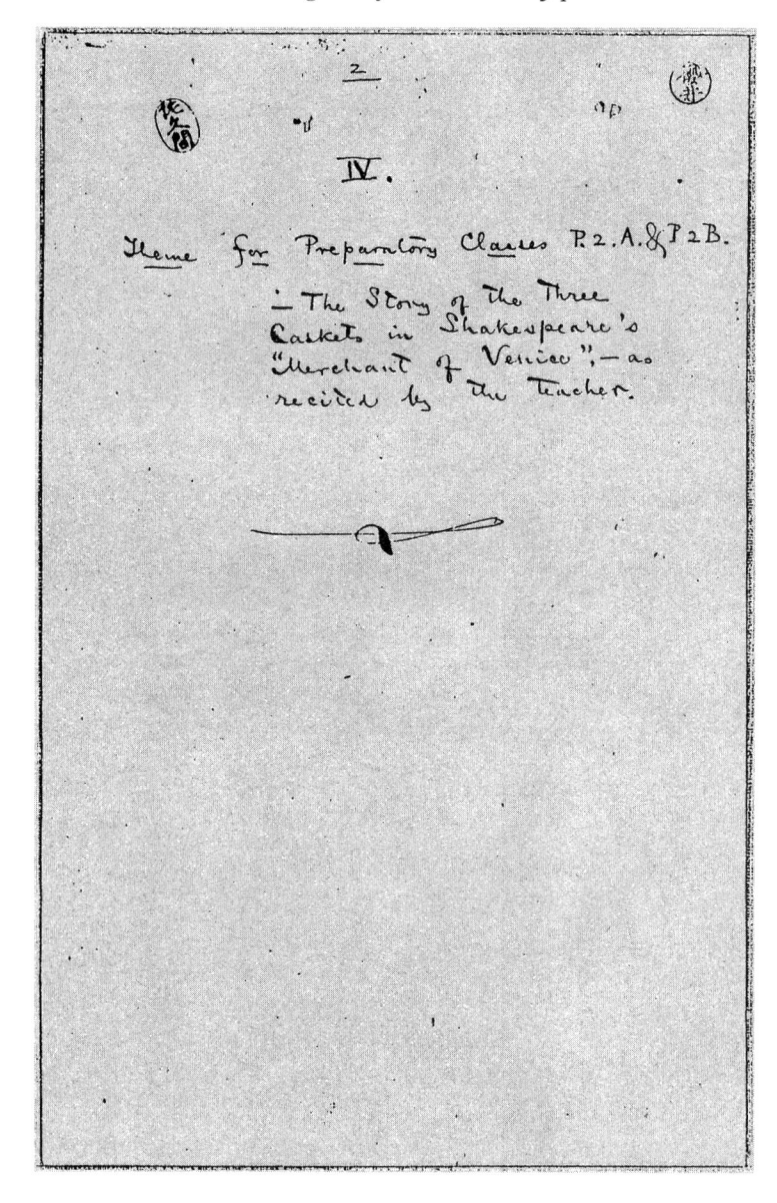

Theme for Preparatory Classes P.2.A.&P.2.B.
— The Story of the Three Caskets in Shakespeare's "Merchant of Venice",— as recited by the Teacher.

APPENDIX VII
HOUSES ASSOCIATED WITH LAFCADIO HEARN – 21 LEINSTER SQUARE AND 3 PRINCE ARTHUR TERRACE, RATHMINES, DUBLIN

In her MUBC thesis *Leinster Square (with Prince Arthur Terrace), Rathmines, Dublin An Early Suburban Speculative Terrace Housing Development 1830-1852*, submitted to University College Dublin in 1995, Anne Lavin, Architect, shows that the numbering of the houses in Leinster Square changed four times over the years since they were built from the 1830s onwards. The location of 21 Leinster Square, in which Lafcadio Hearn lived with his great-aunt, Mrs Sarah Brenane, in 1852-53 is the present 30 Leinster Square since 1954.

Leinster Square and Prince Arthur Terrace are located in a Victorian suburb of Dublin called Rathmines, which is located about two miles south of the city centre. This suburb was created by a generation of entrepreneurial businessmen whose names have been long since forgotten. Declaring themselves an Independent Township in 1847, they administered their own affairs and controlled their own destiny until the Local Government (Dublin) Act, 1929 removed that independence and their Township was absorbed within the boundaries of the City of Dublin in 1930.

Part of the land on which the Square was built was leased for development by John Butler and Arthur Williamson c.1830. C.1851 the three Terraces, Leinster, Ulster and Connaught Place, were collectively renamed Leinster Square and the houses were all renumbered from No.1 to No.27 Leinster Square.

The previous addresses of the present No.30 Leinster Square, Rathmines Road, are:-

    1842 – No.8 Ulster Terrace
    1851 – No.20 Leinster Square South
    1852 – No.21 Leinster Square South
    1954 – No.30 Leinster Square

Mrs Sarah Brenane, according to *Thoms Street Directories* and Valuation Office Records, lived in the house from 1850 to 1853. Lafcadio Hearn went to live with her as a small child of two and three years in 1852-53. The previous addresses of the present No.21 Leinster Square, Rathmines Road are:-

    1834 – No.8 Leinster Terrace
    1851 – No.14 Leinster Square West
    1852 – No.15 Leinster Square West
    1954 – No.21 Leinster Square

(*See page 343 for plan of Leinster Square c.1853.*)

John Butler commenced the building of Prince Arthur Terrace in the Leinster Square area in 1851-52. The street directory of 1852 lists No.1 Prince Arthur Terrace with John Butler, architect, '*and five houses building*'. C.1853 No.1 to No.6 Prince Arthur Terrace were built. *Thoms Directory* shows that Mrs Sarah Brennan (sic) lived at No.3 from 1853 to 1855. Her name has usually been spelt as

'Brenane' and that is what appears on her tombstone in the Molyneux Plot of the Church of the Holy Cross, Tramore, Co. Waterford, but the name would have been interchangeable in practice with 'Brennan'. There can be little doubt but that she was one and the same person as 'Mrs Sarah Brenane'.

The street directories show that Mrs Brennan (sic) lived at No.73 Upper Leeson Street from 1856 to 1863.

Although Mrs Brenane and Lafcadio Hearn as a child did not live in the house that is renumbered since 1954 as No.21 Leinster Square, it was occupied from 1845 to 1864 by Thomas Grubb, the gifted inventor and pioneering amateur photographer, and his talented and famous son, Sir Howard Grubb, who is credited with inventing the submarine periscope, the patent for optical gunsights as well as many photographic lenses. He formed a partnership with another Irishman, Sir Charles Parsons, to continue making astronomical telescopes with a headquarters in Newcastle-upon-Tyne, which operated until 1984.

It is apparent from the foregoing that the plaque in honour of Lafcadio Hearn on the present No.21 Leinster Square is misplaced and should be on the present No.30 Leinster Square. It is also clear that Lafcadio Hearn lived there only briefly as a small child with his great-aunt, Mrs Sarah Brenane, before moving to No.3 Prince Arthur Terrace in 1853.

Appendix

Supplement to Appendix II

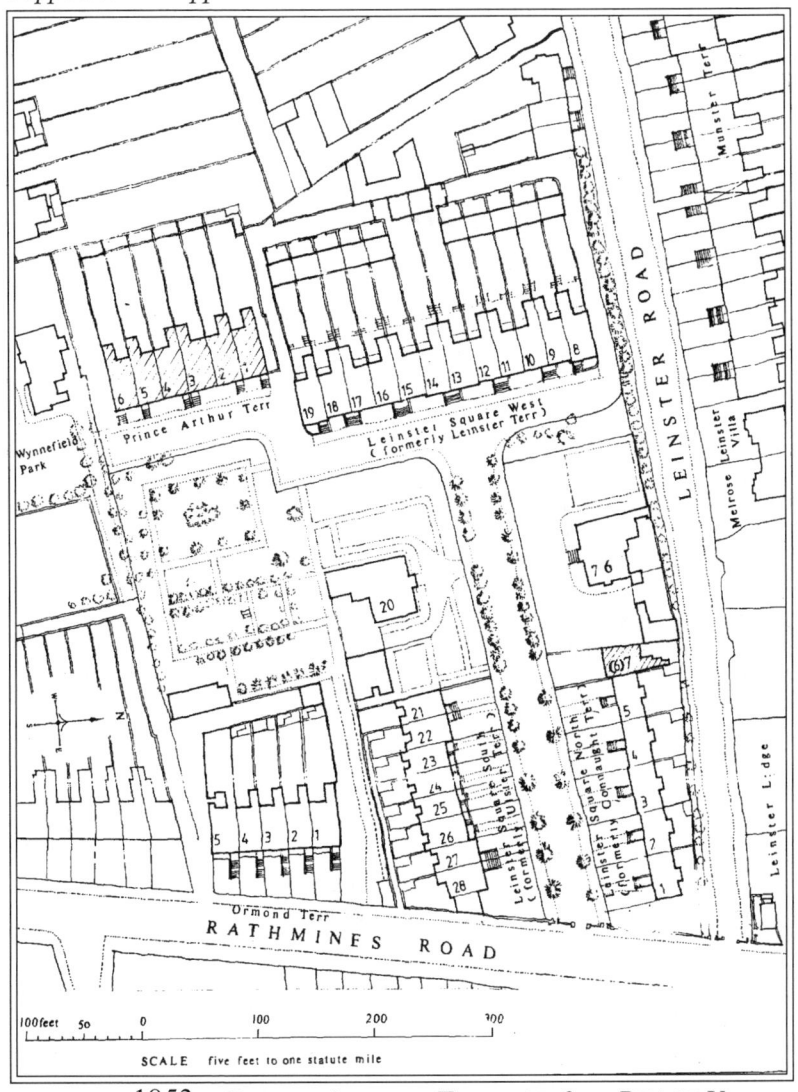

**c.1853 PRINCE ARTHUR TERRACE &   PHASE V
LEINSTER SQUARE (No.7 added)**

(Courtesy of Anne Lavin, Dip.Arch., M.U.B.C., M.I.D.I.,
49 Raglan Road, Dublin 4)

Index

A Japanese Miscellany 83, 86, 150
Allingham, William 22, 183
Amenomori Nobushige 200
America, American 18, 105, 119, 184, 210, 227, 236, 246, 247, 248, 249, 253, 254, 259, 261, 267, 274, 280
Anglin, J.R. 221
Aran Islands 68, 137
Arbuthnot, John 293, 296, 297, 298
Arbuthnot, Sir Robert 293, 297
Arnold, Matthew 80, 134
Ashton-Gwatkin, Frank 165, 170
Aston, W.G. 154, 156, 221
Atkinson, Carleton 281, 282, 301, 303
Atkinson, Charlotte Dorothy 273, 305
Atkinson, John Buckby 269, 270
Atkinson, Minnie xiii, xvi, 11, 258, 265-281, 285, 286, 288, 289, 290, 293, 301, 302, 305, 306
Atlantic Monthly 108

Baker, Page 61
Balcombe, Florence 174
Balzac, Honoré de 179
Barbizon 302, 303
Baudelaire, Charles 61, 80, 146, 179
Beckett, Samuel 64, 179, 184
Berkeley, George 55, 64, 184, 207, 208, 209
Berlioz 179
Bird, Isabella 219
Bisland, Elizabeth (Wetmore) 21, 193, 265, 277, 280, 281, 286, 287, 312
Blake, William 117, 118, 119
Bolger, Ronald 30
Borrow, George 80
Boucicault, Dion 175
Bowen, Elizabeth 180
Brenane, Sarah 9, 10, 14, 15, 16, 17, 33, 39, 47, 59, 60, 66, 77, 122, 141, 142, 174, 175, 176, 259, 261, 263, 266, 273, 291, 298, 299, 301, 308, 310, 314
Brinkley, Frank 221

Index

Browne, Sir Thomas 116
Buddhism, Buddhist 28, 41, 44, 55, 63, 64, 67, 70, 78, 82, 85, 87, 88, 89, 90, 91, 101, 114, 117, 150, 155, 159, 162, 164, 167, 207, 222, 231, 232, 242, 251, 274
Bulmer-Lytton, Edward 146
Burke, Edmund 183, 204-215
Burton, Richard 274
Butler, Marilyn 205
Byron 117, 119, 176

Carlyle, Thomas 212, 213
Carroll, Lewis 56
Cashel 47, 57, 76, 105, 176
Cassimati, Rosa 8, 9, 13, 15, 39, 53, 58, 257, 295, 296, 299, 307, 308, 316
Chamberlain, Basil Hall 24, 56, 146, 152, 154, 155, 161, 162, 164, 167, 168, 169, 185, 193, 202, 220, 221, 223, 247, 282
Chamberlain, Neville Stewart 170
China, Chinese 163, 184, 232, 233, 234, 235, 236, 243, 254
Chita 250
Cincinnati 18, 19, 20, 21, 23, 48, 60, 66, 72, 81, 142, 143, 147, 156, 157, 177, 178, 179, 182, 183, 188, 191, 246, 248, 262, 263, 264
Cincinnati Commercial 20, 21, 60, 147, 192
Cincinnati Enquirer 20, 60, 147, 248
Clontarf, Dublin 141, 173
Coleridge, Samuel Taylor 112, 117
Colm Tóibín 186
Columbia University 111
Cong, Co. Mayo xiv, 16, 66, 142, 229

Congreve, William 183
Connemara 16, 66
Corneille 134
Cornell University 28
Correagh, Co. Westmeath 141, 300, 301
Coulanges, Fustel de 155, 166
County Mayo 175
Cowper, William 118
Crabbe, George 118
Crawford, Alicia 7, 14, 272, 298, 307
Criomhthain, Thomás 132
Crunniac Mac Agnomain 133
Cuchulain 44, 125, 126, 197
Cullinane, Thomas 142

Danatsu Bay 132
Daniels, Gordon 162
Darwin, Charles 113, 249
Deane, Seamus 205, 208
Defoe, Daniel 176, 212
Delaney, Catherine (née Ronan) 18, 142
Donoghue, Denis 197
Dublin xiv, 8, 13, 14, 16, 32, 39, 47, 52, 53, 54, 58, 65, 66, 69, 72, 77, 98, 122, 137, 141, 173, 174, 175, 176, 179, 187, 208, 217, 229, 258, 265, 273, 293, 309
Dunne, Sean xviii

Edgeworth, Maria 176, 177, 186, 187
Eithne 131
Ellman, Richard 174
Elwood, Catherine 10, 66, 142, 151, 174
Emerson, Ralph Waldo 80
Enoshima 82
Erskine, Professor 111, 112

exotic subject matter 249
Exotics and Retrospectives 242, 251

Fabianism 184
Farquhar, George 183
Farson, Daniel 174
Fellers, Bonner, Brig. General 28, 29, 170, 171
Fellers, Nancy 29
Fenollosa, Ernest 75, 79, 94, 196, 197
Ferguson, Samuel xiv, 22, 63, 98, 146, 183, 229
Fianna Cycle 182
Financial Times 171
Flaubert, Gustave 21, 61, 80, 146, 178, 249
Foley, Mattie (Althea) 19, 20, 60
Foster, Roy xvii, 180, 183
Fox sisters, Margaret and Kate 192
France, Anatole 146
France, French 178, 179, 190, 206, 217, 228, 233, 247, 248, 259
Frost, O.W. 295, 299, 300
Fuji, Mount 23, 24, 44, 101, 216, 236
Fukuoka 237

Gautier, Theophile 21, 61, 80, 81, 146, 178
Genji Monogatari 79, 124
Gleanings in Buddha-Fields 83, 156, 160, 162, 224, 251
Glimpses of Unfamiliar Japan 23, 26, 40, 67, 81, 82, 138, 155, 156, 158, 159, 198, 218, 221, 222, 225, 227, 243, 251, 276
Goldsmith, Oliver 183, 208
Goslin, Alicia (Crawford) 7, 14, 272, 294, 307, 313

gothic horror 145, 148, 176, 178, 248
Gotoba 138
Gould, George 170, 264
Greece 13, 47, 53, 57, 58, 71, 72, 141, 224, 257
Gregory, Augusta, Lady 134, 180, 196, 209

haiku 106, 124
Hardy, Thomas 134
Harper's Magazine 23, 24, 50, 54, 62, 66, 81,98, 101, 105, 226
Hasegawa Yoji xviii
Hattori Ichizo 22, 24
Hayley, Barbara xviii
Heaney, Seamus 129, 173, 184
Hearn Library, Toyama University 146
Hearn, Alicia (Goslin Crawford) 14, 272, 294, 307, 316
Hearn, Basil 256, 270
Hearn, Charles Bush 7-11, 13, 14, 15, 34, 35, 39, 53, 57, 65, 76, 141, 257, 258, 271, 289, 293, 294, 295, 296, 297, 299, 300, 301, 302, 304, 307, 311, 313, 314, 316
Hearn, Daniel 256
Hearn, Daniel James (Lafcadio's grandfather) 141, 300, 301, 309
Hearn, Daniel, Ven, Archdeacon of Cashel 105, 292, 297, 298, 300, 301, 309
Hearn, Elizabeth Holmes (Lafcadio's grandmother) 141, 300, 301, 307, 309, 312
Hearn, James Daniel 15, 22, 269, 315, 316
Hearn, Jane 33, 34, 288, 307, 311, 312, 313

Index

Hearn, Lilla 268, 279, 280, 281, 286, 287, 289, 290, 293, 302, 314
Hearn, Mary Dalrymple 292, 293
Hearn, Posey 268, 285, 288, 289, 290, 293, 302, 313, 314, 316
Hearn, Richard 8, 175, 179, 257, 259, 289, 294, 302, 303, 318
Hearn, Robert 257
Hearn, Shane 256
Hearn, Susan Maria 257, 293, 295
Hendrick, Ellwood 119
Hillery, Dr Patrick, 29
Hirakawa Sukehiro xvii, xviii, 167, 170, 229, 236, 239, 243
Hiroshige 228
Hoffman, Ernst 80
Hoffmannsthal, Hugo von 240
Hokusai 5, 101, 159, 222
Holmes, Anne Arbuthnot 297, 303, 307
Holmes, Dorothy 301, 302, 303
Holmes, Oliver Wendell 246
Hone, Joseph 208
Howard, Bob 49
Howells, William Dean 246

Ibaraki Sejiro 111
Ichikawa Ennosuke 131
Imperial University of Kyoto 31, 34
Imperial University of Tokyo 24, 27, 38, 40, 43, 63, 83, 107, 108, 143, 167, 221, 227
In Ghostly Japan 55, 83, 105, 150, 155
Ionian Islands 7, 9, 13, 47, 57, 65, 76, 77, 141, 246
Irish works:
 Annals of Connacht 127
 Buile Suibhne 129
 Dinnsenchas 125
 Leabhar Gabhála Eireann 125, 130
 Táin Bó Cuailgne 124
Ise Monogatari 124
Ishibashi Hiro 53
Ishikawa Riushiro 111
Isshiki Yuri 171
Izumo 2, 136, 139, 224, 225, 251
Izumo Fudoki 125

Japan Gazette, The 221
Japan Mail, The 221
Japan: An Attempt at Interpretation 28, 64, 67, 83, 155, 164, 165, 171, 202, 217, 218, 224, 225, 227, 243, 251, 253, 270
Japanese Fairy Tales 55
Japanese Letters 194, 202
Japanese Miscellany, A 152
Japanese smile 158, 159
Jimmu, Emperor 125, 130
Joyce, James 64, 69, 70, 71, 174, 184, 186

Kagawa Toyohiko 79
Kamakura 24
Kansai 137
Kantō earthquake 220
Kassimati, Rosa 8, 9, 13, 15, 39, 53, 58, 257, 295, 296, 299, 307, 308, 316
Kavanagh, Patrick 186
Kawai Michiko 171
Keio University, Tokyo 38
Kelly, Fergus 127
Kennard, Nina H. xvi, 220, 258, 268, 269, 273, 276, 277, 278, 279, 281, 283, 284, 285, 286, 288, 301, 305, 306
King, Francis 43, 171, 227
Kipling, Rudyard 43, 104, 212
Kishi Shigetsu 111

Kobe 27, 83, 156, 158, 161, 162, 230, 231, 275, 276
Kobe Chronicle 27, 54, 67, 184, 276
Kobinata Sadjiro 111
Kobudera 41
Koizumi Bon xiii, 31, 102, 103, 228
Koizumi Iwao 31, 287, 304
Koizumi Kazuo ('Kajiwo') 28, 29, 30, 31, 33, 34, 142, 171, 265, 268, 270-272, 274, 275, 277-283, 285-288, 290, 301, 302, 306
Koizumi Kiyoshi 31, 287, 304
Koizumi Setsu 25, 26, 31, 35, 40, 62, 67, 83, 102, 138, 261, 265, 274, 275, 279, 281-287, 301, 305, 306
Koizumi So 31
Koizumi Suzuko 31, 302, 304
Koizumi Toki xiii, xvii, 142, 304
Koizumi Yakumo (first use of name) 27
Kojiki 124, 125, 128, 129, 130, 131
Kokorō 83, 156, 160, 161, 225, 227, 230, 231, 236, 239, 242, 243, 244, 251
Konishi Jin'ichi 127
kotodama 127, 128
Kottō 55, 83, 150, 152, 178
Kumamoto xiv, 4, 26, 27, 31, 62, 83, 108, 138, 156, 231, 237, 270, 271, 272, 274, 275, 276
Kunst, Arthur 170
Kurihara Motoi 111
Kwaidan 32, 70, 83, 150, 151, 152, 164, 165, 180, 181, 218, 228, 243
Kyoto 31, 32
Kyoto Imperial University 31, 34
Kythira 13

Kyushu 26
Kyushu Nichinichi Shimbun 239

Labat, Père 177
Le Fanu, Sheridan xiv, 22, 146, 176, 177, 180, 186, 229
Lectures by Hearn:
 Appreciations of Poetry 111
 Books and Habits 112
 Interpretations of Literature 111
 Life and Literature 111, 190
 Pre-Raphaelites and Other Poets 111
 Talks to Writers 111
Lefkas 13, 47, 58, 103, 122, 141
Lever, Charles 183
Lewis, Matthew 176, 264
Longfellow, Henry Wadsworth 246
Loti, Pierre 21, 61, 80, 146, 157
Lowell, James Russell 246

MacArthur, Douglas, General 28, 29, 170, 171, 219
Macaulay, Thomas 212
Macha 133 Mack, Robert L. 186
Manannán Mac Lir 131
Mangan, James Clarence 146
Manyōshū 126
Martinique 22, 34, 50, 54, 62, 81, 98, 143, 247
Mason, Thomas 132
Mason, William B. 281, 282, 283, 285, 286, 289, 306
Matas, Rudolph xviii, 21
Matsue 1, 2, 3, 6, 24, 26, 31, 54, 62, 64, 65, 67, 69, 72, 73, 83, 98, 101, 102, 103, 108, 138, 156, 198, 199, 225, 228
Maturin, Charles xiv, 22, 146, 176, 177, 179, 180, 186, 229
Maupassant, Guy de 146

Index

McCormack, John 174
McDonald, Mitchell 24, 111, 277
McGahern, John 186
McHugh, Roger xviii
McWilliams, Vera 293, 298, 300, 311
Meiji emperor/era, customs etc. 25, 98, 154, 159, 167, 168, 218, 220, 222, 223, 225, 286
Milton, John 109, 176
Minamoto 132
Mionoseki 136
Miyake Tadaaki 34
Molière 134
Molyneux, Henry 17, 54, 60, 142, 259, 260, 263
Molyneux, Isabella 260
Moore, George 175
Moore, Thomas 62, 179
Mordell, Albert 263
Murasaki, Lady 43, 79
Murphy, Joan 256
Murray, Paul xiii, xvii

Nagasaki 157, 266, 270, 306
Nakasone Yasuhiro ix
Nerval, Gerard de 80
New Orleans xviii, 6, 20, 21, 22, 42, 46-51, 52, 54, 60, 61, 62, 66, 77, 81, 98, 143, 157, 179, 183, 186, 193, 246, 248, 253, 264, 272
New York 22, 23, 48, 60, 79, 98, 217, 262
Nihon Shoki 130
Nintoku, Emperor 130
Nishida Sentaro 109
Nogi, Maresuke, General 286
Noh drama 75, 79, 94, 191, 196, 197, 198, 201

O'Brien, Conor Cruise 205, 206, 208, 210
O'Connor. James 42
O'Connor, W.D. 21
O'Conroy, Tadgh 38
O'Grady, Standish 183
O'Sullivan, Seamus 42
Occupation 29
Ochiai Teisaburo 111
Ohashi Bridge 2
Ohio River 18, 20
Ōisín, Ossian 56, 151, 179, 182
Oki Islands 135-139
Oppenheim, Janet 192
Oshima Shotaro 53
Otani Masanobu 111
Oulton, Christopher 256
Oulton, Dr Henry 312
Oulton, Sir Derek 255, 256, 304
Oulton, Susan Stephens 307, 312
Out of the East 40, 83, 151, 156, 160, 161, 200, 218, 227, 251, 273, 276

Paine, Tom 211
Paris, John 165
Parkes, Sir Harry 160
Pater, Walter 213
Perry, Matthew, Commodore 218, 219, 220
Poe, Edgar Allen 80, 145, 146, 213
Portadown 260, 275, 277, 285
Portrait of the Artist 56
Pound, Ezra 75, 79, 94, 196

Quincey, Thomas De 80, 212, 213

Romance of the Milky Way 150, 151
Roquelle, Father 62
Rossetti, Dante Gabriel 80, 109
Ruskin, John 212

Russia, Russian 184, 233, 254, 306
Russo-Japanese War 28, 233

Saga, Emperor 128
samurai 25, 44, 54, 62, 67, 83, 92, 98, 101, 143, 224, 225, 226, 229, 230, 236, 251
Sansom, Sir George 162, 167
Santa Maura 8, 13, 58, 76, 246
Satow, Ernest 154, 156
Scott, Clement 270
Scott, Sir Walter 134, 176
seances 188, 191
Shadowings 150, 194
Sharkey, James 30
Shaw, George Bernard 173, 174, 175, 184
Sheridan, Frances 186, 187
Sheridan, Richard 183
Shimane 2, 136, 138, 224
Shinji, Lake 2, 136
Shinkansen 101
Shinto, Shintoism 63, 91, 101, 155, 162, 164, 165, 169, 171, 180, 196, 197, 202, 232, 242, 251, 276
Showa Emperor 170, 171
Showa Era 34
Sino-Japanese War 163, 231
Sladen, Douglas 219
Social-Darwinism 113, 114
Sokken Yasui 167
Some Chinese Ghosts 149, 187, 249
Sonohito Fujiwara 128
Spectator, The 171
Spencer, Herbert 64, 90, 113, 114, 155, 166, 167, 184, 194. 242, 247, 249, 250, 252, 253
Spencerianism 114, 117, 150, 155, 242, 247, 252, 254
Spiritualist Alliance 191, 196

St Cuthbert's College, Ushaw, Durham 17, 48, 59, 105, 142
St Patrick 132
Stephens, Denis 256
Stephens, Edward M. 288, 289, 290, 291, 292, 293, 295, 297, 298, 299, 300, 301, 308, 311, 312, 313
Stephens, Lilo xviii, 303
Stevenson, Elizabeth 227, 296
Stoker, Bram xiv, 141, 146, 173, 174, 176, 177, 178, 179, 180, 186, 229, 274
Stray Leaves from Strange Literature 148, 187, 193, 249
Sukehiro Hirakawa 206
Sundai School, Co. Kildare 30, 32, 103
Suzuki, D.T. 79
Swift, Jonathan 183, 201, 203, 207
Swinburne, Algernon Charles 80, 134
Symonds, John Addington 80
Synge, J.M. 34, 68, 134, 135, 137, 142, 175, 180, 290

Tabe Yuji 32
Tahiti 157
Táin Bo Cuailgne 133
Takeru Yamato 131
Tanabe Ryūji 111, 283-286
tanka 106
Tanyard Murder report 147
Tennyson, Alfred Lord 109, 134
Tetsujiro Inouye 167
Times Democrat, The 21, 61, 81, 183
Tír na nÓg 132, 151
Tokugawa Shogunate 219, 225, 252
Tokyo 24, 33, 34, 40, 43, 54, 156, 164, 227, 276, 281, 282, 306

Index

Tokyo Imperial University 24, 27, 38, 40, 43, 63, 67, 83, 107, 108, 143, 167, 221, 227
Tottori 136
Toyama Masakazu, Dr 108
Toyama University 146
Tramore, Co. Waterford xiv, 10, 16, 35, 41, 53, 66, 142, 229
Treaty of Kanagawa 219
Treaty Ports 158, 169, 218, 222
Trinity College, Dublin 176
Tsuru Nyobo 133, 134
Tsuruoka Mayumi 32
Twain, Mark 246
Two Years in the French West Indies 250

Uchigasaki Sakusaburo 110, 111
Ulster 44, 133
Ulster Cycle 44, 125
United States xv, xvi, 97, 98, 157, 169, 172, 185, 193, 206, 217, 228, 262, 267, 278
University of Toyama 146
Urashima Tarō 55, 132, 151, 182
Ushaw, Durham xiv, 17, 48, 59, 118, 122, 142, 258, 259, 266, 312, 315
Ushioda Yoshiko 30
Utamaro 228

Vancouver 23, 62, 216
Vendler, Helen 197

waka 124
Wakayama prefecture 130
Waley, Arthur 43, 79
Walpole, Horace 146
Waseda University 27, 31, 54, 110, 227
Watanna Onoto xvi

Watkin, Henry 19, 21, 24, 145, 262, 263
Weatherall, Mrs 272, 273
West Indies 8, 14, 22, 50, 62, 66, 141, 143, 157, 158, 177, 184, 193, 217, 228, 264, 266
Westmeath 141, 300, 301
Whitman, Walt 80, 246
Wilde, Oscar 173, 174, 179, 184
Wisdom, John Oulton 33
Wordsworth, William 116, 117
World Industrial Exhibition of 1884 22
World War II 170, 227
Worth, Katherine 197
Wriedt, Mrs, medium 188, 191

Yaidzu 34, 35
Yano Kazumi 79
Yeats, Georgie (Georgie Hyde-Lees) 191, 196
Yeats, W.B. xiv, 22, 44, 55, 63, 64, 68, 75, 76, 77, 83, 84, 85, 87, 91, 92, 94, 96, 98, 101, 134, 146, 147, 175, 176, 179-182, 184, 187, 188-203, 205-215, 229
Yokohama 24, 51, 100, 111, 156, 160, 216-225, 226, 236, 270, 281, 282, 289
Youma 22, 62
Young, Robert, publisher of *Kobe Chronicle* 282, 283, 306
Yuki Onna 132, 138, 152
Yvetot, Normandy 59, 142

Zenimoto Kenji, Professor 228, 229
Zola, Emile 80, 146, 249
Zoshigaya cemetery 28, 70